Frommer's™

Budapest & the Best of Hungary

8th Edition

by Ryan James

D1056672

WILEY

A John Wiley and Sons, Ltd, Publication

Published by:

WILEY PUBLISHING, INC.

Copyright © 2010 John Wiley & Sons Ltd, The Atrium, Southern Gate, Chichester, West Sussex PO19 8SQ, UK
Telephone (+44) 1243 779777
Email (for orders and customer service enquiries): cs-books@wiley.co.uk. Visit our Home Page on www.wiley.com

UK Publisher: Sally Smith
Executive Project Editor: Daniel Mersey
Commissioning Editor: Stephen Bassman
Development Editor: Fiona Quinn
Project Editor: Hannah Clement
Cartography: Roberta Stockwell
Photo Editor: Richard Fox
Front cover photo: ©Rudy Sulgan/Corbis. Description: Budapest: Chain Bridge over Danube River at Twilight.
Back cover photo: ©Alessandra Benedetti/Corbis. Description: Sziget Music Festival on Obudai Island in Budapest.

British Library Cataloguing in Publication Data
A catalogue record for this book is available from the British Library

ISBN: 978-0-470-55126-4

Typeset by Wiley Indianapolis Composition Services

Printed and bound in the United States of America

5 4 3 2 1

CONTENTS

8 STROLLING AROUND BUDAPEST — 163

9 BUDAPEST SHOPPING — 189

10 BUDAPEST AFTER DARK — 214

11 THE DANUBE BEND — 232

12 THE LAKE BALATON REGION & SOPRON — 246

LIST OF MAPS

ABOUT THE AUTHOR

Dr. Ryan James was born and raised in Long Branch, New Jersey. He earned his doctorate in education from the University of San Francisco and has taught in the American Studies degree program at Eötvös Loránd University in Budapest since 2002. He and his partner own BudaBaB, a bed and breakfast on the Pest side. He welcomes questions and comments about this guide, and his email address is drryanjames@gmail.com.

ACKNOWLEDGMENTS

I am so thankful to my student helpers who came to my rescue when I had questions but was not getting answers: Balázs Varga, Gergely Hubai, Anna Rázsi, and Márton Tévid. Jennifer Norcross, Kim Raney, and Ron Schmitz assisted by joining me for dinners to review restaurants. I am truly indebted to Ron Schmitz (a.k.a. Mr. Map) for his map assistance, his support, and sharing updates on changes in the city. I want to especially thank Stephen Bassman, editor extraordinaire for the tools of the trade he shared with me for the last edition. For this edition, I am indebted to Fiona Quinn, from the London office. Together, we traveled a new journey for this edition.

HOW TO CONTACT US

In researching this book, we discovered many wonderful places—hotels, restaurants, shops, and more. We're sure you'll find others. Please tell us about them, so we can share the information with your fellow travelers in upcoming editions. If you were disappointed with a recommendation, we'd love to know that, too. Please write to:

Frommer's Budapest & the Best of Hungary, 8th Edition
Wiley Publishing, Inc. • 111 River St. • Hoboken, NJ 07030-5774

AN ADDITIONAL NOTE

Please be advised that travel information is subject to change at any time—and this is especially true of prices. We therefore suggest that you write or call ahead for confirmation when making your travel plans. The authors, editors, and publisher cannot be held responsible for the experiences of readers while traveling. Your safety is important to us, however, so we encourage you to stay alert and be aware of your surroundings. Keep a close eye on cameras, purses, and wallets, all favorite targets of thieves and pickpockets.

Other Great Guides for Your Trip:

Frommer's Budapest Day by Day
Frommer's Vienna & the Danube Valley
Frommer's Austria
Frommer's Prague & Best of Czech Republic
Frommer's Europe
Pauline Frommer's Europe
Frommer's Europe from $85 a Day
Frommer's Road Atlas Europe

FROMMER'S STAR RATINGS, ICONS & ABBREVIATIONS

Every hotel, restaurant, and attraction listing in this guide has been ranked for quality, value, service, amenities, and special features using a **star-rating system.** In country, state, and regional guides, we also rate towns and regions to help you narrow down your choices and budget your time accordingly. Hotels and restaurants are rated on a scale of zero (recommended) to three stars (exceptional). Attractions, shopping, nightlife, towns, and regions are rated according to the following scale: zero stars (recommended), one star (highly recommended), two stars (very highly recommended), and three stars (must-see).

In addition to the star-rating system, we also use **eight feature icons** that point you to the great deals, in-the-know advice, and unique experiences that separate travelers from tourists. Throughout the book, look for:

(**Finds**) Special finds—those places only insiders know about

(**Fun Facts**) Fun facts—details that make travelers more informed and their trips more fun

(**Kids**) Best bets for kids and advice for the whole family

(**Moments**) Special moments—those experiences that memories are made of

(**Overrated**) Places or experiences not worth your time or money

(**Tips**) Insider tips—great ways to save time and money

(**Value**) Great values—where to get the best deals

(**Warning!**) Warning—traveler's advisories are usually in effect

The following **abbreviations** are used for credit cards:

AE	American Express	**DISC**	Discover	**V**	Visa
DC	Diners Club	**MC**	MasterCard		

TRAVEL RESOURCES AT FROMMERS.COM

Frommer's travel resources don't end with this guide. Frommer's website, **www.frommers. com**, has travel information on more than 4,000 destinations. We update features regularly, giving you access to the most current trip-planning information and the best airfare, lodging, and car-rental bargains. You can also listen to podcasts, connect with other Frommers.com members through our active-reader forums, share your travel photos, read blogs from guidebook editors and fellow travelers, and much more.

The Best of Budapest

It never occurred to me when living in Modesto, California that someday, I would live in Budapest, Hungary or, even more incredible, be a writer for Frommer's having the opportunity to write two editions of this book and chapters for others.

After graduating with a doctorate in International and Multicultural Education in 2000 (with over 22 years of teaching experience at that point), it was time to make a major move. A year abroad seemed to be in order for me and my partner to revitalize our spirits before transferring to the east coast of the U.S. Our European travels eventually took us to Budapest during a cold spell, and we decided to hunker down and stay until spring. Back then, but no longer, all an American had to do was leave the country for a day and return to refresh your visa for another 90 days—we did this several times. We started teaching English at private schools for the fun of it; when we were told we could avoid work and residency permits if we had our own business, we started a private language school. It turns out we did need those permits after all, which cost us a trip to NYC and a wait in line at the Hungarian Consulate. We submitted our applications and were flying back to Hungary the next day.

After more than three annual visa renewals, we were able to apply for our long-term residency visa, so 8 years later we're still here.

During the first year, we both found university teaching positions and by our third year opened up a bed and breakfast (BudaBaB; p. 83). I am still at the university, but Ron retired from his university position to run the B&B. Budapest and Hungary have grown and evolved before our eyes.

In those days, Budapest was not on the travel radar, still considered too exotic, while many did not realize it was no longer a communist country. (People still ask us this question.) During our first year, Hungary had its third democratic election for prime minister. Each of the three elections put a different political party into control causing continual upheaval in the laws from one party's whims to the next.

Tourism was greatly aided by the budget airlines, which started to spring up in our first 6 years here, but with all of the economic woes, many have dropped Budapest along with other cities from the destinations to which they fly. During the upswing, the hotel industry blossomed. Boutique hotels and new 4- and 5-star hotels were built or took over historic buildings, creating a wide offering of accommodations for budgets from average to luxurious, but the last couple of years there have been poor occupancy numbers.

The restaurant scene also has been in flux during these difficult economic times. It is not uncommon for a restaurant to suddenly close without warning. The Hungarian Restaurant Association had predicted that 30% throughout the country would meet their demise, but it has not been as grave as that. Menus in English were once uncommon, and ordering a meal was a grab-bag surprise; tourism has changed this, but sometimes there is something lost in translation, so what you get is not what you thought you ordered. Culturally, the country (and especially Budapest) continues to thrive, with nightlife, arts, and fashion scenes that are infused with more youthful exuberance than ever before, and an underground party scene that is well worth seeking out. Some districts, however, are implementing laws forcing restaurants to close at 10pm or 11pm for noise control. Each district is autonomous in this law creation.

Since Hungary joined the European Union in 2004, those extended visits we enjoyed in 2001 are no longer valid for most travelers; the official E.U. law still allows 90-day visits, but requires Americans in particular (as well as Canadians and Australians) to leave the E.U. for 6 months before returning. E.U. visitors have no restrictions on their length of stay. I hope that regardless of how long you are visiting, you enjoy yourself enough to extend your stay, just as we did.

1 THE BEST LITTLE ADVENTURES IN BUDAPEST

- **The Best Photographic Viewpoints in the City:** If you want to start at the highest point, you will have to go to János-Hegy (John Hill) where the tower is 529m (1,736 ft) high. On a clear day, you might just see the Tatra Mountains. The best way to get there is the chairlift (p. 150). The next highest vista is the Citadella (Citadel) on Gellért Hill (p. 138). The bus only gets you so far, and then you hike up the rest, but it is worth the effort. This is where you'll find the Lady of Liberty statue viewable from the Pest side. Castle Hill (p. 52) is of course an excellent viewpoint for photographs from both the front of the castle and Fisherman's Bastion. The best view though is from behind the President of Hungary's office buildings (p. 173). Margit Hid (Margaret Bridge, p. 187), the side across from the island, has a breathtaking view of the river from where the bridge elbows.

- **Architecture Not to Be Missed:** Many people don't bother to look up at the top of buildings, missing much. Aside from the historic listings, Posta Takarék-pénzter (p. 178) on Hold utca across from where Perczel Mór utca comes into it is one of my favorite buildings in the city; it is now part of the National Bank. Move around so the trees don't obstruct your view. Párizsi udvar in the Art Nouveau style, where Kigyo utca meets Ferenciek tere, is sumptuous both outside and inside. The building has been sold, so it may not last forever. See it while you can. Walk in the courtyard and look at the ceiling. On the korut, near Blaha Lujza, is the New York Palace built in eclectic style with an emphasis on Italian renaissance and baroque. For something more modern, don't pass up the Lehel tér (p. 209) market at the Blue metro stop by the same name. It looks like a beached boat.

- **Riding the Trams:** With your transit pass in hand, tour the city and orient yourself from the windows of the city's many trams. Hop on a tram and ride it to the end of the line, get out, and take it back again. This is also an inexpensive hop-on, hop-off way to sightsee, checking out things that catch your eye along the way. Tram no. 4 or 6 will take you along the large ring road. Tram no. 2 at night provides a view of Parliament, and Castle Hill all lit up, but parts of the line are under construction. Look for details on public transportation in other parts of the book where they are covered indepth.

- **Packing a Picnic for an Outing:** Any day when pleasant weather is in the forecast, people flock to one of the parks or Margaret Island to enjoy the fresh air and one another's company. Families stroll along with their young children while young lovers enjoy each other's company, and the older folks

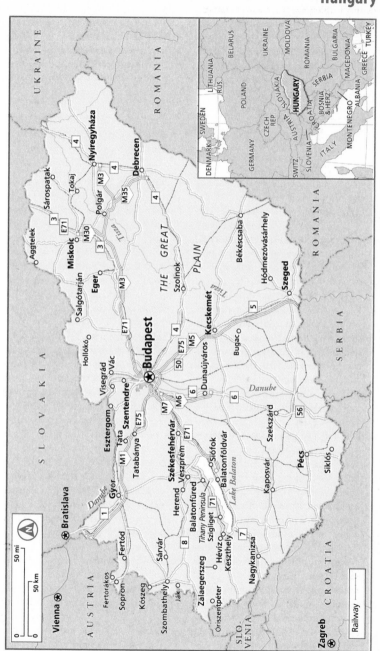

reminisce about the old and better times. A quick and easy way to pack a picnic is to pick ready-made gourmet sandwiches. See the tip on p. 146.

- **Taking a Walk in the Buda Hills:** It's hard to believe that such a large expanse of hilly forest is right here within the capital city. There are hiking trails aplenty; every Budapest native has a favorite—ask around. See chapter 7, "Exploring Budapest," for more activities in the Buda Hills.

- **Strolling through the Jewish District:** Budapest still has a large Jewish population. Pest's historic Jewish neighborhood is disappearing at a sorrowfully rapid rate due to modernization, commercialization, and new construction. Run-down historic areas that once resonated with the magic and tragedy of the past have been bulldozed into oblivion. See "Walking Tour 4: The Jewish District" in chapter 8, "Strolling Around Budapest."

2 THE BEST PLACES TO STOP & SMELL THE FLOWERS IN BUDAPEST

- **Margaret Island (Margit-sziget):** Sunrise to sunset, you can find a number of garden areas on the enchanting island in the Danube. During the summer months, the whimsical fountain, set within one of the beautiful garden areas, plays classical music while spraying water in time to the music. The island did not become a public park until 1908. Before that time only the leaders of the upper classes could set foot on it. Plebeians should take advantage and visit with a picnic. See p. 146.

- **Szabadság tér:** The name is Freedom Square in English. Surrounded by historical buildings, including the U.S. Embassy, this well-tended green space has gardens interspersed with pedestrian walkways. There are plenty of benches under shady trees for relaxing and even a small children's playground for a family rest stop. It is also home to the tall obelisk with a star on top, the last remaining monument to the Soviet Union's liberation of Budapest after World War II. See p. 178.

- **Szent István Park:** This attractive green park in the XIII district is often overlooked by visitors who don't even know it's there. It's a flowering oasis during spring and summer. To reach it, take tram no. 4 or 6 to Jászai Mari tér and

walk parallel to Margaret Island three blocks along the Danube to reach it. The gardens are open from 6am to 8:30pm.

- **Kodály körönd:** If you take the Millennium walking tour (See chapter 8, "Strolling Around Budapest"), you will discover the four pleasant garden areas, each with its own statue.

- **Jókai tér and Liszt Ferenc tér:** Where they are intersected by Andrássy út just past Oktogon, each has attractive flower gardens. The Liszt Ferenc side is always shaped like a giant valentine heart. If you continue down Liszt Ferenc tér, an umbrella of trees will shadow you as you walk along the winding path.

- **Nagymező utca:** Again, just off of Andrássy út in district VI, you will find an extended sidewalk with a planter built up from the ground filled with flowers. Beyond the flowerbeds is a modern, tranquil water fountain. Benches are provided for a rest stop, so give your feet a break and enjoy the views.

- **Hollán Ernő utca:** Just as the street starts off Szent István körút in the XIII district, there is a pedestrian street for one block. Like Nagymező utca, a new pedestrian area has been created complete with flowers and a water fountain decorated with colored lights.

3 THE BEST PLACES TO ENJOY A SUNSET IN BUDAPEST

- **From the Riverside:** As the sun sets, you will find many locals and visitors flocking to the riverside to enjoy people-watching, admire the sunset, and just plain relax. Depending on how busy your day was, you may either want to find a bench to sit on and unwind, or take a stroll onto one of the bridges that span the mighty Danube, the second-longest river in Europe. See chapter 7, "Exploring Budapest," for more about Budapest's bridges and riverside walks.

- **Széchenyi Thermals:** This thermal is open until 10pm. Relax in the hot spring waters while watching the end of the day's sun's rays as they fade into the horizon. For more on the thermals see p. 160.

- **Margaret Island (Margit-sziget):** This island, once called Rabbit Island, was home to the cloistered nuns' convent founded by Princess Margaret, daughter of Béla IV, who promised his daughter to the nunnery. Enjoy the flower gardens or the singing fountain as the sun sinks into the western sky. See p. 146.

- **Fisherman's Bastion:** Sip a glass of wine in this romantic sunset spot. On Castle Hill, it overlooks the city on one side and St. Matthias Church on the other. See p. 139.

- **Academy of Sciences Park:** For a casual place to relax, sit in the park across the street from the academy and take in the engaging architecture, the river view, and a beautiful sunset on Roosevelt tér. See p. 179.

- **The Sculptural Grounds at Buda Castle:** There is a powerful statue called the Matthias Fountain. It is based on a legend of King Matthias, who, while on a hunting trip through the forest, came across a woman stranger, Ilona; she fell in love with him instantly, not realizing he was the king. He reciprocated the love. See p. 172.

4 THE BEST OFF-THE-BEATEN-TRACK MUSEUMS

- **Bélyegmúzeum (Postal Stamp Museum):** Philatelists the world over have recognized the artistic creativity of the Magyar Posta creations. Here you'll find incredibly beautiful and well-organized collections of Hungary's finest stamps and those of many other countries. See p. 127.

- **Miksa Róth Memorial House:** This is the last home of the famed stained-glass and mosaic artist whose work graces the Parliament and other places throughout the city and the world. It is truly an exceptional collection not to be missed. See p. 128.

- **Ráth Gőrgy Museum:** A personal collection of Asian art from different countries, each displayed in separate rooms, makes this Budapest museum a treasure trove of exotic collections, at Varosligeti fasor 12 (© **1/342-3916;** www.hoppmuzeum.hu).

- **Holokauszt Emlékközpont (Budapest Holocaust Memorial Center):** Surrounded by modern architecture is the Páva Synagogue. The center has special exhibits and documents the Jewish history of Hungary during the Holocaust. See p. 123.

- **Underground Railway Museum:** Located at Deák metro underground, this small exhibit shows the history of the tram lines in the city. See p. 165.

5 THE BEST PLACES TO KILL AN HOUR IN BUDAPEST

- **Central Hall Market:** Not only a good place to pick up souvenirs, but also a fun place for people-watching. The balcony overlooking the whole market is an experience you should not miss. See p. 209.
- **Castle Hill:** Ignore the tourist sights for an hour and just stroll along the side streets which wind around, allowing yourself to get lost while admiring the architecture of the area. See p. 52.
- **The Baths:** The Király and Rudas baths are steeped in history and are the perfect way to relax while soaking in the history of the culture at the same time. See "Budapest's Most Popular Thermal Baths" in chapter 7, "Exploring Budapest."
- **A Traditional Coffeehouse:** Coffeehouses are a cultural icon in the city, dating back more than 100 years. Enjoy a cup of coffee or tea and linger with a book or newspaper for as long as you like without feeling any pressure to leave. See "Coffeehouses: Historic & Traditional" in chapter 6, "Where to Dine in Budapest."
- **Browse the Shelves in a Bookstore:** With four English bookstores, there are many opportunities to find something that will catch your eye. Perhaps you will find that special book as a remembrance of your visit. See chapter 9, "Budapest Shopping."
- **Art Factory Gallery and Studio:** Open to the public and located in the ABB Building at Váci út 152–156, it is small enough to enjoy for an hour or longer if you have the time. See chapter 9, "Budapest Shopping."

6 THE BEST HOTELS IN BUDAPEST

- **Best Splurge Hotel:** The magnificent **Four Seasons Hotel Gresham Palace,** V. Roosevelt tér 5–6 (© 1/268-6000), has gained the reputation as Hungary's foremost hotel. The workmanship of the recreated Art Nouveau architecture is breathtaking. Guests get the royal treatment, with customer care that will enamor you for a long time. See p. 67.
- **Best for a Romantic Getaway:** After entering the **Corinthia Grand Hotel Royal,** VII. Erzsébet krt. 43–49 (© 1/479-4000), you will not want to leave the sumptuous building and there's no need to do so with its pool, spa, and restaurants. See p. 66.
- **Best for Families:** The accommodations at **Charles Apartment House,** I. Hegyalja út 23 (© 1/212-9169), are comfortable and clean flats with fully equipped kitchens in a Buda-side apartment building. See p. 79.
- **Best Moderately Priced Hotel:** The jazzy **Cotton House Hotel,** VI. Jókai u. 26 (© 1/354-2600), conveniently located near the Opera House and Liszt Ferenc tér, will soothe the blues away. See p. 71.
- **Best Budget Hotel:** The accommodations at **Medosz,** VI. Jókai tér 9 (© 1/374-3001) are comfortable and clean and close to Oktogon and Liszt Ferenc tér. See p. 75.

- **Best Bed and Breakfast:** Without humility, I have to say it is my own **BudaBaB**, VII. Akácfa u. 18 (© **1/267-5240**), where English is the first language, and which is perfectly located to start your touring or shopping expeditions within easy walking distance of public transportation just two blocks away. See p. 83.
- **Best Views:** This one is a tie between two hotels, one on each side of the river.

On the Pest side, it is the **Four Seasons Hotel Gresham Palace,** V. Roosevelt tér 5–6 (© **1/268-6000**; p. 67), with the Chain Bridge outside its door. On the Buda the **Hilton Budapest,** I. Hess András tér 1–3 (© **1/899-6600;** p. 75), is a luxurious lodging right next door to the Matthias Church and the Fisherman's Bastion square.

7 THE BEST DINING BETS IN BUDAPEST

- **Best for a Romantic Dinner:** At **Hemingway,** XI. Kosztolányi D. tér 2. 1 (© **1/381-0522**), you can dine on the terrace overlooking the lake or in the relaxing Cuban-feeling dining room that would make Ernest feel at home. Excellent service is the order every day, all the while being serenaded by live music at night. See p. 116.
- **Best Decor:** The legends of the benevolent King Mátyás are painted as murals on the walls with stained glass decorating the windows at **Mátyás Pince,** V. Március 15 tér 7–8 (© **1/266-8008**). See p. 92.
- **Best Wine List:** At **Dío,** V. Sas u. 4 (© **1/328-0360**), excellent service with outstanding food can be accompanied by wines with the aid of the sommelier. See p. 92.
- **Best Beer List:** You will have difficulty choosing from a multitude of draft beers or 50 bottled beers at **Mosselen Belgian Beer Café** at XIII. Pannónia u. 14 (© **1/452-0535**). The food is also excellent making it a double treat. See p. 104.
- **Best Wild Game:** At **Paprika Vendéglő,** VII. Dozsa Gyorgy 72, 4½ blocks from Heroes Square (© **06/70-**

574-6508) mobile), you can relish the savory dishes of wild boar or venison. There are many other choices for the less adventurous. See p. 113.
- **Best Traditional Coffeehouse: Centrál Kávéház,** V. Károly Mihály u. 9 (© **1/266-2110**), is the closest to the classic coffeehouse of the city's past traditions. Even today, it is the meeting place for intellectuals, tourists, families, and more. This is a Budapest must-see. See p. 119.
- **Best Nontraditional Coffeehouse:** For coffee or hot chocolate, **Aztek Choxolat Café,** at V. Károly körút 22 or Semmelweiss u. 19. (© **1/266-7113**), has a tremendous selection of both. See p. 121.
- **Best Pastries:** Our favorite pastry shop is the **Művész Kávéház,** VI. Andrássy út 29 (© **1/352-1337**). It has many traditional desserts such as *somlói galuska,* considered a national dessert, plus pastries, and an ice-cream bar. See p. 120.
- **Best Rétes:** Melt-in-your-mouth strudel is available at the **Rétesvar,** I. Balta köz 4 (no phone), the alley on Castle Hill behind the nude woman statue fountain. Look for the red banner hanging outside the brick alleyway. See p. 121.

8 THE BEST DAY TRIPS OUTSIDE BUDAPEST

- **Cruising the Danube:** There's nothing like a boat ride on a fine sunny day. From Budapest, head up the river leading to the charming towns of Vác, Szentendre, and Visegrád along the Danube Bend. See "Railing through the Danube Bend" in chapter 11, "The Danube Bend."

- **Visiting Szentendre:** Only 45 minutes outside the city by HÉV, this small Serbian village boasts a number of tiny museums, shopping opportunities, and pleasant strolls along the Danube. See chapter 11, "The Danube Bend."

- **Vác:** A delightful town that took me 6 years to discover and I wish I'd done so earlier. The center square is a mix of historic buildings with a modern square completed in 2006. The river walk is fantastically beautiful. See p. 239.

- **Visit Esztergom:** Hungary's seat of Catholicism, Esztergom is located 46km (29 miles) northwest of Budapest. St. István, the first Christian king of Hungary, was crowned here on Christmas Day A.D. 1000. The cathedral has impressive views of the Danube

and the rest of the city. See chapter 11, "The Danube Bend."

- **Explore the Monastery at Pannonhalma:** Prince Géza founded the monastery in 969. This is where the gothic cloisters are housed as well as a magnificently ornate 19th-century library, with the most important collection of Hungarian historical documents. It sits on a hill between the forested slopes of the Bakony region and the low-lying *Kisalföld* (Little Plain), with a fantastic view.

- **Sleepy Historical Visegrád:** Located 40km (25 miles) north of Budapest., You first travel to Nagymaros, then take a ferry to Visegrád, you can find the ruins of King Béla IV's reign. The Citadel and the reconstructed Royal Palace are among the places worth seeing. See p. 242.

- **Medve Otthon:** Visit the bears at the bear sanctuary, which houses 42 bears who were once stars in Hungarian movies then rescued due to mistreatment. You can feed them honey and kids can have their faces painted. It is just 1 hour from the city. See p. 62.

9 SOME OF THE BEST THERMALS IN HUNGARY

A vast area of Hungary sits over natural thermal springs providing mineral and curative waters to more than 1,000 wells that produce water of 86° F (30°C). The Romans used these waters to create public baths; in some areas, remnants have survived giving us a peek into their culture during that time.

Later, the Turks built thermals within city walls to have a place to bath during times of war. Arslan, the pasha of Buda, is believed to have started the construction of the **Király** thermal baths in 1565, making

it the oldest thermal in Budapest. It is one of the last tokens of Turkish history within the city. Its water is piped in from the **Lucas** thermals. Although the **Rudas** was believed to have been built in 1550, it was rebuilt by Pasha Sokol Mustafa in 1566, so making the Király the oldest in the city.

Due to space in this book, it is not possible to cover the 150 hot water spas in the country, nor the 36 medicinal spas amongst them. Medicinal thermals are wellness establishments utilizing balneotherapy. **Balneology** is the scientific use of bathing as a treatment for diseases. Goals for these treatments are to enhance the immune system, stimulate the circulatory process including lymph and blood circulation, accelerating cell activity, dilating tissue and vessels while activating the body's own healing process. Medicinal waters have been found to contain various amounts of sodium, magnesium, calcium, and iron, as well as arsenic, lithium, potassium, manganese, bromine, radioactivity, sulfureous acid, salt bromine carbonate, and iodine depending on the area. Not all thermal waters are created equal; it depends on the geography of the areas. Waters at different thermals will have differing compounds and ratios of minerals, while some may be missing a number of them. The medical treatments provided are dependent on the mineral contents of the water. With an increase in tourism, the term wellness has expanded from health wellness to being pampered. Some thermals or wellness hotels offer exotic treatments like a wine, chocolate, or honey massage for example. While this may lift your spirits at the same time as putting a bit of a strain on your bank account, these types of treatments are not intended to provide long-term health benefits. In this section, I will give an overview of some of the physical health wellness treatments available at the various thermals.

Budapest has been called the World's Spa Capital, so starting in the capital the **Király** thermal offers thermal pools of various degrees of increasing temperatures. The waters are believed to be especially healthy for degenerative illnesses of the joints, chronic and semi-acute arthritis, deformations of the vertebral spine, dislocation of vertebral discs, neuralgia, and calcium deficiency.

At the **Rudas**, in addition to the thermals, they have a complex for physiotherapy, a day hospital where they perform physical therapy services. Here you will find radioactive hot spring water with calcium-magnesium-hydrogen-carbonate and other goodies. This water is used for treating the same medical problems as the Király.

The **Gellért's** waters are composed of similar qualities as the others. In addition to the ailments listed above, these waters are recommended for aortic stenosis and problems with blood circulation. The Gellért also has an **Inhalatorium** where they provide treatment for issues with asthma and chronic bronchial complaints. A doctor is on the premises where one can be diagnosed and prescribed a treatment plan all in one place. The Inhalatorium is separate from the thermals, but in the same building.

Széchanyi thermals are probably best known for the ubiquitous pictures of men playing chess in the pool. The waters here are proposed for the same bone problems as the other thermals, but they also have a "drinking cure". Drinking the waters is supposed to bring better health to your internal organs. It will definitely flush your colon in the process, so detoxification is on their list of treatments. With their expanded services, they offer a full-range gym with a trainer. Further information about location and hours of operation for the above can be found in chapter 7, "Exploring Budapest."

The second-largest spa in Hungary, the **Medicinal Spa of Bük** Termál krt. 2, Bükfürdő (*C* **94/558-080**; http://bukfurdo. hu), is just 40km (25 miles) from **Sopron**. Although the list of water properties is longer than my arm, the basics include alkali hydrocarbonate, calcium, magnesium, and fluoride. Water treatment is indicated for cures of all bone and muscle disorders in addition to digestive, chronic gynecological and urological inflammations, and even gout. The drinking cure is recommended for chronic gastritis, ulcers, indigestion, and preventing osteoporosis. With a medical doctor on the premises, you can have an examination and treatment plan created for you on the spot.

Near Eger, is a small village called **Egerszalok** with medical waters and treatments, but no English. The address is Forrás utca 2 (© **30/476-5736** mobile phone only; www.egerszalokfurdo.hu) in the northern part of Hungary, near the Lasko stream, at the foot of Bükk mountain. It is the country's youngest spa. The bath is fed by 2 thermal sources at a blistering 154–158°F (68°C) from a geyser. Curative effects are suggested for joint pain and bone problems. Admission is 1,000 Ft. Hours are summers only from June 15, Monday to Thursday 1pm to 11pm, Friday and Saturday 1pm to 1am.

Hévíz Lake, with its 47,500sq. m (11.74 acres), is one of the best-known spas in Europe. The spring supplies 20,000 liters of water every minute, completely refreshing the lake every 72 hours. In summer, the water is 91–95°F (33–35°C), but never goes below 79°F (26°C) in winter. The inorganic mud combined with the highly organic fango from the bottom of the lake is used as a curative mudpack for rheumatism. See chapter 12, "The Lake Balaton Region and Sopron."

Europe's only cave spa is the **Miskolc-Tapolca Cave Spa**, at Pazár sétány (© **46/ 560–030**). In the cave, the spa is a toasty 86°F (30°C). The medicinal area offers services for hydrotherapy, medicinal and refreshing massages, electrotherapy, and also offers a consultation by a rheumatologic specialist.. The rest of the area is recreational. It is open daily from 9am to 6pm, closed in January. A 4-hour pass for adults is 2,200 Ft or an all-day ticket is 2,700 Ft. Children 5 years and under pay 1,500 Ft or a family ticket for 3 people costs 1,700 Ft.

Budapest in Depth

Budapest, being the capital, is the largest city in Hungary with 1.7 million people within the city proper. However, if the greater Budapest metropolitan area is included, this figure climbs to 3.27 million inhabitants. The metropolis is separated into 23 districts, 6 in Buda, 16 in Pest, and one consisting of Csepel Island making it seem like an immense city at first glance, but the majority of districts are residential and not of interest to most travelers.

1 BUDAPEST FROM THREE TO ONE

Budapest officially became one city with the unification of Buda, Pest, and Obuda on November 17, 1873. One contributing factor was the building of the **Széchenyi lánchíd**, commonly known as the Chain Bridge. This was the first connecting bridge over the Danube in Budapest. It was named for Count Széchenyi who was a major financial supporter of the project. The story goes that Széchenyi was on the Pest side of the river when he received word that his father was on his deathbed. Due to a major storm, Széchenyi was unable to get a boat to traverse the river for a week, thus missing seeing his father one last time before he died. He vowed this would never occur again. Not only did the bridge have practical implications, but it also aided the cultural and economic advancements of the people.

Interestingly, William Tierney Clark, the engineer who designed the Marlow Bridge across the river Thames in Marlow, England designed this bridge as well. Both bridges are similar in design. Construction of the bridge was supervised by a Scottish engineer, Adam Clark, though they were not related. On the Buda side of the bridge is a turnabout named Clark Adam tér. The bridge officially opened in 1849. Its center span of 202m (660 ft) was the largest in the world at that time.

On the ends of the bridge are sculptures of lions, added in 1852, producing a humorous folk legend. When a group of schoolchildren were brought to view the lions and the bridge, the sculptor who was in attendance bragged about the lifelike details of his lions. One child pointed out that the lions did not have tongues. The sculptor was upset over this missing detail; he jumped to his death into the Danube. Of course, this is only a legend as the sculptor lived well into old age.

Budapest is also home to the oldest metro line in continental Europe, the second oldest in the world after London. It has the second-largest Parliament building in Europe, again being beaten only by Westminster in London. The Dohány Synagogue is the second-largest working synagogue in the world after Temple Emanu-El in New York City. Budapest has the world's largest cave system of thermal water with 80 geothermal springs running below it. Széchenyi Thermal is the largest medicinal bath complex in Europe.

Modern-day Budapest is difficult to encapsulate; there are daily changes with international designer stores opening on Andrássy út to the continued construction of Metro four, the newest metro line in the city. The construction has caused public transportation to be rerouted forever on a temporary basis. Margaret Island is a little more difficult to access these days. The Margit Bridge is under reconstruction that will last for the next 2 years, causing the trams to bypass the stop completely.

JEWISH HISTORY IN BRIEF

During the Holocaust, Hungary had a unique situation concerning its Jewish citizens. In order to understand and appreciate the horrific events of World War II, it is important to know the Jewish history of the country.

The Jewish history in Hungary extends to the 2nd or 3rd century A.D., when the first Jewish people came to the area, mainly from Rome. Artifacts dating to 225 have been uncovered, showing a strong Jewish community long before the Magyars conquered the area in 896. When King István I adopted Christianity, declaring it the official religion, he also guaranteed the right to religious freedom, including the practice of Judaism. Religious freedom continued through the Árpád dynasty until it ended in 1301. András II, under pressure from the pope, created a prohibition on mixed marriages in the Golden Bull of 1222, an edict establishing the rights of noblemen. During his reign, he also restricted Jewish people from national and public office, forcing them to wear signs proclaiming their religion. Due to the economic services they provided, some remained in their appointed posts;

one example is Count Teka, who was the Jewish royal chamberlain.

Under threat of invasion by the Mongols, King Béla IV implored Pope Gregory IX in 1239 to allow him to relax the laws, so the national revenues could be controlled by Jews. Béla accomplished this, so during his reign and the reign of his son, István V, there were many Hungarian coins minted with Hebrew characters inscribed on them. This attests to the privileged position of the Jews during this time.

Jewish and Hungarian history has been intertwined for centuries, with the Jews being the welcomed people or the outcasts, flipping back and forth. It was not until the early 20th century that Hungarian Jews were able to hold political positions, but even then, they were not able to make strongholds in creating changes.

The Hungarian regent, Miklós Horthy, of the right-wing Christianized government was in power from 1920 to 1944 and was heavily influenced by the Germans. He and the economic situation at the time pushed the country toward fascism. The Jews realized that efforts to assimilate had been in vain. Horthy aligned Hungary with the Germans and

DATELINE

- **896** Árpád led the Magyars in the Carpathian Basin, becoming the first leader.
- **997** King Stephen of the Árpád dynasty converted the pagans to Catholicism and was proclaimed a saint.
- **1241** The Tartars of Mongolia invaded and devastated the territory.
- **1458** King Matthias reigned until 1490, bringing Italian influence into the country.
- **1526** The Turks defeated the Hungarians, occupying and ruling them for 150 years.
- **1541** Hungary was divided into three parts. The Turks ruled central Hungary, the Habsburgs ruled west Hungary, and the Hungarians had south Hungary.
- **1703** The Prince of Transylvania led a war against the Habsburgs, but was defeated.
- **1848** The Habsburg emperor was dethroned as a result of the Hungarian Revolution, but gained his throne back with the assistance of the Russians.
- **1867** The Habsburgs agreed to a compromise and created a dual-centered monarchy between Vienna and Pest-Buda.
- **1873** Pest, Buda, and Obuda were unified into one city

Italians. He had them promise that the land lost due to the Trianon Treaty after World War I would be returned to Hungary. As Hungary aligned with Germany's Adolf Hitler and Italy's Benito Mussolini, the Jews were no longer in a position to strive for equality. Horthy had come to an agreement with Hitler to save the Hungarian Jews; however, Jews from all over the country were rounded up and many sent to Budapest to live in abandoned factories or "star houses" which were eventually ghettos. They lost everything.

SS Colonel Adolf Eichmann was the official head of deportations from the countryside that started in March 1944. During the last 2 months of World War II, Hungarian police, who were feeling the pressure of Soviet troops getting closer, successfully rounded up and deported 440,000 Jews in more than 145 trains heading primarily to Auschwitz. Thousands of others were sent as workers to dig fortification trenches on the Hungary–Austria border. Those who could not be deported in time were lined up along the Danube by German soldiers and shot in the back, their bodies falling into the river. Those who were killed at the Dohány Synagogue were buried on the grounds, against Jewish law.

Horthy, recognizing that the Axis Powers were not going to win the war, started secret negotiations with the Allied Powers. When this came to light in mid-May 1944, the German Security Police, with the assistance of the Hungarian authorities, methodically began to deport Hungarian Jews. Horthy, under threat of war-crime trials by the leaders of the Allied Powers, decided to stop the deportations on July 7, 1944. The following month, he dissolved his government, trying to create a resolution agreement with the Soviets, who were at Hungary's borders. After finalizing his negotiations with the Soviet commanders in October, Horthy was arrested by the Germans. They created a new government headed by Ferenc Szalasi, the leader of the fascist and radically anti-Semitic Arrow Cross Party.

Under the Arrow Cross regime, members of the party terrorized the Jewish population. Men and women were murdered by the hundreds. Hundreds more died from the brutal conditions of forced labor inflicted upon them. By November 1944, the Arrow Cross rounded up the balance of the 70,000 Jews in Budapest and forced them into a ghetto within an area of .3sq. km (.1sq. mile). During November and December of the same year, several thousand more were forced to march from Budapest to the Austrian border. Those who could not keep up were shot along the way.

continues

In January 1945, Soviet forces were in Pest and had signed a ceasefire. They liberated the Buda side of the city on February 13, 1945, driving out the last of the German troops and their Arrow Cross compatriots by early April 1945.

In 1941, Hungary was home to approximately 825,000 Jews, but 63,000 were killed before the Germans arrived in March 1944. An additional 500,000 died under the Germans from murder or maltreatment. Less than one-third of the total Jewish population of Hungary prior to the war survived the Holocaust; about 255,000 Jews survived.

Many of the survivors owe a debt of gratitude to the Hungarian intellectual class and to government employees of neutral countries who intervened on their behalf, risking their lives in the process. The best known among them was **Raoul Wallenberg**, a Swedish diplomat who processed thousands of Swedish protectorate passports for Jews, so they could escape to Sweden safely. He was arrested by the Soviets in January 1947 and never heard from again. Under pressure, the Soviets claimed he died of a heart attack while in prison, yet this was never confirmed. **Carl Lutz** of Switzerland, as Swiss vice-consul to Hungary, saved Hungarian Jews from deportation by allowing them to immigrate to Palestine under protection of a Swiss safe-conduct, where he housed them

in buildings that he declared part of the Swiss delegation. **Ángel Sanz Briz** was sent to Budapest in 1942 where it is estimated that he saved 5,200 Jews from the Holocaust through his influence as a Spanish diplomat and by using the Spanish embassy. He was aided by **Giorgio Perlasca**, an Italian veteran of the Spanish Civil War who was ordered to leave Budapest in 1944 but continued working with fake documents asserting he was a Spanish diplomat. **Angelo Rotta**, a Catholic priest and a member of the Vatican diplomatic corps, issued 15,000 protection letters to Hungarian Jews and gave them baptismal certificates from the Catholic Church. **Friedrich Born**, a Swiss citizen working for the International Committee of the Red Cross (ICRC), recruited 3,000 Jews as workers in his offices and declared those offices to be under protection of the ICRC.

Several Hungarians were recognized as saviors of the Jews. **Margit Slachta**, who founded the religious order the Sisters of Social Service, was instrumental in saving many Jewish lives. She was an avid protester, raising objections against racial persecution, the anti-Jewish laws, and the deportations. Mother Slachta traveled to Rome in 1943 to appeal to Pope Pius XII to intercede against the persecution of Jews. From the spring of 1944, the mission of the sisters was fully directed at

The Recurring '96'

When the Magyars migrated to the Danube-Tisza in 896, Árpád was chosen as their chieftain. To commemorate this, the highest buildings in Budapest are both 96m (310 ft) high. These are the Parliament building and St. Stephen's Basilica. For the millennium in 1896, the first metro was built to safeguard Andrássy út from being destroyed by an abundance of horse-drawn carriages transporting the crowds to Hősök tere (Heroes' Square) for the celebrations.

helping the Jews. They hid as many as 1,000. One sister, Sára Salkaházi, was murdered by Arrow Cross men on December 27, 1944. She was awarded the title "Righteous among the Nations" in 1969; Sister Margit received the honor 12 years after her death, in 1986.

General Tibor Almásy was an officer in the Hungarian army during World War II. He provided food, medical assistance, and certificates for his Jewish soldiers and was recognized as "Righteous among the Nations" in 1987. Because of his actions, he was arrested and imprisoned in March 1944. Following his release, he was commissioned as the garrison commander of Sopron's prison camp, where 400 Jews were forced laborers. Almásy reassured them that he would protect them as long as he was in charge. When he was ordered to exterminate his servicemen by the Arrow Cross, he saved them by declaring a typhoid quarantine of the entire barracks and erecting huge signs that said DANGER, TYPHOID FEVER: ENTRANCE FORBIDDEN.

Dr. József Antall, the father of a former Hungarian prime minister, was awarded the title "Righteous among the Nations" in 1989, posthumously. As head of the Department of Refugees and the Ministry of Interior, he issued legal permits for thousands of Jewish refugees from other occupied countries to stay in Hungary while at the same time Christianizing them. He opened a boarding school in Vác

for Jewish children who had lost their parents. He was arrested by the Gestapo only to be released in September 1944.

Daily life did not improve for the Hungarian Jews after the war was over. When the Communists came to power in 1948, many of the middle class, including a great number of Jews, were either deported or sent to labor camps. The Jews of the lower classes struggled to survive financially. Their shops were closed or their business licenses were withdrawn, causing further hardships. Religious practices were strictly regulated and limited to ceremonies within the synagogue. It was impossible to raise children in the traditional ways.

Many Jews took part in the unsuccessful revolution of October 23, 1956, including Auschwitz survivor, István Angyal. He, among other Jews, was executed. International relations between Israel and Hungary were abolished and reinstated a number of times. As of 1994, they both abolished visa requirements between the two countries and now have a free trade agreement. This has created a boom in Jewish tourism to Hungary. Today, there are approximately 100,000 Jews living in Hungary, with 80–90% living in Budapest itself, making this the largest population of Jews in Europe.

For more information on the Jewish sights in Budapest, see p. 180, "Walking Tour 4: The Jewish District."

If, like many, you are looking for the old Communist statues that decorated the city, you will be disappointed to find that shortly after the fall of Communism they were moved to **Memento Park** (p. 142) in the XXII district where they are on display. The statues you find around the city celebrate those who have contributed to the historical, political, cultural, and scientific achievements of the country.

ARCHITECTURAL VARIETY

Statues aside, the city is abundantly rich in architectural treasures. Dating back to Roman times when they occupied the area in the 2nd and 3rd centuries, you can visit the Aquincum Museum (p. 139) to see what remains have been preserved.

Gothic-style architecture was a significant style used in the 14th and 15th centuries, but most of the buildings have since been destroyed through wars. Gothic revival was partially used for the Parliament building (p. 131).

The invasion of the Turks brought this part of the world into the Ottoman empire, and they left their mark with their architectural designs. Two places to experience this firsthand are a couple of the thermal baths: the Király was begun in 1565 and the Rudas around 1580. See "Budapest's Most Popular Thermal Baths" in chapter 7.

By the 19th century, architecture adopted the classical style following the precepts of ancient Greek and Roman artistic rules. The most outstanding example of this fashion is the National Museum (p. 126). Adaptation of this can be seen at the Museum of Fine Arts (p. 126), which was created in the neoclassical style, as was St. Stephen's Basilica (p. 134) with its Greek cross ground plan.

BREAKING THE MOLD

Art Nouveau, the international art and architectural form, infiltrated the building designs of Budapest during the late 19th and early 20th centuries. Due to its breaking away from more traditional styles, it is also referred to as secessionist; they incorporate the folk items of each culture, therefore, distinguishing them from country to country. Often, you will hear buildings referred to as Hungarian secessionist. The famous Hungarian architect, Ödön Lechner, has made this form popular. One fine example of his work is the Museum of Applied Arts (p. 128) where his use of Zsolnay ceramics became one of his trademarks. Another delicious example of his originality is the oft-overlooked Postal Savings Bank or Postatakarékpénztár at V. Hold u. 4. Much of the detail is lost from the street view, but if you don't let the trees obscure your line of sight from across the street, you can see the folk symbols of beehives, bees, and birds adorning the side of the building. When Lechner was asked why he would place ornamentation out of people's view, he is said to have replied, "The birds will see it."

At first glance, the Great Market Hall may look like another Lechner design due to the colorful tiles on the roof, however, this building was designed by Samu Petz and built in 1895–97.

Another prime example of Art Nouveau is the well-marketed Gellért Hotel (p. 79). Much of the interior has still not been revamped since it was originally built. The Gellért thermals are also of the Art Nouveau fashion. Owned by the city and not the hotel, they have been completely restored; however, the men's sauna is authentic Zsolnay porcelain, while the women's is imitation.

Bridge Over Political Waters

One of the most-photographed statues is that of Imre Nagy standing on a bridge as he faces Parliament. The statue sits in a small square just off of Kossuth tér. Nagy was the prime minister of Hungary right before the 1956 uprising. His attempt to bridge the old regime with a new one was unsuccessful. The Soviets arrested and later murdered him after promising him his freedom if he left his refuge in the Yugoslavian Embassy.

One building that should not be missed is the Nyugati Train Station, also referred to as the Western Railway Station. It is distinguished as it was designed by Gustave Eiffel studio, of Eiffel Tower fame, in the 1890s. The glass-and-iron construction has a pleasing esthetic appeal. The cafe is now a somewhat tasteful, if not overly lavender, Art Nouveau McDonald's.

In the 1930s and '40s, Hungarian architects embraced the **Bauhaus** mode of design, incorporating modern style with functionality. A group of architects proposed creating a full street in Bauhaus fashion as had been done in Stuttgart, Germany. Much of this is still intact at II. Napraforgó u. 1–22. Twenty-two homes were built surrounding a small square where a commemorative stone lists all the architects involved. Some of the houses needed rebuilding, but the overall character has been kept intact. To explore this area, take bus no. 5 to the end of the line at Pasaréti tér.

Other isolated examples can be viewed in the XIII district at Szent István Park (St. Stephen's Park) and Margit körút where houses are six stories tall. In the same district at Pozsonyi út 53–55 is a Bauhaus building with tiny stores on a triangular area at the corner of Wahrmann Mór köz. Szent Istvánváros Protestant Church complete with belfry is located at Pozsonyi út 58. It was finished in a modern fashion with traditionalist streaks and opened in 1940. Two luxury homes are at Pozsonyi út 38–42. A residential building with a unique entryway with an arched wall at a 45-degree angle was built at Pozsonyi út 33/a. Asymmetric shops combined with a residential building with oversized balconies that cover the facade are located at Tátra utca 5/c. Yet another residential building is on a corner with interesting arched balconies and a capricious facade at Pozsonyi út 19.

THE MODERN AGE

For a sample of "What in the world is that exactly?" you should head on down to gawk at the Lehel Tér market (p. 209) at the Blue metro stop by the same name. It opened in 2002, but it was some time before people could adjust to the fact that it was indeed a market, because it looks like a ship that has badly miscalculated. The architect to credit or hold responsible, depending on your point of view, is László Rajk. Other contemporary buildings are being raised by foreign investors. The Kempinski Hotel is an example of a large building standing out like an orphan at a family reunion. Another example of modernism, built at the foot of the Lágymányosi Bridge, is the National Theatre with its minimalist exterior, using lighting effects to give it additional visual appeal. Alternatively on the same campus is the Palace of Arts (p. 217), which incorporates different styles. Both were based on the designs of Mária Siklós.

Here is a riddle. What do Budapest and Hollywood have in common? Okay, close to Budapest then. Just 26km (16 miles) from Budapest, in a village called Etyek with a population of 3,700, the construction is underway to create the Alexander Korda film studio. At an estimated cost of 150 million euros, the word is that this will be Europe's most modern film production center with some prophesying that "Etyekwood" has the potential to become the "Hollywood of Europe." The majority of the project initiators are Hungarian: producer Andy Vajna, real-estate broker Sandor Demjan, and his now-Canadian business partner Peter Munk are all originally from Hungary. Covering 15 hectares (37 acres), this facility has been designed as the most technically sophisticated international film production to be built yet. Six studios will spread out over 40,000sq. m (430,556 sq. ft). Get the big picture here? Not only will it be the world's largest film studio, but also it will have capabilities for underwater filming.

One often never pays much attention to the ways that the work of an ethnic group adds something to our lives. Although you will not find a plethora of Hungarian movies with English subtitles at your local movie rental outlet, chances are that some Hungarians have been responsible for entertaining you at some point in time. Here is a brief overview of the Hungarian impact on pop culture.

Wilhelm Fried was born to Jewish parents in Tolcsva, Hungary, but at the age of 9 moved to the U.S. with his parents. His name was changed to William Fox. As an adult he created the Fox Film Corporation in 1915, purchasing the equipment to create the Fox Movie, later becoming Fox Movietone sound-on-film system, commercializing talking movies. His name is still associated with 20th-Century Fox Studios and FOX Network News. Adolph

Cukor from Ricse, Hungary was another Jewish immigrant who made film history. Changing his name to Adolf Zukor, he started in the entertainment business by creating a new chain of movie theaters with Marcus Loew. His Famous Players in Famous Plays evolved into Paramount Studios. He introduced the new phenomenon of combining production, distribution, and exhibition all within one company. **George Pal**, born György Pál Marczincsák from Cégled, Hungary was an animator in a few countries before landing in the U.S. to work for Paramount Studios, where he is credited for creating 40 Puppetoon films. As a director, producer, and cinematographer he is best remembered (depending on your age) for his science-fiction movies *The War of the Worlds* (1953), *Houdini* (1953), *Tom Thumb* (1958), and *The Time Machine* (1960), amongst others. He received six Oscars and a special Academy Award. **Ivan Tors** from Budapest was a playwright, screenwriter, film and television producer. His more famous television series included *Sea Hunt* and *Flipper*. His production company, Ivan Tors Films, did the underwater scenes for the James Bond *Thunderball* movie. Andy Vajna, formerly known as András György Vajna, left his home in Budapest in 1956. He joined up with Mario Kassar to form Carolco Pictures, making movie history with a new cinematic hero, *Rambo*. Other Carolco projects include *Total Recall, Air America*, and *Jacob's Ladder*. Vajna is credited with *Die Hard: With a Vengeance*, several *Terminator* movies, *Basic Instinct*, and a list of others.

AT THE MOVIES

If you want to see a bit of Budapest before arriving, you just need to rent the movie *Munich* (2005). Don't be fooled by those Paris scenes; they were filmed in the Paris of the East, Budapest. The whole area of the Opera House was converted to Paris streets. Locals had to remove their cars, so they could be replaced with French cars with French license plates. Stores and restaurants were refitted with French signs and displays. The old dance school across the street from the Opera House was made into a lighting store with an adjoining café. It was quite confusing when I tried going in for a coffee and was kicked off the "lot." The clue should have been the Paris Metro map that was on display when coming up from the metro station.

Two gripping movies tell the story of the Hungarian Holocaust in very different, yet poignant ways. The 1999 release of *Sunshine* follows the lives of three generations of Hungarian Jews. Neither allegiance to their country, celebrity as an Olympic fencing star, nor converting to Christianity is enough to save them. Written and directed by **István Szabó**, the first Hungarian to have won an Oscar.

Based on the book of the same name *Fateless* (Sorstalanság, the Hungarian title), directed by Hungarian Lajos Koltai, is the story of György Köves, a 14-year-old boy who is removed from a bus by the Nazis while on his way to work in a brickyard. He is sent to Buchenwald and into a life of forced labor.

Most of my Hungarian students and friends tell me they don't like Hungarian movies, yet continually I seem to be getting recommendations of what I must see, when they know it is has been subtitled in English. Hungarian movies tend to be dark, yet there are some with comic relief.

If you dare, watch the movie *Kontroll* (2003) before you arrive. It is in Hungarian with English subtitles. The entire movie is filmed in the Budapest metro and follows the life of a ticket inspector or controller named Bulcsú. After the film was released in 2003, some people were fearful to use the metro. Although the controllers have mellowed some since, or perhaps because of this movie, this dark

dramedy (drama with comedy slipped in spots) will entertain and intrigue you, but will leave you with questions unanswered.

A young Hungarian director to keep your eye on is **Krisztina Goda**. She has two movies worth checking out. *Just Sex and Nothing Else* is a romantic comedy about Dora, a 30-something woman looking for that elusive love relationship.

Goda's second movie, *Kaméleon* (English title Chameleon) made its way to the Oscars in 2009 as Hungary's choice for Best Foreign Film. In this comedy/drama, Zsolt Kovàcs cleans offices for a living. However, by going through the trash, he learns more about the people working there than they ever suspect. Taking on different personas, Zsolt performs the ultimate con job.

REQUIRED READING

HISTORY For an in-depth look into the country's history, culture, and economy covering 1,000 years from its inception to the 1988 elections, invest in *A Concise History of Hungary* by Miklós Molnár, translated by Anna Magyar (Cambridge University Press; 2001). Excellently researched and told with precision, *The Hungarians: A Thousand Years of Victory in Defeat* (Princeton University Press; 2004) by Paul Lendvai and translated by Ann Major is a whopping 608 pages. Explore how Hungary fared as the last ally of Nazi Germany in World War II and the destruction suffered as a result in *Hungary from the Nazis to the Soviets: The Establishment of the Communist Regime in Hungary, 1944–1948* (Cambridge University Press; 2009) by Peter Kenez.

A former editor-in-chief of Simon & Shuster, Michael Korda's *Journey to a Revolution: A Personal Memoir and History of the Hungarian Revolution of 1956* (Harper Perennial; 2007) intertwines memoir with history as he visits his father's homeland only to become part of the struggle. George Konrad, a world-renowned essayist and novelist delivers his personal history with *A Guest in My Own Country: A Hungarian Life* (Other Press; 2007). Gathering glimpses of his life from the Holocaust through the Hungarian Revolution of 1956, he transports the reader to another realm.

JEWISH HISTORY For a comprehensive historical overview of Jewish history in Budapest and the region, the best you can get is *Jewish Budapest: Monuments, Rites, History* (Central European University Press; 1999) by Kinga Frojimovics, Geza Komoroczy, Viktoria Pusztai, Andrea Strbik. Filled with photographs, maps, and drawings, it brings the history to life.

HOLOCAUST HISTORY One of my personal favorites is *Nine Suitcases: A Memoir* by Zsolt Béla (Pimlico; 2005). Being a prolific writer, he wrote 10 novels and four plays. Béla was part of the intellectuals who met in the historic coffeehouses of Budapest at the time. What is now in book form, was originally printed in installments from 1946 to 1947 in a Hungarian journal. Kati Marton tells the amazing accomplishments of scientists, computer pioneers, and others who escaped Hungary during troubled times, but in their newly adopted country had spectacular achievements to their credit in *The Great Escape: Nine Jews Who Fled Hitler and Changed the World* (Simon & Schuster; 2007). An excellent accompaniment to any Holocaust collection, Ronald W. Zweig's *The Gold Train: The Destruction of the Jews and the Looting of Hungary* (Harper Perennial; 2003) is a fine account of the false confidence the Hungarian Jews had until the closing days of the war and their subsequent search for the stolen riches after the war was over. Many are familiar with Raoul Wallenberg, but in the book *When Angels Fooled the World: Rescuers of Jews in Wartime Hungary* by Charles Fenyvesi (University of Wisconsin Press; 2003), the author sheds light on other lesser-known names who were just as heroic

in helping the Jews. The author and his family were aided by such "angels" later named Righteous Gentiles and honored in Israel.

ART & ARCHITECTURE *Zsolnay Ceramics: Collecting a Culture* by Federico Santi Federico Santi (Author). Visit Amazon's Federico Santi Page. and John Gacher (Schiffer Publishing; 1998); *Herend: The Art of Hungarian Porcelain* by Gyoza Sikota (Puski; 2nd edition; 1988).

FOR THE KIDS As a former elementary school teacher, I love it when children can be part of the discovery process in travel. The book *Benjamin in Budapest: City Guide for Children* (Palio Kft; www.benjamin guides.com) was written for children and illustrated by children in local schools in Budapest. Follow Benjamin through all seasons as he points out the best places for children to have fun while in the city.

The White Stag by Kate Seredy (Puffin; 1979) is for children 9 to 12 years old. The story is a retelling of the legend of the Huns' and Magyars' long migration from Asia to Europe where they hoped to find a permanent home. The Paul Street Boys by Ferenc Molnar (Corvina; 3rd edition; 1998) is a Hungarian children's classic and still required reading in many schools. The Paul Street boys share in tales of bravery, heroism, patriotism, honor, truth, love, war, and passion in the microcosm of two groups of teenage boys living in Budapest. They are about to fight for a small open space amidst the busy streets of the big city where they can play ball. But that's just the basic plot. It is recommended for pre-teen to young adult readers. *Raoul Wallenberg: The Man Who Stopped Death* by Sharon Linnéa (Jewish Publication Society of America; 1993) exalts the man who is credited with saving thousands of lives during World War II. This book is recommended for young adult readers.

CONTEMPORARY FICTION Hungarians are known for their artistic prowess in creating powerful poetry and extraordinary literature dripping with angst, yet compellingly so. This makes it rather unfortunate that so little of the work is translated into English. Here are some titles worth looking into. *Leopard V: An Island of Sound: Hungarian Poetry and Fiction Before and Beyond the Iron Curtain* edited by George Szirtes (Random House UK; 2004). The chosen pieces for this edited edition reflect the anxiety, disturbances, and murmuring of the Hungarian literary mind. *Niki: The Story of a Dog* by Tibor Dery (NYRB Classics reprint edition; 2009) delivers a parable of love and kindness through a dog's eyes in 1956 Hungary when a fox terrier adopts a family. *Metropole* by Ferenc Karinthy (Telegram Books; 2008) is the story of a Hungarian linguist who boards the wrong plane on the way to a conference and wakes up to find himself in a strange city with an incomprehensible language in an unknown country. This is the basic plot, but more intrigue awaits. Originally written in the '70s, it has just recently made its way into English translation. Some critics call it more Kafkaesque than Kafka himself. *Under the Frog: A Novel* by Tibor Fischer (Picador; 2001) is a story that mingles the evils of totalitarian oppression with the adventures of two members of Hungary's elite national basketball team. Timing is from the end of World War II through the 1956 Hungarian Uprising. *Fateless* by Imre Kertesz (Hydra Books; 1996) is written with a master's stroke as he delivers a novel that follows the life of a 14-year-old who spends a year as a prisoner of Auschwitz. *To Err is Divine: A Novel* (Counterpoint; 2004) by Ágota Bozai is one of the first Hungarian books I read in translation and it was love at first read. Using religious symbolism, our main character, Anna Lévay, a not-so-nice English teacher, wakes one morning to find she has a halo around her head. As she unwittingly starts performing miracles, others realize a business opportunity when they see it. *Prague: A Novel* by Arthur Philips (Random House;

2003) only sounds like it should be in another of our publications, but it is really about Budapest. The story follows the lives of five expats from North America who venture to Budapest in 1990, after the fall of Communism, but have the dream of moving on to Prague.

For some light reading, I truly love the work of Canadian author Lyn Hamilton's archeological mystery series, but in particular *The Magyar Venus* (Berkley; 2005). Lara McClintoch owns an antiques store in Toronto, but when she is prompted to visit Budapest to determine the authenticity of the newly discovered Venus statute, things begin to unwind. It is obvious Hamilton has really researched the city, as you will still find the stores on the streets that she includes in her prose.

CONTEMPORARY NONFICTION *Letters From Budapest* by R. O. Atkins (Merari Fierro Villavicencio Publishing; 2007) chronicles the mundane to the extraordinary twists and turns of life in the fast lane, where one is not exactly sure which direction to take at that fork in the road. Bob, another founding member of my Budapest writers' group, offers a cheerful read in this book. Gastronomy and wine folks will appreciate *Food Wine Budapest* (Random House; 2008) by Carolyn Bánfalvi. As the title suggests, the focus is on Hungarian cuisine and wines. Carolyn shares the history of various Hungarian recipes, cooking methods, where to shop for specialty items, and dining etiquette in addition to providing an overview of various wine region offerings. She includes the other typical Hungarian drinks such as unicum and palinka.

A "NOTE" ABOUT MUSIC

When investigating the musical culture of Hungary, what becomes apparent is that, especially through most of the 18th century, the country was filled with foreign composers, conductors, and orchestras mainly of German or Czech origin. The royal courts and homes of aristocrats brought these musicians to Hungary to have them in-residence becoming their benefactors as their personal musicians. The music of the country was that of the musicians who brought it with them.

Budapest and all of Hungary for that matter is synonymous with Gypsy music. In the late 18th century, *verbunkos* was used to develop an interest in serving for the military. *Verbunkos* is derived from the German word *werbung* meaning "to recruit." *Verbunkos* alternates between a slow (*lassú*) and a fast (*friss*) section. Employed by the emperor, Gypsy musicians were engaged to play *verbunkos* music, while hussars danced to it, creating a hypnotic frenzy that encouraged the youth to join the military before conscription was introduced.

The complete history is not known, but what is known is that the origins were rooted in Hungarian folk music with influences from Slav, Italian, and Viennese music. With its Hungarian origins, it became part of the national identity and was embraced by the Hungarian people. By 1780, beyond the borders of Hungary, Hungarian music was associated with the music of *verbunkos*. Easily recognizable, it had unique characteristics. *Bokázó* is a beat pattern like the clicking of heels, the Gypsy pattern of the *lassú* and *friss* tempos with widely arched melodies and flaming rhythm. This new style transcended other Hungarian musical styles. Liszt created his Hungarian Rhapsodies from the inspiration he garnered from *verbunkos* music. Bartók and Kodály also felt the effect of this music and utilized it for their own work.

Thought to be the premier Gypsy musician of the time, **János Bihari** (1764–1827) created dynamic interpretations suffused with heroism and emotion in his compositions of *verbunkos* style. To expand his repertoire, Bihari tapped into the music of the Kuruc (anti-Habsburgs) era

to create a fusion with the *verbunkos* style. Considered among his contemporaries to be the foremost Gypsy violinist, he was highly sought after to entertain even the highest echelons of society, including the Vienna Royal Court. Bihari composed the musical piece *Rákóczi March,* using old Kuruc pieces of music. Franz Liszt was among his most fervent fans and said of him: "The tones sung by his magic violin flow on our enchanted ears like the tears."

In Pest, in 1837, the National Theatre with **Ferenc Erkel** had the first music director. Erkel composed operas and became known as Hungary's most renowned operatic composer. His creation of Hungarian operas was simultaneous with other European composers creating their own national culture-based operas. Erkel is best known for two works: *Hunyadi László,* composed in 1844 and *Bánk Bán* in 1861. These two pieces continue to be standard fare for opera performances in Hungary.

The best-known musicians of Hungary are **Franz (Ferenc) Liszt**, **Béla Bartók,** and **Zoltán Kodály**. Liszt was born in Doborján, a German-speaking Austrian town that was part of the Austro-Hungarian empire. He never spoke Hungarian, but said "Although, unfortunately, I don't speak Hungarian, I want to remain Hungarian in heart and mind from cradle to grave. I want to work for the development of Hungary's musical culture." Liszt's first visit to Hungary was in 1839. He raised donations to aid the city after Pest was devastated by a flood in 1838. Spending much of his time abroad giving concerts, he was only an occasional visitor to Budapest. However, in 1875, the king appointed Liszt to president of the Academy of Music in Budapest. At the same time, he became the head of the piano department; this is the academy that is now named after him. Note that in October 2009, the academy closed for a 2-year renovation.

Kodály and Bartók started their musical studies at the same time, becoming good friends. They spent summer vacations in the countryside making recordings on wax cylinders of folk songs shared by the villagers. Their collection of 60,000 folk tunes is preserved at the Hungarian Academy of Sciences. Both were professors at the music academy, but Bartók left the country for America before World War II. Kodály is well known for his fierce advocacy of music education in schools. The famous Kodály Method for teaching music was not created by him, but by some of his students based on his educational philosophy. Kodály is considered one of the most famous of the Hungarian composers.

This section would not be complete without touching on *klezmer* music. *Klezmer* originally referred to the instruments used, then to the musicians who played them. It was not until later that it became a genre in music. The music evolved from 15th-century, non-liturgical Jewish music used for celebrations such as weddings. From the 16th century onward, lyrics were added to some *klezmer* and today, the songs run the gamut from celebration to despair, but are usually accompanied by dancing.

5 HUNGARIAN EATS & TREATS

Traditional Hungarian cuisine reflects the rich and varied flavors of many international influences. Since the first Magyars were nomadic people, they learned from the Turkish and other cultures with which they came into contact. Soup was an important staple of their lifestyle. They used a *bogrács*, a large cast-iron pot that hung on an iron rod over the fire, for cooking soups. It was easily transported with the soup in the pot as the Magyars moved from place to place, and the soup was consumed over days. The *bogrács* is a popular cooking utensil even today and soup continues to be an important part of a meal.

Once the Magyars settled in the Carpathian Basin, pork was introduced into the diet with each family raising its own pigs. Culinary transformations occurred through marriage also. After King Matthias and Beatrice of Italy married, she introduced Italian influences into the cooking culture, including turkey, pasta, cheeses, garlic, and onions.

The Turks may have had the greatest influence on gastronomy as they introduced paprika to the culture. Hungary's climate is perfect for growing the red peppers that are ground up to create the spice. At first, the elite only grew paprika peppers for their decorative value, but peasants grew them and used them for cooking. At one point in the 19th century, the rising cost of black pepper convinced the masses to switch to paprika, thus dubbing paprika *török bors* or Turkish pepper. Paprika comes in different varieties. It ranges from spicy hot *(csípős)* to sweet *(édes)* with other varieties in between, depending on the peppers used.

Another way the Turks influenced food habits was by taking all of the domestic animals with them only leaving the pigs as, due to their religion, they did not care about these lowly animals, thus making pork an important meat for the Magyars. Turks are also responsible for introducing *strudel, pilaf, lángos,* and stuffed vegetables. They also introduced plants such as the tomato, sour cherry, corn, and tobacco.

When the Turks gave Hungarians coffee, it changed the culture in astonishing ways. In the late 1800s, there were more than 500 coffeehouses in Budapest alone. Many of the famous ones are where writers, artists, musicians, and other intellectuals gathered.

The Hungarian upper class adopted the French fashion of cooking as did the Austrian aristocrats. Perhaps this is where the love affair with goose liver originated. Middle-class Hungarians incorporated Austrian dishes in their everyday meals, adopting schnitzel, sausages, potatoes, and vegetable stews thickened with flour and lard. Today this vegetable stew is called *főzelék* and is a traditional favorite food.

Different parts of Hungary have regional traditions and favorite recipes, but any good Hungarian restaurant in Budapest incorporates some from each on their menu. Some restaurants specialize in the more exotic fare such as deer, or wild boar. Often, when deer is on the menu, it is translated as deer and not venison. It will be saddle of deer; this is the breast meat. Regardless of what is on the menu, if it is a traditional Hungarian menu, you are guaranteed that food will be plentiful and heavy. Hungarian cooking uses a great deal of pork or goose fat, which adds incredible flavors to dishes. Sour cream, potatoes, or a form of pasta are also added to enrich a dish, adding to that gluttony feeling after you finish. Just so you don't miss any gastronomical experiences, we've put all the foods you should sample while here in a box at the end of this chapter. Some are discussed within this chapter also.

Lunch begins with soup. *Gulyás,* often mispronounced as "goulash," is a meat soup usually made with beef or pork, carrots, and potatoes in a rich broth. Travelers often have the misconception that *gulyás* is a stew. *Babgulyás* is a hearty and delicious bean soup similar to *gulyás.* Hungary is famous for its *gyümölcs leves,* a cold fruit soup, which can be made from sour cherry, peaches, or apricots. Served in summertime, it makes a refreshing way to start a meal. *Sargáborsoleves,* a split pea soup— a good winter seasonal choice— and *halászle,* a fish soup, constitute meals in themselves.

Entrees/main courses are generally some type of meat dish. Try the *paprikás csirke,* chicken cooked in a savory paprika sauce. It's especially good with *galuska,* a pasta dumpling. *Pulykamell,* turkey breast roasted with various fruits and/or sauces, is also delicious. Another great choice is *Pörkölt,* a stewed meat dish that comes in many varieties. *Töltött káposzta,* whole cabbage leaves stuffed with rice, meat, and spices, is another favorite. Cabbage is a winter staple food and appears in pastry also. Remember the word *káposzta* (cabbage) if you don't want it as your savory pastry filling.

Vegetarianism is slowly, ever so slowly, being recognized in Hungarian restaurants; many establishments now offer a vegetable dish, usually consisting of seasonal steamed and grilled vegetables, or cheese plates. Hungarians look on vegetarians with suspicion, regardless of their nationality. Otherwise, vegetarians would do well to order *lecsó tojással* (eggs scrambled in a thick tomato-onion-paprika sauce), *rántott sajt* (batter-fried cheese with tartar sauce), or *túrós csusza tepertő nélkul* (a type of noodle with cottage cheese dish). The kitchen should be able to prepare any of these dishes to order, even if they don't appear on the menu.

Snack foods include *lángos,* a piece of dough pulled into a small pizza shape and served with your choice of toppings: cheese, ham, and garlic sauce are the most popular, but you can also have powdered sugar and whipped cream. *Palacsinta,* a paper-thin crepe stuffed with a multitude of offerings for either a sweet or a savory light bite, is another excellent choice. *Kürtős kalács,* a hollow, tubular honey cake, is an old-fashioned pastry cooked on a wooden bolt; it is sometimes available in metro stations and at outdoor markets and fairs, but is best when freshly baked. *Fagylalt* (ice cream) is the national street food, especially in warm months. Scoops are tiny, so order more than one or you

You Haven't Been to Hungary If You Haven't Tried...

Fözelék. This hearty dish is somewhere between a soup and a stew in consistency, but without any chunks of meat or veg. There are a number of varieties, but green pea, potato, and chicken are the most popular. The vegetable varieties sometimes contain animal fat, so vegetarians should ask ahead of time.

Lángos. Many cultures have their own variety of dough that is deep-fried in fat. Here it's topped with shredded cheese and/or ham, finally sprinkled with garlic juice. There are now many types of toppings, but a *Mexikói* (Mexican) is not authentic. The best place to try them is in the Central Market Hall (Központi Vásárcsarnok, p. 209) upstairs on the right-hand wall of food booths.

Halászlé. This is fish soup, usually made with carp, pike, or perch, but sometimes with a couple of different fish. Widely available in restaurants.

Palacsinta. The French call these crepes. The Hungarians call them a national treasure. There are a number of fillings to make these a complete meal. Some *palacsinta* restaurants have complete menus of entrees and desserts consisting of three to five crepes for a fixed price usually under 800 Ft.

Somlói Galuska. A rich and treasured dessert, this will satisfy a chocolate lover's sweet tooth. Served in a bowl, cubes of spongy cake are sprinkled with a rum flavoring, and then vanilla sauce is poured over the moist cubes followed by a topping of chocolate sauce, which is finished off with whipped cream. It is a dieter's nightmare and often on restaurant dessert menus.

Turós táska (sweet cheese bag). A cheese-filled strudel-type dessert and available in most bakeries.

Túró Rudi. This is so Hungarian, you won't find it outside of the country. Many returning visitors look for it on their first day back. Shaped like a small log, it is a cheese called quark, which is thinly coated with chocolate. The most famous is the "*natur*" flavor, though there are others with fruit added. The original is in a white, red-dotted wrapper. You will not find this on any menu, but if you venture into any convenience store or supermarket, they will be plentiful in the refrigerator case. They are welcome sweets by Hungarian parents for their nutritional value and low cost, about 80 Ft.

will have more cone than ice cream. Fresh fruit flavors are seasonal: in the summer it's *eper* (strawberry) and *meggy* (sour cherry) and in the fall flavors include *szilva* (plum) and *körte* (pear). Summer regulars are delicious *fahéj* (cinnamon), *mák* (poppy seed), and *rizs* (rice).

Hungarian pastries are mouthwatering, but the cakes are not as sweet or moist as other countries' offerings. For the first 2 years, we thought we were being sold stale cakes because we were foreigners. If you like your pastry with some moisture, choose one of the creamy types. The light, flaky *rétes* are filled with fruit (apple, plum, cherry), poppy seeds, or cheese. *Csoki torta* is a decadent chocolate layer cake, and a *Dobos torta* is a layered cake topped with a shiny hard caramel crust. (Hint: Take the crust off first and eat it separately). *Mákos* pastry, made with poppy seeds, is a Hungarian specialty. *Gesztenye* (chestnuts) are another popular ingredient in desserts; some are chestnut cream with whipped cream on top or chestnut cream in a pastry. *Béigli*, a traditional Christmas holiday pastry, appears everywhere during the season. A log-shaped pastry with crushed walnuts or poppy seeds baked in it like a jelly roll, it is sliced into bite-sized portions.

Picnickers should pick up a loaf of Hungarian bread and sample any of Hungary's world-famous salamis. Before you decide to pack some to take home, check the Customs regulations (p. 32). A number of tasty cheeses are produced in Hungary as well: *Karaván füstölt* (a smoked cheese), *Edami* (Dutch cheese), *márvány* (similar to bleu cheese), and *juhtúró* (a soft, spreadable sheep's cheese similar in flavor to feta). In season, fresh produce is cheap and high quality, but variety is limited compared to many other countries. In the winter, fresh fruits and vegetables are slim pickings with apples, pears, cabbage, potatoes, and carrots being the most common choices. In summer, you'll be amazed at the abundance of fresh produce and the low-cost but limited varieties at the colorful markets. One type of berry or another is continually available throughout the summer months: strawberries *(eper)* appear in markets in May; raspberries *(málna)*, blueberries *(fekete áfonya)*, blackberries *(szeder)*, and sour cherries *(meggy)* start hitting the market in June.

BEER, WINE & SPIRITS Hungary never developed a beer culture. Its beer is unremarkable, but don't tell a Hungarian this; they are staunchly proud of anything Hungarian. A number of European beers are now produced under license in Hungary. Your best bet though are Czech beers, such as Budvar, Staropramen, or Pilsner Urquell, which are the real thing.

Hungarian wines are excellent. The most renowned red wines come from the region around Villány, a town to the south of Pécs near the Croatian border. As a result of an aggressive marketing campaign mounted by the former Communist regime, many travelers are familiar with the red wines from Eger, especially *Egri Bikavér* (Eger Bull's Blood). However, Eger wines, though rich and fruity, are markedly inferior to Villányi reds. The country's best white wines are generally believed to be those from the Lake Balaton region, though some Hungarians insist that white wines from the Somló region (northeast of Lake Balaton) are better. *Tokaj* wines—*száraz* (dry) or *édes* (sweet)—are popular as aperitifs and dessert wines. Travelers seeking advice on Hungarian wines are encouraged to visit one of the full-service wine stores in Budapest (see p. 211 for shopping suggestions). You can also pick up the free pamphlet *Wine Regions in Hungary* at Tourinform.

Unikum is the Hungarian national liqueur similar to Germany's Jagermeister or Italy's Fernet Branca. This aromatic bitter liquid is a taste worth acquiring. It is still produced according to the original recipe owned by the Zwack family (the current owner of the company, a Zwack family member, was Hungary's first ambassador to the U.S. after the fall of Communism). The distilled fruit brandy palinka is another variety of Hungarian firewater that is often referred to as schnapps. It is a liqueur with high alcohol content and some fruit or honey flavor. Palinka is traditionally brewed at home where apricots, plums, pears, or honey are plentiful; folk wisdom claims it has medicinal value. Only the better brands have much fruit flavor at all.

COFFEE & TEA Hungarians drink *kávé* (coffee) throughout the day, either in coffeehouses or less seldom in standup coffee bars. The menus in a number of coffee shops have expanded greatly. In general, when ordering coffee in Hungary, you are still ordering espresso. An "American" coffee called *hosszú kávé* (long coffee) will be an espresso with additional hot water added, nothing close to filtered coffee. Espresso drinks are now available in most coffeehouses, as is *koffein mentes* (decaffeinated coffee). *Tejeskávé*, a Hungarian version of café au lait, is another option.

Tea drinkers will have a less difficult time than in the past; most food establishments have come to recognize the tea drinker, offering a selection of tea flavors to choose from. Tea is now readily available in bars and cafes, plus there have been a number of tea cafes that have opened and are prospering (a few tea cafes are listed in chapter 6, "Where to Dine in Budapest"). For more variety and a peek at Hungary's burgeoning world of herbal medicine, look for teas in any of the numerous tea or herbal shops: *gyógynövény, herbárium,* or *gyógytea.*

WATER   While *csapvíz* (tap water) is safe to drink in Budapest, it isn't generally offered in restaurants; when you order water they charge for the bottle. Ask for tap water specifically, stating "not bottled." Hungarians increasingly drink *Ásványvíz* (carbonated mineral water), *szóda víz,* (carbonated tap water), or sz*énsav mentes* (purified bottled water). All these varieties of water are available at restaurants as well as at delicatessens and grocery stores.

Planning Your Trip to Budapest

Having joined the European Union in 2004, the tourism infrastructure has developed at a furious pace in Hungary. There are many high-quality hotels and restaurants for all budgets, yet new hotels and dining opportunities continue to appear on the scene. Major improvements in the service sector have been noticeable over the past few years, but there is always room for improvement.

You will find tourism-related information offices called **Tourinform** (✆ **1/438-8080** or ✆ **06/80-630-800**; www.tourinform.hu), a branch of the Hungarian National Tourist Office, at V. Sütő u. 2, Budapest; open daily from 8am to 8pm. You'll also find a branch office in the heart of Budapest's Broadway, at Liszt Ferenc tér 11 (✆ **1/322-4098;** fax 1/342-2541), open daily from noon to 8pm. These offices distribute pamphlets on events and attractions within the city in which they are located. They can assist you with finding appropriate accommodations and restaurants, but once outside of large cities, the amount of English decreases. The tourism authority, **Magyar Turizmus Rt** (✆ **1/488-8701;** www.hungarytourism.hu), also has offices throughout the world, and it is their mandate to promote Hungary as a destination for tourism.

For general country information and a variety of pamphlets and maps before you leave home, contact the government-sponsored **Hungarian National Tourist Office,** 350 Fifth Ave., New York, NY 10118 (✆ **212/695-1212;** www.gotohungary.com). In London, the **Hungarian National Tourist Office** is at 46 Eaton Place, London SW1X 8AL (✆ **020/7823-1032**). The Hungarian National Tourist Office's main website, a great source of information, is **www.gotohungary.co.uk**.

Other sites with lots of helpful current information including news, shopping, entertainment, and current venues for music, dance, and theatrical events for visitors and English-speaking locals are *Funzine (*www.funzine.hu), published every 2 weeks, and *Where,* published monthly, both free at Tourinform or at many restaurants and hotels. *Time Out,* found in many major cities, started publishing in Budapest in 2009. It is free from the Tourinform or 450 Ft at newsstands. The *Budapest Times* (www.budapest times.hu) both in print at newsstands or online, has news articles with an entertainment section. The Tourinform office puts out a monthly brochure called *Budapest Panorama* listing all of the scheduled events during the month. For news articles about Hungary, check out the Hungarian News Agency at **www.english.mti.hu**. It's updated daily.

For additional help in planning your trip and for more on-the-ground resources in Budapest, please turn to "Fast Facts," on p. 290.

1 WHEN TO GO

I always recommend spring and fall to those who ask what are the best seasons to visit. Hotels are on low-season rates usually until the middle to end of April reverting to them again from about mid-September. Generally, hotels will use their special season rates for Christmas and New Year, but winters generally are cold and gray, casting a dark shadow over a glorious city. Although it does snow here, we have not had any major snowfall for the last 5 years. When it does snow, it generally dissipates within the day. If you choose Christmas time for your holiday, remember to consider that half a day of Christmas Eve, all of Christmas, and the day after are holidays. Many things will be closed for those days; however, some museums open on December 26 if it does not fall on a regularly scheduled closed day. The afternoon of New Year's Eve will have most places shuttered closed with the exception of restaurants, and all of New Year's Day is a legal holiday.

From sometime in April to mid-September, many activities come alive. The outdoor pools are open, and the outdoor squatters' beer pubs start appearing like mushrooms after a rain. Spring is a perfect time to ride the Children's Railroad or the chairlift.

Other activities hibernate during the summer as it can get really warm, especially July and August. Without air conditioning in many venues, like the Opera House, it is too hot to offer regular programming during the summer. There are short-term events held sporadically. Make sure to pack an umbrella. We do get a number of days of rain as you can see from the chart on p. 31 but for the most part, they are passing showers seldom lasting more than a day, but often only lasting hours.

Budapest and the rest of Hungary has been held hostage by the economic crisis, creating a dramatic drop in tourism. Regardless of when you decide to visit, you are sure to find some bargains. With a little planning you can come to Budapest at a time that will coincide with one or more of the city's cultural events; however, if you miss these, there is always something worthy happening; it is a city of festivals. All inquiries about ticket availability and locations of events can first be checked online where you can also buy tickets for many venues at www.jegymester.hu. For other information, contact Budapest's main tourist information office, **Tourinform,** referred to earlier in this section.

MARCH

Budapest Spring Festival (Budapesti Øszi Fesztivál). For 2 weeks, performances of opera, concerts, dance, and drama are held at all the major halls and theaters of Budapest. Simultaneously, temporary exhibitions open in many of Budapest's museums. Tickets are available from the **Festival Ticket Service,** (✆ 1/486-3311, weekdays 10am to 5pm or from http://bof.hu/. If you have questions, write to tickets@festivalcity.hu. Book your tickets as soon as possible as the best shows sell out a few days after they are announced. The festival runs mid- to late March.

Hollókő's Easter Festival. During Easter in this charming, small town in northeastern Hungary, villagers wear traditional costumes and participate in a folk festival featuring traditional song, dance, and foods. For information, contact the **Hungarian Arts Festivals Federation** (✆ 1/202-1095; www.arts festivals.hu). Held on Easter Day, it is as popular with Hungarians as with travelers, so expect a crowd.

JUNE, JULY & AUGUST

Open-Air Theater Programs. Budapest has a rich variety of open-air performances throughout the city during the summer. Highlights include opera and ballet on Margaret Island in the Open-Air Theater; folklore, and dance at the Buda Park Theater; musicals in Margaret Island's Városmajor Theater; and classical music recitals in the Dominican Courtyard at the Hilton Hotel. On the last weekend of June through the second weekend of July, the Chain Bridge has a band on either side with the entire bridge hosting a fair. For information, pick up a copy of *Budapest Panorama* from **Tourinform**, listing all events during the given month. Open-Air events are June through August.

Szeged Summer Festival. Szeged, the proud capital of the Great Plain, is home to a summer-long series of cultural events (ballet, opera, rock opera, and open-air theater). For information, call ✆ 62/471-411; www.szegediszabadteri. hu. June through August.

Organ Concerts, Budapest. Concerts are given in the Matthias Church, in the lovely Castle District of Buda. See p. 217 for details. June through August. In addition, Budapest's largest church, St. Stephen's Basilica (p. 134), also hosts concerts outside the front doors. If you don't care about sitting, you can listen for free. July through August.

International Palace Tournament, Visegrád. Each summer, this ancient town hosts an authentic medieval festival replete with dueling knights on horseback, and early music and dance. Contact **Visegrád Tours,** RÉV u. 15, Visegrád (✆ **26/398-090;** www.palota jatekok.hu). Second weekend in July.

"Budafest" Summer Opera and Ballet Festival, Budapest. This summer festival (usually held during the tail end of July and six times in August) is the only time to see a summer performance at the glorious Hungarian State Opera House in Budapest. Tickets are available at the **Opera House** box office at VI. Andrássy út 20 (✆ **1/331-2550;** www.opera.hu).

International Guitar Festival, Esztergom. This stately town on the Danube hosts a guitar festival that features performers from around the world. The Basilica hosts the classical concert performances. For information, contact **Gran Tours,** Esztergom at Széchenyi tér 25 (✆ 33/502-001; www.guitarfestival.hu). First week of August every other year; the next festival is scheduled for 2011.

Formula One Grand Prix, Budapest. One of the European racing circuit's most important annual events is held at Budapest's HungaroRing in Mogyoród. Hotels increase their rates considerably for this event, so plan ahead. Call ✆ **28/444-444** or check out **www. hungaroring.hu**. First week or second weekend in August.

Island Festival (Sziget Fesztivál), Óbuda Island in the Danube. Established in 1994 as Hungary's very own Woodstock, the Sziget Festival (✆ **1/372-0650;** www.sziget.hu) is a weeklong music festival that draws people from all over Europe, but the scope is now worldwide. It is one of the largest music festivals in Europe, gaining in popularity each year. The event features foreign and local rock, folk, jazz, world music, and other groups on dozens of stages playing each day from early afternoon to the wee hours of the morning. Camping is available. You can get details and pick up a program schedule at **Tourinform** (p. 28) or check out their website. Usually begins the second week of August.

Traditional Handicraft Fair, Budapest. The Castle District is the site of a 3-day annual handicraft fair, which draws vendors from across Hungary and from Hungarian enclaves in neighboring countries, especially Romania. The wares are generally handmade and of high quality. This is part of the St. Stephen's Day celebrations (see below). August 20.

St. Stephen's Day, Budapest. Hungary's national day. The country's first king and patron saint is celebrated with cultural events and a dramatic firework display over the Danube at 9pm. St. Stephen's mummified hand is paraded through the streets. Hungarians also celebrate their constitution on this day and ceremoniously welcome the first new bread from the crop of July wheat. August 20.

National Jewish Festival, Budapest. Celebrating its 11th year in 2010, this annual festival enriches the Hungarian cultural scene. The festival features a variety of Jewish culture-related events. Features range from *klezmer* music to a book fair, from ballet to cabaret, held at various locations for the different venues offered. For information, contact the Tourism and Cultural Center of the Budapest Jewish Community, Síp u. 12 (© **1/343-0420;** www.jewishfestival. hu). Late August into early September; call for exact dates.

Budapest International Wine Festival. This festival, in Budapest's Castle District, features wine tastings, displays, and auctions, as well as folk and classical music performances. Each year, there is a guest country that shares its wines. The sponsor is the **Hungarian Viniculture Foundation,** XI. Bartók Béla út 152 (© **1/203-8507;** www. winefestival.hu). Early September.

Budapest International Fair. For 10 days, Budapest's HungExpo grounds fill with displays of Europe's latest consumer goods. (© **1/263-6000,** www. hungexpo.hu). Mid-September.

Budapest Art Weeks. In celebration of the opening of the fall season, special classical music and dance performances spring up for 3 weeks in all the city's major halls. For information, contact the Hungarian Arts Festivals Federation (© **1/318-8165**) or pick up a *Budapest Panorama* at Tourinform. The festivals' traditional start is September 25, the day of Béla Bartók's death.

Contemporary Music Weeks, Budapest. Held in conjunction with the Budapest Art Weeks, this 3-week festival features contemporary music performances in all the capital's major halls. For information, contact the Hungarian Arts Festivals Federation (© **1/318-8165**). Starts the end of September. Note that the Liszt Ferenc Academy closed in fall 2009 for a 2-year renovation.

For an exhaustive list of events beyond those listed here, check http:// events.frommers.com, where you'll find a searchable, up-to-the-minute roster of what's happening all over the world.

Budapest's Average Daily Temperatures & Days of Rainfall

	Jan	Feb	Mar	Apr	May	June	July	Aug	Sept	Oct	Nov	Dec
Temp. (°F)	31	34	43	51	60	66	69	69	62	51	31	34
Temp. (°C)	3	1	6	10	15	18	20	20	16	10	3	1
Rainfall (in.)	1.3	1.2	1.1	1.5	2.2	2.5	2	2	1.6	1.3	2	1.6
Rainfall (day)	19	17	20	22	25	24	23	20	15	17	19	21

2 ENTRY REQUIREMENTS

PASSPORTS
All citizens of Australia, Canada, Republic of Ireland, New Zealand, the U.K., and the U.S. entering Hungary are required to show a passport that will be valid for their entire length of stay.

VISAS
A specific visa is not required for visiting Hungary for citizens of Australia, Canada, Ireland, New Zealand, the U.K., or the U.S. However, when you enter the country, you are technically entering on a tourist

visa, though there are no preparations needed; it is automatic when you enter the country. All but the British are permitted to stay for 90 days on a tourist visa. The British are allowed a 6-month stay. In order to work or study, you must apply for special visas before leaving your country of citizenship by applying to the Hungarian Embassy or Consulate there.

You may come across information about the Schengen visa. However, citizens from the countries above are exempt from needing this visa. There is a word of caution here. The Schengen countries are not all E.U. countries and not all E.U. countries are Schengen countries. The Schengen Agreement is a treaty between participating countries allowing free movement and travel across borders without passport control. However, there are occasional passport control spot checks. Schengen member states include Austria, Belgium, The Czech Republic, Denmark, Estonia, Finland, France, Germany, Greece, Hungary, Iceland, Italy, Latvia, Lithuania, Luxembourg, Malta, the Netherlands, Norway, Poland, Portugal, Slovakia, Slovenia, Spain, and Sweden. The U.K. and Ireland are not part of the Schengen zone.

The period of stay for citizens carrying passports from Australia, Canada, New Zealand, and the U.S. visiting the Schengen states **is a total of 3 months cumulative stay in the combined member states during any 6-month period.** Passport controllers may check your passport to ascertain whether or not you have overstayed your visa. Stays for longer require special visas issued prior to leaving your home country.

CUSTOMS
What You Can Bring Into Hungary

You're allowed to bring duty-free into Hungary 250 cigarettes, 2 liters of wine, and 1 liter of spirits. There is no limit to the amount of money you may bring into the country. However, you may not take

out of the country more than 1,000,000 forints in Hungarian currency.

What You Can Take Home from Hungary

Returning **U.S. citizens** who have been away for at least 48 hours are allowed to bring back, once every 30 days, $800 worth of merchandise duty-free. You'll pay a flat rate of duty on the next $1,000 worth of purchases. Any dollar amount beyond that is subject to duties at whatever rates apply. On mailed gifts, the duty-free limit is $200. Be sure to keep your receipts or purchases accessible to expedite the declaration process. *Note:* If you owe duty, you are required to pay on your arrival in the United States using cash, personal check, government, or traveler's check, money order, or, in some locations, a Visa or MasterCard.

To avoid paying duty on foreign-made personal items you own before your trip, bring along a bill of sale, insurance policy, jeweler's appraisal, or receipts of purchase. You can also register items that can be readily identified by a permanently affixed serial number or marking, for instance laptops, cameras, and CD players, with Customs before you leave. Take the items to the nearest Customs office or register them with Customs at the airport from which you're departing. You'll receive, at no cost, a Certificate of Registration, which allows duty-free entry for the life of the item.

With few exceptions, you cannot bring fresh fruits or vegetables into the United States; however, if your trip continues from here to other European countries, you will need to know their restrictions also. Some countries in Europe are now restricting the transport of Hungarian salami, of which Pick is a famous brand. Many rules change frequently, so it is best to have the most current information on hand. For specifics on what you can bring back, download the invaluable free pamphlet *Know Before You Go.* Go to www. cbp.gov/xp/cgov/travel and browse "Travel Smart." Alternatively, contact the **U.S.**

Customs & Border Protection (CBP), 1300 Pennsylvania Ave., NW, Washington, DC 20229 (© 877/287-8667) and request the pamphlet.

For a clear summary of **Canadian** rules, write for the booklet *I Declare,* issued by the **Canada Border Services Agency** (© 800/461-9999 in Canada, or © 204/983-3500; www.cbsa-asfc.gc.ca). Canada allows its citizens a C$750 exemption, and you're allowed to bring back duty-free 1 carton of cigarettes, 1 can of tobacco, 40 imperial ounces of liquor, and 50 cigars. In addition, you're allowed to mail gifts to Canada valued at less than C$60 a day, provided they're unsolicited and don't contain alcohol or tobacco (write on the package "Unsolicited gift, under C$60 value"). All valuables should be declared on the Y-38 form before departure from Canada, including serial numbers of valuables you already own, such as expensive foreign cameras. *Note:* The C$750 exemption can be used only once a year and only after a 7-day absence.

Citizens of the U.K. who are **returning from a European Union (E.U.) country** will go through a separate Customs exit especially for E.U. travelers. In essence, there is no limit on what you can bring back from an E.U. country, provided the items are for personal use (this includes gifts), and you have already paid the necessary duty and tax. Customs laws, however, set out guidance levels. If you bring in more than these levels, you may be asked to prove that the goods are for your own use. Guidance levels on goods bought in the E.U. for personal use are 3,200 cigarettes, 200 cigars, 400 cigarillos,

3 kilograms of smoking tobacco, 10 liters of spirits, 90 liters of wine, 20 liters of fortified wine (such as port or sherry), and 110 liters of beer.

The duty-free allowance in **Australia** is A$400 or for those 17 and under, A$200. Citizens can bring in 250 cigarettes or 250 grams of loose tobacco, and 1,125 milliliters of alcohol. If you're returning with valuables you already own, such as foreign-made cameras, you should file form B263. A helpful brochure is available from Australian consulates or Customs offices called *Know Before You Go.* For more information, call the **Australian Customs Service** at © 1300/363-263, or log onto www.customs.gov.au.

The duty-free allowance for **New Zealand** is NZ$700. Citizens over 17 can bring in 200 cigarettes, 50 cigars, or 250 grams of tobacco (or a mixture of all three if their combined weight doesn't exceed 250g), plus 4.5 liters of wine and beer, or 1.125 liters of liquor. New Zealand currency does not carry import or export restrictions. Fill out a certificate of export, listing the valuables you are taking out of the country; that way, you can bring them back without paying duty. Most questions are answered in a free pamphlet available at New Zealand consulates and Customs offices: *New Zealand Customs Guide for Travellers, Notice no. 4.* For more information, contact **New Zealand Customs,** The Customhouse, 17–21 Whitmore St., Box 2218, Wellington (© 04/473-6099 or 0800/428-786; www.customs.govt.nz).

MEDICAL REQUIREMENTS

There are no medical requirements for entering Hungary.

3 GETTING THERE & GETTING AROUND

GETTING TO BUDAPEST
By Plane

The Hungarian flag carrier is **Malév Airlines** (www.malev.com). There are no intra-Hungary flights.

Budapest is served by two adjacent airports, **Ferihegy 1** and **Ferihegy 2,** both located in the XVII district in southeastern Pest. Ferihegy 1 is the airport that all budget airlines use, while Ferihegy 2 (which has a **Terminal A** and a **Terminal B**) serves the flagship carriers and other traditional airlines. The distance between the Ferihegy 2 terminals is about 1 block, so there is no need to be concerned if you arrive at the airport for your flight and are at the wrong terminal, but there is some concern if you arrive at the wrong airport. With Hungary's entry into the Schengen zone, terminal 2A is exclusively used for flights to Schengen countries, so you will pass through security, but not Passport Control. All other flights will depart from 2B and have Passport Control. There are several main information numbers: For airport information, call ✆ 1/296-9696; and for general information, call ✆ 1/296-7000. For ease of language, use the airport's English version website at www.bud.hu/english for flight information. The airport code for Budapest is BUD.

A new airport called FlyBalaton opened and closed in the Balaton region town of Sármellék. The airport code is SOB; however, when Ryanair pulled it from its schedule, Lufthansa's weekend-only services from Hamburg International were not enough to keep the airport open. At this writing, the airport will be closed indefinitely, but for updated information, you should call the Keszthely Tourist Travel Agency at ✆ 83/354-256. There is no domestic air service in Hungary.

Arriving passengers at either airport need to pass through Customs and Passport Control, when appropriate, before they emerge into the bustling arrivals halls of the respective airports.

Ferihegy 1 was remodeled and enlarged just a few years ago, due to the then-expanding number of budget airlines; however, a large number of airlines have pulled out due to lack of demand. **Ferihegy 2** is larger, but still not overwhelming—you shouldn't have any fears of getting lost in it like some other major airports. In each airport, you'll find accommodations offices,

rental-car agencies, shops, exchange booths, plus a Tourinform desk. Exchange rates are much less favorable in airports than in the city, so rather than change money, take it out of the ATM. Even with bank fees, you'll come out ahead in the end. Often, people become confused and anxious with currency in thousands, so to avoid surprises or unnecessary ATM fees, do yourself a favor and print out a currency cheat sheet before leaving home from www.oanda.com/convert/cheatsheet.

Getting into Town from the Airport

You have four general choices to get from or back to the airport depending on your budget. Although in the past airport taxis were notorious for scamming tourists, the airport authority took steps to correct this situation. The airport exclusively contracts with **Zóna Taxi** services (✆ 1/365-5555), making this the official taxi service of both Budapest airports. The fares are fixed rates per cab, not per person and adhere to predestined zones within the city. Fares run from zones 1–4 and cost from 3,500 Ft to 5,400 Ft. These taxis are also metered, so if the metered fare is less than the zone rate, you pay the reduced fare. By law, all taxis must give you a paper receipt for your fare. If you know of another taxi company and prefer them, you will need to call them. The unauthorized taxi stand pick-up area is away from the general taxi area, but there are signs in English.

Airport Shuttle (✆ 1/296-8555; www.bud.hu/english) is a public service owned and operated by the Budapest Airport Authority. There is a clearly visible kiosk for the shuttle in each terminal. If you know you will use this service to return to the airport, a round-trip ticket is less expensive than two one-way tickets. A round-trip fare is 4,990 Ft per person and one way is 2,990 Ft per person. For two traveling together, there is a discount: for one-way, it is 4,490 Ft for two and 8,490 Ft for a round trip. The fares are the same for both airports. Depending on the number of people, you may find the taxi service to be less expensive. When you purchase your tickets for the shuttle, you'll be asked which district you are going to since many districts have streets with the same name. Once a minibus is sufficiently full, the driver will call out your destination, direct you to the vehicle and load your luggage. This can take anywhere from 10 minutes to as much as 1 hour, depending on how busy it is at any given time of day. The shuttle takes you directly to the door of any address in the city. The trip takes from 30 minutes to an hour, depending on traffic and how many stops are made. To arrange your return to the airport from where you are staying, call the number above 24 hours *in advance,* but not longer than 24 hours in advance and absolutely not less than 12 hours in advance. The shuttle office is open from 6am to 10pm, but be warned that you may have to wait on hold for some time and may possibly get disconnected in the process. The shuttle will pick up passengers virtually anywhere in the Budapest area from their front door. You will be given a 10-minute time frame for when the shuttle will arrive to pick you up, based on your flight departure. You will be asked to wait outside the door during this 10-minute period to facilitate the pick-up process.

There are also two public transportation options with the trip taking about 1 hour total on either. Two buses leave the airport for the metro. From **Ferihegy 2,** you will take **bus no. 200E** to the last stop, Kőbánya-Kispest. From there, the Blue metro line runs to the Inner City of Pest. The cost is two transit tickets, which is 540 Ft for both; tickets can be bought from the automated vending machine at the bus stop (coins only and not recommended) or from any newsstand in the airport. From

Ferihegy 1, take **bus no. 93 or 200E** to the same metro stop as above.

As of August 2007, trains stop at Ferihegy 1 only and go to Nyugati train station. After using the highway overpass, stand on the tracks and wait for the train. Take note that there is no station at the airport, but just a siding where the train stops. You must buy the 300 Ft ticket for a one-way journey at the airport. Purchasing a ticket on the train could result in a hefty fine. There are more than 30 trains daily. If you arrive at **Ferihegy 2,** take bus **200E** to **Ferihegy 1** in order to catch the train. Plans to extend the train tracks to the second airport still have not happened.

By Train

Trains arrive regularly from Vienna, Bratislava, and other European cities either as a destination or as a train passing through for somewhere else. It will depend on where your journey began as to which of the three stations you arrive at. In order to curb fare dodging, some of the tracks are barricaded by inspectors who will want to see your ticket when leaving a train as well as boarding it. Don't toss your tickets until you leave the station. For more information about Budapest train stations, see below in the "Getting Around" section p. 37.

By Boat

There are a number of cruise ships on the Danube route making Budapest a stopover or final destination. For those not on a cruise ship, there are hydrofoils that transport passengers between Vienna or Bratislava and Budapest as well as smaller towns within Hungary. For information and schedules in English see www.mahartpassnave.hu after clicking on the British flag.

By Car

Once you arrive in the city, you'll want to either park your car or return it to the rental agency. Driving in the city is hazardous to one's health as there are not as many stop signs as needed. There are many one-way streets, and restrictions on making turns onto major roads, so you'll have to find the right place where you can turn around in order to head in the direction you want.

GETTING AROUND
By Train

The Hungarian railroad system has a website with an English link at www.mav-start.hu. To change to English, look at the top right corner. Another site is more informational, but also has an English link at www.mav.hu.

Budapest has three main train stations. Pályaudvar meaning station is usually abbreviated as pu. **Déli pu** located in district I is the smallest of the three and the only one on the Buda side. It's reachable by Metro 2 (Red line). Of the three stations, it is the farthest distance from downtown Pest—by metro, it would take about 15 minutes to reach it. **Keleti pu**, the largest of the three, is in district VIII and also on the Metro 2 (Red line) and is only one metro stop or two bus stops on the 5 or 7 bus to reach the center of Pest. **Nyugati pu** in district VI was built by the Eiffel Company and sits on the Metro 3 line (Blue). It is on the major ring road, so it is in downtown Pest. Trains from the airport arrive at this station. The trip is 30 minutes.

Within Hungary, Eger, Szeged, and Siófok are a manageable 2 to 2½ hours. Sopron and Pécs are 3 hours away. To travel to Budapest from Vienna will take 3 hours or Bratislava, Slovakia is 2½ hours away.

By Bus

Just like the train stations, Budapest has multiple bus stations as well. Some national and most international destinations arrive or leave from **Népliget bus station** (✆ 1/219-8080) on the Metro 3 line (Blue: Népliget). Information available 6am–8pm. Other domestic buses will pull into and leave from the **Árpád híd bus station** (✆ 1/329-1450). The information office is open 7am–4pm daily. This is also serviced by Metro 3 (Blue line: Árpád hid). If you plan to travel domestically by bus, your only option is **Volánbusz** (✆ 382-0888; www.volanbusz.hu/en). Volánbusz also offers international travel in cooperation with Eurolines bus company. For international travel alternatives check out the newer company **OrangeWays Bus** (✆ 06/30-830-9696 mobile phone only; www.orangeways.com/en). They have new buses, inexpensive fares and provide a number of on-board services. Both companies allow you to book your tickets online if you have access to a printer.

By Car

To rent a car the driver must be 21 years old with no upper age limit. Only the renter is the authorized driver. The driver's license must be at least 1 year old. Some agencies require an international driver's license, so check their website for rules and regulations. Some agencies will require you take their insurance coverage even if you're covered by your credit card company.

You are legally required to carry your passport and your driving license at all times. In addition you must be able to produce your car documents and insurance green card (which is proof of your international insurance) when asked to do so by a police officer. Failure to produce those documents, even if you have them at your hotel, results in an on-the-spot fine. When leaving your car you should also take your car registration documents with you. Renters should note that insurance and VAT taxes are almost never included in quoted rental car rates, so be sure to pay attention when doing an online booking or ask at the rental agency about additional fees. They can add a significant cost to your car rental as insurance is charged per day. Crossing borders within the E.U. is normally sanctioned with car rentals, but some still have restrictions for Romania and Bulgaria. It is best to check if you plan on leaving the country to see if a special permit is required.

All motorways are marked with a letter M and international roads with the letter E. Motorways are gradually spreading throughout the country but the main ones are:

- M0 the ring road round Budapest
- M1 Budapest–Hegyeshalom
- M3 Budapest–Gyöngyös–Füzesabony
- M5 Budapest–Szeged/country border
- M6 Érd–Dunaújváros
- M7 Budapest–Balatonkersztúr

With the exception of motorways in the Budapest suburban areas it is necessary to buy a Motorway Permit before you enter a motorway. There are many garages that display a sign saying that they sell Motorway Permits. You will receive a receipt, which you have to sign and it shows your car registration number. It is very important to retain this receipt for at least 3 months after using the motorways just in case the garage has put the wrong registration number down.

The system of checking car registration number plates is very efficient on Hungarian motorways. Fines are expensive (even for foreign visitors) and you may not know you have a problem for several weeks after returning the vehicle. Rental companies will not become involved with any dispute you may have with motorway authorities.

In the unfortunate event of a breakdown on the motorway, it is of utmost importance that all of the car's occupants move out to wait on the bank of the motorway. There have been a number of accidents where people have been killed while waiting in the car.

You are also required to display a warning triangle (found in the back of the car) approximately 20m (65 ft) from the car. The driver and passengers are also required to wear the luminous yellow jackets that are also provided.

If you do not have a mobile phone there is usually an emergency phone within a kilometer either way.

Be wary of parking within cities. It is best to find a parking garage or lot. Street parking is often time-limited and they love to put the metal clamps on the wheels to prevent you from leaving.

Most destinations within Hungary can be reached within 2 to 3 hours by car. Vienna or Bratislava are about 3 hours each. The number for the Hungarian Automobile Club is ✆ 188.

GETTING AROUND BUDAPEST

Budapest has an extensive, efficient, and inexpensive public transportation system, but locals without global experiences, disagree with this. If you have some patience and minimal skills with reading maps, you can easily learn the system. Public transportation, however, is not without its glitches, due to the construction of a fourth metro line that will continue for the next few years. There have been interruptions throughout parts of the city at various points in time and this is likely to continue until 2013.

They are efficient enough to provide buses to replace any tram or metro that has been disrupted by construction, but it can be confusing.

The biggest disadvantage, however, is that metros and tram routes shut down for the night at around 11:10pm–11:30pm depending on the line (see "Night Service," below). Some areas of the city, most notably the Buda Hills, are beyond the reach of some night bus services making taxi drivers happy to provide those late-night journeys. Increased night bus services to overcome some of these problems have been dramatic, but it is still not perfect with some long waits at dark and lonely bus stops. During rush hours, all forms of transport are crowded making it best to plan your travel around these times. A disadvantage, mostly pertinent to travelers, is that Castle Hill can be reached in only three ways by public transportation and all of these modes of transportation are quite crowded in the high seasons. Most importantly, crowded public transport is the place where you are most likely to be targeted by Budapest's professional pickpockets. Just keep your hand on your wallet and purse.

FARES Fares generally increase in January and July. Fares here were accurate at the time of submission. Transport passes provide unlimited transportation on **all forms of public transportation** (metro, bus, tram, trolleybus (an electric bus evident by the connection to wires above), some portions of the HÉV railway lines, and cogwheel railway) within Budapest city limits. If you are using individual tickets *(vonaljegy),* which cost 300 Ft apiece (children 5 and under or **E.U. citizens 65 and over** travel for free), you are required to validate the tickets as soon as you get on the transport. Each time you change lines, you have to validate a new ticket. You can buy single tickets at metro ticket windows, newspaper kiosks, and the occasional tobacco shop. There are also automated machines in most stations and at major transportation hubs, most of which have been recently modernized or installed and provide a somewhat reliable service, but I wouldn't depend on them. You can also buy a 10-ticket pack *(tizes csomag)* for 2,350 Ft.

I strongly recommend that you buy a transport pass, which does not require validation. They are available for 1 day *(napijegy)* for 1,550 Ft and are good for 24 hours from the day and time marked. The other pass options are 3 days *(turistajegy)* for 3,850 Ft, 7 days for 4,600 Ft or for longer stays, 14 days *(kéthétibérlet)* for 6,200 Ft. The 7- and 14-day passes need to be signed. If your plans are even longer, there is a 30-consecutive day pass *(30 napos bérlet)* at 9,400 Ft, which requires a photo. If you are going to be here for 4 to 5 days, the 7-day *(hetijegy)* pass is still a saving over individual tickets. Passes are so much more convenient than having a handful of tickets that you have to worry about remembering to validate each time or replenishing your stock at odd hours. Honestly, these will save you money in the long run.

While this standard ticket is valid on the metro, there are other types of optional single-ride metro tickets introduced years ago, making ticket buying a bit more complicated for those who want the exactly appropriate ticket for their journey. Personally, I don't think any traveler should waste time caring about this, but I have met some who do. A metro section ticket *(metrószakaszjegy),* at 250 Ft, is valid for a single metro trip stopping at three stations or less. A metro transfer ticket *(metróátszállójegy),* at 470 Ft, allows you to transfer from one metro line to another on the same ticket, without any limit to the number of stations that the train stops at during your journey.

Transportation inspectors are those dreaded people who, like the secret police of yesteryear, whip out a hidden blue or red (the old color, but still sometimes used) armband when approaching you or stand guard at the top or bottom of an escalator at the metro stops, or hop on the tram or buses after the door has closed. Some are uniformed, so you know you are heading into the lion's den. However, many have become trickier and more covert over the years and are often in plainclothes. It is not until they materialize the dreaded armband and greet you, that you realize you have had a false sense of security about having a peaceful ride. There were horror stories for years about how they treated people, screaming and yelling and causing a scene of hysterics when they caught someone without a ticket or an invalid one. Due to the hundreds of letters of complaints filling volumes, the BKV instituted mandatory customer service training meant to file down the teeth of these overly aggressive warriors of transportation justice. For some it has taken hold.

The **fines** for not having a validated ticket or pass are 6,000 Ft if paid on the spot or 10,000 Ft if paid later; this does not include the embarrassment of getting caught. An inspector has the right to ask for your passport (legally, you are required to carry it at all times) or ID and to call a police officer if the need arises. They do not have the authority to harm you or arrest you. Transportation tickets generally have an increase each January and June.

The **Budapest Card,** which is available for 1 or 3 days, does include transportation, but you should look over the other offerings to see if you will maximize your savings by purchasing it. Few museums are free with the card, while others are simply discounted. Realistically, how many museums or discounts included with the card are you really interested in?

4 MONEY & COSTS

The Value of Hungarian Forints vs. Other Popular Currencies

Huf	U.S.$	Can$	UK£	Euro (€)	Aus$	NZ$
100	$0.54	C$0.57	£0.33	€0.66	A$0.59	NZ$0.74

Frommer's lists exact prices in the local currency. In this book, hotels are the exception, because almost all of them quote prices in euros. The currency conversions quoted above were correct at press time. However, rates fluctuate, so before departing consult a currency exchange website such as **www.oanda.com/convert/classic** to check up-to-the-minute rates.

The basic unit of currency in Hungary is the **forint (Ft or Huf).** Coins come in denominations of 5, 10, 20, 50, 100, and 200 Ft. Banknotes come in denominations of 500, 1,000, 5,000, 10,000, and 20,000 Ft. As of November 15, 2009, 200 Ft paper notes are no longer legal tender. If you saved some from a previous trip, they are no longer useable, but you have a lovely green bookmarker.

Telling coins apart can be confusing. The small gold-colored ones are 5 Ft. Ten and 50 Ft coins are both round and silver, but the 50 is larger in circumference. Both the 100 and 200 are dual-colored silver on the inside with a gold-colored band around the outside. The 100 Ft is the smaller of the two.

Paper money with all of the zeros really confuses travelers. The 500 Ft is reddish-brown, 1,000 Ft is blue, but the 2,000 Ft bill is also a brown color, while the 5,000 Ft is a greenish-blue. If you have a purplish-blue bill, it is 10,000 Ft, but the 20,000 Ft note looks like pink was smeared on it. Most importantly from 1,000 Ft and higher, they should all have a silver band on the left face side to be legal. Never exchange currency on the street unless it is at an authorized change kiosk. If you are approached on the street to change money, just walk away; it is illegal. I definitely advocate printing out an exchange rate cheat sheet from www.oanda.com/convert/cheatsheet before leaving home and carrying it in your wallet. When people get to an ATM, they lose all sense of how much money to withdraw because the zeros throw them off.

In Budapest, in the city center, you will find ATM machines from different banks within the same block, but elsewhere in the city there is one within a few blocks. We have no shortage of ATMs in the capital. In other cities and towns, there are fewer, but there are still an ample number.

What things Cost

Some common expenses	
Cup of coffee	350 Ft
Taxi from the airport	3,600 Ft
Transport ticket (single ride)	300 Ft
Moderate 3-course dinner w/out alcohol	4.000 Ft
A night in a moderate hotel	25,000 Ft

Banks do not charge ATM fees other than what your home bank charges. All banks are not equal with their fees, so you should consult with your home bank to find out if they have a cooperative agreement with any banks in Hungary.

All ATM machines accept a four-digit pin code. OTP bank ATMs will accept up to an eight-digit pin code.

Some travelers have reported having problems using their debit cards as opposed to a credit card. In Hungary, which cards an establishment can accept is dependent on which bank they deal with. Not all banks will accept American Express or debit cards, but there is no rule of thumb as to whether to use a debit or credit card. One thing that you should know is that whether or not you use a debit or credit card, the cashier may give you a machine. If it is a debit card, enter your pin code. If it is a credit card, just press the green button, which authorizes the sale.

It is not a rare occurrence when paying the bill in a restaurant to find that suddenly the machine is not working. Sometimes this is due to their Internet connection to the bank, but other times, it means business has not been too good, so that cash influx is necessary.

Insisting you have no cash can sometimes miraculously fix the machine. At other times, someone gets left there, while someone else goes to an ATM.

If you were to leave one credit card at home, contrary to the commercials, it should be your American Express. This is the least widely accepted card here. If you have a Diners Club/MasterCard, you will be fine, but if you have a dedicated Diners Club card without the MasterCard tie-in, your chances of using it are close to nil.

For those with the new chip-embedded credit cards, you should make sure it is able to be swiped, as the chip technology has not hit Hungary as of yet.

Budapest has become increasing costly for residents as well as visitors. When we moved here in 2001, we could buy 3 days worth of groceries for 5,000 Ft. Now, that amount just about buys one day's worth. Inflation on prices has been 8 to 11% annually, including utilities and in the VAT has recently risen to 25% for goods and 18% for hotel rooms. Still a bargain when compared to other major cities like NY, London, and Tokyo, but it really depends on the currency conversion.

Traveler's checks are next to impossible to cash and only a few banks will take them, and not all branches of the banks do. American Express closed their office years ago, but are in conjunction with Western Union, where you will get the worst possible rates of exchange.

5 HEALTH

GENERAL AVAILABILITY OF HEALTH CARE

No shots or inoculations are required for entry to Hungary. To be on the safe side, bring enough of any prescription or other medication you may need. It is also good practice to bring along a copy of all prescriptions in their generic form in case you run out of any medications, but you will need a Hungarian doctor to write a prescription for the pharmacy to dispense it. Not all medications available in other countries are available here, so the doctor may need to substitute. Over-the-counter medications are readily available from a pharmacy, but sunscreen and other toiletries can be purchased at local shops.

COMMON AILMENTS

DIETARY RED FLAGS You will see many people carrying bottles of water, but the tap water is perfectly safe to drink. If you have food allergies, explain it strongly to the wait staff for them to take you seriously. Vegetarians will find it a bit difficult to navigate the meat-loving Hungarian menus; however, there are vegetarian options in chapter 6 "Where to Dine." In non-vegetarian restaurants, innocent dishes could very well have meat included in them without it showing in the English translation. Press the staff for details. For those with religious restrictions, this is especially important. I have ordered a beef dish, only to find it accompanied by a piece of pork chop. I have included Kosher restaurants in this guide and one Indian restaurant that serves Halal dishes.

BUGS, BITES & OTHER WILDLIFE CONCERNS Lake Balaton has had an increasingly bad mosquito infestation and for whatever reason, they have decided not to continue the annual spraying as of this writing.

There have been instances of wild boar sightings in the Buda Hills. Mothers with babies are extremely protective and will attack anyone who is perceived as a threat.

RESPIRATORY ILLNESSES Budapest can get smoggy at times during the summer, but it never lasts longer than a few days before it blows off. Outside of the city, the air is clean.

EXTREME WEATHER EXPOSURE Budapest has been known to have sudden non-predictable storms with torrential rain and heavy winds that seem to come from nowhere. These occur at the end of spring and end of summer, but they pass within hours.

WHAT TO DO IF YOU GET SICK AWAY FROM HOME

For American-type care, we recommend the **First Med Center**, I. Hattyu u. 14, 5th floor (© **1/224-9090**; www.firstmed centers.com), a private outpatient clinic with two U.S. board-certified physicians and several English-speaking Hungarian doctors. There is an OBGYN on staff, and an ultrasound machine on the premises; referrals are available for specialists. It does have a growing list of U.S. insurance companies that it has contracts with and may be able to direct the bill. Otherwise, payment is expected at the time of service (credit cards accepted), but the office will provide coded invoices in English in a form acceptable to most insurance carriers. The clinic is located in a modern building on the street ending at the Mammut shopping mall, just a few minutes by foot from Moszkva tér (Red line).

Also recommended is the Rózsakert Medical Center (© **1/391-5903**) located in the Rózsakert Shopping Center, II. Gábor Áron u. 74–78/a. It has the largest pool of American-trained physicians in Hungary with doctors on call 24 hours.

Another suitable facility is **IMS**, a private outpatient clinic at XIII. Váci út 184 (☏ **1/329-8423**), with English-speaking doctors; it's reached via the Blue metro line (Gyöngyös utca). The same drill applies with respect to payment and insurance claims. IMS also operates an emergency service after hours and on weekends at III. Vihar u. 29 (☏ **1/388-8257**).

6 SAFETY

Overall, Budapest is one of the safest cities in Europe. There are problems with pickpockets on crowded buses, trams, or metros. Caution should also be taken in crowded shops.

The U.S. government as well as others cautions travelers against patronizing certain bars and clubs. You can view the list here: http://hungary.usembassy.gov/tourist_advisory.html.

Due to some political issues, there have been demonstrations that have suddenly erupted during various times of the year. For the most part, they tend to localize in the park in front of the U.S. Embassy, in front of Parliament, and at Heroes Square. In the past, there have not been any threats to tourists, if you just stay clear of those areas on the day of the problems. Most of them are short-lived, so will not disrupt your stay. Your accommodation should be able to give you a warning if something happens to occur during your stay.

Gay travelers should take care and caution during the time of the Gay Pride events, which are no longer specific dates due to problems in the past. They are now held at varied times each year. The conservative right has demonstrated and attacked marchers in the past. Otherwise, there have been no problems for tourists.

Women who are scantily clad may find men will give them the sexist wolf-whistles and comments, but other than that they are harmless. Until recently, men beyond 25 years old or so did not wear shorts in public during warm months, but this is slowly changing. Many men do not wear hats, but a cap is usually a sure sign of a tourist.

Drinking alcohol on the street, when not seated at a cafe, or on public transportation is illegal.

7 SPECIALIZED TRAVEL RESOURCES

In addition to the destination-specific resources listed below, please visit Frommers.com for additional specialized travel resources.

GAY & LESBIAN TRAVELERS

Being part of the E.U., Hungary has had to modify its laws regarding gay and lesbian rights, though some older gay people say they had it better under Socialism. Either way, sexual orientation is not a legal issue in Hungary, but it is still a social one. Gays and lesbians have a tendency to stay invisible as much as possible. Budapest has held an annual Pride March, but in 2007, there was a violent outbreak prompted by far-right protestors. The 2008 parade was attacked with acid-filled eggs by the far right group, the Magyar Garda, causing the 2009 parade to be postponed twice. Other times of the year, there have not been any problems of major concern.

In Hungary, there are far fewer lesbian events and no bars specifically for women. In Budapest, there are only two exclusively gay bars and both are for men only. This is not a hotspot for those seeking a primarily gay orientated vacation. **The International Gay and Lesbian Travel Association (IGLTA; ✆ 800/448-8550** or ✆ **954/776-2626;** www.iglta.org) is the trade association for the gay and lesbian travel industry, and offers an online directory of gay- and lesbian-friendly travel businesses; go to their website and click on "Members."

Spartacus International Gay Guide (Bruno Gmünder Verlag; www.spartacus world.com/gayguide), an excellent travel resource to the top worldwide cities and resorts, includes Budapest and other cities in Hungary. It is available at many bookstores, or from any online bookseller.

TRAVELERS WITH DISABILITIES

Disabilities shouldn't stop anyone from traveling. However, with that said, Hungary is not a disabled-person-friendly country. Access is limited and it is difficult for wheelchairs to get into some hotels, many restaurants, and much of the public transportation. There are only a few exceptions to the rule, the 4 and 6 tram lines have platforms level with the tram door; however, other trams do not have accessibility. The metros have stairs and escalators, not elevators. For the few metro stops that have wheelchair elevators, a key is needed, but there is no attendant available to acquire it. Many sidewalks do not have ramps or slopes for a wheelchair and the majority of the stores have barriers that would make wheelchair access improbable to impossible. The disabled in Hungary have been fighting for better access since the change in government, but change is still slow. In researching this section, I didn't find any escorted tours listed for travelers with limitations to Hungary.

FAMILY TRAVEL

Hungarians tend to be very family focused, making the entire country especially family friendly. When traveling with children,

I highly recommend the Budapest guide for kids "Benjamin in Budapest." See chapter 9, "Budapest Shopping" (p. 189).

To locate accommodations, restaurants, and attractions that are particularly kid-friendly, refer to the **Kids** icon throughout this guide and the section "Especially for Kids" p. 147.

WOMEN TRAVELERS

Budapest is one of the safest cities in Europe. Women travelers alone or in groups have nothing to fear touring the city or the country.

For general travel resources for women, go to www.frommers.com/planning.

MULTICULTURAL TRAVELERS

Since the last edition, I have received a number of e-mails from concerned travelers of African and Asian descent questioning if Budapest is safe for minorities. Budapest has become home for a growing number of refugees who have had to leave their homes in different African nations as well as many immigrants from China and other Asian nations. All have integrated into the fabric of the society, so no longer raise any eyebrows from Hungarians. For African descent travelers, I have included a specialty store for hair products in chapter 9 "Budapest Shopping" (p. 189). Budapest is home to a Chinese-Hungarian bilingual elementary school for further developing relations between the countries. Outside of Budapest, you may encounter long stares, but just curiosity and nothing to fear.

SENIOR TRAVEL

Senior discounts are hit and miss. The general rule for senior discounts, specifically for museum entry, is that they are reserved for E.U. citizens. However, more often than not, the cashier will not question your citizenship when you are purchasing a ticket, so request a senior discount from the start. If they ask for ID, chances are you will be refused if you are not an E.U. citizen, but odds are favorable that they will not ask at all. E.U. citizens 65 years old and over may ride all public transportation within Budapest for free, but you must have a valid ID or passport to show inspectors, especially at the metro stations. All E.U. citizens may tour Parliament for free by providing their passport.

STUDENT TRAVEL

Students can take advantage of the **International Student Identity Card (ISIC)**. Additional museums and entertainment venues have been offering discounts more than they have done in the past. Still some require that you are a student in Hungary, while others will give a discount to any student with an international ID card. If you purchase your airline tickets through STA, you will receive basic health and life insurance and a 24-hour help line. The card is available for $22 from **STA Travel** (*©* **800/781-4040** in North America; or **www.statravel.com**), the world's biggest student travel agency. If you're no longer a student but are still 25 and under, you can get an **International Youth Travel Card (IYTC)** for the same price from the same people, which entitles you to fewer discounts. Travel CUTS (*©* **1/866/246-9762**; www.travelcuts.com) offers similar services for both Canadian and U.S. residents. Irish students may prefer to turn to USIT (*©* **01/602-1904**; www.usitnow.ie), an Ireland-based specialist in student, youth, and independent travel. Also, it is licensed in Australia. Note that in Hungary, student discounts are only given at some hostels, not all of them. Museums and other attractions may reserve the student discounts for Hungarian students only; ask anyway.

8 SUSTAINABLE TOURISM

GENERAL RESOURCES FOR GREEN TRAVEL

Hungary has not jumped on the green bandwagon yet, but these general resources may be helpful. The following websites provide valuable wide-ranging information on sustainable travel. For a list of even more sustainable resources, as well as tips and explanations on how to travel greener, visit www.frommers.com/planning.

Responsible Travel (www.responsible travel.com) is a great source of sustainable travel ideas; the site is run by a spokesperson for ethical tourism in the travel industry. **Sustainable Travel International** (www.sustainabletravelinternational.org) promotes ethical tourism practices, and manages an extensive directory of sustainable properties and tour operators around the world.

In the U.K., **Tourism Concern** (www.tourismconcern.org.uk) works to reduce social and environmental problems connected to tourism. The **Association of Independent Tour Operators (AITO)** (www.aito.co.uk) is a group of specialist operators leading the field in making holidays sustainable.

In Canada, **www.greenlivingonline.com** offers extensive content on how to travel sustainably, including a travel and transport section and profiles of the best green shops and services in Toronto, Vancouver, and Calgary.

In Australia, the national body that sets guidelines and standards for ecotourism is **Ecotourism Australia** (www.ecotourism.org.au). **The Green Directory** (www.thegreendirectory.com.au), **Green Pages** (www.thegreenpages.com.au), and **Eco Directory** (www.ecodirectory.com.au) offer sustainable travel tips and directories of green businesses.

Carbonfund (www.carbonfund.org), TerraPass (www.terrapass.org), and **Carbon Neutral** (www.carbonneutral.org) provide info on "carbon offsetting," or offsetting the greenhouse gas emitted during flights.

Greenhotels (www.greenhotels.com) recommends green-rated member hotels around the world that fulfill the company's stringent environmental requirements. **Environmentally Friendly Hotels** (www. environmentallyfriendlyhotels.com) offers more green accommodation ratings.

For information on animal-friendly issues throughout the world, visit **Tread Lightly** (www.treadlightly.org). For information about the ethics of swimming with dolphins, visit the **Whale and Dolphin Conservation Society** (www.wdcs.org).

Volunteer International (www.volunteer international.org) has a list of questions to help you determine the intentions and the nature of a volunteer program. For general info on volunteer travel, visit **www. volunteerabroad.org** and **www.idealist. org.**

9 SPECIAL-INTEREST TRIPS & ESCORTED GENERAL INTEREST TOURS

SPECIAL-INTEREST TRIPS

Budapest and Hungary are on the top of the list for Jewish travel and tours, but generally these also include a greater scope of travel that includes Prague, Krakow, Warsaw, and Vienna. For Jewish travel within Budapest or Hungary, contact Chosen Tours or Underguide Tours (see chapter 7, "Exploring Budapest").

ACADEMIC TRIPS & LANGUAGE CLASSES

Central European University, V. Nádor u. 5 (© 1/327-3000; www.ceu.hu), boasts students from 90 countries with instructors from 30 countries. Based in Budapest, it is accredited by both the Hungarian and the U.S. accreditation agencies, through the University of the State of New York. The language of instruction is English for the entire extensive list of Master and Doctoral programs. Summer programs are ideal for those who want to take a course without leaving their home university. Generous financial aid is offered to all nationalities.

Many universities are now offering Budapest as an option for a study abroad semester. University students should check with their school for opportunities.

If you think you want to learn Hungarian, one of the schools that brags about having the best reputation and longevity having opened in 1927 is the **Debreceni Nyári Egyetem Budapesti Nyelviskolája** or Debrecen-Budapest Language School. The Budapest location is at V. Báthory u. 4 II/I (© 30/928-6577 mobile phone only; www.nyariegyetem.hu). Summer intensives are available in Debrecen, Sopron, and sometimes Eger. The 60–120 lessons, at 6 lessons per day over 2 to 4 weeks will have you speaking elementary Hungarian. Less grueling schedules are the semester-long programs offered only in Debrecen. They can arrange for accommodations for an extra fee. Course fees run 576€–1,000€ if you opt for accommodations and the meal plan.

BrainTurbo XI. Villányi út 60, 2nd floor (© 30/230-1706 mobile phone only) has an innovative approach, claiming to be four times faster than other language-teaching methods learning 1,500 Hungarian vocabulary words in only 12 weeks without homework. First you lie on your back wearing special glasses, while a series of words and sentences are repeated to you both in English and Hungarian putting your brain in a receptive state for learning. Afterward, a teacher helps you to recall the words and expressions you listened to while relaxed. Because the Hungarian software is fairly recent, there is no track record yet to validate the effectiveness. If you are curious, try out the free trial lesson. The entire 12-week course is a hefty 225,000 Ft. Save 10% by signing up for a free *Funzine* club membership at www.funzine.hu.

ADVENTURE & WELLNESS TRIPS

Much of Hungary is located over natural spring waters allowing many of the towns and cities an opportunity to create wellness oasis spots. You should be aware that the mineral content of the water is believed to have healing properties for diseases and ailments related to skin conditions, respiratory, muscle, or bone problems. Due to this, a good number of the "wellness" centers are also medical centers providing physiotherapy and hydrotherapy. Large spas have doctors on the premises for diagnosis and treatment on the spot. Thermals generally have natural spring pools of different temperatures, wet and dry saunas, and whirlpool baths. As part of the medical treatment, massage is included in the list of services, but other services have been added such as manicures and pedicures.

However, if you are looking for a luxurious pampered wellness opportunity, look over the options of services provided before deciding on a location as the term "wellness" has broad-based usage. Budapest thermals are covered in chapter 7 "Exploring Budapest." Lake Balaton is also popular for wellness spas of the relaxing and luxurious varieties, but as an aid in making a decision **Wellness Weekend** (www.wellnessweekend.hu) has a number of luxury hotels in Budapest, Eger, Heviz, and Sopron with photos and last-minute discounts.

DENTAL & MEDICAL TRIPS

As humorous as it may seem to include dental or medical tourism in a tour guide, Hungary has been known for decades for its high-quality and low-cost dental services. Many Austrians and Germans have been coming here for years and the good word has extended through the rest of Europe and over to the U.S. The dental tourism industry here has complete staff who speak English. Services include whitening, root canals, dentures, and cosmetic implantations. Most have labs on the premises, so there is little waiting time for dentures and if an adjustment is needed, they are on the spot. Some agencies have teamed with plastic surgeons to create a whole new you. I have no personal experience with any of these, but have heard positive reports.

Pasarét Dental II. Pasaréti út 8 (© 1/488–7919; www.pasaretdental.hu) has been around for a long time and has a good reputation for all things dental.

Meditours Hungary VII. Nagydiófa u. 19. (© 1/787-5564; www.meditours hungary.com). The only medical tourism program owned and operated by a medical doctor, American-Hungarian Dr. Randy Simor, takes great pride in arranging the most competent services in the city for medical tourists. Meditours will assist in making all of the necessary arrangements once you arrive, airport meet and greet, accommodations, and handholding every step of the way. Not only do they offer cosmetic dental services, but also cosmetic surgery, anti-aging, and IntraLasik eye sight correction surgery as well as others. Their hosts are on-call 24/7 for any needs you have with the mobile phone they provide for your use during your stay. I used their agency for the IntraLasik eye surgery option and was very impressed.

Kreativ Dent (www.kreativdent.eu) is a New York-based agency that arranges dental tourism packages to Budapest. Outside of Budapest, in the town of Mosonmagyarovar, close to Sopron, you have your choice of over 150 dentists, but you may want to consider **H@ppy Dent** at Zichy Mihály 2 (© **96/566-472**; http://happydent.net). They don't assist with transportation, but they will help with a place to stay. **Diamant Dent** also in Mosonmagyarovar at Regi Vamhaz tér 11 (© **96/579–067**; www.diamantdent.hu) has its own hotel and shuttle to pick you up and transport you to the clinic.

FOOD & WINE TRIPS

If you love food and wine as an introduction into a culture, you may want to try the tours offered by **Taste Hungary** (www.tastehungary.com), co-owned by American Carolyn Bánfalvi, author of *A Food and Wine Lover's Companion to Hungary: with Budapest Restaurants and Trips to the Wine Country*. They only have a website presence and all bookings are through their site. **Wine Time Hungary**, VII. Klauzál tér 13. fszt. 5 (© **1/788-9645**; www.winetime.hu) specializes in wine tours to the regions where the grapes are grown. In Budapest, they offer virtual food and wine tours. Underguide Tours (© **06/30-908-1597** mobile phone only; golocal@underguide) are magicians with creating customized tours and can create the food or wine tour of your choice (for more information, see chapter 7 "Exploring Budapest").

VOLUNTEER & WORKING TRIPS

Habitat for Humanity ★★ (© **1/354-1084**; www.habitat.hu), with an office at VI. Podmaniczky u. 91, has a well-established program in Hungary. None of the building occurs in Budapest, but in smaller villages. They have specific dates when they build; therefore, you will need to schedule your trip around theirs if you want to be part of this endeavor.

Quite a different cultural yet volunteer experience can be had with **Servas International** (http://joomla.servas.org). The program was started in 1949 by Bob Luitweiler as a peace movement. Now active in 100 countries, it is a worthwhile way to experience parts of Hungary as part of their traveler program where Hungarians voluntarily open their home and lives to host you for short periods of time. You need to apply at least 4 weeks before you travel in your home country to be approved.

ESCORTED GENERAL-INTEREST TOURS

Go Today (www.go-today.com) offers a 6-night tour of Budapest or other tours that include Vienna or Prague. **Viking River Cruises** (www.vikingrivercruises.com) proposes travel opportunities via the Danube, including Budapest and other smaller towns along the way as part of their expanded country tours starting in Germany, continuing from here to Bratislava and Vienna.

For more information on Escorted General-Interest Tours, including questions to ask before booking your trip, see www.frommers.com/planning.

---

10 STAYING CONNECTED

For calls within Hungary, but outside of **Budapest,** dial the city code followed by the six or seven-digit number. For calls within Budapest, just dial the seven-digit number. If the number is a mobile phone, to call from a non-mobile phone, you must first dial 06, then the mobile numbers (20, 30, or 70) preceding the seven digits: for example 06/70-315-8828, if you were to call me from a non-mobile phone.

Calls to toll-free area codes **800, 888, 877,** and **866** do not work from Hungary. You should keep notes of non-toll-free numbers for banks and credit card companies in case of emergencies. **International calls** require the use of one of the following services. Credit card calls, collect calls or person-to-person calls using AT&T dial ✆ 06/8000-1112, 1113, or 1114. **MCI** call ✆ 06/8000-1411, or **Sprint** dial ✆ 06/8000-1877. Then follow the voice prompts from there. They will direct you for all of your choices.

MOBILE PHONES

If you have a mobile phone, which is a tri-band phone, it will allow you to use it in Hungary and the rest of Europe. Travelers from Europe, nearly all of North America, Australia, and New Zealand are covered by having this type of phone as it works in your home network as well. U.S. travelers should note that although Sprint phones claim to work in Hungary, so far I have not found one person who has had luck with it.

If you have an unlocked phone, one that is not tied to your home mobile carrier, then you can buy a SIM card from Pannon, T-Mobile, or Vodafone once in Hungary, giving you a Hungarian mobile number. This will greatly reduce the cost of making phone calls as they will no longer be long distance.

Hungarian mobile phone services make it incredibly difficult for anyone other than citizens or legal residents to rent or buy mobile phones. The only alternative is to purchase a phone from a store not associated with a mobile carrier and then purchase a SIM card on a pay-as-you-go plan. Money will need to be added to it to keep it working.

Depending on the company and SIM card, your calls may be restricted to calling domestically only, though you will be able to receive incoming calls from abroad. Domestic calls cost about 25 Ft a minute.

INTERNET & E-MAIL

When you're in Budapest, it is almost impossible not to find somewhere offering Wi-Fi for free or for the cost of a coffee. Look for blue-and-white Wi-Fi signs on doors of restaurants, bars, cafes, bookstores, and even some shops. With a downturn in the economy, this is the hook to get people into an establishment hoping something will strike their fancy once they are in the door. Many hotels now give Wi-Fi away for free as an added attraction to a lackluster occupancy slump. If you didn't pack a netbook or laptop, there are plenty of Internet cafes waiting to serve your need to surf the net or read e-mail. If an Internet cafe is not obvious from the street level, just keep an eye open for an A-frame sign showing the way to a cafe either up or down a flight of stairs. There are no shortages of Internet connections here.

11   TIPS ON ACCOMMODATIONS

Budapest's accommodations run the gamut of categories from beautiful, historic gems to those that have sprung from the ground up, and those that have remained the same from the beginning. They also run the gamut on prices too, but with this sluggish economy, don't hesitate to bargain with the larger hotels for a better rate or an upgrade. Check their website for specials and then follow-up with e-mails. Get the final confirmation in writing, but make sure you have remembered VAT and tourist tax, which can add a substantial amount to an otherwise reasonable room rate.

Bear in mind that many European standards call a room with two twin beds a double. If you want a double bed, you will need to request it specifically.

Extra beds or cots are generally available also. Hungarian hotels often blur the use of the words *apartment* and *suite* to describe bedrooms with a living room in it or connected rooms including a bedroom and living room. Some have a kitchen, while others do not. In chapter 5 "Where to Stay", I have specified if there is a separate living room area and/or kitchen facilities.

During the summer months, air-conditioning can be a major concern; the small hotels, pensions, and hostels are less likely to have it than more expensive properties. Some smaller places may have mobile air-conditioning units available for an added fee.

4

Suggested Budapest & Hungary Itineraries

Most people who only arrange a day or two in Budapest find they have shortchanged themselves and pledge to return for a longer visit in the future. However, if your time in the city is limited, you will find ways in this chapter to maximize your trip. Historic Budapest is basically a small area and many sights are relatively easy to walk to as listed in this book, and you'll have the added pleasure of perusing the architecture along the way. However, if you are severely limited by time, I suggest you invest in a transport pass, covering the number of days you will be here, so you can get around more quickly. Conversely, if you scheduled more than a week in the city, you may want to balance it out with one or two side trips using Budapest as your base. (Be warned that Budapest is my favorite city in Hungary and I will do my best to keep you here.) In an easy day of travel and touring, you can visit the small, quaint villages of Szentendre, Vác, Gödöllő, or Esztergom, each within an hour of the capital.

You may want to consider the information here as a supplement for the itineraries of the walking tours listed in chapter 8, "Strolling Around Budapest."

1 CITY LAYOUT

To really appreciate the city and the layout, you will need a short history lesson. The city of Budapest came into being in 1873, making it relatively young in its present form. It is the result of a union of three separate cities: **Buda, Pest,** and **Óbuda** (literally meaning Old Buda) consisting of 23 self-governing municipal districts. Budapest is divided by the **River Danube (Duna)** with Pest, almost completely flat, on the eastern shore, making up almost two-thirds of the city. On the western bank is Buda and farther yet, Óbuda, which has the hilly areas, these areas being much older settlements. The entire Danube River flows eastward for a distance of some 2,850km (1,771 miles) making some strange twists and turns as it goes flowing through or forming part of a border of 10 European countries, making it the longest river in the European Union.

The stretch of the Danube flowing through the capital is fairly wide (the average width is 400m/1,312 ft), and most of the city's historic sites are on or near the river. Nine bridges connect the two banks, but two are for rail travel only, with five in the city center. The Széchenyi Chain Bridge (Lánchíd) built in 1873, was the first permanent bridge across the Danube uniting Óbuda, Buda, and Pest. Although it was blown up by the Nazis in 1945, it was rebuilt after the war, reopening in November 1949. If you look at a map of the city, you will see that the districts are numbered in a spiral pattern for the most part with districts I, II, and III on the Buda side and then IV starts the Pest side until XI, which again is the Buda side.

Pest

Pest is as flat as a *palacsinta* (pancake), spread over a number of districts, taking in two-thirds of the city. Pest is the heartbeat with the commercial and administrative center of the capital and of all of Hungary. *Central Pest,* the term used in this guide, is that part of the city between the Danube and the semicircular **Outer Ring Boulevard (Nagykörút),** where stretches of it are named after former Austro-Hungarian monarchs: Ferenc körút, József körút, Erzsébet körút, Teréz körút, and Szent István körút, changing names as the district changes. The Outer Ring begins at the Pest side of the Petőfi Bridge in the south and wraps itself around the center, ending at the Margit Bridge in the north. Several of Pest's busiest squares are found along the Outer Ring, and Pest's major east-west avenues bisect the ring at these squares.

Central Pest is further defined by the **Inner Ring (Kiskörút),** which lies within the Outer Ring. It starts at Szabadság híd (Freedom Bridge) in the south and is alternately named Vámház körút, Múzeum körút, Károly körút, Bajcsy-Zsilinszky út, and József Attila utca, depending on the district, before ending at the Chain Bridge. Inside this ring is the **Belváros,** the actual city center and the historic Inner City of Pest. For the traveler, the Pest side is our recommended side for accommodations since this is where the lion's share of the action is and it is easy to walk to where you want to go.

Váci utca (distinct from Váci út) is a popular pedestrian-only, touristy, shopping street between the Inner Ring and the Danube. It spills into **Vörösmarty tér,** one of the area's best-known squares. The **Dunakorzó (Danube Promenade),** a popular evening strolling spot, runs along the river in Pest between the Chain Bridge and the Erzsébet Bridge. The

---

Hungarian Address Terms

Navigating in Budapest will be easier if you are familiar with the following words (none of which are capitalized in Hungarian):

utca (abbreviated as *u.*)	street
út	road
útja	road of
körút (abbreviated as *krt.*)	boulevard
tér	square
tere	square of
köz	alley or lane
körönd	circle
rakpart	quay
liget	park
sziget	island
híd	bridge
sor	row
part	riverbank
pályaudvar (abbreviated as *pu.*)	railway station
állomás	station

historic Jewish district of Pest is in the **Erzsébetváros (Elizabeth Town),** between the two ring boulevards.

Margaret Island (Margit-sziget) is in the middle of the Danube. Accessible via the Margaret Bridge or the Árpád Bridge, it's an enormously popular recreation park with restricted vehicular traffic. It is extremely popular in the summer for sunbathing, sports, jogging, and bike riding. It has a small petting zoo for children and the remnants of an old monastery.

Buda & Óbuda

On the left bank of the Danube is Buda; to its north, beyond the city center, lies Óbuda. Buda is as hilly as Pest is flat and is a good place for hiking. The two most advantageous vista points in the city are in central Buda on Castle Hill and the even higher Gellért Hill. Streets in Buda, particularly in the hills, are not as logically arranged as those in Pest.

Castle Hill is one of the most beautiful parts of Budapest with its magnificent view of Pest. Castle Hill is accessed by steep steps, walking paths, and small roads that are not open to general traffic. There are three less aerobic ways to access Castle Hill for those who want to conserve their energy for other adventures. From Clark Ádám tér (at the head of the Chain Bridge) you can take the funicular; from Várfok utca (near Moszkva tér) you can take the no. 10 bus; or from Deák, take the no. 16 bus, all of which will take you to the top. Castle Hill consists of the royal palace itself, home to several museums. The previous castle was destroyed in World War II, but was rebuilt afterward and named the Royal Palace specifically to house museums. The Castle District has a long history going to pre-Celtic times, but what remains today are the medieval neighborhoods of small, winding streets, circling around Holy Trinity Square (Szentháromság tér), site of the Gothic Church of Our Lady or commonly referred to as St. Matthias Church. There's little traffic on Castle Hill, and the only industry is tourism. Souvenirs, food, and drink tend to be more expensive here than in Pest.

Gellért Hill, to the south of Castle Hill, is named after the martyred Italian bishop who aided King István I (Stephen I) in his conversion of the Hungarian nation to Christianity in the 10th and 11th centuries. A giant statue of Gellért sits on the side of the hill, where legend has it that he was martyred by angry pagans for his efforts. On top of the hill is the Citadella, marked by a 14m (45ft) Liberation Statue of a woman holding a palm leaf to represent victory. It was erected in 1947 and visible from most points along the Danube on the Pest side.

Below Castle Hill, along the Danube, is a long, narrow neighborhood and district known as **Watertown (Víziváros).** The main street of Watertown is Fő utca (Main St.). One of the original market places is off of Batthyány tér in this district. The famous Király thermal bath from Turkish times is right down the street.

Central Buda, the term used in this guide, is a collection of mostly low-lying neighborhoods below Castle Hill. The main square of Central Buda is **Moszkva tér,** just north of Castle Hill, a hub for trams, buses, and the Red line metro, this area is in serious need of revitalizing. Beyond Central Buda, mainly to the east, are the Buda Hills.

Óbuda is on the left bank of the Danube, north of Buda. Although the greater part of Óbuda is lacking any architectural significance, reminding one of the Communist times, the area boasts both a beautiful old city center and the impressive Roman ruins of Aquincum. Unfortunately, the road coming off the Árpád Bridge slices the old city center in half, destroying its integrity. The historic center of the old city is **Fő tér (Main Sq.),** a charming square dotted with small, yet impressive museums. **Óbuda Island (Óbudai-sziget)** is home to an enormous park that swells in size every August when it hosts

Hungary's own annual Woodstock music festival, called the Sziget (Island) Festival. This festival has developed an international following. For more on this event, see p. 30.

FINDING AN ADDRESS Locating addresses in Budapest or anywhere in Hungary for that matter can be an exercise in frustration. Not only is strangeness of the Hungarian language confusing, the difference between an *o, ö, ó, or ő,* can make all of the difference and with 14 vowels to choose from, it can be a real puzzle. However, with a bit of practice and a good map, you should be successful.

Budapest is divided into 23 districts, called *kerülets* (abbreviated as *ker.*). All addresses in Hungary start with a Roman numeral followed by a period signifying the *kerület;* for example, VII. Akácfa u. 18 is in the seventh *kerület.* Many street names are often used repeatedly in different districts, but are not all continuations of the same street. This makes it very important to know which *kerület* a certain address is in. You will also need to pay attention to the type of street. Is it utca, út, tér, or tere? For example, there are streets named Templom (church) in nine different districts with various utca, út, körönd, and so on added to them.

A common mistake made by visitors is to confuse **Váci út,** the heavily trafficked main road that goes from Nyugati Station toward the city of Vác, with **Váci utca,** the pedestrian-only street in the Inner City. Similarly, visitors sometimes mistake Vörösmarty utca, a station on the Yellow metro line, with Vörösmarty tér, the terminus of that same Yellow metro line.

If the address you are hunting for doesn't have a Roman numeral preceding it, look for the postal code for the *kerület.* Postal codes are four digits with the middle two digits representing the *kerület;* thus, Akácfa u.18, 1072 Budapest will be in district VII.

Street signs are posted high up on the corner buildings on a street and on two corners; one showing the even numbers and one with the odd numbers. The information given is the Roman numeral of the *kerület* followed by the name of the district, under this is the name of the street or square, and finally the building numbers found on that block. Look at the arrow on the sign; for example, 29–35 with an arrow pointing to the right tells you that if you walk to the right, the numbers will get higher. You may have to look at all four corners before you see the one you want. Even- and odd-numbered buildings are on opposite sides of the street; however, they do not follow any pattern otherwise. You may be in front of no. 98 on one side of the street and see no. 79 directly across from you. Depending on whether you are looking for an even or odd number on the street, orient yourself with the signs showing the even or odd numbering. Numbers are seldom skipped, but two or more places may share a number; often you'll end up walking longer than you expected to reach a given number. Adding to the "guess where it is" game, many businesses do not have a numeral posted on their doors, so look for other signs.

Many street names were changed following the systemic changes of 1989, reverting for the most part back to their pre-World War II names, aside from a handful of central streets with politically evocative former names, like Lenin körút (now Teréz körút) and Népköztársaság útja ("Road of the People's Republic," now Andrássy út). The one outstanding exception is Moszkva tér.

Floors in buildings are numbered European style, meaning that the floor you enter, is the ground floor *(földszint),* so for the first floor, you have to go up one flight *(első emelet),* and so on. Addresses are usually written with the floor number in Roman numerals and the apartment number in Arabic numerals, following the street name. For example, a full address would be VII. Budapest Akácfa u. 18, IV/24. The district is the seventh in Budapest and the location is on Akácfa u. 18 on the fourth floor, apartment 24.

Read signs carefully and match all of the little marks above those vowels. The Hungarian alphabet has 44 letters, making it very detailed in writing and in speech. Refer to the "Hungarian Address Terms" box above.

STREET MAPS A good map can save you hours of frustration. You can get a decent free map at the Tourinform office. Public transportation lines are shown on the maps, but, in some places, the map is too crowded to make the lines out clearly. If you are really lucky, the BKV térkép (Budapest Transportation Authority map) will be available from metro ticket windows, but they seem to be scarce when needed. If you really want one, at the top of the Red metro escalator at the Deák station, you will find an unnamed bookshop. They seem to have an endless supply of transit maps on sale for 690 Ft. You will also find that Google Maps has done a fine job with Budapest (www.google.com/maps) if you have your laptop or GPRS/WAP-enabled (tri-or quad-band) phone with you.

NEIGHBORHOODS IN BRIEF

BUDA

Castle District (Várnegyed). This district is the city's most beautiful and historic dating back to the 13th century, with some settlements here even earlier. This is **district I**, which is a small district that encompasses the plateau where the grand Royal Palace and grounds fill the southern end above the surrounding neighborhoods and the Danube below. The Castle District is defined by its medieval walls. The northern end is home to small winding streets, with old homes, St. Matthias Church, the Fisherman's Bastion, and the Hilton Hotel.

Watertown (Víziváros). A long, narrow neighborhood wedged between the Castle District and the Danube, makes up **district II**. Víziváros is historically a quarter where fishermen and artisans reside. Built on the steep slope of Castle Hill, it has narrow alleys and stairs instead of roads in many places. Its main street, Fő utca, runs the north–south length of the Víziváros, parallel to and a block away from the river. It is a high-rent district for residents and tourists.

Rose Hill (Rózsadomb). This is the part of Buda Hills and still part of district II, closest to the city center and one of the city's most fashionable and luxurious residential neighborhoods.

Buda Hills. The Buda Hills are numerous remote neighborhoods that feel as if they're nowhere near, let alone within, a capital city. By and large, the hills are considered a classy place to live. Neighborhoods are generally known by the name of the hill on which they stand. Unless you like to walk neighborhoods, there is nothing more for the traveler in this part of the city.

ÓBUDA

Óbuda makes up **district III** and is mostly residential now, though its long Danube coastline was a favorite spot for workers' resorts under the old regime. Most facilities have been privatized, so a large number of hotels are found here. Transportation for the traveler into Pest would be cumbersome, so we do not recommend staying out here. The extensive Roman ruins of Aquincum and the beautifully preserved old-town main square are Óbuda's chief claims to fame.

PEST

Inner City (Belváros). The historic center of Pest, the Belváros, literally meaning "city center" is the area inside the Inner Ring, bound by the Danube to the west. Making up part of **district**

V, it has many of Pest's historic buildings in this area. In addition, a number of the city's showcase luxury hotels and most of its best-known shopping streets are here.

Leopold Town (Lipótváros). The continuation of district V is just north of the Belváros, making Lipótváros a part of central Pest. Development began here at the end of the 18th century, and the neighborhood soon emerged as a center of Pest business and government. Parliament, plus a number of government ministries, courthouses, banks, and the former stock exchange, are all found here. Before the war, this was considered a neighborhood of the "high bourgeoisie."

Theresa Town (Terézváros). The character of Terézváros, **district VI**, is defined by Andrássy út, the great boulevard running the length of the neighborhood from Heroes' Square through Oktogon and down into the Inner City. This grand street has been regaining its reputation of elegance: Andrássy út is once again the "best address" in town, especially since the upper part is now a UNESCO World Heritage site. The Teréz körút section of the Outer Ring cuts through Terézváros; Oktogon is its major square. The area around Nagymező utca is the city's small theater district.

Elizabeth Town (Erzsébetváros). This is **district VII**. Directly to the southeast of Terézváros, Erzsébetváros is the historic Jewish neighborhood of Pest. During the German occupation from 1944 to 1945, this district was where the ghettos were established for the Jewish people. This district is still the center of Budapest's Jewish life. Although it had been exceedingly run-down due to the war, in the last couple of years, it has become gentrified and considered one of the up-and-coming districts to invest in.

Joseph Town (Józsefváros). One of the largest central Pest neighborhoods is **district VIII**. Józsefváros is to the southeast of Erzsébetváros. It has had a reputation of being a less-than-desirable district of Pest, but there are some places in this district worth your time and energy. It should not be dismissed across the board. It is working hard at gentrifying.

2 THE BEST OF BUDAPEST IN ONE DAY

If you only have 1 day in Budapest, you'll want to see a bit of both Buda and Pest, and this tour lets you do both. You'll start off with a cultural and historic tour of Pest, then you'll cross Chain Bridge (an attraction in itself) for a brief tour of the Castle District in Buda, where you can enjoy a meal and a stop in a pub. ***Start:*** Inner Pest.

❶ Inner City & Central Pest ★

Budapest is a city where wide boulevards intersect with some really narrow streets. It is a reminder that it was once part of the Austro-Hungarian empire. Wide boulevards were especially well suited for accommodating the carriages of royals and others of wealth. This is definitely a city to be walked, so start in the center, wander the grand boulevards, and admire the architecture. Make sure you look up. So many interesting features on buildings are not at eye level.

Depending on your travel tastes, you may want to visit a few museums and highlights of the area. You may find the Greek-looking **Hungarian National Museum** ★★ (p. 126), the **Budapest Holocaust Memorial Center** ★★ (p. 123), or the **Inner City Parish Church** ★ (p. 134) to your liking.

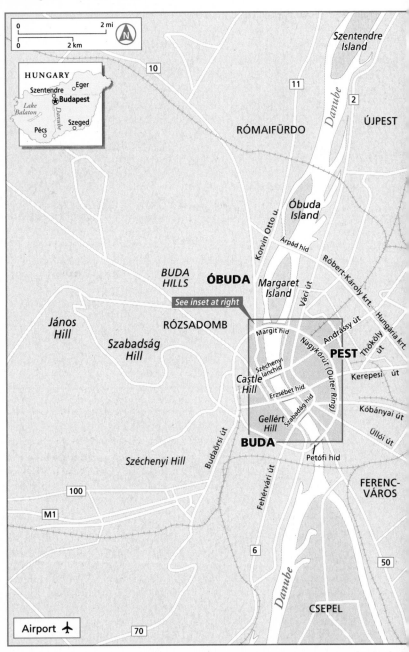

0   2 mi
0   2 km

N

HUNGARY

Szentendre   Eger
Lake Balaton   ★Budapest
Danube
Pécs   Szeged

10

11

Danube

2

Szentendre Island

RÓMAIFÜRDO

ÚJPEST

Korvin Otto u.

Óbuda Island

Árpád híd

Róbert-Károly krt.

Hungária krt.

BUDA HILLS

ÓBUDA

Margaret Island

Váci út

János Hill

RÓZSADOMB

See inset at right

Margit híd

Andrássy út

Thököly út

Szabadság Hill

Nagykörút (Outer Ring)

PEST

Kerepesi út

Castle Hill

Széchenyi lánchíd

Erzsébet híd

Szabadság híd

Kóbányai út

Gellért Hill

Üllói út

Budaörsi út

Széchenyi Hill

BUDA

Petófi híd

FERENC-VÁROS

100

M1

Fehérvári út

6

50

Danube

Airport ✈

70

CSEPEL

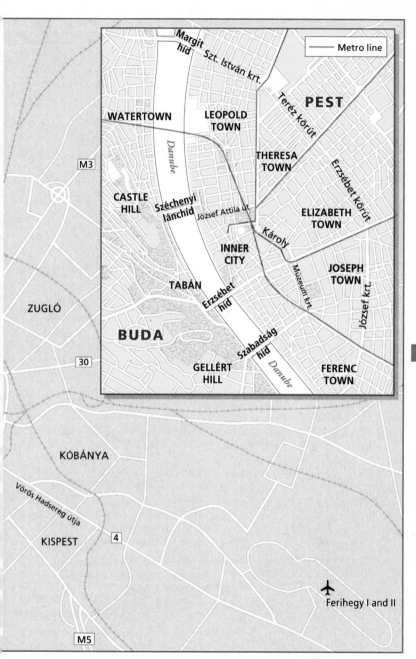

As you wander through the area, remind yourself of two facts: unlike Prague, much of Budapest was bombed during World War II; and the Communist regime only ended in 1989. In a relatively short time, the city has made tremendous strides, although it still has far to go. Many historic buildings have been torn down to be replaced with modern conveniences such as boutiques, apartment complexes, or restaurants. Others have been renovated to their former glory, but in my opinion, certainly not enough. History is being replaced by sterility of the new and modern.

Váci utca is the perennially favorite shopping and walking street of Budapest. Developed after the regime changes in 1989, it has blossomed with many international stores and some Hungarian ones as well. For examples of Hungarian crafts, visit the **Vali Folklór** folk craft shop (p. 206), the **VAM Design Gallery,** at Váci utca 64, and various clothing stores (avoid the touristy cafes here).

Walk from Váci utca to the Danube Promenade and stroll along the river. Following the no. 2 tram line, you will be making your way to Kossuth tér for:

❷ Parliament ★★★

Budapest's exquisite Parliament building is the second largest in Europe after England's Westminster. I've taken the tour six times and could still do it again. The main facade faces the Danube. Designed by Imre Steindl and completed in 1902, the building mixes neo-Gothic style with a neo-Renaissance dome reaching 96m (315 ft), significant as the country's millennium was 1896 and the conquest of the kingdom of Hungary was 896. St. Stephens is also 96m (315 ft) high for the same reasons. It is by far one of our favorite buildings in Budapest. At the top of a grandly ornamented staircase, there is a hexadecagonal (16-sided) central hall that leads to an impressive chamber. The fabled Hungarian crown jewels of St. Stephen are on display. Unfortunately, you can enter only on guided tours (the ¾-hour tour is worth the chance to go inside). See p. 131 for tour times and information.

❸ SZABADSAG TÉR (FREEDOM SQUARE) ★

This beautifully maintained park is the home of a large obelisk statue that commemorates when the Soviet Union liberated Hungary at the end of World War II. It is the last remaining memorial to the Soviet Union in the city. You may want to rest in the park or have a coffee at Farger's Café at Zoltán u. 18, right on the square. You will be directly across from the U.S. Embassy.

Walk back to Parliament and then south about .4km (¼ mile) toward the historic Chain Bridge, which you will see in the distance:

❹ Chain Bridge ★

Known as the Széchenyi Bridge or the Chain Bridge, this bridge holds the distinction of being the first permanent crossing to link Buda and Pest. The idea for the bridge was instigated and funded by 19th-century Hungarian reformer, Count István Széchenyi. Legend has it that due to storms, he was not able to cross the river to be with his dying father. While Széchenyi waited 8 days for the storms to subside so he could cross the river, his father died and he missed the funeral. Designed by William Tierney Clark, an Englishman, the bridge was also one of the largest suspension bridges of its time when it opened in 1849. According to legend, the omission of sculpted tongues on the lions, which guard the bridge at either end, caused the sculptor to drown himself in the river out of shame; however, the lions do have tongues, just not visible from the ground. See p. 140. (*Note:* You might duck into the **Four Seasons Hotel Gresham Palace** ★★★ while you're here to view its breathtaking interiors and use the bathroom; p. 67).

Walk across the Chain Bridge, and take the funicular up to the:

❺ Castle District ★★

Castle Hill, a UNESCO World Cultural Heritage site, consists of two parts: the Royal Palace itself and the so-called Castle District. Most of this area is a reconstructed medieval city, but the original castle was destroyed in World War II and replaced with the current Royal Palace. For a detailed 3-hour itinerary of this area, see "Walking Tour 2: The Castle District," in chapter 8, "Strolling Around Budapest."

This is an interesting area for walking and wandering. There are many cobblestone streets, so choose your shoes carefully. You might also wish to stop and visit the **Hungarian National Gallery** ★ (p. 138) and the **Budapest History Museum** ★★ (p. 137).

> **RIVALDA CAFÉ & RESTAURANT** ★
>
> After a long day of walking and sightseeing, one option for a meal while still on the hill is the Rivalda Café & Restaurant. This restaurant is housed in a building that was once a monastery of Carmelite monks who disbanded in 1786. The building was then given to the people of Buda by Joseph II to become a theater. Open as a restaurant in 2000, it has saxophone or piano music nightly. I. Színház u. 5–9; *©* 1/489-0236. See p. 117.

After dinner, you might head back to your hotel to relax for a bit so you'll be ready to:

7 Socialize at a Bar, Club, or Bistro
Budapest has a variety of lively nightlife possibilities to suit every taste. You'll find all levels of partying available, whether you're looking for hardcore clubbing or just a pub for drinks with the locals. Clubs such as **The Old Man's Music Pub** (p. 223) and **Paris, Texas** (p. 224) have nightly music. Both are quite popular places for nighttime drinks and socializing, where you'll find locals of all ages mingling here. See chapter 10, "Budapest After Dark."

3 THE BEST OF BUDAPEST IN TWO DAYS

Once you have discovered the charms of Inner Pest and the Castle District on Day 1, it is time to broaden the scope with a walk around the **Outer Ring Boulevard** *(körút)*. Note that as you walk the *körút,* the name changes from district to district. ***Start:*** New York Palace Hotel.

1 New York Palace Hotel ★★
The New York Life Insurance Company originally commissioned the building, which opened on October 23, 1894. During the 1900s, its cafe was a center of intellectual life in the city, with writers and journalists as frequent patrons. After many years of remodeling and revitalizing the original eclectic style with a strong Italian renaissance influence, the Boscolo hotel chain reopened the hotel and its legendary cafe in 2006. The detailed reconstruction is worth admiring and returning to see in the evening when lit up. Walk toward Oktogon, noting the grand turn-of-the-20th-century architecture of Pest. At Oktogon turn right and walk up to Andrássy u. 60:

2 Terror Háza (House of Terror) ★★
First the headquarters of the secret police of the Nazi Arrow Cross regime, when the Soviets liberated Hungary, it immediately turned into the headquarters for the Communist secret police. This building is the setting of some of the most horrific days of 20th-century Hungary, which lasted for more than 50 years. Hundreds were tortured and murdered in the basement by both regimes. The Nazis' primary victims were Jews, but the Communists targeted anyone who spoke out against the government. The building is a museum functioning as a

memorial to the victims of both Fascism and Communism and is an everlasting reminder of the effect of oppressive regimes in Hungary. However, it has caused continual controversy since it opened in 2002, especially because the building's overhang has the word "TERROR" stenciled on it, which is quite striking when the sun shines through it.

❸ Andrássy Boulevard ★

Strolling up the majestic Andrássy Boulevard toward Heroes' Square and City Park, you are taking the UNESCO World Heritage Site tour. The boulevard is lined with trees and a wealth of beautiful apartment buildings, many of which are now used as embassies. In addition, there are restaurants and museums scattered along the way leading to Heroes' Square. This is Pest's greatest boulevard.

If you are ready for a break:

---

❹ KOGART GALLERY AND RESTAURANT ★★★
Designed by Ignác Alpar, who also designed the Vajdahunyad Castle in City Park, this historic building is now home to a beautiful cafe and restaurant. Take your coffee and read a paper while sitting on a leather sofa in a quiet corner of the room. If you are so inclined, the art gallery upstairs has rotating exhibits of superior quality. Andrássy út 112. ✆ **1/354-3830.**

Once you reach the end of Andrássy Boulevard, adjacent to the Museum of Fine Arts, the Múcsarnok, and City Park, you'll find:

❺ Heroes' Square ★★

Heroes' Square was created for the millennium in 1896 (remember the reoccurring 96), which celebrates the arrival of the Magyar tribes in the Carpathian Basin in 896. The statues represent the chronology of some 1,000 years of Hungarian history. The seven statues on the left side are all Hungarian kings. On the right side, they are all famous Hungarians, but only one was a king. In 1896 during the famous world exhibition, this space was the apex of

some 200 pavilions that made up the festivities. Many festivals are still held here.

To your left you will find the **Museum of Fine Arts** ★ (p. 126). The museum is the main repository of foreign art in Hungary. It has one of central Europe's major collections and it is considered one of the most important art collections in Europe. Free 1-hour tours are offered by highly trained docents Tuesday through Friday at 11am and 2pm and Saturday at 11am.

Walk through the park and you will arrive at:

❻ The Széchenyi Baths ★★

After a long day, you deserve to rest and relax. Nothing could be better after a day of touring than a soak in a thermal. This is one of the largest spa complexes in Europe and the first thermal bath on the Pest side. Chances are if you have seen photos of men playing chess on floating chessboards, the men were in this thermal. It is mixed men and women and bathing suits are mandatory.

See p. 159 and the box, "Thermal Bathing 101," on p. 160.

After your afternoon of thermal bathing, you may want to head back to your hotel to rest, but if you have done so at the thermals, then head out for dinner. You can take the Yellow metro from Széchenyi and go one stop to Mexikói or choose a dining spot from chapter 6, "Where to Dine in Budapest," but either way make a reservation.

❼ Trófea Grill Étterem ★★★

You have had a full day of exercise, so treat yourself to the best Hungarian all-you-can-eat restaurant in the city. With more than 100 choices from soups to desserts and everything in between, everyone is sure to leave satisfied. See p. 114.

❽ Attend Some Nighttime Culture ★★

Spend an evening attending an opera at the **Opera House** ★★★. It is a premier venue. The Opera House is magnificently beautiful inside. The fine arts are alive and well in Budapest, and a nighttime cultural event is the way to round out your short stint in the city. Note that performances usually start at 7pm not the customary 8pm.

Now that you've had a taste of Budapest, perhaps you want to experience other parts of the country and see how life differs outside of the capital. Since the average visitor to Hungary usually spends a few days in the country, we've opted to give you a few side-trip options from Budapest, rather than a 1-week or longer tour of the entire country. All rail tracks lead to Budapest, so regardless of which direction you go chances are you will have to return to Budapest when changing from one geographical area to another, making a full Hungarian tour both difficult and time-consuming. You'd need several weeks to see it all. Traveling by bus is even more time-consuming and not as comfortable as the train. Driving a car can be downright dangerous if you're not used to European driving, not to mention the cost. Trains, though not quite luxurious, are easy and safe, and they usually cost less than 6,000 Ft round-trip, depending on the destination.

For more information on the following regions, see the regional chapters later in the book.

Option ❶: A Day in Szentendre ★★

After some time in Budapest, you might visit Szentendre (pronounced *Sen*-ten-dreh), just north of Budapest on the Danube and one of the most-visited spots in all of Hungary. Take the HÉV (regional train) from Budapest's Batthyány tér metro for a 45-minute ride.

Visit the **Margit Kovács Museum** ★★★ and see the interesting collection of the late Margit Kovács. She was primarily a ceramicist, and her depictions of peasant life in Hungary are charming. Have a late lunch at the **Aranysárkány Vendéglő** ★, and take a walk along the river. Then spend your afternoon exploring the many shops, museums, churches, and galleries in town. Fő tér, the main drag, is enticing, but explore all the side streets of this small, manageable town. Try **Chez Nicolas Restaurant** ★★ Kígyó utca 10.

For more information on Szentendre, see chapter 11.

Option ❷: A Day in Vác ★★★

Just past Szentendre along the Danube, but actually faster to reach, Vác can be reached by direct train from Budapest in as little as 25 minutes. This is a very historic town, and it also has one of the most

beautiful Danube parks I have seen. All along the river is a wide promenade with winding walking and biking paths with play areas for children interspersed along the way. To the side of these are wide sidewalks providing a relaxing walk under the chestnut-tree-lined street.

Vác is a town for strolling, since most of the historic sites are to be seen from the outside, with the exception of peeking through the glass of the doorways of churches and one must-see museum. Starting at the main square, **Március 15 tér** ★★★, there is the historic **White Friar's Church** ★★ and the impressive statute and fountain of **St. Hedwig** on the side of the church. Directly across from the church is the **Memento Mori** ★★★ with the preserved crypts that were uncovered accidentally when renovations took place on White Friar's Church. Also on the square are many historic and interesting baroque buildings. The **Cathedral of the Assumption** on Konstantin tér is the only building in Hungary influenced by Parisian revolutionary architecture. At Géza Király tér is the **Franciscan or "Brown" Church,** which sits next to the castle, the oldest building in Vác. An Italian architect designed the synagogue on Eötvös utca in romantic style. The river walk is a glorious relaxing escape.

For more information on Vác, see p. 239 in chapter 11.

Option ❸: A Few Hours in Gödöllő ★

Gödöllő is the home to the largest baroque palace in Hungary, which was originally built for the aristocratic Grassalkovich family. Later Franz Josef, emperor of Austria, king of Hungary, and his wife Elisabeth, or "Sisi" as she was affectionately known, used this as their summer residence. Gödöllő is less than an hour away from Budapest by HÉV, making this an ideal getaway for a short day trip. At Christmastime, the decoration of the palace is well worth seeing. While in Gödöllő, you may want to have dinner at **Kastélykert Étterem** (Palace Park Restaurant) at Szabadság út 4; ✆ **28/527-020.** They are open daily from noon to 11pm.

Option ❹: Visit the Bears ★★ (Kids)

Medve Otthon or Bear Sanctuary is the place to go when the kids, or the adults for that matter, are tired of the city and need some nature-loving activity. Here you can visit the 42 brown bears at the bear sanctuary, just 50 minutes from Nyugati Station. Some of the bears were stars in Hungarian films, but were rescued due to mistreatment. Don't ask for their autographs, but you can feed them honey bought from the gift shop using a long spoon. If you find this unbearable, there are two packs of 26 wolves living here also. On weekends, there are pony rides, a bouncy castle, and face painting. The sanctuary is located at Patak u. 39, Veresegyház and it is open daily from 8am to 7pm. Take the train from Nyugati Station to Ivacs, the nearest station. Depending on the train, the tickets will cost either 480 Ft or 955 Ft with the less expensive trains actually being faster: 45 minutes as opposed to 1 hour

and 5 minutes. From the train station, follow the clearly marked route 2km (1.2 miles) to the sanctuary. Admission is 200 Ft per person. Hours are March to September 8am to 7pm. October to February 9am to dark.

Option ❺: Győr ★★

Győr is located halfway between Budapest and Vienna (131km/81 miles) in the northwestern corner, making it a perfect stop if you are coming from or going to Vienna. Considered one of the more important cities in Hungary, it is known as the town of rivers; it sits at the meeting point of three rivers, the Danube, Rába, and Rábca. There are six fast trains leaving Budapest, which will get you into Győr in 1½ hours for 2,700 Ft, but you will need a reservation for these trains.

First inhabited by the Celts, then the Romans in the 1st century B.C., Győr has been populated ever since. During the Ottoman invasion, the commander of the town didn't think it was worth defending, so he ordered the entire town to be burned to the ground. When the Ottomans arrived, they only found piles of ashes. When they left, the town was rebuilt and the top Italian builders completed the work, filling the city with baroque buildings. World War II brought destruction, but a massive campaign in the '70s renewed the buildings to their former status, thus earning them the European Award for monument protection. Buildings surrounding each square give them a unique feel from the others.

Things to see include the Győ Basilica on Káptalandomb, where King Stephen established the Episcopate in his first decade as king. The baroque church with its Blessed Virgin picture is one of the most significant pilgrimage sites in Hungary. It is open 8am to noon and 2pm to 6pm. The Esterházy Palace at Király u. 17 (✆ **96/ 322-695**), consists of three monumental buildings from the 18th century. Originally the palace of Count Gábor Esterházy, it is now the City Art Museum, open Tuesday through Sunday 10am to 6pm. At the **Zichy-Palota** on Liszt Ferenc utca 20 (🕿 **96/311-316**), you will find the permanent puppet collection of 72 puppets, accessories, and furniture. It is open Tuesday through Thursday 8am to 3:30pm and Friday 8am to 1pm. If you miss the bath experience in Budapest, you can visit the **Rába-Quelle Medicinal, Thermal and Pleasure Bath** at Fürdő tér 1 (🕿 **96/514-900**). It is open 9am to 10pm. If your visit brings you here between April and August, the city has a number of fairs and celebrations. One dining option among the many is Komédiás Étterem at Czuczor G. utca 30 (🕿 **96/527-217**). It is open 11am to midnight and accepts all credit cards.

For hotel recommendations or further information, contact Tourinform in Győr at Árpád utca 32 (🕿 **96/311-771;** www. gyortourism.hu). From June through August it's open weekdays from 8am to 8pm and weekends 9am to 6pm, and during the rest of the year, it's open weekdays 9am to 5pm and weekends 9am to 1pm.

Option ❻: Two Days in Keszthely ★ & Héviz ★★

Keszthely and Héviz are located on the western corner of Hungary's very own "sea," Lake Balaton, almost 200km (124 miles) from Budapest. The towns sit right in a microclimate area, with warm summers, clear skies, and beautiful vistas and hills.

From Budapest, take a 3-hour express (*gyors*) train from Déli or Keleti stations to Keszthely. Then explore the **Festetics Mansion** ★, **Carriage Museum,** or try the **Dolls Museum,** which has Europe's largest collection of dolls, with the **Parliament of Snails.**

After roaming around Keszthely, have a traditional Hungarian meal, with a traditional Unicum, at the **Margaréta Étterem.** At night, you may want to consider an

event at the **Balaton Congress Center and Theater,** and stay either in a "private room" or at the **Barbara Wellness Pension.**

The next day take a bus to Héviz, 8km (5 miles) northeast of Keszthely. Here you'll find a wide range of hotel choices from pensions to five-star luxury hotels to fit any budget. One choice is **Hotel Erzsébet** in the town center. Take a dip in **Europe's largest thermal lake,** or spend your whole day unwinding at the hotel. Spa treatments include a selection of health cures, sports, wellness, or even medical treatment programs.

You might shorten this trip by heading straight to Héviz, then tour Keszthely and relax in the spa hotel at night.

For more information about Keszthely, see chapter 12, p. 253.

Option ❼: Two Days in Pécs ★★★

The popular Pécs is the most culturally vibrant Hungarian city outside of the capital—warm and arid, with lots of museums, galleries, and a large student population from the university.

Take an early morning InterCity train from Budapest's Déli Station to Pécs, a 3-hour ride. Walk down Káptalan utca, the street of museums which are all housed in medieval houses. Visit the **Tivadar Csontváry Museum** ★, the institution that celebrates one of Hungary's most notable artists. In the **Zsolnay Museum** ★★★, housed in a Gothic residence, you'll find displays of the finest pieces of award-winning porcelain, even paintings. Then check out the hustle and bustle of the **Pécsi Vásár** ★★ flea market, and shop for traditional Hungarian wares. Head uphill for dinner at the **Vadasztanya (Hunters' Lodge)** ★★, where you can enjoy a fine Hungarian wine before checking in at the fun, centrally located **Hotel Főnix** ★★.

For a mid-morning snack, stop for coffee and pastry at the **Mecsek Cukrászda** before checking out Pécs' houses of worship, the **Pécs Cathedral,** the **Pécs Synagogue** ★, and the largest-standing Turkish structure, the **Mosque of Pasha Gazi Kassim.**

For more information about Pécs, see chapter 14.

Option ⑧: Two Days in Szeged ★

The southeastern town of Szeged is the cultural center of the region. With a thriving university, it is overflowing with students. If you're in Hungary in the summer, come for the **Szeged Summer Open Air Festival ★★** in Dóm tér, which offers rock operas, classical music, ballet, and contemporary dance in July and August, making it the largest festival of its kind in Hungary.

From Budapest, take the train from Nyugati Station for a 2½-hour ride. Start off with a coffee and pastry at the famous **Virág Cukrászda.** Enjoy some of the impressive architecture; visit the Votive **Church of Our Lady of Hungary ★★★,** the cathedral built in Hungarian Ecclesiastic architecture.

Take a walk on the river's edge, then head back to **Kárász utca ★★**, the main walking street which is usually bustling with students. Have a casual dinner on the terrace at the **Gödör Restaurant** or for a more upscale meal try **Göry Restaurant & Terrace ★**. Try to get a room at the reasonably priced and clean **Family Pension,** not far from the train station and Dóm tér.

On your second day here, check out the **Polish Market (Lengyel Piac) ★** on the southern edge of town and visit the beautiful and historic **synagogue ★**. Then head for some hearty fish stew at **Kiskörössy Halaszcsarda ★** for which Szeged is famous, which uses fish from the Tiza River, not the Danube.

For more information about Szeged, see p. 284 in chapter 14.

Where to Stay in Budapest

A few new hotels such as the **Buda Castle Fashion Hotel** and **Promenade City Hotel** opened late in 2008, while more hotels are being built as of this writing. The Mercure Hotel Budapest Nemzeti is closed for remodeling and rebranding, and (at the time of writing) will not reopen until spring 2010 as a Mercure MGallery Hotel. The most distinctive of the Budapest hotels include the historic **Gresham Palace Four Seasons, Corinthia Grand Hotel Royal,** and **Castle Hill's Hilton Hotel,** being among the city's most elite lodgings.

Lodging rates in Budapest have risen considerably, becoming more comparable to the rates of other European capitals. With that said, hotel occupancy has been decreasing over the last few years and dramatically in 2009. Reports have shown that many hotels are fewer than 50% occupancy during some peak periods, so deals can be had if you are a savvy Internet bargain hunter. After doing your research, compare the rates you have found with the hotel's website to look for specials. Don't stop until you try e-mailing the hotel directly to see if there are any unadvertised specials or discounts they are willing to offer.

In the past, during the high season from April or May to the end of September, it was difficult to get your first choice of a room in your first choice of hotel, but this has eased over the last few years. However, if you wait for the last minute to book, it could still hold true. During the Hungarian Formula One weekend or the Sziget Festival (both in August), it can be quite difficult to secure a hotel or pension room or even a hostel bed, so make reservations and get written confirmation well in advance of your stay.

BUDGET LODGINGS There are a number of recommendable budget accommodations in Budapest. Travelers have the advantage of choosing from a wealth of perfectly acceptable options. Small pensions sometimes called *panzios,* self-catering apartments, and a number of good youth hostels make the city inviting to travelers on any budget. Remember the realtor phrase: *location, location, location.* The location of your accommodations is a significant factor in cost. Normally, one can expect to pay more for the location, the history, and the reputation of a place; being in the center of the city will inflate the cost. Note that with construction of the new metro 4 line, transportation services on the Buda side are continually in flux. This can make it difficult to get to and from your hotel. Returning late in the evening to some parts of the city can be trickier than in the past. Question the transportation options carefully. There is nothing worse than having to end a pleasant evening early just to catch the last transport back to your hotel. Remember, time is precious and you don't want to spend too much of it on public transport.

ACCOMMODATIONS AGENCIES I generally hesitate recommending a private accommodation for most people, because of potential language barriers. Hungarian is so different a language that travelers may feel isolated if they book with non-English-speaking families. However, if you are feeling brave and want to try this option, the most-established accommodations agency is the former state-owned travel agent **Ibusz**. The main **Ibusz reservations office** is at Ferenciek tere 10 (© **1/501-4911**; fax 1/**501-4915**; www.ibusz.hu), accessible by the Blue metro line. This office is open year-round Monday through Friday 9am to 6pm.

SEASONS Many, but not all hotels and pensions in Budapest, divide the year into three seasons. **High season** is roughly from March or April through September or October. Easter week and the period of the Budapest Spring Festival (mid- to late March) are also considered high season by some hotels. **Special season** includes the weekend of the Hungarian Formula One in August, and New Year's Eve. A few places consider Easter part of this season also, but it seems fewer than in the past. **Low season** is roughly November through February, with the exceptions above. Some hotels discount as much as 30% in low season, while others offer no specified winter discounts, yet with occupancy rates at an incredible low they do sneak in web specials, so be sure to inquire.

PRICE CATEGORIES The majority of hotels and pensions in Budapest list their prices in euros, so the rates are listed in this book as the hotel designates. Listing rates in euros is not just intended as a means of transition to the E.U. currency (Hungary is not expected to join the euro zone until 2012 at the earliest and most likely later), it is also a hedge against forint inflation (though the forint has had significant highs and lows over the past few years). All hotels in Budapest accept payment in Hungarian forints as well as in foreign currencies, but their rates will be much more to their advantage than yours.

If paying with a currency other than Hungarian forints or euros, exchange your currency on the street at authorized booths and then pay the hotel. Exchange rates fluctuate daily, of course, so the price of a room in euro-to-forint and other currencies will change accordingly.

All hotels are required to charge a whopping 18% value-added tax (VAT), an increase instituted in July 2009. Most build the tax into their rates, while a few tack it on top of their rates. When booking a room, ask whether the VAT is included in the quoted price. Unless otherwise indicated, prices in this book include the VAT.

Hotels in Hungary are rated by the international five-star system. In our view, however, the ratings are somewhat arbitrary and are not included in our entries for that reason. You can find an explanation of the Frommer's star ratings used throughout this guide in the front matter.

Note: I have discovered that just about every accommodation has some Internet specials or packages on its website. Just like the airlines, hotels continually gauge their occupancy and change rates according to room availability; but they all say that the early bird gets the biggest discount. Unless noted otherwise, the hotels listed have Internet deals, so check their website. Once you have booked, confirm the rate and the room desired by getting a confirmation number.

I have found that smaller hotel and pension websites are not frequently updated with respect to rates. If they don't have online booking capabilities, make sure to call or e-mail them to confirm rates. If you can book online, the rates should be current and accurate.

1 THE INNER CITY & CENTRAL PEST

VERY EXPENSIVE

Corinthia Grand Hotel Royal ★★★

One of the grand dames of Budapest, originally built in 1896 by architect Rezső Ray, this hotel reopened in its current grandeur fashion in 2003. It exudes opulence the minute you walk in. There is a staircase to the baroque grand ballroom, where balls and conferences are often held. Paintings of famous Hungarians hang on the walls. The secessionist splendor of the rest of the hotel continues throughout. The guest rooms come in two categories: superior and executive. All are beautifully appointed to meet every need a traveler could have. When you climb into the bed, it caresses your body. The bathrooms are done in marble tiles with separate showers and tubs. Bathrobes and slippers are waiting for you to cozy up in on the sofa with a glass of wine. Executive rooms give access to the exclusive business lounge, breakfast area, and lounge where snacks and drinks are offered complimentarily. This is a place to be pampered.

VII. Erzsébet krt. 43–49. ℃ **1/479-4000.** Fax 1/479-4333. www.corinthia.com. 414 units. High season 230€ superior; 600€ deluxe. Low season 140€ superior; 350€ deluxe; Executive Club all seasons 60€ superior; included with deluxe. Breakfast 28€ per person. Children 11 and under stay free in parents' room. AE, DC, MC, V. Secure underground parking. Tram: 4 or 6 to Király u. **Amenities:** 3 restaurants; 2 bars; 1 cafe; babysitting; bikes; concierge; executive-level rooms; Jacuzzi; large indoor heated pool; room service; sauna; smoke-free rooms. *In room:* A/C, TV/DVD, hair dryer, minibar, movie library from concierge, Wi-Fi.

Four Seasons Hotel Gresham Palace ★★★

This hotel is so remarkable, tour buses stop here to allow people to look over the lobby. This Art Nouveau building, one of the most elegant and majestic properties in the city, stands as one of the finest in the world. With the Chain Bridge directly opposite the front doors, it has a picture-perfect view of the Buda Castle making this the most picturesque location of any hotel in the city. Originally built as the Gresham Life Assurance Company in 1906, it awed the world even then with the craftsmanship provided by the most acclaimed craftsmen of the time. Nearly destroyed by World War II and subsequent vandalism, it was restored over 5 years using and matching every single piece of remaining item of decor to bring it back to its original glory, even returning to the original manufacturers when possible. The doors reopened on June 18, 2004. As is Four Seasons tradition, guests are pampered in every way possible. While all rooms are beautifully decorated with mahogany furniture, the most expensive suites are equipped with bedroom sets made of mother-of-pearl and some have fireplaces. Every bathroom is fitted with Italian and Spanish marble with deep-soak bathtubs. No detail in design has been overlooked, and each room has been recreated in its original glory.

V. Roosevelt tér 5–6. ℃ **800/819-5053** in North America or ℃ **1/268-6000.** Fax 1/268-5000. www.fourseasons.com/budapest. 179 units. Year round rates 300€–790€ double; 1,000€–5,000€ suite. Rates do not include VAT or tourist tax. Children stay free in parents' room. Breakfast 8,600 Ft per person. AE, DC, MC, V. Parking 12,000 Ft per day. Metro: Deák tér (all lines). **Amenities:** 2 restaurants; bar; concierge; exercise room; massage; pool (luxurious heated indoor); room service; sauna; smoke-free rooms. *In room:* A/C, TV, fax machine (on request), hair dryer, Internet high-speed access (for a fee), minibar, newspapers, robe, slippers.

Le Méridien Budapest ★★★

Centrally located on Deák tér is Le Méridien, a member of the leading hotels of the world. It was originally designed in 1913 for the Italian Adria Insurance Company; the building was completed in 1918. After World War II, the Budapest Police made this their home until 1997. The original structure is a protected monument, thus it still has its austere exterior. The structure was beautifully renovated and reopened at the end of 2000. Elegant architectural details are evident in the lobby as well as the hallways, which are surrounded by wrought-iron railings. These overlook the stained-glass dome topping the breakfast area below. Guest rooms are beautifully appointed with French classical decor in a navy and beige color scheme, luxurious

Andrássy Hotel **17**
Art'Otel Budapest **8**
Atlas Hotel **38**
Atrium Hotel **32**
Baross Hotel **29**
Beatrix Panzió **4**
BudaBaB **28**
Buda Castle Fashion Hotel **5**
Burg Hotel **9**
Charles Apartment
    House **12**
City Hotel Mátyás **39**
City Ring Hotel **14**
Corinthia Grand Hotel
    Royal **22**
Cotton House Hotel **18**
Domina Hotel Fiesta **23**
Domino Hostel **41**
Fortuna Botel & Hostel **3**
Four Seasons Hotel
    Gresham Palace **10**
Gellért Danubius Hotel **45**
GG Panoráma Panzió **1**
Gerlóczy **33**
Hilton Budapest **7**
Hilton Budapest
    WestEnd **15**
Hotel Anna **37**
Hotel Carat **24**
Hotel Kálvin House **44**
Hotel Kulturinnov **6**
Hotel Panda **2**
Hotel Zara **42**
Ibis Budapest Centrum **43**
Ibis Heroes' Square **16**
King's Hotel **27**
Le Méridien Budapest **25**
Leo Panzió **36**
The Loft Hostel **40**
Marco Polo Hostel **31**
Medosz **19**
NH Hotel **13**
Novotel Budapest
    Centrum **30**
Pilvax City Hotel **35**
Promenade City Hotel **34**
Sofitel Budapest Chain
    Bridge **11**
Spinoza Self-Catering
    Apartments **26**
Star Hotel **20**
Unity Hostel **21**

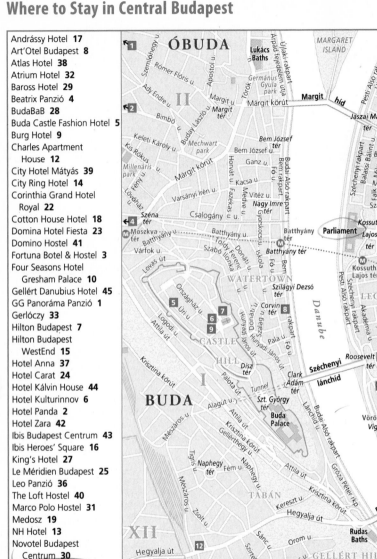

Information
Metro
District
boundary

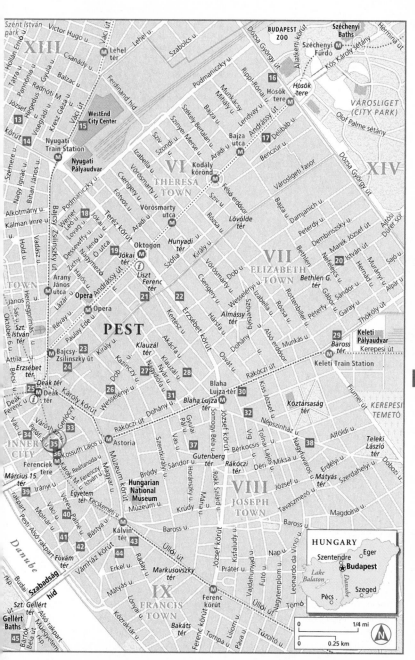

fabrics, and mahogany furniture. The suites are sumptuously grand, some with artificial fireplaces, kitchenettes, and dining areas ranging from extra large to huge.

V. Erzsébet tér 9–10. ✆ **800/253-0861** in North America, ✆ **0845/6000-778** in Britain, or ✆ **1/429-5500**. Fax 1/429-5555. www.lemeridien.com/budapest. 218 units. High season 159€–239€ double; 269€–1,599€ suites. Low season 109€–169€ double; 209€–1,299€ suites. Special season 299€–359€ double; 299€–3,000€ suites. Rates do not include VAT or city tax. Children 12 and under stay free in parents' room. Breakfast 25€ per person. AE, MC, V. Parking 9,000 Ft per day. Metro: Deák tér (all lines). **Amenities:** 1 restaurant; bar; babysitting; concierge; exercise room; massage; pool (indoor heated); room service; spa; Wi-Fi on conference floor. *In room:* A/C, TV, hair dryer, minibar, Internet (for a fee; free in suite), MP3 docking station (on request), stereo (in suite).

EXPENSIVE

NH Hotel ★★★   We don't usually associate modern elegance with a homey atmosphere, but this Spanish-owned chain has accomplished this. Built from the ground up in 2003 directly behind the Vigszinház Theater, this hotel has taken a modern, minimalist approach oozing a warm welcome. The use of a variety of textiles in the room decor spanning shades of browns and tans with rich dark wood adds a cozy warmth to a spacious room. Add to this, the mottled brown and tan marble used in the bathroom, the feeling of quiet elegance is carried throughout. Sleep-inducing beds bring it all together for a perfect night's sleep. Although the exercise room on the eighth floor is limited, it is beautifully executed with the most modern exercise equipment, separate changing rooms for women and men, a solarium (for a fee), and a relaxation room with beautiful lounge chairs. It's eco-friendly to boot.

XIII. Vigszinház u. 3. ✆ **1/814-0000**. Fax 1/814-0100. www.nh-hotels.com. 160 units. High season 196€ double. Low season 99€ double. No special season rates. Rates include VAT. Breakfast 17€ per person. AE, DC, MC, V. Secured parking 16€ per day. Metro: Nyugati (Blue line) or tram 4 or 6. **Amenities:** Restaurant; bar; bikes; exercise room; LAN connection free; room service. *In room:* A/C, TV, hair dryer, minibar, Wi-Fi.

Novotel Budapest Centrum ★★   Originally built in 1911, this is another Art Nouveau example of Budapest's past glory, which reopened in 2002. The fifth floor is the executive floor, where all rooms have an espresso machine, free mineral water, movies, Wi-Fi or LAN connection, local calls, a bathrobe, and slippers. All rooms have been transformed with modern blond furniture, beige-on-beige print wallpaper, blue drapes, and tangerine-color pillows and chairs. Standard rooms are comfortable, but not luxurious. Bathrooms are tiled and of adequate size. There is a smoking floor, while all others are nonsmoking. All rooms range from 23 to 28sq. m (248–301 sq. ft).

VIII. Rákoczi út 43–45. ✆ **1/477-5450**. Fax 1/477-5454. www.novotel.com. 227 units. High season 165€ double, 190€ executive. Low season 130€ double, 155€ executive. Special season 250€ double, 275€ executive. Breakfast 17€ per person. Children 15 and under stay free in parents' room. AE, DC, MC, V. Parking 17€ per day. Metro: Blaha Lujza tér (Red line). **Amenities:** Restaurant; bar; Jacuzzi; room service. *In room:* A/C, TV, hair dryer, LAN Internet (for a fee), minibar.

Sofitel Budapest Chain Bridge ★★★   This is the only Sofitel in Hungary. Rooms on floors one to seven have a tub/shower combo, while those on the eighth-floor executive level have separate showers and bathtubs plus access to the executive lounge where snacks, drinks, and a special breakfast is served. Junior suites on several floors have kitchenettes and a combined living and bedroom area. Rooms have been decorated with soft beige-on-beige designs and the beds have luxuriously huge pillows. Bathrooms are ample sized with marble tiles and countertops of gray and cream. The fitness center is decked out with a large indoor pool, exercise room, massage area, and sauna. Smoking and nonsmoking rooms are available.

V. Roosevelt tér 2. ℂ **1/266-1234.** Fax 1/266-9101. www.sofitel-budapest.com. 350 units. High season 219€ superior; 319€ executive floor; 429€ suites. Low season 119€ superior; 219€ executive floor; 239€ suites. No special season rates. Rates do not include VAT. Breakfast 29€ per person. AE, MC, V. Parking 7,500 Ft per day. Metro: Vörösmarty tér (Yellow line). **Amenities:** 2 restaurants; bar; cafe; concierge; executive lounge; exercise room; massage; pool; room service; sauna; nonsmoking rooms; Wi-Fi. *In room:* A/C, TV, hair dryer, LAN Internet, minibar, robe, slippers.

MODERATE

City Hotel Mátyás ★★   Old world charm lives within this simplistic hotel. Some rooms have a fantastic view of the Buda Castle District. When reserving, you should request this view to assure it. The hotel is located on a busy traffic street, but I was not disturbed by noise. The rooms are plain, with minimal decor, clean white walls, and comfortable beds and linens. A pie-slice-shaped shower takes up little space, leaving room for a second person to use the sink at the same time. One drawback was an insufficient number of electric outlets. In 2008, there were plans to remodel the front of the building and the rooms, but instead it was sold to Taverna Hotels, so all rooms were painted, but the outside still has the same charming character. Breakfast is served in the adjoining famous Mátyás Pince Restaurant (p. 92), a restaurant with outstanding decor.

V. Marcius 15 tér. ℂ **1/338-4711.** Fax 1/317-9086. www.cityhotel.hu, 85 units. High season 88€ double. Low season 60€ double. Special season 146€ double w/3-night minimum; extra bed 20€ all seasons. Rates include full breakfast. AE, MC, V. Limited street parking. Metro: Ferenciek tere (Blue line). **Amenities:** Restaurant; bar; Internet access (for a fee); nonsmoking rooms. *In room:* A/C, TV, fridge, hair dryer (on request).

City Ring Hotel ★★★   Perfectly located for the train traveler coming or going from Nyugati train station, this hotel is only one block away, making it ultra-convenient. Situated on the ring road, you have access to transportation, shopping, and restaurants just outside your door. The rooms are a bit overwhelmed by the modern furniture giving it a crowded feeling, but if you are out all day touring, they are more than adequate, impeccably clean, and the beds are comfy. We could have used thicker pillows, but they were sufficient. One caution is that the shower is on the small side, which may pose a challenge for larger people. Free Wi-Fi is only available in some rooms. Clientele seem to be 30-somethings and over. Rooms are located in a different building than the reception area, so you have to cross a small corridor and go up a short flight of steps before reaching the elevator. The staff will assist with luggage for those in need, but there is no bellhop service per se. The hotel is now operated by Taverna Hotels.

XIII. Szent István krt. 22. ℂ **1/340-5450.** Fax 1/340-4884. www.cityhotel.hu. 39 units. High season 78€ double. Low season 51€ double. Special season (3-night minimum) 115€ double. Deluxe double add 15€ per night to double room rate and 20€ per night to double room rate for all seasons. Rates include full breakfast. AE, MC, V. Metro: Nyugati (Blue line) or tram 4 or 6. **Amenities:** Nonsmoking rooms. *In room:* A/C, TV, fridge, hair dryer (on request).

Cotton House Hotel ★★★ (Finds)   You will see stars at this hotel for sure. As you walk into the lobby, you feel transported back in time to 1930s' Americana. Each room is named for some famous personality and decorated with his or her pictures. All rooms have beautifully replicated '30s furniture, down to the old cradle phone modernized with buttons. Although the beds may look old, the mattresses are modern and comfortable. The tiled bathrooms are definitely 21st century, some with Jacuzzi tubs, and others with hydro showers. Sink and tub fixtures are brass adding to the authenticity. The Al Capone room is the largest with a sitting area, while Humphrey Bogart did not fare as well, his room is smaller, but still a comfortable size. Liza Minnelli is sized between the two others. Room service is available in the larger rooms where space permits a table.

VI. Jókai u. 26. © **1/354-2600.** Fax 1/354-1341. www.cottonhouse.hu. 23 units. High season 130€–150€ double. Low season 80€–120€ double. Special season (3-night minimum) 130€–150€ double. Rates include breakfast, VAT, and 1 fitness center visit. AE, MC, V. Limited street parking. Metro: Opera (Yellow line). **Amenities:** Restaurant; bar; exercise area; Jacuzzi; room service; nonsmoking rooms; cigar room. *In room:* A/C, TV, hair dryer, minibar, Wi-Fi.

Domina Hotel Fiesta ★★ Once an apartment building, the Italian Domina Hotel Group transformed the building to a hotel with creative accomplishment, but they took out all the balconies in doing so. The high ceilings of the former residences add a spacious feeling to all categories of rooms: classic, superior, or the four family rooms, the latter are basically two bedrooms open to each other. Rooms are cozy and comfortable; not overly spacious, but roomy enough for two to share. Each has modern wood furniture, including a desk and small sitting area with a sofa. Bathrooms have showers only. Currently, the majority of their clientele arrive from Italy and Spain, where the chain is better known.

VI. Király u. 20. © **1/328-3000.** Fax 1/266-6024. www.dominahotels.com. 112 units. High season 159€ standard double. Low season 79€ standard double. Special season (3-night minimum) 130€–150€ double. Add 20€ a night to standard rate for superior double in all seasons; 25€ for third person, 25€ for four family rooms. Rates include breakfast, VAT. AE, MC, V. Public parking nearby. Metro: Deák tér (All lines). **Amenities:** Restaurant; bar; room service; nonsmoking rooms. *In room:* A/C, TV, hair dryer, minibar, Wi-Fi.

Gerlóczy ★★ (Finds) Just above the popular triangular restaurant by the same name, this small hotel opened in 2008. The building dates to 1892, so the concept for the hotel was to retain the flavor of the times; therefore, four rooms have claw-footed tubs only, the others have hand-held showers. Each room is spacious, yet the large windows give an expanded feel to it overlooking the historic courtyard. This was the starting point for the War of Independence from the Habsburgs in 1848. The furniture fits the period, but the beds are comfortable. Breakfast is an additional mandatory fee of 10€ per person, whether or not you choose to eat in the restaurant.

V. Gerlóczy u. 1. © **1/501-4000.** Fax 1/501-4001. www.gerloczy.hu. 15 units. All year, all rooms are 85€ plus a 10€ per person fee. 11 rooms with hand-held shower. MC. Limited street parking. Metro: Deák tér (all lines). **Amenities:** Restaurant. *In room:* A/C, TV, minibar, Wi-Fi.

Hotel Anna ★ This very cozy, in a mundane sort of way, small Hungarian hotel is located on a quiet street. It has been around for a number of years without much remodeling to bring it up to date, but this actually adds to its homey charm. To reach the rooms, you need to walk through the lobby and then back outside again where the double rooms use a different entrance than the suites. Although the room decor is unremarkable to the point of being dull, the rooms are comfortably large and sparkling clean. The suites are composed of a living room and bedroom, with no kitchen facilities except a coffeemaker. For breakfast you can choose to sit indoors in the breakfast room or take it to the outside dining area, a covered space with tables and chairs. This also functions as the smoking area since the hotel is all nonsmoking.

VIII. Gyulai Pál u. 14. © **1/327-2000.** Fax 1/327-2001. www.annahotel.hu. 36 units. High season 118€ double, 132€ jr. suite, 149€ deluxe suite, 42€ extra bed. Low season 79€ double, 86€ jr. suite, 117€ deluxe suite, 29€ extra bed. Special season 154€ double, 182€ jr. suite, 209€ deluxe suite; 33€ extra bed. Rates include breakfast, and city tax. MC, V. Parking 15€. Metro: Blaha Lujza (Red line). **Amenities:** Bar; Wi-Fi in lobby. *In room:* A/C, not all rooms, TV, fridge (in suite), high-speed Internet access.

Hotel Carat ★★★ This classy hotel opened in 2007 on the gentrified Király utca. Almost all rooms have twin beds pushed together to form a double, but can be separated upon request. Rooms sporting a true double bed are slightly larger. Nearly all rooms have bathroom with a tub with a hand-held shower, but there are some with showers only. The simple, but novel stenciling on the walls adds a touch of class to rooms that range from a bit smallish to adequate pace for two people. All rooms are nonsmoking, but the fifth floor has seven rooms with a balcony, so smokers are wise to request one of these rooms. Seven triple rooms can accommodate families. The fitness room has three modern exercise machines, a small Jacuzzi, and a tiny sauna.

VI. Király u. 6. ☏ **1/428-0143.** Fax 1/428-0144. www.hotelcarat.hu. 50 units. High season 100€ double, 130€ triple. Low season 80€ double, 110€ triple. Special season 160€ double, 195€ triple. Rates include full breakfast, VAT and city tax. AE, MC, V. Metro: Deák (all lines). **Amenities:** Restaurant; bar; room service. *In room:* A/C, TV, iron (on request), minibar, Wi-Fi.

Hotel Kálvin House ★★

After being tipped off by a reader, I went to tour this hotel that opened 10 years ago in what was once a 19th-century apartment building. Spread over four floors with a lift in the building, the rooms are huge. If you want to dance all night, there is plenty of room to do so without leaving your room. Furnished with turn-of-the-century furniture, each room has a distinctly different personality, but all are bright and fresh. Rooms vary with twin beds and double beds, so if you have a preference, make it known at the time of booking. Smoking and nonsmoking rooms are available. Váci utca and the central market are within a few minutes' walk.

IX. Gönczy Pál u. 6. ☏ **1/216-4365.** Fax 1/216-4161. www.kalvinhouse.hu. 38 units. Rates are dependent on occupancy, not necessarily season. 65€–95€ double; extra bed or suites are plus 20€ to double rate. Rates include full breakfast, VAT, and city tax. AE, MC, V. Metro: Kálvin tér (Blue line). **Amenities:** Snack bar; Wi-Fi. *In room:* TV.

Hotel Zara ★★

Located on a small side street off of Váci utca, the pedestrian shopping street, this hotel is just two short blocks from the great market, a convenient location for shoppers. Having opened in 2006, this small boutique hotel is the first of others planned by this company. The decor is a beautifully executed mix of eclectic styles with Murano glass light coverings to Thai designs for the carpeting and drapery, created by Hungarian craftsman. Rooms seem small at 18sq. m (194 sq. ft), since most of them sport a queen-size bed, a rarity in less than a five-star hotel, but roomy enough to be comfortable. The furniture style is Asian modern with a soft pink and chocolate brown theme, while the bathrooms are tiled in browns and beiges, with showers only. Each corridor has only five rooms for an intimate feeling with designated smoking and nonsmoking floors. Excellent staff adds to the stay here.

V. Só u. 6. ☏ **1/577-0700.** Fax 1/577-0710. www.zarahotels.com. 74 units. Weekdays 70€–90€ double; weekends 80€–120€. Special season 150€ double. Children up to 12 stay free in parents' room. Rates include breakfast and city tax. AE, MC, V. Parking 18€. Metro: Kálvin tér (Blue line). **Amenities:** Restaurant; bar; room service; Wi-Fi in public areas. *In room:* A/C, TV, high-speed Internet access, minibar.

Ibis Budapest Centrum ★★

The location of this hotel is ideal, based at the foot of Ráday utca, one of the major dining streets in the city and a street that is becoming a cultural-event hotspot. By the time you read this, the whole hotel will have been remodeled in the new Ibis design. A 2-minute walk away is the National Museum, while Váci utca is 5 minutes away, where shopping and a multitude of dining options are available. The Ibis chain has a 15-minute satisfaction guarantee so if there is something wrong with a room and it is not taken care of in 15 minutes, you get one night free. Rooms are basic, adequately sized, not huge, but impeccably clean. There is a peaceful garden terrace on the first floor where you can sit and relax. If you are very sensitive to sound, you should request a room overlooking the terrace rather than Ráday.

IX. Ráday u. 6. ☎ **1/456-4100.** Fax 1/456-4116. www.ibishotel.com. 126 units. High season 63€ double. Low season 52€ double. Special season 75€–125€ double. VAT is not included in rates. Breakfast 7.60€ per person. AE, DC, MC, V. Parking 20€ Metro: Kálvin tér (Blue line). **Amenities:** Bar; computer in lobby; snacks 24 hr; T-Com mobile Wi-Fi vouchers available; nonsmoking rooms. *In room:* A/C, TV.

King's Hotel ★★ (**Finds**) The King's Hotel opened for business in 1995 in a beautifully renovated and restored *fin de siècle* building in the heart of Pest's Jewish District. Rooms resonate with a 19th-century atmosphere due to the plainness of the furniture. All of the beds are twins, but they don't mind if you push two together. Many rooms have small balconies overlooking the quiet residential street. The reception is uniformly friendly and helpful. There is an adjoining restaurant, but it is no longer kosher. Due to its location and the former kosher restaurant, it has been an attractive choice for Jewish travelers.

VII. Nagydiófa u. 25–27. ☎/fax **1/352-7675.** www.kingshotel.hu. 78 units. High season 80€ double, 100€ triple. Low season 60€ double, 80€ triple. Special season 100€ double, 120€ triple. Rates include breakfast. AE, DC, MC, V. Metro: Astoria (Red line). **Amenities:** Restaurant; bar; babysitting. *In room:* A/C, TV, fridge, Internet.

Leo Panzió ★★ (**Finds**) This small pension sports a fantastic location in the downtown area of Budapest close to the heart of the business and shopping area, and within a stone's throw of the Blue line metro station. Váci utca and all of the other shopping opportunities are minutes away. The hallway and bedroom walls are decorated with framed antique Budapest postcards. Dark red wood in the bedrooms is accented by the deep red patterned drapes and bedspreads that evoke a feeling of embracing the past, while living in the present. The rooms are on the smallish side with the double bed and desk overpowering the room, but it is adequate, as is the bathroom in each room. If charm and location are more important than living space, then this is the hotel you want, although don't count on the charms of the reception; we would best describe the man who helped us as apathetic, but he may have been having a bad day.

V. Kossuth Lajos u. 2/A. ☎ 1/266-9041. Fax: 1/266-9042. www.leopanzio.hu. 14 units. High season 99€ double; 118€ triple. Low season 76€ double; 99€ triple. Special season 119€ double, 148€ triple. No Internet deals. Rates include breakfast. DC, MC, V. No parking. Metro: Ferenciek tere (Blue line). **Amenities:** Fax. *In room:* A/C, TV, hair dryer, minibar, Wi-Fi.

Pilvax City Hotel ★★ The best word to describe this hotel is *charming;* you'll be overcome by a snuggly, comforted feeling as soon as you enter. Located on a pedestrian street, there is only traffic on one small one-way street, keeping noise to a minimum. Having so few rooms has its advantages, and personalized service is excellent. With only two floors the hotel lacks an elevator and instead has a grand winding staircase. Each room is well equipped for the weary traveler, all perfectly quiet for a good night's sleep on an excellent mattress with matching quality pillows. No one should feel cramped in these well-appointed rooms. The bathroom is equally as comfortable, but the quarter-circle shower is a bit small. Once a Mellow Mood property, it is now part of the Taverna Hotels chain.

V. Pilvax köz 1-3. ☎ **1/266-7660.** Fax 1/317-6396. www.cityhotel.hu. 32 units. High season: 88€ double. Low season: 60€ double. Special season 146€ double; extra bed 20€ all seasons. Rates include full breakfast. AE, MC, V. No parking. Metro: Deák tér (all lines). **Amenities:** Restaurant; bar; nonsmoking rooms. *In room:* A/C, TV, hair dryer (on request), fridge.

Promenade City Hotel ★ First impressions matter; my first thought was 'bed in a box'; a plain, simple room without decor if you don't count the runner across the bed, just the basic bed and pillows. The balcony is inaccessible; one window opens about 6 inches, while the other looks like it was meant to be a door, but without a handle to open it. These were effective for noise control from the pedestrian street below, which was a plus. Being a Mellow Mood property, the ultra-firm mattress was no surprise, but the pillows were rock hard. The bathtub is the strangest I have seen, shaped like an old-fashioned coffin, with a hand shower on a pole, but no door or curtain to keep the floor from getting a good soaking. If location is more important than ambience, then this is just the place. All rooms are nonsmoking, so head to the street if you need a puff.

V. Váci u. 22. ✆ 1/799–4444. Fax 1/799–4455. www.promenadehotelbudapest.com. 45 units. High season 90€ double. Low season 70€ double; extra bed for high and low season 20€ extra, special season 50€ extra. Rates include full breakfast. AE, MC, V. No parking. Metro: Ferenciek tere (Blue line) or buses 5, 7, or 105, Ferenciek tere. **Amenities:** Nonsmoking rooms. *In room:* A/C, TV, minibar.

INEXPENSIVE

Medosz ★   The hotel, formerly a trade-union hotel for agricultural workers, retains its Communist utilitarian appearance with tread-worn carpeting and ugly halls. Those staying here certainly do not do it for the decor or the beauty of the rooms; the rooms are simple, on the smallish side, but clean. The location cannot be beaten. Jókai tér is less than one block from the bustling Oktogon and across from Liszt Ferenc tér with a dozen restaurants. Because of this, it can be noisy at night with the many restaurants and clubs in the area. Courtyard-view rooms are subject to neighbor noise from other apartments, but not nearly as bad as the front of the hotel. The hotel remains good value given its location. A reader in the past reported their bed had springs popping from the mattress; my advice is to check out the mattress immediately upon checking in and ask for a room change if needed. The entire hotel is nonsmoking.

VI. Jókai tér 9. ✆ 1/374-3001. Fax 1/332-4316. www.medoszhotel.hu. 68 units. High season 59€ double; 69€ triple; 79€ quad. Low season 49€ double; 59€ triple; 69€ quad. Special season same as high season; extra bed 6€. Extra bed 10€ per night. Rates include breakfast and all taxes. DC, MC, V. Metered on-street parking; indoor garage nearby. Metro: Oktogon (Yellow line). **Amenities:** Restaurant; bar. *In room:* TV, no phone in most rooms.

2 OUTER PEST

VERY EXPENSIVE

Hilton Budapest WestEnd ★★   Shop until you drop has new meaning with this hotel conveniently located in West End City Center, one of the largest shopping malls in Central Europe. Situated next to Nyugati train station, it is convenient for train travelers. This Hilton is geared for the business set, but it welcomes leisure travelers as well. Opened in 2000, it was a start-up player in the new group of five-star hotels. Each room is stylishly decorated with extra-large beds and a large ergonomic lounge chair offering luxurious relaxation. The room color scheme of plum, dark green, and tans is standardized throughout all rooms. The fourth floor executive lounge (and its panoramic view) makes check-in quick and easy, and it offers snacks and drinks throughout the day. The suites are extremely roomy, with executive suites sporting two rooms. The chic and ultramodern Zita cafe on the ground level attracts many people from the area with their lunch specials.

VI. Váci út 1–3. ✆ 1/288–5500, 800/445-8667 in North America, ✆ 0870/590-90-90 in U.K. Fax 1/288-5588. www.budapest-westend.hilton.com. 230 units. High season 135€–190€ double; 185€–240€ jr. suite.

Low season 110€–190€ double; 160€–240€ jr. suite. Special season 260€ double; 310€ jr. suite. Lower weekend rates. Rates do not include VAT or city tax. Breakfast 27€ per person. AE, MC, V. Parking 4,000 Ft per day. Metro: Nyugati pu (Blue line). **Amenities:** Restaurant; bar; cafe; babysitting; concierge; exercise room; room service; sauna; secretary services; Wi-Fi (for a fee). *In room:* A/C, TV, minibar, hair dryer, robe, slippers.

EXPENSIVE

Andrássy Hotel ★★   The Andrássy Hotel started as the Bauhaus boarding house for Jewish children in 1937. Under the Communist regime, it was the official hotel of the Ministry of Foreign Affairs, then it was called the Hotel Central. The hotel has been fully renovated a number of times, the last being the end of 2007. It continues to recreate a fresh image to be fully worthy of its exclusive upscale boutique-hotel status featured in "Small Luxury Hotels of the World" (www.slh.com); there are only two in Hungary. With each change, it only gets better, which is difficult to imagine of this treasure of a hotel, located in an exclusive embassy neighborhood. It is just a few minutes' walk to Heroes' Square and the City Park, and a 1-minute walk to the nearest metro station. The lobby is sleek, spacious, and tasteful, with everything done in shades of orange and etched glass. All of the rooms are newly redecorated in relaxing grays, greens, and browns, with burnt-orange sofas and chairs combined with contemporary design blond wood furniture and modern Asian prints. The holistic mood is a Zen feel making it perfectly relaxing. The spacious suites are worth the splurge. Most rooms come with terraces. No fitness facilities here, but guests can use those at a partner hotel located nearby. *Note:* This hotel also arranges special Budapest/Tokaj packages with Gróf Degenfeld Castle Hotel (another member of the Small Luxury Hotels of the World) on their vineyard in the Tokaj region.

VI. Andrássy út 111. ☎ **1/462-2100.** Fax 1/322-9445. www.andrassyhotel.com. 70 units. High season 129€–179€ classic; 149€–219€ superior; 169€–239€ deluxe; 229€–299€ jr. suite; 319€–399€ ambassador suite. Low season 109€–159€ classic; 129€–179€ superior; 149€–199€ deluxe; 209€–259€ jr. suite; 299€–349€ ambassador suite. No special season rates. AE, DC, MC, V. Parking 16€ per day. Metro: Bajza u. (Yellow line). **Amenities:** Restaurant; lounge; concierge; room service. *In room:* A/C, TV, DVD/VCR (on request), fax, hair dryer, bathrobes, minibar, slippers, umbrella.

Atrium Hotel ★★   Reopened in March 2007, this ultramodern hotel part of the Mellow Mood chain is a breath of fresh air in the area, only one block from the Red metro. Attention to detail was obvious when this former post office was converted into its current incarnation, a completely nonsmoking hotel. The greenish-gray walls mixed with the blues in the carpeting make the rooms feel airy and roomy, yet they exude a warmth that will welcome even the finicky guest. The extra-large built-in double closet is convenient for a long-term stay, where luggage and clothes can be stored without taking up space in the room. Rooms have soundproof windows. The desk has three outlets at the back, making it convenient for plugging in devices while working. A table lamp uses a low light that's not obtrusively bright. For those who like to read, a comfortable chair is set by the desk with a floor lamp nearby. This is suited to travelers of all ages, and all ages were represented during my stay.

VIII. Csokonai u.14. ☎ **1/299-0777.** Fax 1/215-6090. www.hotelatrium.hu. 57 units (22 with double beds; 35 with twin beds). High and special season 122€ double, 162€ triple. Low season 84€ double, 104€ triple. Rates include full breakfast. AE, MC, V. Parking 5,000 Ft per day. Metro: Keleti (Red line). **Amenities:** Bar; room service; babysitting. *In room:* A/C, TV, minibar, fridge, hair dryer, Wi-Fi.

MODERATE

Atlas Hotel ★   If Keleti train station fits into your plans, this hotel is very close and convenient. The inside of the hotel has a comfy feel, but the neighborhood is on the

sketchy side; although not a dangerous area, it won't win any beauty contests. The rooms
will not give anyone claustrophobia; they are generous with space. An oversize maple-colored wardrobe is generously covered with panels of mirrors on the doors. There are fixed wall lamps for plenty of lighting. I was disappointed that the few electric outlets in the room were being used by other lamps, making it impossible to plug in a laptop while at the desk without performing contortions to unplug something first. The bathrooms are highly inadequate, lacking large towels or even an outlet.

VIII. Nepszinhaz u. 39. © **1/299-0256.** Fax 1/299-0255. www.atlashotel.hu. 136 units. High season 85€ double, 100€ deluxe double, 121€ triple, 161€ quad. Low season 58€ double, 73€ deluxe double, 80€ triple, 106€ quad. Rates include breakfast. MC, V. Parking 3,000 Ft per day. Metro: Blaha Lujza tér (Red line). **Amenities:** Bar. *In room:* A/C, TV, hair dryer (on request), minibar.

Baross Hotel ★   For rail travel convenience, you couldn't ask for a better location; this hotel is located across the street from Keleti train station, literally 1 minute away. To add icing on the cake, the metro Red line is just outside the door, along with four bus lines. On the negative side, Baross tér is where one of the Metro 4 stations is being built, causing construction confusion. With that said, this hotel is a little diamond with all rooms having been redecorated in 2008 giving them a fresher and roomier feeling. I suggest requesting a room with a courtyard view for plenty of natural light. Flower pots hanging on the railings give a minigarden effect. The apartments have kitchenettes. The entire building, even the non-hotel floors, has been well maintained. Guests run the gamut from seniors to young travelers with smoking and nonsmoking rooms, in this Mellow Mood hotel. Baross tér is a busy street, so a room on that side may be noisier late at night.

VII. Baross tér 15. © **1/461-3010.** Fax 1/343-2770. www.barosshotel.hu. 49 units. High season 108€ double, 126€ triple, 152€ quad. Low season 80€ double, 99€ triple, 110€ quad. Rates include breakfast. AE, MC, V. Metro: Keleti (Red line). **Amenities:** Internet access (for a fee); nonsmoking rooms. *In room:* A/C, TV, minibar, hair dryer (on request).

Fortuna Botel and Hostel ★★ **Kids**   Ahoy matey; if you like boats, you'll love this hotel. It is on a ship built in 1967, which once cruised on the Danube as a holiday ship for trade unions. It was retrofitted in 2000, all of the cabins were enlarged, and an English Pub was created in the former engine room. The hotel section has rooms on the upper and main decks each with en-suite bathrooms, including four superior rooms. Some of my older friends stayed here and gave it a first-rate review. A hostel area is on the lower deck in the hull with shared bathrooms and showers. Each of the rooms is named after a famous sailor or pirate. All rooms are nonsmoking.

XIII. Szent István Park, also rakpart. © **1/288-8100.** www.fortunahajo.hu. 42 units. High season hotel rooms with shower 55€. Hostel rooms 30€ double; 40€ triple. Low season hotel rooms with shower 40€–45€ double; hostel rooms 23€ double; 30€ triple. Superior rooms and suites add 25€ to hotel room rate. Special season rates are not published, so contact directly. Rates include VAT and tourist tax. Breakfast 8€ per person. AE, MC, V. Tram: 4 or 6 to Jászai Mari tér. **Amenities:** Restaurant; bar. *In room:* A/C, TV, minibar.

Ibis Heroes' Square ★★   Formerly the Hotel Liget, Ibis Heroes' Square is an unusual modern design by the Hungarian architect Jozsef Finta. The location is excellent, across the street from the zoo, the Museum of Fine Arts, and Heroes' Square. Accor bought the property in 2007 and have completely remodeled it in the company's new Accor "poppy" theme. The color scheme is poppy red with beiges and tans throughout the hotel and rooms. Each room is 20sq. m (215 sq. ft) furnished with modern sleek furniture and wood floors. The terracotta, beige walls and deep red curtains are quietly soothing. Bathrooms are equipped with showers only, no tubs in any of the rooms.

Unlike its predecessor, the hotel focuses on business and leisure travelers, not families. Both smoking and nonsmoking floors are offered. For the best view of the zoo across the street, request room no. 420.

VI. Dózsa György út 106. ☎ **1/269-5300.** Fax 1/269-5329. 139 units. High season 51€–59€. Low season 42€–49€. Special season 108€. Rates do not include VAT or city tax. Breakfast 9.50€ per person. AE, DC, MC, V. Metro: Hősök tere (Yellow line). **Amenities:** Restaurant; bar; bike rental. *In room:* A/C, TV, hair dryer, Internet connection, Wi-Fi (for a fee).

Star Hotel ★   This small Mellow Mood hotel was spruced up in 2008, giving the rooms a rejuvenated fresh appearance, still roomy and painstakingly clean. Guests run the gamut from seniors to young backpackers, mostly Europeans. The modern furniture is simple, yet functional with the bed in a box frame, so watch your toes. The mattress is firm, but not stone-slab hard and there are extra large pillows that are not as firm as some places. The TV desk has plenty of room to share with a laptop, or to just sit and write, although there is a shortage of plugs, something has to be traded out. There are also apartments that can sleep up to four people, but they don't have kitchens. Having a competent multilingual staff adds to the enjoyment of the property. All rooms are nonsmoking. It is a bit out of the city center, but a trolleybus line stops right in front of the hotel, making it very convenient to access with less noise to worry about.

VII. István u. 14. ☎ **1/479-0420.** Fax 1/342-4661. www.starhotel.hu. 48 units. High season 100€ double, 120€ triple, 150€ quad. Low season 78€ double, 96€ triple, 104€ quad. Rates include full breakfast. AE, MC, V. Limited street parking. Trolleybus: 74. **Amenities:** Bar. *In room:* A/C, TV, hair dryer (on request), minibar.

---

3 CENTRAL BUDA

VERY EXPENSIVE

Art'Otel Budapest ★★★   Opened in 2000 by the Park Plaza hotel group, this is the first Art'Otel outside Germany. The distinguishing concept of this chain is that each property spotlights the work of one particular artist, thus you are staying in a gallery of modern art. At this hotel, the artist is Donald Sultan, an American modernist. More than 600 pieces of his work grace the hotel's walls from the lobby to the hallways and guestrooms. He also designed everything from the carpets to the dinnerware. The modern side of the hotel is a seven-story building facing the Danube, with a walkway leading to four 17th-century, two-story, baroque town houses, which now serve as rooms, suites, and the Chelsea Restaurant. Many pieces of the original houses are protected by historical conservation laws, so were incorporated into designs. Somewhere in each room there is a bird on a perch designed by Sultan. Rooms on the top three floors of the new building facing the Danube command the best views. Rooms ending with 17, 18, 19, and 20 have especially spectacular views, thus called the Danube view rooms with a higher price tag. Rooms in the old houses have higher ceilings, some unusual doors and locks from their original time, but no view. Executive rooms have a living room in the bedrooms, while the art suites are separate rooms.

I. Bem Rakpart 16–19, Budapest. ☎ **800/814-7000** or ☎ **1/487-9487.** Fax 1/487-9488. www.artotels. com. 165 units. High season 139€ double non-Danube view; 20€ Danube view supplement; 30€ Executive room supplement; 60€ Art suite supplement. Low season 99€ double non-Danube view. Supplement as for high season above. No special season rates. Children 12 and under stay free in parents' room. Breakfast 12€ per person. AE, DC, MC, V. Self-parking or valet parking 15€ per day. Metro: Batthyány tér

5

Gellért Danubius Hotel ★★   Built in 1918, this was at the time the only hotel on the Buda side making it the Buda Grand Dame and a protected historical site. Outside it still has all the grand status appeal; however, inside it is dated. Only 40 doubles and 16 suites have been refurbished, while others may never be. Those that have been redone have air-conditioning either built in or portable units, while all others only have fans. Being an old building, the rooms are spacious, yet furniture pieces in some rooms have a considerably old-fashioned flair. The remodeled rooms with renewed furniture have pieces with Zsolnay porcelain inlaid. These also have the best views of the river or Buda Hill, so ask for a room ending with 8 to 18 on any floor. Beds and pillows are ultra comfortable, neither too soft nor firm. About 40% of the guests are over 50 years old, either European or returning expats with pleasant childhood memories of events, which were held here. Hotel accommodation includes free and unlimited private entry access to the adjoining Gellért Thermals through a cooperative agreement. You will find a bathrobe in your room expressly for this service, but the thermal is not owned by the hotel. Staying here is like visiting an old relative's home whom you have not seen for a long time, but who have never modernized their living space. In that regard, the service people make you feel like a long-lost welcomed relative.

XI. Gellért tér 1. ✆ **1/889-5500.** Fax 1/889-5505. www.danubiushotels.com. 234 units. High season 170€ standard double; 194€ Danubius guestroom double; 216€ renovated double; 268€ suites. Low season 135€–152€ standard double; 159€–176€ Danubius guestroom double; 181€–198€ renovated double; 233€–250€ suites. An extra bed is 40€ in all seasons. Full buffet breakfast is included. Thermal entry is included. AE, DC, MC, V. Limited parking. Tram: 19, 47, or 49. **Amenities:** 2 restaurants; cafe; bikes; Internet (business center for a fee); room service; smoke-free rooms. *In room:* A/C, TV, hair dryer (in deluxe room; on request for standard room), minibar, Wi-Fi (for a fee).

MODERATE

Charles Apartment House ★   After opening in 1991, owner Károly Szombati has accumulated 73 apartments in a group of buildings in a less-than-eye-appealing Buda-side neighborhood. The apartments are a 15-minute walk at a good pace or a 15-minute bus ride from downtown Pest. The last refurbishment was in 2006; although the rooms are pleasant enough, they are nothing spectacular. The furnishings are comfortable, clean, and for the most part new with the last remodel. All apartments have full bathrooms and kitchens; some kitchens are part of the bedroom, while others have them in a separate room. The kitchens are stocked with dishes, cups, silverware, and other things can be borrowed from reception. Hegyalja út is a very busy street, but only two apartments face out onto it (avoid these); the rest are in the interior or on the side of the building. Also take note that only deluxe rooms have air-conditioning. A nearby park has tennis courts and a track. There is a new restaurant in the apartment complex. The staff is friendly and speaks English. The reception desk is open 24 hours. The clientele are the more sedate who are not interested in nightlife and therefore are not concerned with transportation after hours.

I. Hegyalja út 23. ✆ **1/212-9169.** Fax 1/202-2984. www.charleshotel.hu. 73 units. High season 65€ double; 72€ deluxe double; 89€ triple; 99€ apt for 1–4 people. Low season 39€ double; 45€ deluxe double; 49€ triple; 55€ apt for 1–4 people. Special season 85€ double; 99€ deluxe double; 99€ triple; 120€ apt. Breakfast is 8€ per person. AE, DC, MC, V. Parking 2,500 Ft per day. Bus: 78 from Keleti pu. to Zsolt u. stop, then a 200m (656ft) walk; buses 8 or 112 stop in front. **Amenities:** Restaurant; bar; babysitting; bikes; Wi-Fi. *In room:* A/C, TV, hair dryer (in deluxe room; on request for standard room), minibar.

MODERATE

Buda Castle Fashion Hotel ★★★ (Finds) Set on a quiet street between the main square and the viewing terrace of Buda Hills, you can be assured of a restful night in this small, but stylish hotel. The trade-off is that none of the rooms offer a view of the hill. This newest addition to the Castle District is another Mellow Moods property opened in late 2007. My room for the night was large enough to hold a family reunion and with such elegant modern decor I would have been proud to do so. Lamps are strategically placed so one can go to sleep, while another stays up to read, both in comfort. My mattress was too firm for my liking, but comfortable for a temporary stay. A room with the toilet is separate from the rest of the bathroom, making it ideal for privacy for two people. The bathroom has an extra large shower in addition to a second shower as part of the tub. The bar serves as the breakfast room in the mornings, with a courtyard patio for outdoor eating during warm weather.

I. Úri u. 39. ✆ **1/224-7900.** Fax 1/201-4903. www.budacastlehotelbudapest.com. 25 units. High season 149€ double. Low season 110€ double. Special season same as high season. Rates include breakfast and city tax. AE, DC, MC, V. Parking 25€ per day in public garage. Bus: 16a from Moszkva tér or 16 from Deák tér. **Amenities:** Bar. *In room:* A/C, TV, bathrobe, hair dryer, minibar, slippers, Wi-Fi.

Burg Hotel ★★★ An overlooked treasure on Castle Hill, this hotel was highly recommended by a friend, so we had to investigate it. Sitting on a corner directly across from St. Matthias Church, it is an excellent location. The multilingual staff is as friendly as they are talented with languages. The rooms are spacious and beautifully decorated in muted greens, rose, and beige with modern comfortable furniture from their last remodel in 2007. The corner room is extra large, but any room would be comfortable. The blue-tiled bathrooms are simple, but sizeable. All rooms have a view of Trinity Square. Wi-Fi is provided free throughout the hotel. Breakfast is served in a large room with windows overlooking the square. There is no lift, but it is only three floors above the ground-floor entrance.

I. Szentháromság tér 7–8. ✆ **1/212-0269.** Fax 1/212-3970. www.burghotelbudapest.com. 26 units. High season 115€ double; extra bed 39€. Low season 99€ double; 29€ extra bed. Special season 175€ double, 39€ extra bed. Children 13 and under stay free in parents' room. Rates include breakfast and city tax. AE, MC, V. Parking 16€ per day in public garage. Bus: 16A from Moszkva tér or 16 from Deák tér. **Amenities:** Bar. *In room:* A/C, TV, hair dryer, minibar.

Hilton Budapest ★★★ This Hilton has the most enviable piece of real estate in Budapest, sitting right next door to St. Matthias Church with part of the Fisherman's Bastion behind it. The hotel's award-winning design incorporates both the ruins of a 13th-century Dominican church (the church tower is alongside the hotel) and the baroque facade of a 17th-century Jesuit college, which makes up the hotel's main entrance. The hotel was renovated in 2007; the rooms are now a uniform rose, green, and beige color scheme. The corner suites are beautifully decorated with separate sitting areas, a dining area, and bedroom with oversize windows for a spectacular view of the Bastion and Danube. The elegant Baroque Room is three levels and has a fully equipped kitchen. Two floors are nonsmoking.

I. Hess András tér 1–3. ✆ **1/899-6600.** Fax 1/899-6644. www.hilton.com. 322 units. 90€–140€ advanced purchase over 21 days ahead; 95€–145€ advanced purchase 3–21 days ahead; 110€–180€ flexible rate; 30€ Danube view supplement; 50€ executive floor supplement. Rates do not include VAT or city tax. One child per adult stays free in parents' room. Breakfast 28€ per person. AE, DC, MC, V. Parking 25€ per day in public garage. Bus: 10 from Moszkva tér or 16 from Deák tér. **Amenities:** Restaurant; bar; exercise room; concierge; shops; room service; babysitting; Wi-Fi in lobby. *In room:* A/C, TV, minibar, hair dryer, Wi-Fi (for a fee in standard room).

Hotel Kulturinnov ★ ⓥ **Value** For those with cultural interests or a burning desire to stay on Castle Hill, this is a modest alternative. The actual hotel is located on the first floor in the building of the Hungarian Culture Foundation, built in the early 20th century. The foundation's mission is to promote the culture of Hungarians living outside of the country. The building has an impressive entrance. Entering one long hall, the rooms are at the end. The rooms are small, impeccably clean, with very high ceilings. None of the rooms have exceptional views, except perhaps no. 10, which overlooks the garden. However, for the location, the price is a bargain, but without luxury; this is just a place to sleep when you intend to have a full day touring the city. The staff is warm and friendly.

I. Szentháromság tér 6. ⓒ 1/224-8100. Fax 1/375-1886. www.mka.hu. 16 units. High season 24,000 Ft double; 30,000 Ft triple. Low season 19,000 Ft double (discount for booking more than 2 nights during low season); 22,000 Ft triple. Closed December 20 to January 3. Children 5 and under stay free in parents' room. Rates include breakfast and all taxes. MC, V. Parking 10€ per day. Bus: 16A from Moszkva tér or 16 from Deák tér. **Amenities:** Wi-Fi; snack bar. *In room:* Hair dryer, minibar.

---

5 THE BUDA HILLS

Unless you have some special reason to want to stay in the Buda Hills, be aware that you will be using precious time to travel to the Pest side where the lion's share of sights are located. These accommodations are good, but they take two transport connections to reach the center of Pest.

MODERATE

Beatrix Panzió The Beatrix Panzió opened in 1991 as a modern pension with clean, comfortable rooms, but the furniture dates back to that era, though still very clean. Seven rooms have private balconies; suites have kitchen areas with two burners for cooking. Guests are welcome to use the sun deck with the landscaped garden and a goldfish pond; in good weather, breakfast is served in the garden. Staff assists with making tour arrangements and restaurant reservations. Although the pension is located on a small street about a 10-minute walk from the tram stop, it took me the better part of an hour to reach it from central Pest. I do not suggest this as a place for the energetic "I want to see all of Budapest" traveler as the commute will really cut into your time. Trams stop at 11:30pm. Those driving may find this convenient. A well-stocked grocery store is conveniently located down the street. There are no rooms that do not allow smoking, since they cater to European guests, mostly from Germany.

II. Széher út 3, 1021 Budapest. ⓒ 1/275-0550. Fax 1/394-3730. www.beatrixhotel.hu. 22 units. High season 70€ double; 80€ triple; 90€–120€ suite. Low season 60€ double; 70€ triple; 60€–90€ suite. Special season depends on occupancy. Breakfast is included. No credit cards. Free parking in secured lot. Tram: 61 from Moszkva tér to the 7th stop. **Amenities:** Bar; room service. *In room:* TV, kitchen (in suite), fridge.

GG Panoráma Panzió ★ Gábor and Éva Gubacsi, an English-speaking Hungarian couple, run this panzio. I have to say they were the most gracious people I have met in a long time. Guest rooms now span the house, which is located on a steep, but quiet street in the Rose Hill (Rózsadomb) section of Buda. Don't be alarmed by the gates and guards on the street; the Israeli Embassy is their neighbor. The rooms are small to comfortable, furnished tastefully with simple-styled furnishings and en-suite bathrooms with a shower. Each room shares a common balcony to view the Buda Hills. The common kitchen has full facilities and a dining area with access to an outdoor garden space in which to relax. Two apartments sit on the top floor with a common kitchen, dining room, and living room, also with a huge balcony. The entire building is nonsmoking, but permitted on balconies. It's a place to relax. The Gubacsis are reportedly sincerely concerned about their guests' comfort. There are two bus lines down the hill and fairly close to the neighborhood providing access to the center of the city. Be warned: you will need to take a bus and then either the metro or tram from there to get to the city center.

II. Fullánk u. 7, 1026 Budapest. ©/fax **1/394-4718** or © **1/394-6034**. www.ggpanorama.hu. 7 units. High season 50€ double, extra bed 10€; 70€ apartments. Low season 10% discount on high season, but further discount for large groups. Breakfast 5€ per person. No credit cards. Parking available in the yard. Bus: 11 from Batthyány tér or no. 91 from Moszkva tér. **Amenities:** Common kitchen; Wi-Fi. *In room:* TV, radio.

Hotel Panda This hotel sits on Pasaréti Square, a neighborhood with a modern Catholic church, grocery store, and other businesses in a very busy square. The staff are friendly, efficient, but they speak limited English. Unfortunately, the desirability of the rooms varies greatly, but the furniture is dated in all of them. Rooms facing the front (10 in all) have terraces, with a southern exposure and views of the Buda hills. Rooms elsewhere in the hotel have smaller windows and no terraces, inviting stuffiness in warm weather. Every bathroom has a window. Only nine rooms in the hotel have air conditioning, some in each category. While the larger suites are quite big, the smaller ones are identical in size to normal double rooms. Most of the clientele are European, mostly from Germany. All rooms are nonsmoking. This is a good location if you want a relaxing vacation as the transport to the city center in Pest will take the better part of an hour.

II. Pasaréti út 133, 1026 Budapest. © **1/394-1935** or © **1/394-1932**. Fax 1/394-1002. www.budapest pandahotel.hu. 28 units. High season 80€ double; 99€ triple and suite. Low season 70€ double; 80€ triple and suite. Special season 100€ double; 110€ triple, 120€ suite. Rates include breakfast and VAT, but not tourist tax. AE, MC, V. Limited free parking. Bus: 5 from Március 15 tér or Moszkva tér to Pasaréti tér (the last stop). **Amenities:** Restaurant. *In room:* TV, fridge.

6 ALTERNATIVES TO HOTELS

Let me first state that not all hostels are created equal and should not be considered for young party people only. There are alternatives out there and I have listed a couple of good ones. There is intense competition in Budapest between the leading youth hostel companies and various privately run hostels since there are more than 85 hostels in the city.

Representatives from the Budapest Tourinform office sometimes board inbound trains early to pass out tour information and maps. In the past, international trains arriving in Budapest were also assaulted with people trying to book backpackers into their property. Some representatives even boarded Budapest-bound international trains at the Hungarian border crossing so that they could work the backpacking crowd before the train reached Budapest. This is not as common as it once was, but your best bet is to book a bed in advance at one of the recommended hostels. Otherwise you can check with the booking agency at the train stations or airport for assistance once you arrive. You can try your luck with a hostel hawker, but for your own safety, it is wise not to. Shop around and don't let yourself be pressured. If they are pushing you, you have to wonder why they need to do so. Most hostels that solicit at the station have a van parked outside. The ride to the hostel is usually free, but you may have to wait a while until the van is full.

Mellow Mood Ltd. operates a youth hostel placement office for their own hostels at Keleti Station (© 1/343-0748), near the Baross Restaurant. This office is open daily 7am to 9pm. For other hostels, check out the website **www.hostelworld.com** for other offerings in the city.

In July and August a number of university dormitories and other empty student lodgings are converted into hostels. Their locations (as well as their condition) change from year to year, so we haven't reviewed any of them in this guide. The youth hostels and budget lodgings listed below are all open year-round. All hostel rates are per person, not per room.

INNER CITY & CENTRAL PEST

BudaBaB ★★★ (Value) Throwing humility to the wind, here is the full disclosure: my partner and I are the owners of this B&B. We have been open for 8 years, and have had guests from 19 countries. We thrive on the interaction with guests, which was the motivating reason for opening our home. Being small allows us to give individualized attention to meet guests' needs. Plus, you can tell your friends you stayed with the author of this guide, get it autographed, pick up expert advice along the way, and share your own experiences. Seeing the city through others' eyes refreshes our appreciation for it. In 2009 we totally remodeled the kitchen; however, the mural painted by American artist Scott Allen is still intact, especially since he is becoming known for his murals around the globe. Each room has been painted and decorated with trinkets from our own travels, providing a relaxed atmosphere. We have put in new ultra-comfy sofa beds in each room to increase the number of guests we can accommodate. Situated at the edge of the historic Jewish ghetto, we are only two blocks from two tram lines, the Red metro, and two bus lines. Keleti train station is one metro stop away. Smoking is allowed in common rooms, but not the bedrooms. Whether you stay here or not, feel free to contact me before or while you are here. Toll-free calling from all English-speaking countries is available.

VII. Akácfa u. 18 © **1/267-5240**. www.budabab.com. 2 units. No seasonal rate changes. Double 45€–55€, triple 55€–70€, quad 85€. Breakfast included. Closed December 15–January 15. No credit cards. Metro: Blaha Lujza (Red line). **Amenities:** Communal areas; computer center; film library; hair dryer. *In room:* Wi-Fi.

Domino Hostel ★★ (Finds) For a hostel, this location could not be more perfect. Mellow Mood opened this hostel in 2007 on Váci utca, the ideal place for eating, drinking, and shopping, not to mention close to public transportation. The new bunk beds are stainless steel-framed for support and comfort. Larger rooms have tables and chairs for guests to work or read. Linens are provided. The place is very clean, and the staff is friendly. Reception is open 24 hours giving you free access to come and go as you please. Each bed has its own locker for safe storage of your goods. The large common room is a perfect place to meet other guests, watch TV, or play some darts. This is a nonsmoking facility. Rates are per person.

V. Váci u. 77. © **1/235-0492**. Fax: 1/216-4733. www.dominohostel.com. 26 units (146 beds). All rates are per person. High season 15€ 8-bed dorm; 17€ 6-bed dorm; 18€ quad; 28€ twin. Low season 11€ 8-bed dorm; 13€ 6-bed dorm; 15€ quad; 23€ twin. 10% discount for IYHF members or ISIC cardholders. No credit cards. Metro: Kálvin tér (Blue line). **Amenities:** Restaurant; communal kitchen; hair dryer (for fee); Internet access (for fee).

The Loft Hostel ★★★ (Value)   True to its name, this hostel, which opened in 2007, is on the top floor of a building with dormer loft-type ceilings. It has an elevator, but regrettably, the elevator only goes to the third floor, so there is one short flight to climb. Run by a young Brit and a Hungarian, both are in a band that has just cut its second album. The kitchen area is spacious and well supplied for cooking meals; tea, coffee, and hot chocolate are free at all times. A common room is huge, with sofas, bean bag seats, and TV. The rooms have skylights giving an extra airy feeling to them and the ability to air them out. Bed linens and towels are provided free. There are two bathrooms that are shared by all. The owners want to provide more for less, but they also want to keep their lease, so this is not a late night party place. Tours are also booked at cost, with no commission. Access is 24/7 with a code to the front door and a key.

V. Veres Palne u. 19 IV/6 bell 44. ℂ/fax **1/328-0916.** www.lofthostel.hu. 3 units (20 beds). High season 4,000 Ft–5,000 Ft quad; 3,500 Ft–4,500 Ft 6-bed dorm; 3,000 Ft–4,000 Ft 8-bed dorm. Low season is 1,000 Ft lower for each category. Special season add 500 Ft to high season rates. Weekends add 500 Ft to high season rate. No credit cards. Limited street parking. Metro: Ferenciek tere (Blue line). **Amenities:** Communal kitchen; hair dryer (on request), Wi-Fi.

Marco Polo Hostel ★   Calling this establishment a youth hostel is a bit of a misnomer, since it closely resembles a hotel. This place is not just for backpackers as just about anyone would be comfortable spending the night here. The central location is ideal for hopping on a bus or catching the metro. The rooms have clean and attractive linens, and each bed has its own large wardrobe with a lock. The dorm rooms are separated with walls with a bunk bed in each section and a curtain separating it from the narrow common area of the dorm. You can have privacy or sit out and meet others here or in the well-appointed common room. This is a very good deal with no curfew and a 24-hour reception. For party animals, the bar in the basement is open 24 hours, but music stops at 10pm. Open year-round, the hostel is operated by Mellow Mood. There are safes available at the front desk.

VII. Nyár u. 6. ℂ 1/413-2555. Fax 1/413-6058. www.marcopolohostel.com. 47 units (156 beds; double, quad, and 12-bed units have shower and toilet within the unit). High season 17€ 12-bed dorm; 23€ quad; 25€ triple; 33€ twin. Low season 11€ 12-bed dorm; 15€ quad; 19€ triple; 23€ twin. Rates include breakfast. 10% discount for IYHF members. MC, V. Limited street parking. Metro: Blaha Lujza tér (Red line). **Amenities:** Restaurant; bar; communal kitchen; Internet access (for fee). *In room:* TV (in double and quad), hair dryer (for fee).

Spinoza Self-Catering Apartments ★★★ (Finds)   Located next to the Spinoza cafe, these self-catering apartments opened in September 2007. They are all fully furnished for filling your everyday needs, including cooking if you wish to do so. Everything is modern and ready to go. They have four nonsmoking apartments, which will accommodate from one to eight people. Rates depend on the apartment and the number of people. If you wish, you can have breakfast in the restaurant for 5€.

VII. Dob u 15. ℂ **1/413-7489.** www.spinozahaz.hu. 4 units. All year rates are 40€–120€ double to 8 people. No credit cards. **Amenities:** Restaurant. *In room:* TV, kitchen, linens, towels, washing machine, Wi-Fi.

Unity Hostel ★★ (Value)   This hostel takes quiet time seriously. To stay here you need to sign a statement saying that all loud noise ends at 10pm and the common room should be empty by midnight, making it a perfect place for older travelers or those with children. They happily accommodate all. Located on the third floor of a building with an elevator, all of the rooms are bright and clean. The common room has a TV with cable, a video library, and a computer that is free to use. The kitchen area is fully equipped to prepare meals. One room has a shower with bathrooms outside; the other rooms share a bathroom and showers. Linens are provided and towels can be rented for 500 Ft per stay. Each bed has a security locker and a lock. For sun lovers, there is a rooftop terrace that overlooks the Liszt Music Academy lending itself to free concerts or just a relaxing space. The location is perfectly located with Liszt Ferenc tér less than a minute away and the ring road one block away. Access is 24/7. Péter, the owner, has spent many years in the hospitality business.

VI. Király u. 60. III/15. (C) **1/413-7377.** Fax 1/413-7378. www.unityhostel.com. 5 units. 4,300 Ft double; 3,400 Ft triple; 3,100 Ft quad; 3,000 Ft dorm. Add 500 Ft for high and special seasons. Breakfast is included. No credit cards. Limited street parking. Tram: 4 or 6: Király u. **Amenities:** Communal kitchen, hair dryer (on request), Wi-Fi.

Where to Dine in Budapest

The Budapest restaurant scene has been hard hit by the global crisis, in addition to the Hungarian downturn in the economy. The former means less tourism creating a "now you see it, now you don't" situation with some restaurants lasting only 3 months before throwing in the frying pan. Here today, gone tomorrow. The Hungarian Restaurant Association in 2009 predicted that 30% of all restaurants in the country would close. There is nothing I fear more than getting an e-mail from a reader who thinks I did not do my research by suggesting a defunct eatery. Bearing this in mind, I have tried to include those restaurants that seem to be stable enough to continue to exist when you arrive.

Of course, the best part of travel is sampling the culture's cuisine; ample opportunities await to choose either traditional or nouveau Hungarian recipes from these listings. There is a diverse range of restaurants, including some traditional eateries that have negotiated the economic tides over time. Many ethnic restaurants are listed for those who feel the national cuisine has been adequately sampled.

For a list of snacks and meals that should not be missed in this gastronomic culture, see "Hungarian Eats & Treats," p. 23 for suggestions. At times you may want to nibble, not wanting a full meal; for this reason, I have also included snack places for a quickie bite.

Most restaurant kitchens close an hour earlier than the posted closing hours of the restaurant, but if a restaurant is open until or past midnight, the kitchen will be closed by 11:00pm. Exceptions are rare.

Something fish-less is going on here: Do take into consideration when ordering fish that this is a landlocked country. Unless it is fish that has come from one of Hungary's rivers or lakes, it is imported and was most likely frozen for shipment. If this is of importance to you, you should question your waiter before ordering. One Hungarian national dish is a particular fish soup, which is also part of the traditional Christmas meal. Most famous among these soup recipes are those of Szeged where fish from the Tisza River are used to prepare it. If you enjoy fish, you will find this item on many traditional restaurant menus.

Food Warning and Allergies: When we ate out for the last edition of this book, I don't recall finding bacon either explicitly described on the menu descriptions or just implanted in a recipe without warning. This time around, I have been pleasantly shocked at how many dishes, regardless of the main meat, have bacon stuck in there somewhere when the menu did not offer a clue. I love pork of all sorts, but for people with religious restrictions and even vegetarians, you should question the server before placing your order.

An ever-increasing number of people suffer from food allergies, especially the ubiquitous peanut allergy, so for those of you who do, you should keep the following phrase handy when dining. It is purposefully dramatic, since wait staff give little credence to other phrases. *Ha bármi mogyorósat eszek, meghalok.* "If I eat anything with nuts in it I will die."

WHERE TO EAT There are many words used for eateries; few have clear-cut boundaries. *Étterem* is the most common Hungarian word for restaurant and is applied to everything from cafeteria-style eateries to first-class restaurants. A *vendéglő,*

Tips **Hints for a Better Dining Experience**

Reserving a table for most Budapest restaurants is almost always necessary. It is not unusual for a table that has been reserved by someone for 9pm to sit empty even if you happen to show up at 6pm. They will not allow you to use that table although there should be ample time to change the linens between guests. Call the restaurant to make your reservation or ask your hotel to do it for you. If you call, speak slowly. To reserve for the half-hour, use the phrase "and a half"—for example "seven and a half," not "seven-thirty." You will want to avoid the downstairs restaurants in summer months; they can be brutally hot. Almost no restaurants offer air-conditioning, even if it says so on their window. Mysteriously, it is just not working on the day you show up for dinner. Before you order wine, take a good look at the menu. Glasses of wine are priced by the deciliter (dl) and you should order how many decis you want. If you don't, you may receive a full glass of wine with a surprisingly large bar tab. 1 dl = approximately 3.3 ounces.

an inn or guesthouse, is a smaller, more intimate restaurant, often with a Hungarian folk motif; a *csárda* is a countryside *vendéglő* (often built on major motorways and frequently found around Lake Balaton and other holiday areas). An *önkiszolgáló* indicates a self-service cafeteria. *Büfés* (snack counters) are not to be confused with buffets in English. They are found all over the city, including transportation hubs. A *cukrászda* is a bakery for pastries and a coffee, while a *kávéház* is a coffeehouse that generally has a limited selection of pastries. Traditionally, many coffeehouses are places to sit for hours to meet with friends, read a book, or just sit and people-watch. Today, some establishments use the word *kávéház* in their name, but really are restaurants providing full meals. You will be able to tell the difference if you scope out the menus.

Other establishments you will come across in your travels are those whose primary function is to serve liquor, but some also serve meals or snacks. A *borozó* is a wine bar; these are downstairs off the street (they are likely to include the word *pince* (cellar) or *barlang* (cave) in their name), and generally feature a house wine. A *söröző* is a beer bar; these places, too, are often found in downstairs locations. Sandwiches are usually available in *borozós* and *sörözős*. Some are excellent places,

while others are dives where cheap drinks are served to the less economically advantaged.

MUSIC Live Gypsy music is often touted in traditional Hungarian restaurants as a tourist marketing tool. Most often, this is not authentic Gypsy music but a fair imitation for the unbeknownst traveler who can say they heard Gypsy music. One exception is the **Mátyás Pince** (p. 92). Chances are a member, or the whole band, will rotate playing a song or two at your table. If you feel uncomfortable or this is disrupting your conversation, politely decline his or her offer to play for you as soon as they approach your table. If, however, you allow them to play, then you have committed yourself to giving them a tip. The appropriate amount varies whether it is one person or more and the price category of the restaurant itself. Giving 1,500 Ft to 2,000 Ft is an example for a single musician.

With the shifting economy over the last couple of years, I have not ducked out from beefing up the budget dining options for when you really want to pork out, but not risk having your bank account go out on the lamb. All jesting aside, I have added more budget food options in this edition.

PRICE CATEGORIES For the purposes of this book, I have classified restaurants as

Fizetek, kérem! = "Check, Please!" & Other Tipping Tips

One of the glorious holdovers from times past is the ability to sit in any drink or food establishment without concern of being hurried out the door. Unless the doors are closing for the evening, no one will approach you to pay your bill until you signal that you are ready; therefore, you can linger for hours on end. In 8 years, I have only found one exception to this. It is for this reason that the reservation issue described above is such a sticky issue.

Don't be surprised if the person who comes to collect your money is not the person who served you. Many places have a designated cashier who will arrive at your table to collect your money. It may be a few minutes before they arrive, so be patient. Smaller restaurants still have this annoying habit of giving you a small piece of paper with a list of numbers and nothing else to associate them with. If you have questions about it, ask to see a menu to match the charges on the list before you pay or ask the cashier to explain it. If there is a mistake, challenge it and it will be corrected.

Always ask if a service charge is already included. It should show somewhere on the bill, but it is worth asking to make sure. If the service is included, you are not expected to tip. If no service charge is included, **add 10% to the bill** (15% for exceptional service in high-priced restaurants only—though note that the waiter very rarely gets a share of the tip). I like to hand the tip directly to our waiter to make sure he receives it. Never leave the tip on the table and walk out.

The cashier will often remain at your table after delivering the bill, waiting patiently for payment. State the full amount you are paying (bill plus tip), and the waiter will make change on the spot. If the restaurant accepts credit cards and you are using one, then the cashier will bring a portable card reader to your table to swipe the card. If you want to add the tip to the charged amount, you need to say so before the charge is processed; it can't be added to the bill later. When I really appreciate our server, I slip some money to him or her privately to make sure the server receives some compensation. During tough economic times, it happens often that when paying by credit card, "suddenly" the credit card machine has died and you will be asked for cash. If you insist that you have no cash and refuse to run to the local bank machine, mysteriously, their credit card machine resurrects from the dead and can handle the transaction. My restaurant friends tell me this is to aid the establishments' cash flow and avoid paying taxes. Don't be part of their scheme if you really want to use plastic.

It is rare the restaurant that will give separate bills to one table. If you ask, they will often say they can until it comes time to pay, then suddenly they can't do it any longer. If you are sharing a bill, you may want to keep note of your charges to make things easier when it comes time to split the bill.

follows: A restaurant is inexpensive if the average main dish is $10 or under; moderate, between $10 and $20; expensive, between $20 and $30; and very expensive, $30 and over. Bargain meals are becoming a thing of the past, but a few still exist. Having lived here for 8 years, basically living on a Hungarian salary, watching the cost of dining out soar has been inhibiting. However, guests from urban areas with more expensive restaurant meals generally find some menus more reasonable than I do. For this reason, I have tried to provide a wide range of choices to fit any mood and budget. One day you may feel like splurging on a top restaurant, but other days you may want something more moderate.

Credit cards are still not as ingrained in all businesses as they are elsewhere, so check with a restaurant if you need to use a credit card. I have listed the cards accepted at the time of this writing, but things change. Unless otherwise noted in the review, an English-language menu is available in all of the restaurants listed, although it may not be posted outside with the Hungarian menu. Don't hesitate to go in and ask to see a menu before you decide to stay.

For eating on a budget, almost all restaurants now have a day menu or weekly special menu for lunchtime meals under 800 Ft, usually available until 4pm. Sometimes other dinner special offerings are posted either outside or on an inner wall, not appearing on the menu. Ask your server about specials and the cost before ordering, to avoid any embarrassment. If a restaurant doesn't list drinks on the menu, which is rare, feel free to inquire about the price before deciding. Cocktails are extremely costly, while wine and beer are reasonable.

WARNING The U.S. Embassy provides a list of restaurants that engage in unethical business practices, such as excessive billing, using physical intimidation to compel payment of excessive bills, and assaulting customers for nonpayment of excessive bills. However, it states that this list is not comprehensive. At all costs, you should avoid these establishments. The list includes **Városközpont** (accessible by outside elevator), Budapest V district, Váci utca 16; **La Dolce Vita,** Október 6. u. 8; **Nirvana Night Club,** Szent István krt. 13; **Ti'Amo Bar,** Budapest IX district, Ferenc körút 19–21; **Diamond Club,** Budapest II district, Bimbó út 3; and **Pigalle Night Club,** Budapest VIII district, Kiss József utca 1–3. If a woman approaches you and asks for directions, but then asks you to buy her a drink, red flags should shoot into the air. The embassy cannot offer too much assistance in these situations due to Hungarian laws that are ineffective. Buyer beware.

You can always check the U.S. embassy website for updated information: visit http://hungary.usembassy.gov/tourist_advisory.html.

1 RESTAURANTS BY CUISINE

AZERBAIJAN
Marquis de Salade ★★ (The Inner City & Central Pest, $$, p. 103)

COFFEEHOUSES
Aztek Choxolat Café ★★ (The Inner City & Central Pest, p. 121)
Café Noé ★★★ (The Inner City & Central Pest, p. 121)

Centrál Kávéház ★★★ (The Inner City & Central Pest, p. 119)
Fröhlich Kóser Cukrászda ★ (The Inner City & Central Pest, p. 121)
Gerbeaud's (The Inner City & Central Pest, p. 119)

Key to Abbreviations: $$$$ = Very Expensive $$$ = Expensive $$ = Moderate $ = Inexpensive

Lukács Cukrászda (The Inner City
& Central Pest, p. 119)
Művész Kávéház ★ (The Inner City
& Central Pest, p. 120)
Rétesvar ★★★ (The Castle District,
p. 121)

DUTCH
Mosselen Belgian Beer Café ★★★
(The Inner City & Central Pest, $$,
p. 104)

GREEK
Taverna Dionysos (The Inner City
& Central Pest, $$, p. 107)
Zorbas Taverna ★★ (The Inner City
& Central Pest, $$, p. 108)

HUNGARIAN MODERN
Angelika Kávéház és Étterem ★★
(Central Buda, $$, p. 116)
Blue Tomato Pub ★★★ (The Inner
City & Central Pest, $$, p. 96)
Buena Vista ★★ (The Inner City
& Central Pest, $$, p. 96)
Café Eklektika ★★★ (The Inner City
& Central Pest, $$, p. 97)
Café Kör ★ (The Inner City &
Central Pest, $$, p. 97)
Dió ★★★ (The Inner City &
Central Pest, $$$, p. 92)
Firkász ★★★ (The Inner City
& Central Pest, $$, p. 99)
Gerlóczy Kávéház ★★ (The Inner
City & Central Pest, $$, p. 100)
Hemingway ★★★ (Central Buda,
$$$, p. 116)
Kőleves Vendéglő ★★★ (The Inner
City & Central Pest, $, p. 111)
Kossuth Museum Vénhajó
Étterem ★★★ (The Inner City
& Central Pest, $$, p. 102)
Menza ★★★ (The Inner City
& Central Pest, $$, p. 103)
Red Pepper ★★ (The Inner City
& Central Pest, $, p. 112)
Remiz ★★★ (The Buda Hills, $$,
p. 118)
Rivalda Café & Restaurant ★★★
(The Castle District, $$, p. 117)

Spinoza Étterem ★★ (The Inner City
& Central Pest, $$, p. 106)
Vista Café & Restaurant ★★★ (The
Inner City & Central Pest, $$, p. 107)

HUNGARIAN TRADITIONAL
Alföldi Kisvendéglő ★★ (The Inner
City & Central Pest, $$, p. 96)
Arany Tálca Önkiszolgáló Étterem ★★
(The Inner City & Central Pest, $,
p. 108)
Bagolyvár ★★★ (Beyond Central
Pest, $$, p. 113)
Café Csiga (Beyond Central Pest, $,
p. 115)
Fatál ★★★ (The Inner City &
Central Pest, $$, p. 99)
Fészek ★★ (The Inner City &
Central Pest, $$, p. 99)
Főzelékfalo Ételbar ★★ (The Inner
City & Central Pest, $, p. 109)
Frici Papa Kifőzés ★ (The Inner City
& Central Pest, $, p. 110)
Gundel ★ (Beyond Central Pest,
$$$$, p. 113)
Kulacs Étterem ★ (Beyond Central
Pest, $$, p. 102)
Mátyás Pince ★★★ (The Inner City
& Central Pest, $$$, p. 92)
Nagyi Nonstop Palacsintázója ★★
(The Inner City & Central Pest, $,
p. 111)
Önkiszolgáló vendéglő ★★ (The
Castle District, $, p. 111)
Paprika Vendéglő ★★★ (Beyond
Central Pest, $$, p. 113)
Szent Jupát ★ (Central Buda, $$,
p. 116)
Szép Ilona ★ (The Buda Hills, $$,
p. 118)
Tabáni Terasz ★★★ (Central Buda,
$$, p. 117)
TreffOrt Vendéglő ★★ (The Inner
City & Central Pest, $, p. 112)
Trófea Grill Étterem ★★★ (Beyond
Central Pest, $$, p. 114)
Vörös Postakocsi Étterem ★★ (The
Inner City & Central Pest, $$,
p. 108)

INDIAN

Bombay Express ★★ (The Inner City & Central Pest, $, p. 108)

Govinda Vegetariánus Étterem ★★★ (The Inner City & Central Pest, $, p. 110)

Kohinoor Étterem★★ (The Inner City & Central Pest, $$, p. 102)

Shalimar ★★★ (The Inner City & Central Pest, $$, p. 106)

INTERNATIONAL

Amstel River Café ★★ (The Inner City & Central Pest, $$, p. 93)

Cactus Juice ★★★ (The Inner City & Central Pest, $$, p. 96)

Café Alibi★★ (The Inner City & Central Pest, $, p. 109)

Crazy Dzsungel Café es Étterem ★★★ (The Inner City & Central Pest, $$, p. 98)

Karma ★★★ (The Inner City & Central Pest, $$, p. 101)

M ★★★ (The Inner City & Central Pest, $$, p. 102)

Menta Terasz ★ (The Inner City & Central Pest, $$, p. 103)

Mokka ★★★ (The Inner City & Central Pest, $$$, p. 92)

Noir et L'or ★★★ (The Inner City & Central Pest, $$, p. 105)

Soul Café ★★★ (The Inner City & Central Pest, $$, p. 106)

Stex Ház ★★ (The Inner City & Central Pest, $$, p. 107)

ITALIAN

Club 93 ★★ (The Inner City & Central Pest, $, p. 109)

Il Terzo Cerchio ★★ (The Inner City & Central Pest, $$, p. 100)

Olíva Étterem és Pizzéria ★★★ (The Inner City & Central Pest, $$, p. 105)

Pink Cadillac ★★ (The Inner City & Central Pest, $, p. 112)

Pomo D'oro ★★ (The Inner City & Central Pest, $$, p. 106)

JAPANESE

Momotaro Metélt ★★ (The Inner City & Central Pest, $$, p. 104)

Wasabi Running Wok & Sushi Étterem ★★ (The Inner City & Central Pest, $$$, p. 93)

JEWISH (KOSHER)

Carmel Restaurant (The Inner City & Central Pest, $$, p. 98)

Hanna's Orthodox Restaurant (The Inner City & Central Pest, $, p. 110)

MEDIEVAL

Sir Lancelot ★★ (The Inner City & Central Pest, $$$, p. 93)

MEXICAN

Iguana Bar & Grill ★★ (The Inner City & Central Pest, $$, p. 100)

SCOTTISH

Caledonia Scottish Pub and Restaurant ★★ (The Inner City & Central Pest, $$, p. 98)

SPANISH

Két Szerecsen ★★ (The Inner City & Central Pest, $$, p. 101)

Pata Negra Tapas Bar ★★ (The Inner City & Central Pest, $$, p. 105)

TEAHOUSES

Tea Palota (Tea Hall; The Inner City & Central Pest, $, p. 122)

Teaház a Vörös Oroszlánhoz (The Red Lion Teahouse; The Inner City & Central Pest, $, p. 122)

Zöld Teknős Barlangja (Green Turtle Cave; The Inner City & Central Pest, $, p. 122)

VEGETARIAN

Eden ★ (Central Buda, $, p. 117)

Hummus Bar ★★★ (The Inner City & Central Pest, $, p. 110)

Napos Oldal Café ★★ (The Inner City & Central Pest, $, p. 111)

EXPENSIVE

Dió ★★★ (Finds) HUNGARIAN MODERN   Being frugal when eating out, I often bypass the more expensive eateries, but this one received such rave reviews from a reader, I could not miss out on the experience he described. Recreating Hungarian folkart with oversized carved dark wooden panels on the walls interspersed with etched glass mirrors, the dining room has a cozy hearth-like warmth. Service was beyond reproach, but the food was a competitive shining star. I splurged by having the tapa starter of three pieces of pumpkin and spinach pie. It was heavenly and I could have stopped there and been satiated, but I went forth with the duck breast served with sweet potato soufflé with fig and thyme mousse. My dining companion decided on the Mangalitsa pork chops stuffed with goat cheese and chandelle mushrooms accompanied by a potato cake. Whoever believes that money cannot buy happiness has not eaten here. Not only will the food and service be beyond reproach, but the memories will live on.

V. Sas u. 4. (*C*) **1/328-0360.** www.diorestaurant.com. Reservations recommended. Main courses 2,880 Ft–4,680 Ft. AE, MC, V. Daily noon–midnight. Metro: Bajcsy-Zsilinszky út (Blue line) or Deák Ferenc tér (all lines). Note that this restaurant shares the same street address as Mokka.

Mátyás Pince ★★★ (Moments) HUNGARIAN TRADITIONAL   Art, history, or music buffs will love this restaurant established in 1904, named for King Mátyás; the myths and legends of his reign grace the walls in magnificent style. The frescoes and stained glass decorating the dining areas were registered as national monuments in 1973. Music is provided by the Sándor Déki Lakatos Gypsy music dynasty every night but Monday from 7pm until closing, creating an all-round romantic experience. I sampled the cold blackberry soup, rich in creamy fruit flavor. The main course was King Mátyás's favorite menu of sirloin of beef on a spit, leg of duck, goose liver wrapped in bacon, roast sausage, onion potatoes, steamed cabbage, and letcho. Beautifully presented, every morsel was delectable, and certainly fit for a king or anyone aspiring to eat like one. The service was impeccable. The menu is extensive and the combination of an excellent meal and entertainment makes for an enjoyable evening out.

V. Március 15 tér 7-8. (*C*) **1/266-8008.** www.cityhotels.hu. Reservations recommended. Main courses 3,500 Ft–10,900 Ft. AE, MC, V. Daily 11am–midnight. Metro: Ferenciek tere (Blue line).

Mokka ★★★ (Moments) INTERNATIONAL   Close to the basilica on Sas utca, Mokka creates a dramatic first impression: dark orange walls, etched bamboo designed glass, masks on the walls, and the horizontal bamboo art over the bar area. Orange glass balls as hanging lights make for a romantic tryst. The menu contains the most imaginative combinations of foods I have seen on a Budapest menu. I gave in and tried the wild boar, hearing it does not taste like pork. It arrived in thick filet mignon style with two halves of baby squash and a potato cake. Tasting similar to beef, the boar was excellent. The potato cake was layers of micro-thin slices of potato that must have had each layer brushed with butter. It looked like a large muffin. It was outstanding. My guest had St. Peter's butterfish with honey-bacon sauce and spinach cous-cous. Both dishes arrived magazine perfect, but looking scarce on the large plates; however, after finishing, there was surprisingly no room for dessert. Our dining gratification was enhanced by the superior service. The menu changes seasonally due to the chef's commitment to using the freshest ingredients available.

V. Sas u. 4. ℂ **1/328-0081.** www.mokkarestaurant.hu. Reservations recommended. Main courses 2,580 Ft–8,980 Ft. AE, MC, V. Daily noon–midnight. Metro: Bajcsy-Zsilinszky út (Blue line) or Deák Ferenc tér (all lines). Note that this restaurant shares the same street address as Dió.

Sir Lancelot ★★★ (Kids MEDIEVAL   Plan for a "knight" of excitement when you enter this medieval cellar venue decorated with stone, stained glass, and lion-head fountains. Eat as in times of yore with a knife and spoon, but no fork; eating with your hands is encouraged. Candle lighting and flute music add to the atmosphere as costumed servers place humongous dishes of food such as Saint Grill, Virtue of Womanfolk, or Basket of Merlin before you. As you are eating, don't be surprised if a swordfight breaks out between two rival knights or a fire-eater decides to dine on flames right next to you while a belly dancer is shimmering down the aisle. Set menus are available for three, four, or six people, fixed knight's meals are for one person, and individual menu items are available for your choosing. No matter which you pick, have a big appetite ready and be open for the excitement that follows.

VI. Podmaniczky u. 14. ℂ **1/302-4456.** www.sirlancelot.hu. Reservations recommended (72 hours in advance preferred). Set menu for 2–6 people 11,900 Ft–36,900 Ft; knight's meal 4,390 Ft–5,390 Ft; entree 2,190 Ft–5,390 Ft. AE, DC, MC, V. Daily noon–1am. Tram: 4 or 6, Nyugati.

Wasabi Running Wok & Sushi Étterem ★★ JAPANESE   An unusual concept for an all-you-can-eat restaurant; you will find the dining area is one long room tastefully set out with one wall of all exposed rock, while the other wall has large windows with Japanese-style amber-simulated paper lantern lights. Tables can seat up to four, so larger parties have to separate. Down the center of the room separating the tables is a 25m (82 ft) two-level, glass-encased, metal conveyor belt. On the upper conveyor, all hot dishes will roll by, while cold dishes pass on the lower level. Each section is temperature controlled. By each table, there are sliding doors, so when a tasty morsel is within reach, you open the door and snatch it. You have to be friends with your dining companions, since competition can be fierce for certain selections. On our most recent visit many cold selections were sushi with some desserts and cold salads. The hot selections included meats, noodles, and other fish, but they removed the doors on the hot section, so the food was tepid, not hot. For the best and first selection, ask to be seated on the right side closest to the kitchen for first pick of what the chef sets out. Sixty wok dishes and eight sushi rolls are offered, but drinks are not included. The Buda location is at III. Szépvölgi út 15, ℂ **1/430–1056.** Daily 11am–11pm.

VI. Podmaniczky u. 21. ℂ **1/374-0008.** www.wasabi.hu. Reservations recommended. Lunch Mon–Tues 3,990 Ft, Wed–Fri 4,490 Ft; dinner Mon–Tues 4,490 Ft, Wed–Fri 5,490 Ft, Sat–Sun all day 5,490 Ft. Children 2 and under free. MC, V. Daily lunch 11:30am–5pm; dinner 5–11:30pm. Tram: 4 or 6, Nyugati.

MODERATE

Amstel River Café ★★ INTERNATIONAL   Looking like a Dutch pub inside is no accident as the owner is a gay man from the Netherlands. Just off Váci utca, the pedestrian shopping street, this cafe is the perfect place for lunch or dinner. I have been coming here for years; sad to say, I am in a rut. The Indonesian satay chicken is my repeat choice. The skewered chunks of chicken are marinaded and served with a picante peanut sauce served with French fries. My partner has tried the broccoli soup and chicken wrapped in bacon, which he raved about. The soup was flavorful without the veggies being overcooked. The chicken was moist with the bacon crisp. They offer free Wi-Fi. Weather permitting, choose the outdoor seating for people-watching.

V. Párizsi u. 6. ℂ **1/266-4334.** www.amstelrivercafe.com. Main courses 1,690 Ft–3,390 Ft. No credit cards. Daily noon–midnight. Metro: Vörösmarty (Yellow line).

WHERE TO DINE IN BUDAPEST

6

THE INNER CITY & CENTRAL PEST

Alföldi Kisvendéglő **65**
Amstel River Café **59**
Angelika Kaveház és Étterem **7**
Arany Tálca Önkiszolgáló
  Étterem **55**
Aztek Choxolat Café **58**
Bagolyvár (Owl Castle) **83**
Blue Tomato Pub **21**
Bombay Express **32**
Buena Vista **35**
Cactus Juice **30**
Café Alibi **64**
Café Csiga **72**
Café Eklektika **41**
Café Kör **44**
Café Noé **54**
Café Vian **36**
Caledonia Scottish Pub
  & Restaurant **31**
Carmel Restaurant **51**
Centrál Kávéház **61**
Club 93 **73**
Crazy Dzsungel Café es
  Étterem **26**
Dió **46**
Eden **6**
Fatál **63**
Fészek **77**
Firkász **19**
Főzelékfalo Ételbar **40**
Frici Papa Kifőzés **38**
Fröhlich Kóser Cukrászda **52**
Gerbeaud's **14**
Gerlóczy Kávéház **57**
Govinda Vegetariánus
  Étterem **15**
Gundel **84**
Hanna's Orthodox
  Restaurant **49**
Hemingway **12**
Hummus Bar **78**
Iguana Bar & Grill **18**
Il Terzo Cerchio **74**
Karma **34**
Két Szerecsen
  (Two Brothers) **37**
Kohinoor Indian &
  Pakistani Étterem **76**
Kóleves Vendéglő
  (Stone Soup) **50**
Kossuth Museum Vénhajó
  Étterem (Old Ship) **13**
Kulacs Étterem **75**

Lukács Cukrászda **81**
M **80**
Marquis de Salade **42**
Mátyás Pince **60**
Menta Terasz **1**
Menza **33**
Mokka **45**
Momotaro Metélt **17**
Mosselen Belgian Beer Café **20**
Müvész Kávéház **39**
Nagyi Nonstop Palacsintázója **5**
Napos Oldal Café **29**
Noir et L'or **48**
Olíva Étterem és Pizzéria **43**
Önkiszolgáló vendéglő **8**
Paprika Vendéglő **82**
Pata Negra Tapas Bar **66**
Pink Cadillac **70**
Pomo D'oro **16**
Red Pepper **22**
Remiz **3**

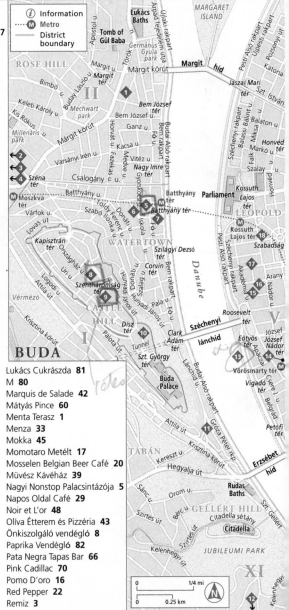

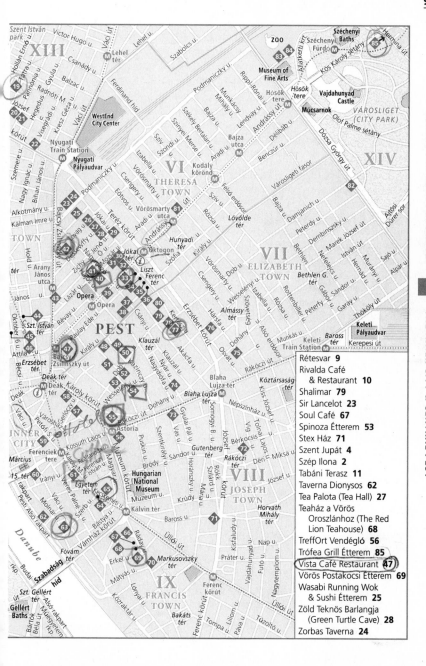

Rétesvar **9**

Rivalda Café
& Restaurant **10**

Shalimar **79**

Sir Lancelot **23**

Soul Café **67**

Spinoza Étterem **53**

Stex Ház **71**

Szent Jupát **4**

Szép Ilona **2**

Tabáni Terasz **11**

Taverna Dionysos **62**

Tea Palota (Tea Hall) **27**

Teaház a Vörös
Oroszlánhoz (The Red
Lion Teahouse) **68**

TreffOrt Vendéglő **56**

Trófea Grill Étterem **85**

Vista Café Restaurant **47**

Vörös Postakocsi Étterem **69**

Wasabi Running Wok
& Sushi Étterem **25**

Zöld Teknős Barlangja
(Green Turtle Cave) **28**

Zorbas Taverna **24**

Alföldi Kisvendéglő ★★ HUNGARIAN TRADITIONAL   Alföldi is named after Hungary's flat plain region and is paneled with horizontal brown wood-stripped walls with assorted old plates above, creating a homey country feel. The dining room offers wooden booths or tables with traditional country hand-embroidered tablecloths and placemats in folk designs. Each table has a basket of spicy homemade *pogácsas* (a type of biscuit), and you will be charged for each one eaten, but it's worth the nominal charge. Here the Hortobagy pancakes have a different flavor to the paprika sauce, but were delectable. The buttered veal scallops were ultra tender with a light buttery sauce that was used for the potatoes and rice that came with it. The pork medallions were also splendid, served without any flare, in a down-home country manner.

V. Kecskeméti u. 4. ℂ **1/267-0224.** www.alfoldivendeglo.hu/hun/. Main courses 1,440 Ft–5,140 Ft. MC, V. Daily 11am–midnight. Metro: Astoria (Red line) or tram 47 or 49 to Kálvin tér.

Blue Tomato Pub ★★★ HUNGARIAN MODERN   Don't let the "Pub" in the name fool you, this is a serious place for treating your tastebuds with tasty morsels. The dark woody walls are plastered with old Americana and European advertisements, creating a cozy relaxing atmosphere. The smoking section is fully segregated from the non-smokers, a real plus in Hungary. Again I had the corn soup with bacon and almond slivers as a starter. Not as thick as in the past, but just as creamy, and with the chunks of bacon and lots of almonds, it was bowl-licking delicious. Quite embarrassing for my guest, actually. I tried the chicken served in the earthenware dish, which was layered chicken breast with sliced potatoes, tomato, onion, bacon of course, and a creamy cheese Dijon sauce over the entire dish. It was something to crow about. A fellow diner had chicken breast with green mascarpone sauce with forest mushrooms. Fantastic food at reasonable prices (that have not changed in more than 2 years) with good service always wins me over.

XIII. Pannónia u. 5–7. ℂ **1/339-8099.** www.bluetomato.hu. Reservations recommended. Main courses 1,390 Ft–3,900 Ft. MC, V. Mon–Sat noon–midnight; Sun noon–10pm. Tram: 4 or 6, Jászai Mari tér.

Buena Vista ★★★ HUNGARIAN MODERN   Reportedly this restaurant is named for the famous Buena Vista Social Club that performed at this location before the restaurant opened. Perhaps the success of the band has lent its success to its namesake. This is one of the oldest restaurants on this square (Liszt Ferenc tér), and it has thrived for more than 9 years. The interior, brick and stone on multiple levels, is not that memorable; it could be any other restaurant in the city. What makes this restaurant stand out from the crowd is its service and food. Now offering 18 tapas (choice of four for 2,500 Ft) in addition to their regular menu, gives them an edge. I savored the garlic milk-marinaded pork filet served with minced cabbage mixed with ewe cheese and Hungarian dumplings. Also receiving two thumbs up was the Valencia paella full of mussels and chicken chunks. In the warm months, the outdoor seating is the only place to be, to see or be seen by the many people walking up and down the tér, and because there is no air-conditioning inside. Due to its longevity and outstanding reputation, this is one of the most popular hotspots in the area.

VI. Liszt Ferenc tér 4–5. ℂ **1/344-6303.** www.buena-vista.hu. Reservations recommended. Main courses 2,200 Ft–5,800 Ft. AE, MC, V. Daily 10am–11pm. Metro: Opera (Yellow line).

Cactus Juice ★★★ (Finds) INTERNATIONAL   Listen up pard'ner, this old west feelin' joint will transport you in time, but tickle your tastebuds while doing it. It may look like something from an old western movie set, but there is nothing staged where the food is concerned. My dining companion is a professional chef who proclaimed the chicken tarragon soup the best ever. My pork cutlet with fried onions was served over gnocchi blended with ewe cheese. I would rob a stagecoach to sample this again. After the kitchen closes around 10pm, the place transforms into a swinging saloon with music and dancing.

VI. Jókai tér 5. ✆ **1/302-2116.** www.cactusjuice.hu. Reservations recommended. Main courses 1,980 Ft–3,750 Ft. AE, MC, V. Mon–Thurs noon–2am; Fri–Sat noon–1am; Sun 4pm–2am. Metro: Oktogon (Yellow line).

Café Eklektika ★★★ (Value HUNGARIAN MODERN   With tables and booths, a mellow mood is created by the soothing vocals with a cabaret feel serenading in the background, the monthly changing artwork on the walls, and the dependably excellent service. The chicken dish I loved was replaced with chicken breast stuffed with spinach served with a potato pie layered with cheese. It was good enough to make me forget the other dish I longed for. My dining guest had gnocchi with mozzarella balls and olives. He said the sauce was excellent. During the summer on weekdays only, they offer an all-you-can-eat buffet from noon–4pm. At other times, you may just find weekly specials on the blackboard or ask the wait staff. Outside seating is available in good weather, but inside you will be treated to free unlimited Wi-Fi, for the price of a coffee. No one will rush you out; this is a place to call home away from home.

V. Nagymező 30. ✆ **1/266-1226.** www.eklektika.hu. Reservations recommended. Main courses 1,490 Ft–2,390 Ft. Pizza 1,290 Ft–1,890 Ft. Cash only. Mon–Fri 10am–midnight; Sat–Sun noon–midnight. Metro: Opera (Yellow line).

Café Kör ★ HUNGARIAN MODERN   It has escaped my imagination why so many travel writers award grandiose praise to this restaurant, making me wonder if they have actually eaten here or copied text from one enthusiastic writer in years past. I have eaten here. The decor is simplistic with stucco-colored walls and low-hanging lighting, within one large room. When the dining room is full, which is often, tables and chairs are crammed together. The wait staff is extensive and often chatting with each other at the bar, but the service is not neglected. They get points for service. Specials are written on brown paper on one wall causing people to hover around an already crowded room to see what is not on the menu. Request a seat far from the specials to avoid feeling smothered. I ordered a salad with avocados, large enough to share. My entree was beef tenderloin steak sidelined by potato jackets with Roquefort sauce. As tender as the steak was, it was incredibly salty putting my arteries on high alert. The boiled potatoes had a dab of sauce on top making them disappointing. The alternative entree chosen by my guest was the goose risotto from the specials list. It was served al dente with large chunks of goose, mixed with small cubes of carrots and a handsome sized liver on top.

V. Sas u. 17. ✆ **1/311-0053.** www.cafekor.com. Reservations recommended. Main courses 1,890 Ft–4,290 Ft. No credit cards. Mon–Sat 10am–10pm. Metro: Bajcsy-Zsilinszky út (Blue line) or Deák Ferenc tér (all lines).

Café Vian ★ HUNGARIAN MODERN   When a street has 14 eateries in one block, you really have to try excelling to beat the competition. Café Vian needs to learn this lesson. I am not certain how it has lasted for years, but if my chicken paprikash is an example, I am truly puzzled. The platter held a chicken thigh and leg that looked the size of a pigeon, not a grown hen. The paprika sauce lacked zest, though it was dark enough to have been dowsed with paprika. Not even the sour cream dollops aided the flavor. My dining partner's beef stew in wine sauce with dumplings was agreeably disagreeable in the gastronomic list of first choices. The one bright spot was the exemplary service. Inside is retro-looking with high-back stuffed chairs and sofas with large button-backs, nothing extraordinary. If you try your luck, eat outside. Watching others pass by will distract your attention from the food.

VI. Liszt Ferenc tér 9. ✆ **1/268-1154.** www.cafevian.com Reservations recommended. Main courses 1,230 Ft–4,990 Ft. AE, MC, V. Daily 9am–1am. Metro: Oktogon (Yellow line) or Tram: 4 or 6, Oktogon.

Caledonia Scottish Pub and Restaurant ★★ SCOTTISH   If whisky comes to mind when you think of Scotland, this pub will not disappoint with its 40 varieties of the finest malts. The wood-paneled walls and soft lighting provide a relaxing atmosphere to enjoy a drop or to have a hearty meal. We especially enjoy their all-day Scottish break-fast featuring a fried egg, sausages, fried mushrooms, gammon steak, beans, tomatoes, black pudding, and toast. Okay, we leave the black pudding on the plate, but the rest makes for a perfect brunch outing. On our return, we went the diner route, choosing the steak and Belhaven Ale pie. Served like a stew with a crust in a large ramekin, there were plenty of beef chunks and veggies in thick brown gravy to call this a satisfying meal. For the more familiar, try the fish and chips. The lightly battered cod with large fries was declared a real treat. For a larger group, reserve a table on the mezzanine to eat and enjoy a lofty feel overlooking the main dining room and the goings-on below. If this has not convinced you, they put up big screen television for major sports events, there is free Wi-Fi, and a small Scottish gift shop.

VI. Mozsar u. 9. ✆ **1/311-7611.** www.caledonia.hu. Reservations recommended. Main courses 1,200 Ft–4,000 Ft. AE, DC, MC, V. Sun–Thurs 11am–midnight; Fri–Sat 11am–1am; kitchen closes at 10pm. Metro: Oktogon (Yellow line) or Tram: 4 or 6, Oktogon.

Carmel Restaurant JEWISH   Now stating they are Glatt Kosher, they have Jewish and international cuisine on the menu. When you enter, go down the stairs to find the restaurant. It opened in 1987 and is a long room with an outdated motif, probably the original and in dire need of renovations. Four diners ventured here, I had the Jewish beef with dumplings, which was two slices of a pot-roasted beef with four grapefruit-sized bread dumplings. The gravy made the meal, but for 3,700 Ft, I felt it was exorbitantly priced as an a-la-carte dish. My fellow diners enjoyed their meals as well, but also stated each was overpriced for the quantity and quality. During the summer on Thursday nights, you can be entertained by the Klezmer concerts held here for the price of a dinner. We were in a back room for smokers, but the band was so loud, we had to scream at each other; this is not to say they were not good. This is one of the popular dining spots for Jewish tours in the city.

VII. Kazinczy u. 31. ✆ **1/322-1834.** Fax 1/461-0024. www.carmel.hu. Reservations recommended. Main courses 2,000 Ft–6,000 Ft. Daily noon–11pm; closed Sat in summer. AE, MC, V. Metro: Astoria (Red line) or Deák (all lines).

Crazy Dsungel Café es Étterem ★★★ (Kids INTERNATIONAL   It may be perfect for kids, but this restaurant packs in the adults. It consists of several rooms, each with its own identity and decor. There is the jungle room, the savannah room, the ocean room, and even a pirates' room. Throughout, there is a glass walkway with different objects to set the mood of the room. Seashells and sand are used in the ocean room for example. The pirates' room has life-size pirate dolls climbing ship's ropes and locked in the brig. The menu is equally inventive with a page devoted to each theme and menu items named accordingly. With all of this fun, the six of us dining here had a ball sur-rounded by the jungle theme. They have added kangaroo, crocodile, and ostrich to the menu. Three of us had enough to bring home for a full lunch the next day. We highly recommend the Pirates Legend, pork stuffed with cabbage and served with polenta dotted with pumpkin seeds. The pork stuffed with feta cheese and prune had two of my friends bragging about their choice for hours. Fun times, delicious food, and outstanding service make this a winner for sure.

VI. Jókai u. 30. ℂ **1/302-4003.** www.dzsungelcafe.hu. Reservations recommended. Main courses 1,990 Ft–3,690 Ft. AE, MC, V. Daily noon–1am. Tram: 4 or 6, Nyugati.

Fatál ★★★ (Value) HUNGARIAN TRADITIONAL   The name means "wooden plate". This is one of my favorite restaurants in the city, but I can rarely get others to join me. The basement restaurant fills with expats and tourists, creating a noise chamber in the long semi-barrel-shaped dining room. However, they have now opened their second dining room upstairs, open to the street. We sat in the new dining area outside, but I am still a creature of habit. My meal of choice here is always the crispy leg of pork with noodles, mushrooms and brown gravy served in a medieval-looking covered metal bowl nestled on, what else, a wooden plate. The other choice selection is the duck with cabbage and pasta. Each serving is enough for two moderate appetites, so bear this in mind. The service is slow upstairs, because the kitchen is still down below, giving the wait staff quite a work-out, but the food is worth the wait.

V. Váci u. 67. ℂ **1/266-2607.** www.fatalrestaurant.com. Reservations recommended. Main courses 2,390 Ft–7,690 Ft. No credit cards. Daily upstairs noon–10pm, downstairs (entrance on Pintér u.) noon–midnight. Tram: 47 or 49, Fővám tér.

Fészek ★★ (Value) HUNGARIAN TRADITIONAL   You may do what we did and walk past this restaurant time and again, before realizing it is a dining place. Fészek, which means nest, is situated in the center of an old grand building that has seen better days. The building's exterior entry courtyard displays photos of famous Hungarian entertainers; this historic building has been popular with artists of all types for the last century. Once you traipse through a rundown lobby and enter the interior courtyard you realize a restaurant is located here. The inner ring has tables both in a covered circular terrace area and in the exposed center courtyard, where 100-year-old chestnut trees canopy the tables. Service can sometimes be at a snail's pace so if you are in a hurry, avoid it. Choosing the veal paprikash with Hungarian noodles was a wise choice. Chunks of tender meat floated in a rich brown gravy alongside a field of freshly made noodles. Chicken coated in parmesan was a flattened breast served with a heaping mound of mashed potatoes. Live music entertainment is offered each night, ranging from American show tunes to Gypsy fusion. In the winter, portable heaters are used to make the dining experience a year-round dining adventure. Because of its reputation for having Hungarian show people, it is often filled with stargazing Hungarian diners.

VII. Kertész u. 36 (corner of Dob u.). ℂ **1/322-6043.** www.feszeketterem.hu. Reservations recommended. Main courses 1,790 Ft–2,890 Ft. MC, V. Daily noon–midnight. Tram: 4 or 6, Király utca.

Firkász ★★★ HUNGARIAN MODERN   The name means scribbler in English; referring to journalists who scribble their notes. Looking around, it is noticeable that the decor matches the name. Walls are covered with old newspapers from the early 20th century, accented with old typewriters; clocks; shadowboxes of old pens, erasers, and pencil sharpeners; and other memorabilia of yesteryear. Wine bottles litter the shelves all around, which is appropriate for the vast menu selection of vino. Because I try to have a fresh view, I never read my last review before returning to the restaurant. Hence, I ordered the crispy pork with cabbage yet again. Luckily, though the menu had not changed in 2 years, the quality did. The pork was crispy on the edges, but the tender meaty medallions were moist. A side of pan-fried potatoes was a delightfully large serving of mashed potatoes fried with onions. My fellow diner ordered the batter-dipped fried mushrooms with ewe cheese and leek sauce, which he was pleased with. If you choose the smoking area, request a seat away from the piano player who plays from 7pm to midnight, or it will be difficult to carry on a conversation. Nonsmokers can dine in a second quieter room. This is one of the few restaurants of its class to add a 15% service charge to all tabs.

XIII. Tátra u. 18. ✆ **1/450-1118.** www.firkaszetterem.hu. Reservations recommended. Main courses 1,290 Ft–4,690 Ft. MC, V. Daily noon–midnight. Tram: 4 or 6, Jászai Mari tér.

Gerlóczy Kávéház ★★ HUNGARIAN MODERN I just hate when I want to show off a restaurant to a visiting friend and it fails to live up to my recommendation. On a late Sunday afternoon, I took my friend here for lunch. The outdoor seating was filled, but an abundance of staff should have been able to meet everyone's needs. Seated quickly, served drinks, and then forgotten, I started to rethink my previous reviews. This could have been an off day, but not one waiter seemed to be interested in being there. I chose a weekly special, a cassoulet of white beans with a sausage and piece of chicken. My friend had chicken breast with taboule mixed with dried tomato. Both dishes were appetizing and tasty, but not extraordinary. Perhaps it is the harp music Tuesday to Saturday evenings that adds the special touch that I missed, but the lack of attention from the staff was also a disappointment. I do hope this was just an off day, because I have fond memories of excellent dinners here in the past and want to have more in the future.

V. Gerlóczy u. 1. ✆ **1/501-4000.** www.gerloczy.hu. Reservations recommended. Cold main courses 900 Ft–2,750 Ft; hot main courses 1,350 Ft–4,900 Ft. MC. Daily 7am–11pm. Metro: Deák tér (all lines).

Iguana Bar & Grill ★★ (Kids) MEXICAN Colorfully decorated and always buzzing with activity as an expat hang-out, reservations should be made for lunch or dinner. Opened in 1997, Iguana attracts those who have cravings for Mexican food, although this is closer to Tex-Mex than authentic Mexican. Over the years, the quality of the food has sometimes faltered, but it comes through in a pinch. It is family-friendly, but families with young children should go in the earlier hours. The decor includes old Mexican posters and Diego Rivera reproductions. The menu consists of Mexican classics, including a selection of quesadillas, chilis, fajitas, burritos, and enchiladas. Jenö's Quesadilla is my favorite, but I opted for the *enchiladas de mole* and was disappointed. (I forgot to read my review from the last time.) The sauce was overly thick and did not have much flavor, so stick with other choices. Enchiladas with especiale sauce usually get rave reviews. An ample selection of vegetarian dishes offered will not make anyone feel left out. There are special parties for Mexican holidays. Friday and Saturday, the kitchen is open until midnight.

V. Zóltán u. 16 ✆ **1/331-4352.** www.iguana.hu. Reservations recommended. Main courses 1,790 Ft–2,690 Ft. AE, MC, V. Sun–Thurs 11:30am–12:30am, Fri–Sat 11:30am–1am. Metro: Kossuth tér (Red line).

Il Terzo Cerchio ★★★ ITALIAN The restaurant's name, which means the third circle, has this inside the menu: "In the 3rd level of Dante's *Inferno*, gluttony was punished with acid rain. In our hell, tasty and fresh food is the punishment." If this is punishment, punish me regularly. The oversize windows, the whitewashed walls, the brick concave ceiling, and the exposed kitchen creates a real Tuscany feel, making you want to cozy up with some comfort food. I especially love the gnocchi with gorgonzola, pecorino, and cream sauce, but have difficulty deciding between this and the pizzas, which have the delectable thin crusts of my childhood. But I have to confess: we have been here repeatedly and have

---

> ### (Fun Facts) Cows & Pigs on the Menu
>
> Hungary has its own breed of cows and pigs that you will see on some menus. Magyar *szürke szarvasmarha* or gray cow is a breed that was brought to the Carpathian basin in the 9th century. The Hungarian Mangalica pig breed, characterized by its long curly hair, was developed in the 19th century. It doesn't need any special breeding or feeding, but has fatty meat making it ideal for sausage and salami, but sometimes it is served in cooked dishes. The other pork you will find served in restaurants is wild boar, a little gamier tasting than domestic pork.

---

not had a bad meal yet. Pizzas are cooked in a brick oven and some of the cooks are imported from Italy along with the ingredients they use. No matter how crowded it happens to be, you still feel the intimacy of those you are with; the ceilings absorb the sound from those around you. The waitstaff are attentive without being overbearing and help each other, so three or four people may be serving your drinks, food, or the replacement fork you dropped.

VII. Dohány u. 40. ✆ **1/354-0788.** www.ilterzocerchio.hu. Reservations recommended. Main courses 2,750 Ft–4,750 Ft; pizza 1,750 Ft–2,450 Ft. AE, MC, V. Daily noon–11pm. Metro: Blaha Lujza (Red line).

Karma ★★★ INTERNATIONAL   For the last book, I gave this place a scathing review, but have been back a few times since to give them the benefit of another chance. As you can see from the stars, they have turned themselves around. The interior is charmed with decor in a mix of Indian and Asian styles, with Buddha looking over the serving of meals. They have a large patio where every table is full in clement weather, but with those drinking and not always with diners. If you like turkey breast and sun-dried tomatoes, you will love this offering as I did. Served with risotto mixed with minced asparagus, it was delightful. My guest had tomato chicken breast with fresh tomato and mozzarella, to which he gave two thumbs up. Service has improved tremendously; we have been continually impressed over the last year.

VI. Liszt Ferenc tér 11. ✆ **1/413-6764.** www.karmabudapest.com. Reservations recommended, especially for outdoor seating. Main courses 1,090 Ft–3,600 Ft. MC, V. Daily 11am–1am. Metro: Oktogon (Yellow line).

Két Szerecsen (Two Brothers) ★★★ (Kids) SPANISH   This restaurant opened in 2000, and only gets better with time. In 2006, it underwent a dramatic remodel and expansion of the interior, creating equal sized smoking and nonsmoking rooms, decorated with deep orange walls and pounded-metal lamps with multicolored glass pieces dangling. The walls display old advertisement signs and posters featuring two black men. We learned that two black men from Africa had a coffeeshop in this spot more than 100 years ago, thus the restaurant's name and decor is a tribute to them. Nine choices of tapas make a considerable snack or meal. Regular menu items are not extensive, but are supplemented by imaginative daily specials. One example is the mustard-yellow chicken curry with big cubes of pumpkin, which I tried and will return for again. The spice level was perfect for a lunch. My friend had the ricotta ravioli with artichokes. The portions are very generous. Sitting outdoors under the huge tree is relaxing.

VI. Nagymező u. 14. ✆ **1/343-1984.** www.ketszerecsen.hu. Reservations recommended. Main courses 1,690 Ft–3,990 Ft; tapas 790 Ft–1,590 Ft. AE, DC, MC, V. Mon–Fri 8am–midnight, Sat–Sun 9am–midnight. Metro: Opera (Yellow line).

Kohinoor Indian and Pakistani Étterem ★★ (Finds) INDIAN   In my 8 years in Budapest, this is the fourth restaurant to try this location, but has gone beyond its 2-year anniversary, so I think it is a keeper. I believe this is the only restaurant where I have seen "HALAL," the designation for Muslim dietary laws on the menu. Pakistani offerings are minimal, but the Indian dishes are satisfying enough to avoid caring. We eat here regularly, so it was disappointing when my favorite dish of chicken korma, cubes of meat in a white cashew sauce with raisins, was creamy, but bland; a real anomaly. However, the kasuri methi karahi, chicken with onions, tomatoes, and ginger, more than made up for it with spiciness to awaken our tongue. They have the largest selection of naan breads to complement any meal. I have not given up on the chicken korma yet either.

VII. Wesselényi u. 49. ✆ 1/787-9105. www.kohinooretteren.hu. Reservations recommended. Main courses 850 Ft–2,600 Ft. MC, V. Daily 11am–11pm. Tram: 4 or 6, Wesselényi.

Kossuth Museum Vénhajó Étterem (Old Ship) ★★★ (Kids) HUNGARIAN MODERN   One hundred years old and one of the last remaining paddle boats in Hungary, this old ship serves as both a museum (opened in 1986) and a restaurant (added during 2004 remodeling). Docked on the Pest side directly across from the Castle and facing the Széchenyi Chain Bridge, it has the most romantic and spectacular view when the sun goes down and the castle and bridge are lit. Of the boat restaurants docked in a row, this one is at the forefront of the three with a better view. In good weather, request a table on the outer and upper deck. Two of us had the duck with red pepper sauce served with potato doughnuts sitting in their own caramel sauce. Another had a chicken dish on the weekly special menu. Our server provided one of the best dining experiences we have ever had, being beyond charming and attentive. Live music entertains every night, except Monday, from 8pm onward. The boat does come out of dock at times for dinner cruises, so call ahead.

V. Vigadó 2. ✆ 1/411-0942. www.europahajo.hu. Reservations recommended, especially for outdoor seating. Main courses 1,450 Ft–4,950 Ft. MC, V. Daily 11am–11pm. Tram: 2, Eötvös.

Kulacs Étterem ★ HUNGARIAN TRADITIONAL   I have a love-hate relationship with this place. All nooks and crannies are filled with decor that must have been excavated from an old-fashioned country home. The back wall behind the Rezsö Seres Gypsy band has a large mural. This neither adds nor negates my dining experience; the food is always delicious (love), but the service is atrocious (hate). After ordering the stuffed cabbage listed under beef, it arrived with a pork chop and sausage. Fine, I love pork, but my Jewish fellow diner would not have been amused. It took another 20 minutes for the side of French fries. My fellow diners had a cheese platter and soup. All portions are hearty and delectable once they arrive. The band plays nightly and so loudly, we three had to scream at each other to hear. Band members roam to the tables; we asked the violinist to leave. The waiters cluster around the computer for entering orders, while the owner or manager is playing casino games on it. Love the food, which would get them three stars, but hate the lack of service. This is where the song "Gloomy Sunday" was written by Rezső Seres. It figures.

VII. Osváth u. 11. ✆ 1/322-3611. www.kulacsetterem.hu. Reservations recommended. Main courses 2,500 Ft–4,800 Ft. AE, MC, V. Daily noon–midnight. Metro: Blaha Lujza (Red line).

M ★★ INTERNATIONAL   This unassuming restaurant is easily overlooked, with only two tables visible, but there are more upstairs. For 6 months it was closed and had changed owners. Things went from good to awful. That has changed with new management, so things are on the up again, much to my delight. Menu choices change weekly;

a vegetarian surprise is just that. Begging will not get you information. Here, the snappy, **103** yet subtle decor entertains me while waiting for my food. Walls and ceiling are covered with brown wrapping paper with black line drawings of furnishings found in a home. There are piles of books, lamps, and a parrot in a cage, vases, and a phone on a stand. This place has a warm, creative atmosphere to simulate being in someone's home. You can check the website for the week's menu. Reserve for outside or on the main level in warm weather; upstairs is hot.

VII. Kertész 48. ✆ **1/322-3108.** www.metterem.hu. Reservations recommended. Main courses 1,600 Ft–2,900 Ft. No credit cards. Daily 6pm–midnight, Sat–Sun menu noon–4pm. Tram: 4 or 6, Király u.

Marquis de Salade ★★ (Moments) AZERBAIJAN   We discovered this restaurant on our first trip to Budapest in 1998 and loved it then. Twelve years later it is still going strong. The entrance is on the street level, but the restaurant is downstairs in a cavelike atmosphere, decorated with Asian rugs on the walls and ceiling. Beyond the first dining area, there is another room for a group of six and yet another room in the back suitable for two for a romantic interlude. The latter is more like a Pasha's den with low seating and lots of cushions. Our group of three started with the Marquis's salads, which is a sampler platter of six different salads. Along with the bread, this about constituted a diversely sumptuous meal, but we plunged forward with entrees; lamb shank with sweet red peppers, chicken with shrimp sauce and coconut, and steak topped with mushroom sauce. The last two received mixed reviews, so I would avoid them, but the salad is a meal for three without ordering more. This is a small intimate restaurant so the service is impeccable.

VI. Hajós u. 43. ✆ **1/302-4086.** www.marquisdesalade.hu. Reservations recommended. Main courses 2,600 Ft–3,900 Ft. No credit cards. Daily 11am–1am. Metro: Arany János (Blue line); bus: 70 or 78 to Bajcsy-Zsilinszky út.

Menta Terasz ★ INTERNATIONAL   The last time we were here, I was not impressed with the food, but the multisensory style of the restaurant drew me back as it is like visiting an eccentric relative's bizarre villa home. The garden has beautiful hand-made wooden chairs and tables with Italian mosaic panels gracing the walls. Downstairs is the music area where live performances are held, until the DJ takes over at 10pm. On the rooftop, discover the colonial gardens with loads of plants and relaxing lounge chairs under a bamboo roof. Once again, this engaging decor is undermined by mediocre food. How can you ruin a Chicken Caesar salad? Use cheap lettuce; overcook the chicken. The pork dish ordered by my fellow diner was barely warm. Sending it back to the kitchen, it reappeared 30 minutes later, still cool to the touch, although there were only 10 diners in the entire place. In disgust, we finally had it boxed to go. Many accolades to the waiter who was so apologetic, he took our beers off of the bill, a first in Budapest. Sadly enough, service here is always exceptional, but they don't get the cooperation from the kitchen. Skip the food, go for a drink, and soak up the atmosphere instead of calories. Thankfully, the kitchen closes by 11pm.

II. Margit krt. 14. ✆ **1/336-1250.** www.mentaterasz.hu. Reservations recommended. Main courses 1,290 Ft–3,290 Ft. AE, MC, V. Sun–Wed 11am–2am; Thurs–Sat 11am–4am. Tram: 4 or 6 Margit Híd, Budai Hídfő, then walk around the corner.

Menza ★★★ HUNGARIAN MODERN   With a name that my students tell me translates to "canteen," like the cafeteria at a school, the '60s and '70s retro style, the orange, green, and brown decor with emphasis on shades of orange, takes some adjustment. The walls, especially so since they are blooming with black-and-white oversized flowers. The outdoor seating is the most popular, perhaps to avoid the decor; even in colder months, there are heaters to utilize the space. Menu choices are varied, so all diners will be accommodated, plus there is a changing weekly menu. I started my meal with the garlic soup served with a mini *lángos* stuffed with creamy cheese and grated cheese piled on top; a perfect touch for the creamy soup. The roasted (yes, roasted) steak had a mountain of fried onions smothering it and the French fries below. What looked like a waste dump received all of my attention being an onion lover. Another diner had veal stuffed with parma ham and spinach, which he proclaims is one of the best meals in our weeks of restaurant hopping. The servers are generally exceptionally attentive and aware of guest needs, without hovering, but this time it was a bit slack. This restaurant has continually been popular for years and there does not seem to be any economic slowdown in their future. On the edge of the tér, it is location, location, location.

VI. Liszt Ferenc tér 2. ✆ **1/413-1482.** www.menza.co.hu. Reservations recommended. Main courses 1,390 Ft–3,790 Ft. AE, MC, V. Daily 10am–1am. Metro: Oktogon (Yellow line).

Momotaro Metélt ★★ JAPANESE *Metélt* means noodle, but the waiter told me that the name is based on a Japanese legend about a peach boy. According to the server, the menu is a combination of Japanese and Chinese. Regardless of its name, this once-huge restaurant has shrunk in size, reserving its large banquet hall for special groups only. Now, a cozy, simple environment with plain wooden tables and stools in a nonsmoking environment, it is perfect for enjoying the tangy steamed pork dumplings. The two in a serving are the size of grapefruits, so share without feeling cheated. The crispy duck was lean and lightly battered complementing, not detracting from, the flavor and was served with a cabbage/carrot salad. Noodles with cabbage made an excellent accompaniment. No one will leave here hungry; the portions were sufficient to ask for a take-away container at 100 Ft apiece. The telling tale is the number of people waiting for a table. There are many selections available at the lower end of the price range with specialty items at the higher end of the range.

V. Széchenyi u. 16 near Nádor u. ✆ **1/269-3802.** Reservations not accepted. Main courses 1,500 Ft–4,500 Ft. No credit cards. Mon–Fri 11am–midnight, Sat–Sun noon–midnight. Metro: Kossuth Lajos tér (Red line).

Mosselen Belgian Beer Café ★★★ (Finds) BELGIAN *Mosselen* means mussel in Flemish, but before you push the door open, you'll notice the names of different famous beer brands etched into the glass panels on the doors alongside the "Best of Budapest" award stickers on other glass panels. Once you step into this L-shaped restaurant, the world around you changes to a Belgian feeling. The dark wood bar has to be huge to accommodate the 10 different beers on tap, plus the further selection of at least 50 others. Each beer is distinctively served in a glass appropriate for the brand with a coaster to match, and the prices widely range from 790 Ft to 5,900 Ft for an 11oz (⅓) glass. The brew view of beer here is taken seriously. The wainscoted walls of similarly deep rich wood continuing around the bar maintains the motif. The numerous old metal advertisements, bottles, pictures, and stenciled words are reminiscent of an old-time pub. Cabinets of old beer bottles and an antiques store add to the homey atmosphere. The menu has an interesting selection of fish dishes from tuna steak to prawns, but meat and vegetarian options are also available. The plates of food are the most artistically presented I have seen in Budapest. My choice was the grilled pork stuffed with hot peppers and feta cheese and a bacon topping. Guests loved the Dijon salmon with pesto dressing, and

another the grilled chicken breast baked with mozzarella and pesto. The accompanying
salad had a cucumber carved as a leaf with endive lilies, complete with a pepper stamen.

XIII. Pannónia u. 14. ✆ **1/452-0535.** www.mosselen.hu. Reservations recommended. Main courses 2,390 Ft–4,890 Ft; beer 790 Ft–5,900 Ft. AE, DC, MC, V. Daily noon–midnight. Tram: 4 or 6, Jászai Mari tér.

Noir et L'or ★★★ INTERNATIONAL Not entirely black and gold, the walls are dark, but there are tangerine orange box lights providing subdued lighting. Yes, there are gold cherubs flocking on one wall above the bar, creating a strange hangout for angelic figures. Perhaps they are overseeing the service, which is as superior as the food is delicious. With a party of 15 already seated, we did not have high hopes of good service, so we were utterly impressed that the manager jumped in to wait on us. I tried the sweet pea soup, much different from split pea. I would return for this alone. Dare I say heavenly? The chicken breast stuffed with marinaded feta cheese, black olives, and capers was delectable. The other choice excelled also; the medallions of pork tenderloin with goat cheese flamed in cognac, topped in mustard sauce, served with grilled vegetables and rosemary potatoes were also exemplary. The menu changes seasonally, but I hope the sweet pea soup is a keeper.

VII. Király u. 17. ✆ **1/413-0236.** www.noiretlor.hu. Reservations recommended. Main courses 1,990 Ft–4,490 Ft. MC, V. Daily 11am–midnight. Tram: 4 or 6, Király.

Olíva Étterem és Pizzéria ★★★ ITALIAN When a restaurant serves excellent Italian food, but also has Hungarian items on the menu, it makes it difficult to pigeonhole it into a category. Walking into Olíva is like entering an old-fashioned Italian country farmhouse, with country-style plates and knick-knacks in shadowboxes decorating the walls and the red-checked tablecloths adding to the country charm. In spite of the busy large room, there is still a sense of coziness that envelops each table, blocking out the rest of the surroundings. My partner and I have returned here often, but this time specifically for a review. As in the past, the service was efficient throughout the evening. We shared a Caesar salad, which really was a meal in itself, but I had the gray cow steak smothered in onions with side order of steak potatoes. Ron had a pizza smothered in artichokes, olives and mushrooms. We were both satiated with the food and the service, but the decor really makes the meal special. At the end of the meal, we were given Limoncello, the Italian lemon liqueur, to end an enjoyable evening.

VI. Lázár u. 1. ✆ **1/312-0080.** Reservations recommended. Main courses 1,250 Ft–2,990 Ft; pizza 990 Ft–1,790 Ft. MC, V. Daily noon–midnight. Metro: Arany János (Blue line).

Pata Negra Tapas Bar ★★★ (Value) SPANISH I am confused as to how the name black foot or paw fits this establishment, but the food is too good to care about Spanish semantics. The space's *au courant* brick ceiling complements the colorful Spanish tiles that cover the wall behind the bar, along with rows and rows of wine bottles, like vino soldiers. Other walls are graced with Spanish prints between the oversize windows; Spanish ballads play softly in the background. However, the main attraction here is the menu; it is primarily a tapas restaurant with which you will not be disappointed. Tapas are appetizers, but many make them a full meal, which I did again by ordering three: garlic spinach with cream and Serrano ham; white beans with spinach and chorizo; and garlic chicken with hot peppers. All three were so delectable I was tempted to order more, but was dining alone. The service remains exemplary over the years. Due to the construction of the metro 4 line, which will continue for some years, this restaurant is hidden from view from the street, but is worth hunting for. There are many choices at the low end of the price range, but they also have some full meals.

IX. Kálvin tér 8 (where Ráday starts). ✆ **1/215-5616.** www.patanegra.hu. Reservations recommended. Main courses 850 Ft–2,200 Ft; tapas 350 Ft–1,950 Ft. No credit cards. Mon–Fri 11am–midnight, Sat–Sun noon–midnight. Metro: Kálvin tér (Blue line).

Pomo D'oro ★★★ ITALIAN   All palates lead to the power of the tomato in this restaurant. The menu treats us to a legend that goes like this: in the 16th and 17th centuries the tomato was thought to be an aphrodisiac used by alchemists in various curative potions. Menu items are not the typical Italian fare, thus I jumped at the chance to try the tortellini stuffed with pumpkin covered in a cream sauce flecked with spinach. My fellow diners tried the salmon ravioli with caviar cream sauce and green lasagna with beef. All three of us were self-congratulatory about our choices. The food was only usurped by the exemplary service. The two-level restaurant itself is massive and impressively made of walls of stone, divided into four sections on differing levels. The loft is above the pizza oven, so beware of heat.

V. Arany János u. 9. ✆ **1/302-6473.** www.pomodorobudapest.com. Reservations recommended. Main courses 1,990 Ft–5,990 Ft. Pizza 1390 Ft–2,790 Ft. MC, V. Mon–Fri 11am–midnight; Sat–Sun noon–midnight. Metro: Arany János u. (Blue line).

Shalimar ★★★ INDIAN   Many have walked right by this unpretentious, downstairs restaurant due to its small outdoor sign. Being among the first Indian restaurants in the city, it has reinvented itself a number of times, but it remains a perpetual award winner in Budapest culinary competitions. The menu features typical items from the northern Indian Mughlai cuisine. They are typically rich meat dishes in various sauces, grilled meats using an enormous array of spices cooked in a tandoor along with different breads. Decorated with false backlit stenciled windows, it maintains a fresh new appearance. We have been here so often over the years that we have sampled almost everything on the very extensive menu. Pork Vindiloo is served in lavish red gravy made with a coconut milk base. Chicken in spicy spinach with cheese is still one of my favorites. Order different naan breads to enrich your meal; they are baked in a tandoori clay oven, fired with charcoal. The portions may require you to ask for the balance to be wrapped to go. Fixed business lunch specials are available.

VII. Dob u. 50. ✆ **1/352-0305.** www.shalimar.hu. Reservations recommended. Main courses 680 Ft–3,690 Ft; business lunch special 1,100 Ft–1,300 Ft. AE, MC, V. Daily noon–4pm; 6pm–midnight. Tram: 4 or 6, Király u.

Spinoza Étterem ★★   This eclectic restaurant was opened by a Hungarian woman who had spent many years in the Netherlands, but who, on returning to Budapest, wanted to combine the Dutch and Jewish philosophical cultures for her restaurant located in the historic Jewish quarter. I tried the chicken breast with feta cheese served with tomato salsa, finding it moist, tangy and delicious. The marinaded goose breast with stewed plum sauce is another favorite. A pianist will entertain you while dining each evening from 7pm to 11pm; on Tuesdays and Fridays the music is available at lunchtime. The small cabaret theater in the back offers music and theatrical events on a regular basis. The schedule is posted in the window of the cafe. Every Friday night at 7pm, there is a Klezmer concert for 2,000 Ft or combined with dinner for 5,000 Ft.

VII. Dob u. 15. ✆ **1/413-7488.** www.spinoza.hu. Reservations recommended. Main courses 1,650 Ft–2,350 Ft. Weekday lunch specials 800 Ft. MC, V. Daily 11am–11pm. Bus: 74 to Dohány Synagogue, walk to Dob and turn right for one block.

Soul Café ★★★ INTERNATIONAL   Inside you will find a large room filled with tables, low lighting and warm-colored walls covered with carpet weavings in frames.

Soulful ambience. The summer months allow the expansion of this restaurant with tables along the side of the building in addition to a massive area across the street that fills quickly. I had the chicken stuffed with soft cheese blended with sun-dried tomatoes and olives over pasta. My partner had a pork medallion special of the day with sweet potato quiche. We competed in raving about our good fortune in our selections, offering frugal tastings to each other to prove our point, but it was a draw. The service was some of the best we have experienced in the city.

IX. Ráday u. 11–13. ✆ **1/217-6986.** www.soulcafe.hu. Reservations recommended. Main courses 1,600 Ft–3,350 Ft. AE, MC, V. Daily noon–1am. Metro Kálvin tér (Blue line).

Stex Ház ★★ ⟨**Value**⟩ INTERNATIONAL   Who wants to gamble eating at a casino? After being cajoled into eating here once by a group of people, I was so impressed with the food, I knew I had to return. With a rag-to-riches story on the cover of the menu, it is worth the read. Hungary for pizza, I had the Penelope with tomatoes, ham, onion, mushrooms, and hot pepperoni peppers. Ron choose a more traditional meal of turkey strips lightly battered, served with a Greek salad and potatoes. The inside of the restaurant looks like a mini Viva Las Vegas, but not noisy enough to be disturbing; however, in agreeable weather, we always sit outside. Excellent service, good food, and fair prices were a real treat. Most items are at the lower range below.

VIII. József krt. 55–57. ✆ **1/318-5716.** www.stexhouse.hu. Reservations recommended. Main courses 1,150 Ft–3,790 Ft, pizza 1,250 Ft–1650 Ft. No credit cards. Mon–Sat 8am–4am, Sun 9am–2am. Kitchen closes at midnight. Tram: 4 or 6, Baross tér.

Taverna Dionysos ★★★ GREEK   You will feel like you have been transported to a Greek isle at this authentic-looking Greek tavern, located on Pest's Danube embankment. It serves all the typical Greek specialties you would expect if you were sitting in a Greek village tavern. The menu comprises an extensive fish selection, shrimp, lobster, as well as souvlakia, and other delicacies all in a Mediterranean environment. The restaurant is located in a typical Greek whitewashed building, and you are served on blue-and-white tablecloths. We have found the food here to be on par with what we had in Greece. The moussaka was superb with a creamy béchamel sauce. The Greek hamburger was oversized ground meat stuffed with feta cheese with a side of feta cheese. On a Wednesday night, it was surprising that the place was jam-packed with diners. Weather permitting, sidewalk dining overlooking the Danube is available, but call in advance to reserve.

V. Belgrád rakpart 16. ✆ **1/318-1222.** www.dionysos.hu. Reservations recommended. Main courses 2,050 Ft–13,980 Ft. MC, V. Daily noon–midnight. Metro: Ferenciek tere (Blue line).

Vista Café Restaurant ★★★ HUNGARIAN MODERN   This place is so convenient since it is right in the center of town. It serves hardy meals and is associated with the popular Vista travel agency across the street. The restaurant is airy, with high ceilings, and the works of local artists and special themes are eye-candy for the walls. The non-smoking section is far enough away from the smoking area to make a difference, something unusual in Hungary. I was in hog heaven when I received my crispy pork roast smothered in just as crispy onions and oven roasted potatoes. Another recommended option is chicken breast stuffed with plums and bacon. Sensational food, excellent presentation, first-rate service, but there is more. A pianist entertains daily from 6pm to 10pm. Internet-connected computers are free for restaurant guests.

VI. Paulay Ede 7. ✆ **1/268-0888.** www.vistacafe.hu. Reservations recommended. Main courses 1,250 Ft–3,930 Ft. AE, MC, V. Daily 11am–midnight. Metro: Deák tér (Red line).

Vörös Postakocsi Étterem ★★★ HUNGARIAN TRADITIONAL   The eclectic building on the very busy Ráday utca was built in 1876, where it once served as a coffeehouse. The restaurant opened in 1970, named after the Hungarian writer Gyula Krudy's book *The Red Post Coach,* which is on display in the entry. The restaurant reflects the tone of the novel with an early-20th-century feel inside with heavy dark furniture and old-fashioned wallpaper; it is like eating in a history lesson. Food selections embrace traditional as well as fresh new Hungarian recipes. As a starter, the Hortobágyi pancakes, are stuffed with minced veal, topped with a rich dark paprika sour cream sauce. This starter is sufficient as a meal for a light eater, but I plunged on in the name of research and sampled the pork marinaded in beer, stuffed with salami served with red cabbage and minced potato, all of which put me in hog heaven. My fellow diner chose the turkey breast au gratin topped with the ever present bacon, sun dried tomatoes, and melted mozzarella cheese. A side dish of Caesar salad was close to perfection. Live music is provided daily, except Mondays. They will serenade you while you eat indoors or outside, thanks to the oversize windows that signal no air-conditioning inside. We found the service significantly improved over time. The wait staff was quick and efficient.

IX. Ráday u. 15. ℭ **1/217-6756.** www.vorospk.com. Main courses 1,300 Ft–3,90 Ft. AE, DC, MC, V. Daily 11:30am–midnight. Metro Kálvin tér (Blue line) or trams 47 or 49 to Kálvin tér.

Zorbas Taverna ★★★ GREEK   Although this Greek restaurant does not have a Danube view, you will feel like you are in a Greek village once inside. Typical rough whitewashed walls are heavily decorated in Greek regalia to transport you to the Mediterranean. This place is large enough to hold the population of a small island, but the service is quick and efficient. Excellent food with portions more substantial than we can finish makes this one of our favorites. My pork chops with garlic and lemon were perfectly spiced and moist. My companion's choice of moussaka was proclaimed the best meal she'd had in the city. There are a number of choices for seafood, lamb, poultry, and pork, although the beef is neglected, but not missed. Most main dishes are entrees only, but the sides are reasonably priced. Friday nights you will be entertained by Greek music and dancing.

VI. Podmaniczky u. 18. ℭ **1/332-7900.** www.zorbastaverna.hu. Reservations recommended. Main courses 1,460 Ft–3,420 Ft. Mon–Sat 10am–midnight; Sun 10am–10pm. Tram: 4 or 6, Nyugati.

INEXPENSIVE

Arany Tálca Önkiszolgáló Étterem ★★ HUNGARIAN TRADITIONAL   No decoration to stimulate your senses, there is full reliance on the food to do so. And it will in this cafeteria restaurant. Take a tray, look over the selections, see what looks good, and go back to point to it. Both locations fill up at lunchtime, but it is usually local workers, so they don't linger long. Tables are easy to come by. Portions fill the plate; choices rotate daily. If they have chicken paprikash, I recommend it. It is the best and cheapest I have had in the city. At the Dohány location only, very near the synagogue, there is a 10% discount on all food after 4pm. Side dishes run from 200 Ft to 320 Ft.

VII. Dohány u. 3. No phone. Reservations not accepted at either location. Main courses 540 Ft–660 Ft. No credit cards. Mon–Fri 8am–6pm. Metro: Astoria (Red line). VII. Wesselényi u. 35 corner of Akácfa u. No phone. Mon–Fri 9am–7pm.

Bombay Express ★★ INDIAN   Once a very expensive but beautiful Indian restaurant was at this address, but it was transformed into an Indian fast-food restaurant. Three years later, this cafeteria-style restaurant has successfully found its niche. Owned by the people who own Salaam Bombay, the food is perfect for a budget diner; the portions are generous. With your tray in hand, you have choices of tandoori wraps with chicken, mincemeat, or vegetables. There are express meals with chicken, beef, lamb, or vegetables and they come with rice and naan bread. Samosas and potato bombas are also available. Nothing is overly spicy, so ask for hot sauce if you want some fire in your food. I have tried most of the menu with enjoyment. You won't leave here hungry or broke.

VI. Andrássy út 44. (℃) **1/332-8363.** www.bombayexpress.hu/galleryhun.htm. Reservations not accepted. Wraps 690 Ft–890 Ft; main courses 1,200 Ft–1,800 Ft. No credit cards. Daily noon–midnight. Metro: Oktogon (Yellow line).

Café Alibi ★★ (Value) INTERNATIONAL

Sitting on a corner across from the university for law is this pearl of a cafe with its limited food menu. Inside is cozy and meant to have an old-cafe feel with the old-fashioned chairs, the streetlamp lighting, and the prints hanging on the wall. The antique cash register adds to the flavor of the place. Personally run by the owner, Laszlo Vagi with an efficient staff, it continues to thrive by accommodating guest wishes whenever possible. I stopped by with a student for the tuna salad, which was quite a large and tasty serving. Breakfast is served until noon, and then the lunch menu starts. Best of all, if you sign up for their newsletter on their website, you can get a code for a free coffee. Special wine dinners for a fixed price are also available at different times; the notices come in the e-mails or check the website for dates.

V. Egyetem tér 4. (℃) **1/317-**4209. www.cafealibi.hu. Breakfast 790 Ft–1,690 Ft; main courses 1,290 Ft–1,890 Ft. No credit cards. Restaurant Mon–Sat 8am–10pm. Metro: Kálvin tér (Blue line).

Club 93 ★★ (Value) ITALIAN

This gay-friendly restaurant welcomes all hungry diners with abundant portions of food whether you choose pizza or another dish. I have enjoyed their pizza, but a real treat is the *Gnocchi di Toscana* where the gnocchi pasta is smothered with smoked ham, bacon, and onion all coated with a cheese sauce. My other favorite is the broccoli-bacony chicken. Tender, but not mushy broccoli is stuffed in a chicken breast and then wrapped in bacon, keeping it all moist. Most of the seating in this tiny place is upstairs where the smokers gravitate. Downstairs has minimal seating, but in suitable weather, the outdoor seating is prime real estate. In winter months at the owners' whim, they shorten their opening hours to 5pm to midnight.

VIII. Vas u. 2. (℃) **30/630-7093** (mobile phone only). www.club93pizza.hu. Reservations not accepted. Pizza 1,300 Ft–1,790 Ft; main courses 1,390 Ft–1,790 Ft. No credit cards. Daily 11:30am–midnight in summer, winter hours fluctuate. Metro: Blaha Lujza (Red line).

Főzelékfalo Ételbar ★★ (Value) HUNGARIAN TRADITIONAL

Don't expect to sit down and be served. You have to go to the counter and order. No worries, they attract plenty of tourists, so they do go the mile to help you without using English. This tiny restaurant is so popular with Hungarians there is a line out the door at lunchtime. *Főzelék* is a cross between a soup and a stew, though it is puréed, and this wisp of a restaurant has been voted the best in the city by all who have been polled. *Főzelék* is a national dish and treasure, so if you have not tried it, you have not officially been to Hungary. Inside there are only bar tables and stools, but if the weather is good, the sidewalk will be packed with tables. Take it to go if you have to; they will give you a spoon. The blend comes in a number of varieties, but green pea and potato are the most popular. If you want something heartier, they sell fried chicken too. This is the cheapest, filling meal you will find in the city. If you still want some dessert, they serve *palacsinta* (Hungarian crepes).

VI. Nagymező 18. No phone. Reservations not accepted. Main courses 380 Ft–580 Ft. Salads 180 Ft per dkg. No credit cards. Mon–Fri 9am–10pm; Sat 10am–9pm; Sun 11am–6pm. Metro: Opera (Yellow line).

Frici Papa Kifőzés ★ ⓥ**Value** HUNGARIAN TRADITIONAL   This used to be a restaurant with attitude, not for the decor, but from the staff. In the past, they could be downright surly, but on recent visits, they have actually been pleasant. Honestly, it detracts from the fun of eating here. This is a plain, down-home place with no frills and the prices reflect it. The daily offerings from soup to desserts and everything in between are posted with signs hanging on a pegboard near the front windows. When they run out of something, it comes off the board. The regular menu is limited and nothing is translated into English. Everything is a la carte, even ketchup will cost you extra. The portions are humongous, cheap, and tasty. We had the chicken breast and a roasted pork dish, both on the board that day, supplying a good hearty Hungarian meal. Lunch or an early dinner is best for the full day's selection. After 7pm, you are taking your chances. Now take a deep breath and order everything you think you translated correctly and hope for the best. This is a fun adventure in eating.

VI. Király u. 55. No phone. Reservations not accepted. Main courses 649 Ft–699 Ft. Cash only. Mon–Sat 11am–9pm. Tram: 4 or 6, Király u.

Govinda Vegetariánus Étterem ★★★ ⓥ**Value** INDIAN   Once you descend the steep steps to enter this restaurant, you will find a simply decorated ultraclean restaurant that is run by the local Hari Krishna-type group here in the city. Eliminate any negative thoughts; proceeds from this restaurant support their efforts in feeding the homeless of the city through a monthly food giveaway. Delicious vegetarian food is served in a tranquil, smoke-free environment with Indian gods and goddesses looking over your shoulder. As a self-service system, you can choose from different dishes, each at a set price, or from two daily menu options written on a blackboard. For others, there is a small or large sampler platter. Items might include stuffed squash with Indian ragout and brown rice; or a potato-pumpkin casserole with garlic Roquefort sauce. Unless you have a really healthy appetite, I recommend the small sampler which is ample. Seating is plentiful, but this place can be packed at lunchtime on weekdays, so you may have to wait in line. The staff speaks English and will explain each dish. There is a small yoga center and shop in back, stocked with New Age and Eastern literature, clothes, candles, and incense.

V. Vigyázó Ferenc u. 4. ⓒ **1/269-1625.** www.govinda.hu. Reservations not accepted. Main courses 220 Ft–650 Ft; small sampler meal 1,550 Ft; large sampler meal 1,850 Ft; student menu 760 Ft. Cash only. Mon–Fri 11:30am–8pm, Sat noon–8pm. Metro: Kossuth Lajos tér (Red line).

Hanna's Orthodox Restaurant JEWISH   If you happen to be at the Orthodox Kazinczy Synagogue, you will see signs for this restaurant next to two oversize metal doors with a buzzer you push to be let into the courtyard. Note that this is the back entrance. One of two kosher restaurants in the city, this one has a large room with simple tables and chairs that lack any decoration. Serving good kosher meals at low prices is the utmost concern, not making this a place to linger about. On the wall is a framed certificate of kosher authenticity. We have had a number of guests who have reported complete satisfaction with the food. The other positive is that the cashier will sometimes try to get someone to open the synagogue for viewing in the afternoons if it is not already open—an added benefit to having a meal here.

VII. Dob u. 35. ⓒ **1/342-1072.** Main courses 1,100 Ft–1,900 Ft. Sun–Fri 8am–10pm, Sat 11am–3:30pm. No credit cards. Bus: 74 to Kazinczy Synagogue.

Hummus Bar ★★★ ⓥ**Value** VEGETARIAN   This is the most popular hummus and falafel bar in the city and the proof is that they now have three locations. You can eat in, seating is upstairs, or you can take it with you. Either way, the food is delicious and very

inexpensive. Several varieties of hummus and salads are offered to go with the falafel.
While you are waiting, don't be surprised if you are offered some tea or samples of other
items. All of the limited choices are made fresh. At V. Alkotmány u. 20 ✆ **70-932-8029**
(mobile phone only) open daily 10am to 10pm, you will find the same veggie offerings
as the premier restaurant. Vegetarians, close your eyes for a minute, because the third
location also serves meat (VI. Október 6 u. 19, ✆ **1/354-0108**). The hours are daily
11:30am to 10:30pm.

VII. Kertesz u.39. ✆ **06/70-378-7293** (mobile phone only). Reservations not accepted. Menu items 1,200
Ft–1,800 Ft. No credit cards. Daily noon–11pm. Tram: 4 or 6, Király u.

Kőleves Vendéglő (Stone Soup) ★★★ (Finds) HUNGARIAN MODERN   If you
remember the story of *Stone Soup*, the playfulness of this establishment will charm you with
light fixtures made of inverted glasses and cheese graters, the pieces of contemporary art
that grace the walls, and the soup bowls adorning the bar. But the real delight comes with
the food, made from preservative-free ingredients. The menus are printed on individual
disposable sheets, because the menu changes monthly. I love the corn soup with chilis; it is
thick and tangy. A reoccurring offering is chicken with Roquefort dressing, which is
delightful. Some dishes are a la carte with a suggested side dish that is extra, at 360 Ft to
400 Ft, but others are complete meals. Either way, it is still a bargain for such delicious
treats. They have carved a spot for themselves with a loyal clientele, so join the fun.

VII. Kazinczy u. 35. ✆ **1/322-1011.** www.koleves.com. Reservations recommended. Main courses 1,350
Ft–3,560 Ft. AE, MC, V. Daily noon–midnight. Close to Dohány Synagogue on the corner of Kazinczy u.
and Dob u.

6

Nagyi Nonstop Palacsintázója ★★ (Value) HUNGARIAN TRADITIONAL
Whether you are having a snack attack at 3am, craving something sweet, or wanting a
full inexpensive meal, this is your place. *Palacsintá* is the Hungarian version of crepes. At
this restaurant, you can find fixed menus of three or four crepes as well as individual
crepes in savory or sweet categories. Crepes are made within the hour and are prepared
in front of you. It is the perfect place for a quick snack, a budget dinner, or to refuel after
leaving the clubs. There are multiple locations; the two most popular are on Batthyány
tér and Petófi Sandor utca.

I. Batthyány tér 5 and V. Petófi Sandor u. 17–19. No phone. www.nagyipali.hu. Reservations not accepted.
175 Ft–990 Ft. No credit cards. Daily 24 hr. Metro: Batthyány (Red line) and Deák tér (Yellow line).

Napos Oldal Café ★★ VEGETARIAN   This shop has attracted my attention for
years, but I only seem to remember it when writing this book. It's a combo bioproduct
store, small restaurant, and tea and coffee cafe all lumped into one cute little shop. But this
is not to say it is cramped. The biostore section sells a range of goods from soap to shampoo
on the right side of the store, while on the left, the display case of fresh salads and baked
goods, including organic and sugar-free pastries, will grab your attention. Do some shopping, have a bite to eat, and relax over a cup of tea, coffee, freshly squeezed juice, or homemade ginger ale, before continuing on with your day. The staff here is friendly and warm
adding to the general-store feeling of the place. Y'all come back now, ya hear?

VI. Jókai u. 7. ✆ **1/354-0048.** www.naposoldal.com. Daily menu 1,200 Ft–1,300 Ft; salads 290 Ft–350 Ft
per 10dg (3.5 oz.); drinks 110 Ft–450 Ft. Mon–Fri 10am–9pm, Sat 10am–2pm; biostore Mon–Thurs
10:30am–6pm, Fri 10:30am–5pm, Sat 10am–1pm. Metro: Opera (Yellow line).

Önkiszolgáló vendéglő ★★ HUNGARIAN TRADITIONAL   Only open for
lunches, this buffet-style restaurant is popular with residents and workers on Castle Hill.
The selections change daily, but the portions are bountiful and inexpensive. It is a bit

difficult to find since there is no exact address, so go to Hess András tér 4 where you will find the Fortuna Passage. Pass the restaurant on the ground floor, find the second wooden door on the left side where you will see the sign for this restaurant. Take the stairs up one flight. It is worth seeking out for a hearty lunch.

I. Hess András tér 4. No phone. 500 Ft–800 Ft. No credit cards. Mon–Fri 11am–2pm. Bus: 16 from Deák tér or 16a from Moszkva tér.

Pink Cadillac ★★ ITALIAN   Who would have thought to name an Italian restaurant Pink Cadillac? But it seems to have worked. This is one of the longest-surviving restaurants of the ever trendy Ráday utca. After a number of remodels, it looks fresh, but retains some '50s flare of tackiness with the half-pink Cadillac crashing through the wall. The tiled areas on the walls also add that yesteryear flavor. The inside seating fills fast due to the free Wi-Fi. In summer, you will want to sit outside, where mists of water are lightly sprayed into the air to cool down the temperature. We love the table-side buzzer for calling the waitstaff, who responds almost instantly. What has not changed over the course of time is the quality of the food, which is fantastic. Pizza is the specialty, but a full range of Italian selections are also excellent choices. I tried the carmiano shrimp in garlic butter with creamed cheese sauce over spaghetti. This lived up to their motto of "good mood food." It is a repeat selection for the future.

IX. Ráday u. 22. ✆ 1/216-1412. www.pinkcadillac.hu. Reservations recommended. Main courses 1,240 Ft–2,440 Ft; pizza 1,460 Ft–2,310 Ft. AE, MC, V. Mon–Fri 11am–midnight; Sat–Sun noon–midnight. Metro: Kálvin tér (Blue line).

Red Pepper ★★ HUNGARIAN MODERN   This long, half-barrel-shaped basement restaurant with rounded brick ceilings continuing for half of the wall on one side, is minimally decorated. The large curved windows on the street side, allow light to pour in during the day, but the fashionable lighting is sometimes too much illumination the rest of the time. Intimate space is not what this restaurant is known for, so they have to rely heavily on their food offerings, and this is where they should excel. Chicken breast stuffed with smoked cheese and broccoli was a tempting offering for a pleasant marriage of flavors. The generous portion of two chicken breasts with the thick cut French fries were appealing both visually and in taste, but the chicken could have been a little warmer to heat up the broccoli. The service people are attentive and friendly, but being a cellar restaurant, you will want to avoid it in the hot months. There is no air-conditioning and it gets hot and stuffy.

XIII. Visegrádi u. 2. ✆ 1/352-1394. www.redpepper.cjb.hu. Reservations recommended. Main courses 1,050 Ft–2,790 Ft. MC, V. Mon–Sat 10am–midnight. Metro: Nyugati (Blue line).

TreffOrt Vendéglő ★★ (Finds) HUNGARIAN TRADITIONAL   Okay, let's take the phrase "old school" to a new level, since this cafeteria is located in the lobby of Eötvös Loránd University, lovingly referred to as ELTE, one of the oldest universities in central Europe. This building is new, so no worries. Not only is the food delicious, but you will get an abundant amount of it. This is a hotspot for local businesses, so from noon to 1pm there is a long line waiting for gastronomic tastes just like mama makes. With two lunch specials, either a soup and entree or an entree and dessert set at 550 Ft–630 Ft, it is not difficult to understand why. Get there early or late for a shorter wait or to get your meal to go and then head to a park to eat. When you get to the address, there are two oversized green doors. Bypass the restaurant on the right-hand side and walk straight back. You cannot miss the glass walls with the food service behind it.

VIII. Rákóczi út. 5. No phone. Reservations not accepted. Main courses 490 Ft–5,90 Ft. No credit cards. Mon–Fri 11am–3:30pm. Metro: Astoria (Red line).

VERY EXPENSIVE

Gundel ★ (Overrated) HUNGARIAN TRADITIONAL   Budapest's fanciest, most famous, probably most expensive, and most overrated restaurant, Gundel reopened in 1992. It was sold to the Danubius Hotel Group about 4 years ago and, according to insider information, it has gone downhill since then. The restaurant is the place for the Hungarian elite and other dignitaries to see and be seen dining in the opulent dining room adorned with 19th-century paintings. Lamb and wild-game dishes are house specialties. The Gundel menu also includes four sets of gourmet choices with fixed prices, but menu items do not include the 12% service charge. Jackets are required for men. There are many other choices in the city for excellent meals at a lower cost. For a Gundel experience try their more moderate restaurant Bagolyvár below.

XIV. Állatkerti út 2. ✆ 1/468-4040. www.gundel.hu. Reservations recommended; jackets required for men in the evening. Main courses 3,990 Ft–10,620 Ft; dinner prix-fixe menu 22,000 Ft–39,900 Ft; lunch prix-fixe menu 3,800 Ft–5,900 Ft; Sun brunch buffet 5,800 Ft; children 5–15 2,900 Ft; children under 5 free. AE, DC, MC, V. Mon–Sat noon–4pm and 6:30pm–11pm; Sun 11:30am–3pm (brunch) and 6:30pm–11pm. Metro: Hősök tere (Yellow line).

MODERATE

Bagolyvár (Owl Castle) ★★★ (Kids) HUNGARIAN TRADITIONAL   Bagolyvár is a less expensive alternative to Gundel. Both were created by the same people, but the prices here are reasonable. Housed in a Transylvanian manor house, the idea, as sexist as it may be, is that you are dining in your mother or grandmother's place; therefore, you are served only by women who care for your gastronomic needs. The size of the room negates any romantic notions of family-style intimacy, but the female waitstaff does provide excellent service; the female kitchen people do produce excellent food. The only male in attendance is the one playing the cimbalom each evening. Dining on the terrace, surrounded by the edges of the City Park, was an escape from the city. The Bagolyvár menu is limited; a dozen main courses are supplemented by daily fixed-menu three-course meals. I went traditional this time having the duck leg with red cabbage and potatoes; my partner chose the salmon with sorrel sauce with sliced potatoes. Not being familiar with sorrel, he was pleasantly amazed at the sensory awaking freshness it added to the salmon and to our gastronomic palate. We rounded off the evening with a fresh fruit salad and a walnut *palacsinta*. I left wondering why we don't treat ourselves to dinner here more often.

XIV. Állatkerti út 2. ✆ 1/468-3110. www.bagolyvar.com. Reservations recommended. Main courses 2,670 Ft–4,230 Ft. AE, DC, MC, V. Daily noon–11pm. Metro: Hősök tere (Yellow line).

Paprika Vendéglő ★★★ (Finds) HUNGARIAN TRADITIONAL   If you want to escape to the Hungarian countryside to sample the cuisine without leaving the city, this is the place. Still my number one favorite place in the city, set out in an old-fashioned earthen oven, the oversize cooking utensils, and the log-cabin interior will mellow you in rustic comfort. The chairs and benches are also made of logs adding to the country ambience. Let yourself go hog wild and try the roasted wild boar with brandy or saddle of deer. My personal favorite had gotten me into a rut as I continually order the leg of goose Vadazsdi style, oven roasted served with red cabbage and parsley potatoes. Not feeling so adventurous? No problem, they have other dishes to choose from on a liberal menu. The Hortobagy pancakes are filled with minced meat and the sauce is superb. No matter what

Uncork, Swirl, Sniff, Taste: Hungarian Wine Culture

The wines of Spain, South Africa, and Hungary have one thing in common: governmental changes thwarted their production and development for periods of time. Before Communist times, Hungarian wines were developing into a mature market, but one that never reached much beyond its borders. During the politically difficult times, winemakers' efforts were stomped and trampled and only the cheapest and most insignificant wines could be produced and mostly sold only to other Soviet bloc countries. The few wines that did make the export list were the insignificant offerings that did nothing to put Hungary on the winemaking radar for sommeliers. When the climate changed in the early 1990s, the winemakers found themselves starting from the beginning, not only creating new varieties of grapes, but developing their wines, and struggling for international recognition to abolish the reputation of the past.

One of the major achievements of the industry was the creation of an annual festival to bring attention to the wines of the country. If you are a wine buff or if you just like to drink it, you will surely want to plan your trip around the second week of September when Budapest celebrates the first wheat harvest and the largest wine festival of the year held atop Castle Hill. The celebration begins with the Harvest Parade, and people from different regions of the country (dressed in traditional clothing) dance, play folk music, and sell their crafts. Each year, a celebrated wine-producing country is invited to share the spotlight with Hungarian winegrowers and their many varieties of wines. Check the website (www.aborfesztival.hu) for exact dates; it changes year to year.

The winemakers created the foundation Hungarian Viti- and Vini-cultural Public Benefit Company, a trade group to market their wines by bringing wineries to international competitions as well as hosting them. In June 2007, they

you order, the portion will be generous; don't hesitate to ask to have leftovers wrapped to take home. There are separate dining areas for smoking and nonsmoking.

VII. Dozsa Gyorgy 72. **①** **06/70-574-6508** (mobile phone only). www.paprikavendeglo.hu. Reservations recommended. Main courses 1,550 Ft–3,900 Ft. AE, MC, V. Daily 11am–11pm. Metro: Hősők tere (Yellow line) 4¹/₂ blocks from Heroes' Square.

Trófea Grill Étterem ★★★ (Finds) HUNGARIAN TRADITIONAL   Prepare to starve yourself the whole day before heading off to this restaurant and you will not be sorry you did. The interior is decorated like an old hunting lodge, filled with cozy booths and tables. This is the best all-you-can-eat restaurant in the city providing a selection from more than 100 different dishes. Once the waiter brings your drinks, you are on your own, but he will return to clear all dirty dishes or replenish the drinks. Start with a choice of five soups, and then work your way over to the numerous salads, followed by a choice of six different entrees and the vegetable bar. If the prepared entrees are not to your liking, move on over to the section of marinaded meats and bring them to the grill to be cooked while you wait. Save some room though, because there are about 15 desserts waiting to be sampled. There is more: it is all you can drink, too. You have choices of tap hosted the 30th Congress and 5th General Assembly of the Organization of Internationale de la Vigne et du Vin (OIV), where 500 member organizations converged on the city. This and other international events bring further exposure of Hungarian wines to international audiences.

For a Hungarian wine education, be sure to consider one of the many wine tours offered by Wine Time. See Chapter 7, p. 157 for more information.

Wine Primer: Hungary has 22 wine regions and cultivates more than 93 varieties of wine grapes, producing the full spectrum of reds, whites, roses, and sparkling wines. Serious wine enthusiasts will know that varietals indigenous to Hungary are referred to as Hungaricum and are only grown here. Some such varieties are Budai Zöld, Furmint, Juhfark, Hárslevelű, Kadarka, Kéknyelu, and Királyleányka.

Best Regions for Whites: White wine is still the major product of Hungarian wineries with each region producing its own distinctive variety. Somló produces some of the country's best whites, which are usually acidic. Tokaj produces world-famous dessert wines under the name "Tokaj." Tokaj's vineyard area is strictly delimited, less than 5,463 hectares (13,500 acres) in 26 villages with well-defined regulations going back to the 16th century. It was declared a UNESCO World Heritage Site in 2002. The Balaton regions, particularly Badacsony, make excellent whites, as does Gyöngyös in the Mátraalja region.

Best Regions for Reds: Hungary has been producing increasingly greater amounts of reds due to international demands. Villány has achieved recognition as the Bordeaux of Hungary. Szekszárd, Sopron, and Eger also produce fine reds. But great reds also come from regions better known for their whites, like Balatonlelle.

beer, house wine, champagne, sodas, coffee, espresso drinks, and tea. Everything is included in one price if you don't order wine off the wine list or from the new cocktail bar. Each Sunday, a playroom is set up for children with qualified kindergarten teachers supervising. Note: there are four locations with the same name, but they are owned by different companies. This location is the only one we recommend.

XIV. Erzsébet Királyné útja 5. (✆ **1/251-6377.** www.trofeagrill.com. Reservations recommended. Lunch Mon–Fri 2,999 Ft; dinner Mon–Thurs 3,999 Ft; dinner Fri and all day Sat–Sun or holidays 4,599 Ft. Half-price for children up to 150cm (59 in.). No credit cards. Mon–Fri noon–midnight; Sat 11:30am–midnight; Sun 11:30am–8:30pm. Playroom Sun 11:30am–5pm. Metro: Mexikói (Yellow line).

INEXPENSIVE

Café Csiga (Finds) HUNGARIAN TRADITIONAL   Owned by an Irish expat, this small cafe is the perfect hiding place for a relaxing cafe latte or an unhurried lunch, where you can sit with your book for hours. Set back on a corner off of a square, it is a bit difficult to find as a metro 4 station is under construction the block in front of it. However, the laidback atmosphere, the country-style tables and chairs, and the funky artwork on the walls draw us back repeatedly. We have eaten from the ever-changing menu, so I hesitate to make suggestions here. This restaurant does a good catering business, so the menu for those events are the daily offerings written on the blackboard in Hungarian only. The coffee and even the latte is served hot, which are bonus points in my regard. What the staff lack in English skills, they make up for in friendliness.

VIII. Vásár u. 2. ☎ **1/210-0885.** www.cafecsiga.org. Reservations not accepted. Menu items 1,500 Ft–2,600 Ft. Daily 11am–1am. Kitchen closes at midnight. Tram: 4 or 6, Rákóczi tér. Hidden behind Metro 4 construction.

4 CENTRAL BUDA

EXPENSIVE

Hemingway ★★★ (**Moments**) HUNGARIAN MODERN   You will feel like you are escaping the city when visiting this restaurant next to a small lake with plenty of trees. Opened 9 years ago, it has gained in popularity year after year making reservations well in advance a necessity. The interior of the venue always makes us feel like we have joined Hemingway in one of his favorite Spanish getaways; the room is open and airy. Most of the tables sit on a platform, with the nonsmoking section in another room. The piano and bass duo adds to the relaxing Casablanca atmosphere with the Latin music. It may seem contradictory that the cuisine is Hungarian, but the fusion of food and atmosphere blend once you take your first bite. Try either of the indigenous Hungarian fares; the famous Mangalica pork is served as a crispy knuckle with cabbage noodles baked in freshly made strudel and fried onion strands. The most expensive menu item is the Hungarian Grey beef served as a Chateaubriand with tomato-bacon steak potato. A sommelier can assist in choosing the perfect wine to accompany your meal; the waiter service is superior. In fine weather, reserve a table outside on the terrace overlooking the water.

XI. Kosztolányi D. tér 2, Feneketlen tó. ☎ **1/381-0522.** www.hemingway-etterem.hu. Reservations recommended. Main courses 1,980 Ft–8,900 Ft. AE, DC, MC, V. Mon–Sat noon–midnight. Bus: 7 toward Buda from Ferenciek tér to Feneketlen tó, a small "lake." Trams: 19 or 49 to Kosztolányi Dezső tér.

MODERATE

Angelika Kaveház és Étterem ★★ HUNGARIAN MODERN   Angelika is housed in a historic building next to St. Anne's Church and was once part of the church's ministerial buildings on Buda's Batthyány tér. Better known as a place for drinks and pastries on a summer's day, their multilevel terrace has perfect views of Parliament across the Danube. Inside you will find extra-large rooms where smokers and nonsmokers are truly segregated. Each room has Art Deco love seats and well-padded individual chairs to match in blue, maroon, and beige. The menu has expanded over time. I enjoyed the pork chops with cheese and beer sauce served with mashed potatoes and Roquefort salad; however the pork with BBQ sauce was appealing, the meat was mixed with a lot of bone. The vegetable soufflés served with it were a pleasant change of pace for a vegetable side dish.

I. Batthyány tér 7. ☎ **1/201–0668.** www.angelikacafe.hu. Main courses 1,090 Ft–3,990 Ft. MC, V. Daily 9am–midnight. Metro: Batthyány tér (Red line).

Szent Jupát ★ (**Finds**) HUNGARIAN TRADITIONAL   My guess is that St. Jupát has something to do with fishermen. Along with the rustic wood booths with tables, there stands a life-size wood-carved statue bringing back childhood memories of the boxes of frozen fish sticks. That, and the fish dishes, was yet another clue to the restaurant's namesake. The menu has shrunk since the last visit, but the portions were amply filled with starches. I had pork that looked like it had been run over by a steamroller, it was so thin, but topped with mushrooms, two slices of ham, and melted cheese. To top it off, add to this new potatoes and rice as the additions. The other choice, equally disappointing, was chicken stuffed with ewe cheese, but there was so little cheese, stuffed is a hyperbole. Leave your cholesterol counter at home.

II. Dékán u. 3 (corner of Retek u.). ℂ **1/212-2923.** www.stjupat.hu. Reservations recommended. Main courses 1,490 Ft–3,590 Ft. No credit cards. Thurs–Mon noon–6am. Metro: Moszkva tér (Red line).

Tabáni Terasz ★★★ HUNGARIAN TRADITIONAL   The last time I reviewed this restaurant, I dined outside and had to sneak a peak in. This time, it was the reverse. Inside you will find different small rooms each with only a few tables and chairs so as not to overcrowd the room, while at the same time oozing with warm feelings of visiting a distant relative's home. Decorated with wall hangings, some paintings, and other regional touches, it is branded with personality. The dishes are all prepared with a variety of vegetables, which is unusual for Hungarian cuisine. Dishes are the traditional fare, heaping portions. Gnocchi with turkey, bacon, and slices of Parmesan was covered in a mild, but savory white sauce encouraging all flavors to meld to perfection. Turkey stuffed with goose liver was enjoyed by my dining companion; it was served with mashed potatoes and onions. It is a bit difficult to get to from the Pest side, but worth the effort.

I. Apród utca 10. ℂ **1/201-1086.** www.tabaniterasz.hu. Main courses 2,500 Ft–4,700 Ft. MC, V. Daily noon–midnight. Bus: 86 or tram 18 to Döbrentei tér.

INEXPENSIVE

Eden ★ (Finds) VEGETARIAN   Vegans can celebrate for this historic building houses the first and only vegan restaurant in Buda. The building was restored in 2001 and this vegan buffet restaurant opened. All ingredients are natural and fresh without any coloring, additives, or preservatives. After making your selection from the limited offerings, you have the choice of sitting in the charming country-cozy dining room or in the atrium garden. The food is quite tasty, so meat will not be missed. Their selection of 12 juices freshly squeezed from fruits or vegetables will quench anyone's thirst. When you order, take note that the price for salad is by weight and the drinks are by volume.

I. Iskola street 31, Batthyányi sq. ℂ **06/20-337-7575** (mobile phone only). www.edenetterem.hu. 590 Ft–890 Ft. Cash only. Sun 11am–9pm; Mon–Thurs 7am–9pm; Fri 7am–6pm; Sat closed. Metro: Batthyányi (Red line).

5 THE CASTLE DISTRICT

MODERATE

Rivalda Café & Restaurant ★★★ HUNGARIAN MODERN   The building has much history to tell, once being a monastery and later a theater with a casino in the 17th century. In the summer months, you will be pleased to be seated in the huge courtyard with wicker tables and chairs, hurricane lights, and either a pianist or violinist with a saxophonist serenading diners while the stars shine in the sky. Peeking inside, we found the interior to be pleasantly decorated with Impressionist scenes from theater productions, actual theater lighting directed at the small stage at the end of the room, and gossamer hanging lucidly from the ceiling. Rivalda has a simple, but varied menu. I tried the hazelnut mozzarella on a bed of greens. The Mediterranean chicken stuffed with goat cheese, roasted peppers, and wrapped in bacon was excellent. Braised leg of goose with prune-infused cabbage, accompanied by bread pudding with sausage, was imaginative and worth the price. We three diners were pleased with our choices, the atmosphere was sensational and though fully booked, the service was excellent.

I. Szinház u. 5–9. ✆ **1/489-0236.** www.rivalda.net. Reservations recommended. Main courses 2,700 Ft–5,400 Ft. AE, MC, V. Daily 11:30am–11:30pm. Bus: 16 from Deák or Várbusz from Moszkva tér.

6 THE BUDA HILLS

MODERATE

Remiz ★★★ (Value) HUNGARIAN MODERN   Remiz is defined as the place where trams spend the night, and such is the location of this restaurant. It can be an adventure to get to from the city center, but you will be well rewarded, especially in summer. This is when they crank up the lava stone barbecue outside in the gazebo for their ultimate special dish, spare ribs. Unlike any we have ever tasted, the two extra large racks of ribs sans any sauce were incredibly meaty and flavorful. This dish unique to Hungarian menus has been perfected here, making it their hallmark dish. A sea of diners on the tree-and-umbrella-covered terrace with plates of ribs in front of them is a common occurance during the summer months. During the rest of the year, the tram-shaped restaurant, which is decorated with early-20th-century posters is the setting for delicious meals, but the ribs are what keep me returning for more.

II. Budakeszi út 5. ✆ **1/275-1396.** www.remiz.hu. Reservations recommended. Main courses 2,180 Ft–4,560 Ft. AE, DC, MC, V. Daily 9am–midnight. Bus: 22, three stops from Moszkva tér (departs from the bus stops by the 4 or 6 tram area).

Szép Ilona ★ HUNGARIAN TRADITIONAL   If you remember the fountain on the castle with King Matthias from the 15th century, who came across a maiden in the woods and then fell in love, you will recognize Ilona as the maiden. *Szép* means beautiful and as legend has it, this love tryst happened where this restaurant is now located. Once styled in Socialist-outdated, it has been completely revamped inside and out creating a romantic or relaxing dining experience. We were thrilled to see the changes when we brought our visiting friend. The food continues to be served in hearty, delicious portions. When weather permits, sit on the terrace. For a starter, I cannot resist the Hortobagy pancakes, meat wrapped in a thin crepe with a creamy paprika sauce poured over the top finished by a dollop of sour cream. The pork with Julienne vegetables and the pork with Hungarian noodles were tenderly cooked to perfection. Although located in a Buda neighborhood that is a bit of a trek to reach, the food is scrumptious and sitting under the trees is relaxing.

II. Budakeszi út 1–3. ✆ **1/275-1392.** Main courses 1,250 Ft–3,600 Ft. MC, V. Daily 11am–10pm. Bus: 22 from Moszkva tér.

7 COFFEEHOUSES: HISTORIC & TRADITIONAL

As part of the Austro-Hungarian empire, Budapest (just as in Vienna) developed a coffeehouse culture where people of like minds met to discuss politics, literature, or music.

Each coffeehouse has its own story as to which literary movement or political circles favored their establishment. More than one claims the legend that someone stole the keys to the front door to keep their favorite cafe from ever closing. During the Communist era, these traditions evaporated into history, though a few of the coffeehouses did survive those strained times. With full freedoms returned, some coffeehouses have been restored to their previous glory. Other more modern coffeehouses have sprung up to create a new legacy of java traditions; see "Coffeehouses: Modern & Fun," below.

All the classic coffeehouses offer a variety of traditional pastries and coffee, with pastries displayed in a glass case. Some also serve ice cream, while others offer bar drinks. As in restaurants, there is no need to rush; no one will push you out the door when you finish your drink or pastry.

Centrál Kávéház ★★★   Coffeehouse culture is ingrained in Budapest history; this coffeehouse is one of the historic places where writers and artists gathered. Today it is a perfect replica of the original establishment, which opened in 1887. Although the restaurant served meals as well, the menu is limited, thus its reputation is best known as a coffeehouse. Restored by one of Hungary's own millionaires, Imre Somodyt, to its former richness, it is a hotspot, not only for tourists, but also for locals. With its perfect location, it is always busy with a mix of tourists, businessmen, locals, and local celebrities coming in for a pastry or meal. When mellowing in this coffeehouse's calm green interior with lavishly attractive ceilings, and brass hanging lamps with glass shades, you feel transported to an earlier era while keeping a foot in the present by browsing the free copies of various newspapers over a coffee and a fresh croissant. A cup of coffee at Centrál will cost you 600 Ft to 1,000 Ft, add on a pastry ranging from 390 Ft to 900 Ft, and you have paid for the ambience but it is worth the price. If you order a *torta*, a piece of cake, after 10pm, you will receive a 30% discount on it.

V. Károlyi Mihály u. 9. ✆ 1/266-2110. www.centralkavehaz.hu. Main courses 2,300 Ft–3,900 Ft. AE, MC, V. Daily 8am–midnight. Metro: Ferenciek tere (Blue line).

Gerbeaud's (Overrated)   Perhaps the most famous of the Budapest coffeehouses, Gerbeaud's is more than likely the most overrated also. Founded in 1858, it has stood on its current spot since 1870. There is no denying that the exterior and interior are elegant and may transport you to times past—the late 19th century. However, the pastries and coffee are no better than many of the better shops in the city where prices are lower. The extravagant prices are for the window dressing, not the goods. Walk in, see the interior, say you've been there and leave. Coffees cost 680 Ft to 780 Ft, but add a pastry and you are looking at an additional 420 Ft to 1,100 Ft. From the looks of business when I am in the area, it seems others are thinking along the same line as I am.

V. Vörösmarty tér 7. ✆ 1/429-9000. www.gerbeaud.hu. AE, DC, DISC, MC, V. Daily 9am–9pm. Metro: Vörösmarty tér (Yellow line).

Lukács Cukrászda (Overrated)   After my last review, I received a harshly worded reprimand from the manager for stating this establishment was overpriced and having complained about not being able to get tap water with our coffee. He countered that the tap water was not "high enough quality to be served", but obviously the 1,100 Ft bottled water is fine. So with two friends in tow who did not know the past incident, I had two objective opinions to draw from. Each of us had a pastry and an espresso of some variety. At 1,500 Ft for a pastry, it may well be similar quality to Paris or Rome as the manager argued, but this is not Paris or Rome and definitely does not command the prices of those cities. The bill came to a little over 7,000 Ft, but we did get a glass of tap water and

Our Favorite Sweets

Hungarians love their sweets, as you will discover by all of the pastry shops and bakeries everywhere. There will be some type of confectionery to satisfy everyone. The cakes are much drier than most people are used to and they seem stale at first, but they aren't. Only the pastries with fruit or creams are likely to be moist.

Flódni is a central European layered pastry of apples, poppy seeds, and walnuts only available at **Café Noé,** Wesselényi u. 13 (© **1/321-7145**) as far as we know. They also have a selection of diabetic pastries.

Found only in Hungary, **Dobos torta** is a light chocolate layer cake with a caramelized frosting. Take the topping off before cutting into the cake and then eat the topping separately. **Ischler** dates back to Viennese times. It is two short-bread cookies with apricot jam filling, sometimes dipped in dark chocolate.

Meggyes rétes (*rétes* is a strudel) comes with sour cherries and is a traditional favorite as is the **Mákos rétes, Alma rétes** (apple), or my favorite **Szilva rétes** (plum) when in season. All of them have flaky pastry and are delicious snacks. The best we have had is from **Rétesvar** ★★★ at Balta köz 4 in the Castle Hill district.

Somlói galuska is a national treasure in the dessert world. See p. 25.

Kürtőskalács is an interestingly different honey bread. You can watch them wrap the dough around a cylindrical piece of wood shaped like an oversized rolling pin and bake it in an extremely hot oven. It's not available in regular shops or cafes, but readily available at festivals and craft fairs.

If you like cinnamon, Hungarian **cinnamon ice cream (fahej)** is unbeatable for flavor. And if you come across the rarest of its varieties, cinnamon rice ice cream *(fahejes rizs),* by all means try it. **Rizs** alone is also common in the summertime.

the service was good. Having to admit the pastries were delicious, we still could not justify the cost.

VI. Andrássy út 70. © **1/373-0407.** www.lukacscukraszda.com. AE, MC, V. Mon–Fri 8:30am–7pm, Sat 9am–7pm, Sun 9:30am–7pm. Metro: Vörösmarty u. (Yellow line and not to be confused with Vörösmarty tér, both are on this line).

Művész Kávéház ★ Diagonally across Andrássy út from the Opera House, Művész (artist) was one of Budapest's finer traditional coffeehouses, dating back to 1898. In the late part of 2008, they remodeled, but left some of the elegant interior of the long-gone past with marble tabletops, crystal chandeliers, and mirrored walls. Művész is still a casual place to just unwind. On offer are many of the traditional desserts such as *somlói galuska* and an ice-cream bar, but for my money, the orange chocolate cake bursts with a citrusy tang when combined with dark chocolate. The dessert display is now in the rear right of the dining room with prices from 550 Ft–690 Ft and coffee to wash it all down is 350 Ft–400 Ft. This room can get quite smoky at times, so the tables in the front room or on the street, weather permitting are a pleasant alternative.

VI. Andrássy út 29. © **1/352-1337.** www.muveszkavehaz.hu. Reservations not accepted. No credit cards. Daily 9am–11:45pm. Metro: Opera (Yellow line).

Rétesvar ★★★ (**Finds**) To say that this bakery has the absolute _rétes_ (strudel) we have ever had is no exaggeration. Warm out of the oven, the flaky pastry was just enough to hold the warm cheese filling inside. It is melt-in-your-mouth scrumptious. They have a variety of other _rétes_ and some other savory small pizza-type pastries. The place is small, though there are benches outside to sit and enjoy. It is a bit difficult to find. When you come to the nude woman fountain, the brick alleyway (_köz_) is immediately behind her. If you arrive at the little convenience store, you have passed it.

I. Balta köz 4. No phone. No credit cards. Daily 9am–8pm. Bus: 16A from Moszkva tér or no. 16 from Deák tér to Castle Hill. Funicular: From Clark Ádám tér to Castle Hill.

---

8 COFFEEHOUSES: MODERN & FUN

THE INNER CITY & CENTRAL PEST

Aztek Choxolat Café ★★★ (**Finds**) If you have seen the movie Chocolat and dreamed of finding a cafe where you could indulge in the hot chocolate served in the movie, you are in for one extraordinary treat. Being such a small place, you would never expect it to be a chocoholic's fantasyland, with a hot chocolate called Secret of the Mayas with a blend of six herbs and spices mixed in hot molten chocolate, my personal favorite. For the less adventurous, there is chocolate with sour cherry and coriander; chocolate with amaretto, ginger, and nutmeg; and 10 other combinations. If your taste buds run more to java than chocolate, there are treats in store for you also. The coffees come in 20 combinations, many that the big chains have not yet discovered, but also in three sizes. If you supersize it here, you will be floating out. In agreeable weather, they have four tables in the passageway; otherwise, you will have to scramble for one of the three tables inside. And did I mention that all of their spices can be bought mixed for 400 Ft a bag to be added to your own cocoa when you return home? They also sell pralines in imaginative flavors, beautiful designs, and placed in a box ready for gift giving. You can enter the short passageway from either street, but keep your eyes open, it is sometimes easily missed.

V. Karoly korut 22 or Semmelweiss u. 19. ✆ **1/266-7113.** Hot chocolate 490 Ft–810 Ft; coffee 310 Ft–810 Ft; pastries 200–260 Ft. MC, V. Mon–Fri 7am–7pm; Sat 9am–2pm. Metro: Deák Ferenc tér.

Café Noé ★★★ For a delectable pastry treat called flódni this small pastry shop is the only place to find it. Flódni is an old Eastern European Jewish traditional layered pastry with apple, poppy seed, walnuts, and plum jam. Every pastry we have sampled has been fresh and delectable. A rarity in Hungary, they also have diabetic pastry and homemade ice-cream selections. The regular ice cream is also homemade. Order a coffee and wander upstairs to their funky nonsmoking cafe area and bring your laptop, the Wi-Fi is free at both locations. They have a second location called the Bulldog Cukrászda. You can also order a custom cake from their website and have it delivered to someone special in Budapest; if you need my address, drop me a line.

VII. Wesselényi u. 13. ✆ **1/787-3842.** www.torta.hu. AE, MC, V. Mon–Thu 10am–7pm; Fri 10am–5pm. Or Bulldog Cukrászda V. Veres Pálne u. 31 Mon–Fri 10am–6pm.

Fröhlich Kóser Cukrászda ★ KOSHER If you want your baked goods kosher or you just want them tasty, this is the place to go. It is a basic type of bakery, where atmosphere is not high on the priority list, but good baked goods are sold. There are a couple of not-too-comfortable tables to sit for a coffee and pastry, but take-away is the best option, enjoying your wares in a park. The staff does not speak English, so you have to point to your selection.

VII. Holló u. 1. © **1/267-2851**. Cash only. Sun–Fri 9am–6pm. A short walk from Dohány Synagogue.

---

9 TEAHOUSES

Tea drinkers are finally being recognized with their own places to sit, relax, and savor a pot of tea of their choosing with a limitless variety of teas available. Just like the coffeehouses, you are welcome to unwind as long as you wish without concern of overstaying your welcome. This is just a sample of teahouses; they are cropping up all over the city.

Tea Palota (Tea Hall)   Come here if you want to free Tibet or even just feel free in Tibet. Entering this tea shop, you'll find a huge mural of a Tibetan mountain on the wall; you can use your imagination to feel the cool mountain air in summer, since they don't have airconditioning. They do have relaxing ambience in a Zen-like atmosphere. For larger groups with good backs, you can venture upstairs to a room full of pillows and Japanese-style tables for lounging while sipping your tea. At the top of the stairs is a smoking room for those who like to mix their tea with nicotine. Teas are available in a wide range, but sadly the menu is in Hungarian only. If you describe your desires to the waitstaff, they will make recommendations.

VI. Jókai u. 20. © **1/354-1453**. MC, V. Mon–Fri 11am–11pm; Sat 4pm–11pm; Sun 5–11pm.

Teaház a Vörös Oroszlánhoz (The Red Lion Teahouse)   This is a place to hide from the tourists and with multiple locations you have choices too. You can choose from various "atmospheres": Business-talk-like chairs and tables, friendly bean bags, or intimate private rooms with mattresses. Within the shop, a small yet fitting bookstore features a selection of esoteric, literary books in English as well. Tea lovers will be amazed at the countless high-quality tea offerings from Indian green teas and Chinese black teas to healing teas.

IX. Ráday u. 9 © **1/215-2101**; VI. Jókai tér 8. © **1/269-0579**; XI. Villányi u. 12. © **1/279-1133**. www.vorosoroszlanteahaz.hu. MC, V. Mon–Sat 11am–11pm; Sun 3pm–11pm at all locations. Metro: Kálvin tér (Blue line); Metro: Oktogon (Yellow line).

Zöld Teknős Barlangja (Green Turtle Cave) ★★ **Kids** A Native American teahouse seems out of place in Budapest, but it's still fun to see how other cultures interpret some aspects of Hungarian culture. It looks overwhelmingly like a tourist trap, but step downstairs for the real fun. Down in the nonsmoking section, the room is decorated in a rustic, log-cabin style—a comfy spot for a pot of tea. Even better: To the left of the staircase are intimate nooks for two, and behind those doors you'll find small rooms with comfortable chairs and a fake fireplace for inviting tea parties. Smokers can head to the first floor (one up from the street), where Native American motifs add to the ambience— right down to the chief sitting with his hollowed-out log fire as an ashtray. Pressing a silent bell button will call the waitstaff to take your order for a pot of tea from over 50 different choices, all with Native American names.

VI. Jókai u. 14. © **1/302-0024**. www.zoldteknosbarlangja.hu. AE, MC, V. Sun–Thurs 3am–11pm; Fri–Sat 3pm–midnight. Metro: Opera (Yellow line).

7

Exploring Budapest

Historic Budapest is smaller than people realize when they first arrive. Since this is an ideal walking city, many attractions listed in this chapter are easily reached on foot from the city center or if you would rather save some time, public transport will get you there too. As you stroll from one place to the next, look up at the buildings even if you have to stop a minute. There are so many missed treasures above normal views that go underappreciated by many. Regardless of a building's decay, take into consideration it probably has a long and interesting history associated with it. Many people have commented to me about how fine some of the buildings would be if they were restored, but they forget this city was heavily bombed during World War II. That rubble falling from the facade most likely has a story to tell. Clean and neat buildings are easy to look at, but what historical secrets have they sandblasted away? It is like telling your grandmother you would enjoy looking at her more if she had a facelift.

This city is a grand old dame that has seen plenty and survived the hardships.

1 THE TOP ATTRACTIONS ON THE PEST SIDE

Museums

Museums are closed on Monday, except where noted. Museums sometimes offer senior discounts for E.U. citizens or student discounts with an international ID; however, if it is not posted, ask anyway. If a senior discount is posted, there are times when a cashier is willing to bend the rules in your favor, so I have listed senior discounts here to let you know to attempt it. Up until January 2008, a good portion of museums had free entry to the permanent exhibits. The good times are over; there are few freebies any longer. Entry fees are usually posted in English next to the ticket window. A few museums offer a family rate. Many museums are open on non-religious holidays and some actually have free admission on those days. All museums have coat-check rooms. You are expected to check your coat and bags, but women can keep their purse. This is a fairly standard rule. Unlike many countries, museums in Hungary allow photos and videotaping, which thrills a shutterbug like me, but they charge for the privilege. In the listing details, I have included the cost of a photo and video ticket if they offer it so you can determine if it is worth your while to carry the equipment. Where photos or video are not allowed, there are no ticket prices.

Holokauszt Emlékközpont (Budapest Holocaust Memorial Center) ★★★

Opened in 2004 to coincide with the 60th anniversary of the Holocaust, this is the first government-funded Holocaust memorial center in central Europe. Architecturally, it is a combination of classical and modern creating asymmetrical lines. All of the distorted symmetry is intentionally symbolic of the warped, perverse history of the Holocaust. In the center is a refurbished eclectic-style synagogue that was originally designed by Leopold Baumhorn, a famous architect of synagogues at the turn of the 20th century. The space has a permanent exhibition, a research center, and an excellent bookshop with

ATTRACTIONS

Belvárosi Plébániatemplom
(Inner City Parish Church) **47**

Bélyegmúzeum
(Postal Stamp Museum) **42**

Buda Palace **14**

Budapesti Történeti Múzeum
(Budapest History
Museum) **16**

Dohány Synagogue **41**

Fóvárosi Állat és Növénykert Zoo
and Botanical Gardens **25**

Füvészkert Botanical Garden **52**

Gellért Hegy (Gellért Hill) **18**

Gül Baba Türbéje
(Tomb of Gül Baba) **3**

Gyermekvasút
(Children's Railroad) **6**

Hadtörténeti Múzeum
(Museum of the History
of Warfare) **9**

Halászbástya
(Fisherman's Bastion) **12**

Holokauszt Emlékközpont
(Budapest Holocaust
Memorial Center) **51**

Hósök tere (Heroes' Square) **31**

Institute for Musicology **10**

Iparművészeti Múzeum
(Museum of Applied Arts) **50**

János-Hegy Libegó
(János Hill Chairlift) **5**

Kerepesi Cemetery **44**

Kozma Cemetery **45**

Kózépkori Zsidó Imaház
(Medieval Jewish Prayer
House) **11**

Közlekedési Múzeum
(Transport Museum) **28**

Liszt Ferenc Emlékmúzeum
(Ferenc Liszt Memorial
Museum) **32**

Ludwig Múzeum
(Ludwig Museum of
Contemporary Art **49**

Magyar Állami Operaház
(Hungarian State
Opera House) **35**

Mátyás Templom
(Matthias Church) **13**

Miksa Róth Memorial House **43**

Millenáris Park **4**

Múvészetek Palotája
(Palace of Arts) **49**

Nagy Cirkusz (Great Circus) **26**

Nemzeti Galéria (Hungarian
National Gallery) **15**

Nemzeti Múzeum (Hungarian
National Museum) **46**

Nemzeti Zsidó Múzeum és Levéltár
(National Jewish Museum
and Archives) **40**

Néprajzi Múzeum
(Museum of Ethnography) **23**

Parliament **22**

Postamúzeum
(Post Office Museum) **37**

Semmelweis Orvostörténeti Múzeum
(Semmelweis Museum of
Medical History) **17**

Széchenyi Lánchíd
(The Chain Bridge) **21**

Szent István Bazilika
(St. Stephen's Church) **36**

Szépművészeti Múzeum
(Museum of Fine Arts) **30**

Természettudományi Múzeum
(Museum of Natural History) **53**

Terror Háza (House of Terror) **33**

Vajdahunyad Castle **29**

Vasuttortentipark (Hungarian
Railway Museum) **24**

Vidám Park (Amusement Park) **26**

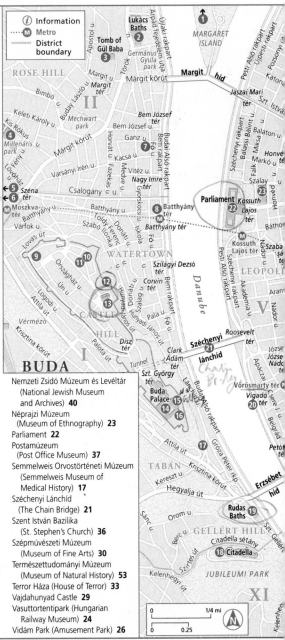

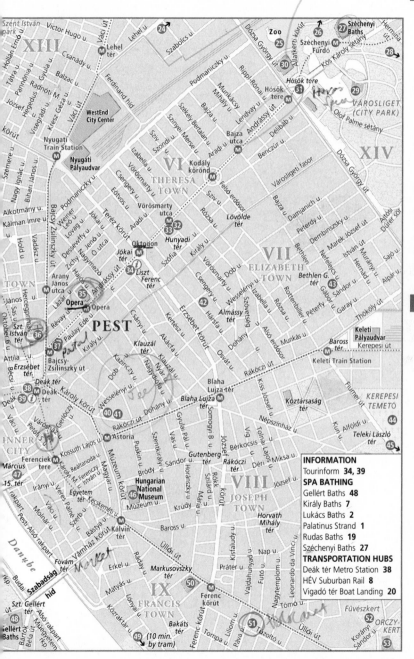

Fire Arts

INFORMATION
Tourinform **34, 39**
SPA BATHING
Gellért Baths **48**
Király Baths **7**
Lukács Baths **2**
Palatinus Strand **1**
Rudas Baths **19**
Széchenyi Baths **27**
TRANSPORTATION HUBS
Deák tér Metro Station **38**
HÉV Suburban Rail **8**
Vigadó tér Boat Landing **20**

many English selections. Temporary exhibitions are local and international. A large wall surrounds the courtyard serving as remembrance for the Hungarian victims of the Holocaust. The names of the victims are engraved onto the glass wall.

IX. Páva u. 39. (© **1/455-3333.** www.hdke.hu. Admission 1,200 Ft adults, free for students with International ID and seniors. Tues–Sun 10am–6pm. Metro: Ferenc krt. (Blue line).

Nemzeti Múzeum (Hungarian National Museum) ★★ The Hungarian National Museum was founded in 1802 thanks to the numismatic, book, and document collections of Count Ferenc Szénchényi. One of my favorite buildings in Budapest, this enormous neoclassical structure was finished in 1846. It was here that the poet Sándor Petőfi and others of like mind are said to have roused the emotions of the people of Pest to revolt against the Habsburgs on March 15, 1848. If you look carefully, you will find a column on a plinth on the left side of the entrance that was given to Hungary by Mussolini. The column was from the Forum in Rome. Due to its negative history, the plague now states "A gift from the Italian nation."

The permanent exhibit holds more than one million pieces of Hungarian historical artifacts, including the main attraction, a replica of the so-called crown of King St. Stephen. Stephen was the first king of Hungary and brought Christianity to the land, thus he made it to sainthood upon his death in 1000. The original of what is referred to as King St. Stephen's crown is in the Parliament building. It was stored in the Pentagon in the U.S. after World War II and returned in 1978. Hungarian historians state that the crown was not St. Stephen's; its lower part is believed to have been a gift to King Géza I (1074–77), and its upper part was built for Stephen V, who reigned almost 250 years after the first Stephen's death. The permanent exhibition is the History of Hungary from the Foundation of the State to 1990. Featured are various objects and documents illustrating the migratory history of the early Hungarians from Siberia to the area now known as Hungary, and other displays of their military and social history up to the freedoms regained in 1990. A second permanent exhibit is Lapidarium Roman Stone Finds located in the basement.

VIII. Múzeum krt. 14. (© **1/327-7700.** www.mnm.hu. Admission for permanent exhibits 1,040 Ft, children and seniors 520 Ft; temporary exhibits vary. Free admission on March 15, August 20, and October 23. Photo 3,000 Ft; video 5,000 Ft. Tues–Sun 10am–6pm. Metro: Kálvin tér (Blue line).

Néprajzi Múzeum (Museum of Ethnography) ★★ **Kids** One of the largest specialist museums in Europe, it contains more than 139,000 Hungarian and 53,000 international art objects. Housed in the former Hungarian Supreme Court building, directly across Kossuth tér from the House of Parliament, the museum has the pleasure of being in a Renaissance, baroque, and neoclassical building. The lavish interior alone is worth a visit. A ceiling fresco of Justitia, the goddess of justice, by the well-known artist Károly Lotz, dominates the lobby. The permanent exhibition named From Primitive Cultures to Civilization needs a good dusting, but nevertheless, it is fascinating and holds my attention on each visit. It features dioramas with articles from all periods of early Hungarian history. There is more to see in this museum than my fortitude allows in one visit, so I often return for another sampler. Temporary exhibits rotate often. Check their website for the seven free admission dates.

V. Kossuth tér 12. (© **1/473-2400.** www.neprajz.hu. Admission 800 Ft. Photo 300 Ft; video 1,000 Ft. Tues–Sun 10am–6pm. Metro: Kossuth tér (Red line).

Szépművészeti Múzeum (Museum of Fine Arts) ★★★ During the 1896 millennial celebration of the Magyars' settling and forming a nation in 896, the plans were proposed for the Museum of Fine Arts. Ten years later in the presence of Franz Josef, the king and emperor of Austria and Hungary, the Museum of Fine Arts was opened at the left side of Heroes' Square. This was the last great monument to be built during the most prosperous period of Hungary's history. Designed in the Beaux Arts style, the main facade has three classical Greek temples connected by colonnades. The temples represent the grove of muses, a place of relaxation. The Greek influence is further incorporated with the Corinthian columns and sculpture in the pediment: the Battle of the Lapiths and the Centaurs from the Temple of Zeus at Olympia. The museum is the main repository of foreign art in Hungary and it houses one of central Europe's major collections of such works. The initial collection was donated by Count Széchenyi who presented a number of portraits. A significant part of the collection was acquired in 1871 from the Esterházy collection, an enormously wealthy noble family who spent centuries amassing great art. There are eight sections in the museum: Egyptian art; antiquities; baroque sculpture; old masters; drawings and prints; 19th-century masters; 20th-century masters; and modern sculpture. Most great names associated with the old masters: Tiepolo, Tintoretto, Veronese, Titian, Raphael, Van Dyck, Brueghel, Rembrandt, Rubens, Hals, Hogarth, Dürer, Cranach, Holbein, Goya, Velázquez, El Greco, and others are represented here. Delacroix, Corot, and Manet are the best-represented 19th-century French artists in the museum. The overall collection consists of more than 3,000 paintings, 10,000 drawings, and 100,000 prints. Trained docents offer a 1-hour guided tour, in English, free of charge. Stand by the cashier's desk close to the starting time and a docent will announce the tour. They are offered Tuesday through Friday at 11am and 2pm and Saturday at 11am. Ask the docent which gallery the tour will focus on. They rotate galleries with each tour.

XIV. Hősök tere. ✆ 1/469-7100. www.szepmuveszeti.hu. Admission 1,400 Ft for permanent collection; temporary exhibits are in addition and vary. Photography only permitted in the permanent collection. Photo 300 Ft; video 1,500 Ft. Tues–Sun 10am–5pm. Every 2nd Thurs on odd weeks until 10pm. Metro: Hősök tere (Yellow line).

2 MORE PEST MUSEUMS & SIGHTS

PEST

Bélyegmúzeum (Postal Stamp Museum) ★ When I had the personal mission to visit every museum in Budapest one summer, I thought this would be one I could spend 10 minutes in and check it off of my list. Almost 3 hours later, I left in awe. Beyond the unappealing entry, the museum itself is modern, bright, and air-conditioned. Admittedly this is my first stamp museum ever, but the displays were ingenious with rack after rack of the country's finest stamps starting from the first stamps ever ordered by royalty to almost current times totaling more than 12 million. The Madonna with Child in **Rack 49,** which was mistakenly printed upside-down, is said to be Hungary's most valuable stamp. Variations on Lenin and Stalin can be seen in **Racks 68 to 77,** and **Racks 70 to 80** ★★ contain numerous brilliant examples of Socialist Realism. Aside from Hungarian stamps, stamps from around the world are just as impressive, though obviously not as complete. Make sure you go into the dark room with the audio in English that plays while you view a U.S. stamp with a magnifying glass. The staff seldom sees visitors so they are extremely friendly and welcoming. My only regret is that photos are not allowed, even for a price.

VII. Hársfa u. 47. ℭ **1/341-5526.** www.belyegmuzeum.hu. Admission 500 Ft adults and 250 Ft students. Apr–Oct Tues–Sun 10am–6pm; Nov–Mar Tues–Sun 10am–4pm. Tram: 4 or 6 to Wesselényi u.

Füvészkert Botanical Garden ★★   This is the botanical garden of Eötvös Loránd University, containing a plethora of flora with more than 7,000 species including at least 800 varieties of cactus. It was established here in 1847 after being started by Cardinal Péter Pázmány in 1635, in what is now Slovakia. The garden was uprooted and replanted a few times, before finding its Budapest home. The gardens also contain a palm house and Japanese garden complete with pond and goldfish. Reconstruction will continue through 2010, making the opening times difficult until it is completed.

VIII. Illés u. 25 (entrance is on the corner of Illés u. and Korányi Sándor u.). ℭ **1/314-0535.** www. fuveszkert.com. Admission 600 Ft adults, 300 Ft students and children. English audio CD rental 2,200 Ft. Gardens Mar 1–Oct 31 Daily 9am–5pm; Nov–Feb 9am–4pm. Greenhouses 9am–noon and 1pm–4pm. Bus: 99 to Diószeghy Sámuel and then walk.

Iparművészeti Múzeum (Museum of Applied Arts) ★★   You have to see this building and not just from the outside. Even if you are not interested in the collections, walk into the lobby and take a peak. It makes me imagine what being inside a wedding cake must be like. Architect Ödön Lechner was the designer of the museum along with Gyula Pártos in what is called Secessionist or Hungarian Art Nouveau in the 1890s. The roof is done in Zsolnay ceramic tiles. Lechner left his stamp in other parts of the city as well as the country. If you like this building, visit the former Post Office Savings Bank on Hold utca. Permanent exhibits, which are made up of antique decorative arts from all over Europe, are divided into five sections: furniture; textiles; metalwork; ceramics, porcelain, and glass; and an eclectic display of books, leather, and ivory. I find the temporary exhibits far more interesting than the permanent ones, which are fortunately given more space. Unlike the other museums, you have to pay the special exhibit fee when there is one in order to enter the regular collection. Regardless, you have to see the interior, so if you don't want to pay, just walk in the door and gawk from there.

IX. Üllői út 33–37. ℭ **1/456-5100.** www.imm.hu. Admission 1,000 Ft adults, 500 Ft students and seniors for permanent exhibit. Temporary exhibits are variable, but generally 800 Ft extra. Photo 2,000 Ft; video 2,000 Ft. Tues 2pm–6pm Wed, Fri, Sat and Sun 10am–6pm and Thurs 10am–10pm. Metro: Ferenc krt. (Blue line).

Miksa Róth Memorial House ★★★   This museum is in the artist's last home, making it sometimes difficult to find, but well worth hunting for. Róth was a mosaic and stained-glass artist who gained worldwide acclaim for his work. He has pieces in the Parliament, on public buildings, and in Mexico and other countries. His stained glass is breathtaking, as is the method of painting on glass that he developed. Once you have been to this museum, you will become aware of how prolific an artist he was. This is one of my favorite museums of the small variety.

VII. Nefelejc u. 26. ℭ **1/341-6789.** www.rothmuzeum.hu. Tues–Sun 2pm–6pm. Closed August. Admission 500 Ft adults, 250 Ft students. Photo 2,000 Ft. Tram: 4 or 6 Wesselényi and then walk.

Nemzeti Zsidó Múzeum és Levéltár (National Jewish Museum and Archives) ★★   Sitting to the left of the Dohány Synagogue (p. 134), the museum contains an excellent collection of Judaica, which survived the war by being housed in the basement of the National Museum. The permanent collection contains devotional objects for Jewish holiday celebrations, everyday objects, and a special room with the History of the Hungarian Holocaust exhibit. Outside there is a plaque stating that

Theodor Herzl, the founder of Zionism, was born on this spot. The museum is only four rooms, but it is a powerful display. Note that admission includes the museum.

VII. Dohány u. 2–8. ☏ **1/342-8942.** Admission 1,600 Ft adults, 750 Ft students. Photo 500 Ft synagogue, free for museum. Mar 1–Oct 31 Sun–Thurs 10am–5:30pm; Fri 10am–2:30pm; Nov 1–Feb 28 Sun–Thurs 10am–3:30pm; Fri 10am–1:30pm. Closed national holidays and Jewish holidays, except for services. Metro: Astoria (Red line) or Deák tér (all lines); bus: 74.

Postamúzeum (Post Office Museum) ★★ (Finds) This museum is often overlooked, but like the Museum of Applied Arts, you should come here to see the historic building interior. The stained glass in the entryway is only the beginning of the razzle-dazzle to follow. It surprised me how interesting the collection was once I was immersed in the grandeur of my surroundings. There are explanation sheets in English, so you self-tour around the pieces of post, communications, and program broadcasting historical pieces. The collection comprises 20,000 items, but don't fear, you can do this museum in an hour or less if you rush through. The apartment and furnishings were owned by the Sexlehner family who were obviously a prosperous clan. Chandeliers hang royally from the frescoed ceilings, and intricately carved wood moldings trim the walls, making this a must for anyone interested in history, design, or antiques.

VI. Andrássy út 3. ☏ **1/269-6838.** www.postamuzeum.hu. Admission 500 Ft adults, 250 Ft students. Photo 300 Ft; video 1,000 Ft. Tues–Sun 10am–4pm. Metro: Bajcsy-Zsilinszky út (Yellow line) or Deák tér (all lines).

Terror Háza (House of Terror) ★★ You will have to brace yourself before going into this historical building. Also bring your reading glasses; all of the information in English is on copious sheets of paper in each room. This is the former headquarters of the ÁVH secret police. This building is witness to some of the darkest days of 20th-century Hungary and is now a chilling museum. The goal was to create a memorial to the victims of Fascism and Communism, the successive oppressive regimes in Hungary, but according to critics, it misses the mark by putting more energy into the Communist times. The Nazis headquartered here in 1944 used the basement for torture and murder of suspected traitors and others they thought were undesirables. The Communist secret police wasted no time at all in taking over the building and continuing the reputation the Fascists started. The fact that it is now a museum has caused much debate amongst locals who feel it is glorifying the evil past. The artsy roof that overhangs its stenciled letters onto the street doesn't help the cause with Andrássy út being a UNESCO World Heritage site.

VI. Andrássy út 60. ☏ **1/374-2600.** www.houseofterror.hu. Admission 1,800 Ft adults, 900 Ft students w/ student card, 800 Ft for temporary exhibits. Tues–Sun 10am–6pm. Metro: Oktogon (Yellow line).

Vajdahunyad Castle ★★ (Kids) Many refer to this castle as a replica of a Transylvanian castle, but actually it was built for the 1896 millennium celebration. The purpose was to highlight the different architectural styles of the past with detailed replicas of historic buildings in Hungary incorporated into the design. The main section is a copy of the Vajdahunyad Tower, giving it its name. Interestingly, the original was made of cardboard, and of course disintegrated. Now the building houses the Museum of Agriculture, an interesting place to visit, not only for the interior of the building, but also for the exhibits, such as how bees produce honey, for which Hungary is famous. They are surprisingly captivating.

XIV. City Park-Városliget. ☏ **1/422-0765.** www.mmgm.hu. Admission 600 Ft adults, 300 Ft students. Photo free. Apr 1–Oct 31 Tues–Sun 10am–5pm, Nov 1–March 31 Tues–Fri 10am–4pm and weekends 10am–5pm. Metro: Széchenyi fűrdő (Yellow line).

Vasuttortentipark (Hungarian Railway Museum) ★★ **Kids** Occupying the former site of the Budapest North Depot of the Hungarian State Railways, this is the first European interactive railroad museum, which opened in July 2000. With a roundhouse and 34 bays, there is plenty of room to keep the vintage railroad engines and cars including a steam engine from 1840. The pride of the vintage fleet is the elegant teak dining car built for the Orient Express in 1912. Not only can you admire the old machines, but you can also try them out. You can drive a steam engine, travel in a car converted for rails, operate a handcart, and ride on the turntable or the horse-drawn tram. For the serious railroad buff, Hungary has a wide assortment of seasonal vintage and narrow-gauge railroad excursions. Check their website for dates and times; there is an English link or contact Tourinform (p. 28).

XIV. Tatai út 95. ✆ **1/238-0558.** www.vasuttortenetipark.hu. Admission 950 Ft adults, 300 Ft children, 1,900 Ft family. Photo 200 Ft; video 800 Ft. Apr–Oct Tues–Sun 10am–6pm. Bus: 30 from Keleti Station; tram: 14 from Lehel tér, both to Rokolya u. stop; a vintage rail diesel runs from Nyugati Station to the museum during the season.

Historic Squares & Buildings

Hősök tere (Heroes' Square) ★★★ **Kids** If you want a dramatic experience, come up from the Yellow metro station at Hősök tere from the city center at night. When Hősök tere is lit it is majestic in its splendor, not to say that it is not impressive during the day too. Located at the end of the grand World Heritage Boulevard, Andrássy út, the square is the entryway into the best-known park in the city, City Park (Városliget). Like so many other things in the city, the square and park were planned and built to celebrate the arrival and settling of the Magyars' forming a nation in 896. The tricky part was that, at the time, Hungary was part of the Austrian empire, yet celebrating their independence as a nation. The monument you see was not completed until 1929, which had the collapse of the empire precede it.

In the center of the monument is a column 37m (120 ft) high, topped by a large statue of Gabriel, the Archangel. The sculptor György Zala won a prize for his work at the World Exhibition in Paris after it had been shipped where it waited out testing of the strength of the column to support it. If you look at Gabriel's hands, he is holding a crown. Legend has it that Stephen, the first king, had a dream where Gabriel appeared to him and prompted him to continue his efforts to convert his people to Christianity.

At the base of the column are statues of the conquerors on horseback. The one in the forefront is Árpád, the leading chieftain who led the six other Magyar tribal leaders in conquering the land. To the sides of the column in a colonnade, are seven heroes of Hungarian history on each side. Starting from the far left you will find King Stephen I, the country's first Christian king, followed by six other kings who followed him. On the right side, only the second statue is a royal: King Matthias Corvinus, who presided over Buda's golden age in the 15th century (sixth from right). Other statues found atop the colonnade are immediately to the left and right of the column, the chariots of peace and war. At the forefront top on the left and right sides are statues representing work and welfare, while on the other side glory and knowledge.

Heroes' Square is a popular place with kids who come with their parents, but also local kids and teens who generally arrive with their skateboards after the throngs of tourist buses leave the area. Many concerts, fairs, and political demonstrations are held on this plaza throughout the year.

Two of Budapest's major museums, the Museum of Fine Arts and the Exhibition Hall, flank Heroes' Square.

Metro: to Hősök tere (Yellow line).

Fun Facts   Check Mate!

Budapest-born Zsuzsanna (Susan) Polgár made chess history in July 1984 when, at the age of 15, she was the top-ranking woman chess player in the world. Susan is also the first woman to earn the title of Chess Grandmaster in regular competition. She was followed by her sister Judit Polgár, who also achieved the Grandmaster title at the age of 15 years and 4 months, making her the youngest person to do so as of 1991. This was the result of an educational experiment conducted by their father László, who believed if trained properly "Geniuses are made, not born."

Magyar Állami Operaház (Hungarian State Opera House) ★★★   Built in a neo-Renaissance style, this is the most beautiful building of this style on Andrassy út. The architect was Miklós Ybl, the most successful and prolific architect of his time. He created what many agree is one of the most beautiful opera houses in Europe. It was completed in 1884. It is Budapest's and Hungary's most celebrated performance hall; the Opera House boasts a fantastically ornate interior featuring frescoes by two of the best-known Hungarian artists of the day, Bertalan Székely and Károly Lotz. Both inside and outside are dozens of statues of such greats as Beethoven, Mozart, Verdi, Wagner, Smetana, Tchaikovsky, and Monteverdi. In corner niches you will find the muses Terpsichore, Erato, Thalia, and Melpomene representing dance, love poetry, comedy, and tragedy. Home to the State Opera and the State Ballet, the Opera House has a rich and evocative history, which is related on the guided tours given daily at 3pm and 4pm (these can be arranged in English). Well-known directors of the Opera House include Gustav Mahler and Ferenc Erkel, the composer of the Hungarian national anthem. See p. 216 for information on performances. You may enter the lobby without charge, but the only way to tour the interior is with the guided tour.

VI. Andrássy út 22. ✆ **1/332-8197.** www.opera.hu. Tour 2,800 Ft adults, 1,400 Ft students with international ID. Photo 500 Ft; video (with small camera) 500 Ft. Tours daily 3pm and 4pm. Metro: Opera (Yellow line).

Parliament ★★★   Budapest's great Parliament, the second largest in Europe after London, is an eclectic design mixing the predominant Gothic revival style with a neo-Renaissance dome. Construction began in 1884, 16 years after Westminster, and was completed in 1902. Standing proudly on the Danube bank, visible from almost any riverside point, it has from the outset been one of Budapest's proud symbols, though until 1989 a democratically elected government had convened here only once (just after World War II, before the Communist takeover). Before entering, take note that the top of the building is 29m (96 ft) high at its peak, commemorating the 896 conquest. St. Stephen's Basilica is the same height.

It used to be a bicameral parliament with an upper and lower house, but now is unicameral with coalitions having to be formed. As you walk up the imposing staircase, you are led under the dome along a 16-sided hallway with 16 statues of rulers. In the center floor under the dome is a glass case with the legendary jeweled crown and scepter of King St. Stephen. Historical records have shown that the crown is of two parts and from two different eras, neither from King St. Stephen's time, but Hungarians want to believe it was Stephen's. Nevertheless, it is one of the oldest royal crowns in history. You will notice

Kerepesi Cemetery ★★★

You may find visiting a cemetery a strange vacation attraction, but those interested in history, art, or nature will not be disappointed. Here is the final resting place of Hungary's richest and most prominent men and women in one of the most beautiful parks in the city. Fantastic sculptured monuments are often suggestive of the deceased's life's work and are scattered among many chestnut trees giving the place a unique, almost classical air. As you stroll down arcades, you will see extraordinarily huge mausoleums, artwork gracing graves, and alongside memorials to Communists of a previous era. After All Saints' Day, the graves are covered with flowers. Half the streets in Hungary are named after people buried here; names will be familiar as you venture round the city.

Straight through the gate, 50m forward on the left are the Hungarians who fought with the Communists against their countrymen. Others who died in the 1956 uprising can be found in plot 21. Walking down Arkádsor (see map), on each side are the glorious home-sized richly ornate mausoleums with Róth Miksa mosaics, while at the end of these on the left rests **Blaha Lujza**, the Sarah Bernhardt actress of Hungary. Her reclining full-figured body is juxtaposed by small angels surrounding her. In the center is the monument to Jókai Mór, a celebrated dramatist and novelist. **Arany János**, the noted Hungarian poet, rests in section 14. One of my favorite memorials is for **Ligeti Miklós**, a sculpture, in section 18/1. Here you will find a chair with a coat draped over it accompanied by a hat and cane.

Have you gone to Gerbeaud's café? The man responsible is **Gerbeaud Emil** resting in section 26. **Lechner Odon** the famous architect whose polychrome tiles and mosaic work is evident on many buildings throughout the country is in section 28 along with **Antall Jozsef**. Antall was the first prime minister of Hungary after the fall of Communism; his grave is marked by an eerily bizarre statue. **Erkel Ferenc** (section 29) composed the first Hungarian opera, *Bank Ban*, and was the father of composer and writer, **Erkel Sandor**. Considered one of the most important artists of 19th-century Hungarian art, **Munkacsy Mihaly** lies in rest in section 29. If you love the architecture of the Opera House and St. Stephen's Basilica among other buildings in the city, **Ybl Miklós** the architect responsible is resting in 31/1. The "Mother's Savior" **Semmelweiss Ignac**, is the first man to realize that germs carried by doctors' hands caused transmitting infections. He is the proponent of hand washing, causing a dramatic decrease in infections. He rests in section 34/2.

Three free-standing mausoleums are highlighted in the park with free-standing memorials. **Kossuth Lajos** (1802–94), the governor-president of Hungary in 1849, regarded worldwide as a freedom fighter and proponent of democracy. **Deák Ferenc** (1803–76), known as "The Wise Man of the Nation" was a Hungarian statesman and minister of justice. **Batthyány Lajos** (1807–49) was a descendant of the Capet kings of France and a long line of counts. He was the first prime minister of Hungary and was convicted of high treason by the emperor of Austria when the Hungarian Revolution of 1848–49 failed.

VIII. Fiumei út. Free admission. Opening time is daily at 7am all year. Oct–Mar closing 5pm; Apr and Aug closing 7pm; May–July closing 8pm; Sept closing 6pm. Metro: Keleti Station (Red line) and then tram 24 one stop. Take note that the entrance gate is near the tram 24 stop.

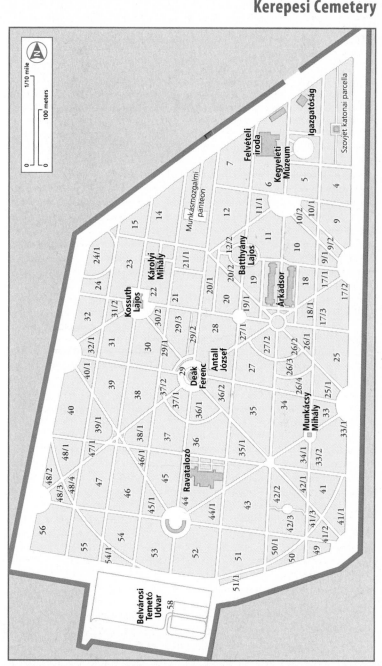

0 1/10 mile

0 100 meters

Belvárosi Temető Udvar

Ravatalozó

Deák Ferenc

Antall József

Kossuth Lajos

Károlyi Mihály

Munkásmozgalmi panteon

Batthyány Lajos

Árkádsor

Munkácsy Mihály

Felvételi iroda

Kegyeleti Múzeum

Igazgatóság

Szovjet katonai parcella

56 55 54 54/1 53 52 51 50 50/1 51/1 49 41/2 41/1 41/3 42/3 42/1 42/2 41 43 44/1 44 45/1 45 46 47 48/4 48/3 48/2 48/1 47/1 46/1 37 38/1 39/1 40 39 40/1 38 37/1 37/2 36 36/1 36/2 29 35/1 35 34 33/1 33/2 34/1 42 33 25/1 26/4 26/3 26/2 26/1 27 27/2 25 17/2 17/3 17/1 9/2 9/1 10/1 9 10/2 4 5 6 7 11/1 11 10 18 18/1 19/1 19 20 20/1 21 22 23 24 24/1 15 14 12 12/2 20/2 28 29/2 29/3 30/2 30 29/1 31 31/2 32 32/1 31 27/1

the bent cross on the top; although there are many legends as to why it is bent, no one knows for sure. In St. Matthias Church on Castle Hill, there is a small, but impressive museum dedicated to the crown (p. 138).

V. Kossuth tér. ⚞ **1/441-4415**. Tourist.office@parliament.hu. Admission (by guided tour only) 50-min. tour in English 2,640 Ft adults, 1,320 Ft students, free admission for E.U. passport holders with passport. Photo free. Tickets available at gate X for individuals; pre-booking for large groups mandatory by e-mail or phone ⚞ **1/441-4904** or ⚞ **1/441-4415**. English tours year-round daily 10am, noon, and 2pm. Ticket office opens Mon–Fri 8am–6pm, Sat 8am–4pm, Sun 8am–2pm. Closed to tours when Parliament is in session, usually Mon and Thurs. Metro: Kossuth tér (Red line); tram 2 or 2A Szalay u.

Churches & Synagogues

Belvárosi Plébániatemplom (Inner City Parish Church) ★ The Inner City Parish Church dates back to the 12th century and is built in the Romanesque style, on the site of the grave of Bishop Gellért, the martyr who was said to have been killed by angry pagans. This is the oldest church in Pest. Nothing from the original building exists any longer having been built over through the centuries with Gothic features. In the 17th century, the Turkish invaders turned it into a mosque. After a fire destroyed part of the church in 1723 the rebuilding included the baroque style with an interior of neoclassical features. From the outside, it looks rather dilapidated, but inside, the attractive features are the Gothic chapel, the neo-Gothic carved pulpit, the 15th-century Italian frescoes, and the 20th-century main altar. Daily mass is held at 6:30am and 6pm; Sunday mass is at 9am, 10am, noon, and 6pm.

V. Március 15 tér. ⚞ **1/318-3108**. Free admission. Mon–Sat 6am–7pm; Sun 8am–7pm. Metro: Ferenciek tere (Blue line).

Dohány Synagogue ★★★ Built in 1859, this is the second-largest working synagogue in the world (the largest is in New York City), and the second-oldest large building of those still standing. The oldest is the National Museum. In 2009, it celebrated its grand 150-year anniversary. The architect was non-Jewish Lajos Förster who designed it with Romantic, Moorish, and Byzantine elements. The synagogue's interior is a mix of Orthodox and Reformed Judaism for the Hungarian Neolog Jewish denomination, which seems to exist only in Hungary. Due to this, many are surprised to see an organ in the loft. They had to, and still have to, have a non-Jewish organist to play it. The synagogue has a rich, but tragic history; it was one of many detention areas for Jews during the Holocaust. A Jewish museum next door traces the origins of Hungarian Judaism and features exhibits of ceremonial Judaica throughout the centuries. The museum periodically puts on excellent temporary exhibitions. The Holocaust Memorial and Heroes' Temple in the courtyard are well worth visiting. Note that the Holocaust Memorial Museum is at a different location.

VII. Dohány u. 2–8. ⚞ **1/413–5500**. Admission 1,600 Ft adults, 750 Ft students. Photo 500 Ft synagogue, free for museum. Mar 1–Oct 31 Sun–Thurs 10am–5:30pm; Fri 10am–2:30pm; Nov 1–Feb 28 Sun–Thurs 10am–3:30pm; Fri 10am–1:30pm. Closed national holidays and Jewish holidays, except for services. Metro: Astoria (Red line) or Deák tér (all lines); bus: 74.

Szent István Bazilika (St. Stephen's Church) ★★★ The country's largest church, this basilica took more than 50 years to build (the 1868 collapse of the dome caused significant delay) and was finally completed in 1906, which explains the differences in architectural designs. Szent István Square, a once-sleepy square in front of the church, was elegantly renovated in the autumn of 2002 and the entire church was given a good cleaning in 2003. The plaza area was converted along with several neighboring streets into a pedestrian-only zone, now surrounded with restaurants. As you wander into the church and to the left in the back chapel you can view St. Stephen's mummified hand or you can wait until August 20, his feast day and see it for free when it is paraded around the city. To get the box to light up to actually see it, you will have to spring for 100 Ft.

V. Szent István tér 33. ☎ **1/318-9159.** www.basilica.hu. Church free admission; treasury 400 Ft; panorama tower 500 Ft, students and seniors 400 Ft. Photos free. Tour 12,000 Ft. Church Mon–Fri 9am–5:15pm, Sat 9am–1pm, Sun 1pm–5pm. Services at 8am, 10am, noon, 6pm, 7:30pm; treasury daily 9am–5pm; Szent Jobb Chapel Mon–Sat 9am–5pm, Sun 1pm–5pm; panorama tower daily 10am–6pm. Metro: Arany János u. (Blue line) or Bajcsy-Zsilinszky út (Yellow line).

Cemeteries of Historical Interest

Kozma Cemetery ★★   The city's largest Jewish cemetery dates back to 1868, when the land was given to the Jewish community. The cemetery was designed by architect Freud Vilmos and the building was completed in 1896. More than a half-million Jews are buried here. Those memorialized include the 10,000 Hungarian Jews who fought in World War I and those who are victims of the Holocaust. Alfréd Hajós, the Hungarian Olympic champion and architect (the first Hungarian to win a gold medal), made the memorial possible. A set of nine large walls with pillars are inscribed with the names of victims with family and friends having hand-filled in others. About 6,500 names appear including the 2,000 victims of the Klauzál tér ghetto, who perished during the last months of the war. The cemetery is still in use today, and the many monuments and ornate headstones are worth visiting as a reminder of man's injustice to man. Situated in the eastern end of the Kőbánya District, it is a tram ride away from the center of town.

X. Kozma u. 6. Free admission. Mon–Thurs 8am–4pm; Fri & Sun 8am–2pm. Tram: 37 from Blaha Lujza tér to Új köztemető (Kozma utca) one stop before the end of the line.

3 SITES OF JEWISH INTEREST

MEMORIALS

Along the Danube, on the embankment between the Chain Bridge and the Parliament building is a row of 60 pairs of bronze shoes that look suddenly abandoned. The memorial was created by sculptor Gyula Pauer. He named it *Shoes on the Danube Promenade* to commemorate those who were shot to death on the riverbank as the Allies were approaching the city. On the sidewalk, you will find a mosaic monument not far from the shoes. The inscription is in Hungarian, and states: "In memory of the Hungarians who fell victim to the Arrow Cross terror in the winter of 1944–45."

There are a number of memorials to **Raoul Wallenberg,** the Swedish diplomat who saved the lives of so many Jews. *Snake Killer* is a statue created by sculptor Pátzay Pál as a tribute to Wallenberg's work and it is in XIII. St. István Park. It was completed in 1949 and destroyed, but renewed and erected in 1999. You can get there by tram 4 or 6. Raoul Wallenberg utca is named in his honor and is where he established the "Swedish houses." There is a relief of Wallenberg on a wall with an inscription that translated says: "Raoul Wallenberg, The Deputy of the Swedish Nation. From the beginning of July 1944 until January 1945 he coordinated the brave and noble humanitarian activity of the Royal Swedish Embassy in Budapest. He became a legendary hero in that dark period of destruction. May this monument announce our imperishable gratitude in the middle of the city, which people were protected by his persistent humanity in an inhumane era's night." Another Raoul Wallenberg memorial created by Imre Varga is in Erzsébet Szilágyi Fasor a park in the second district consisting of a statue of the hero between two large rose-colored blocks of stone. Inscribed on the back of the stones is an imprint of the *Snake Killer* statue with the Latin phrase: "Donec eris felix multos numerabis amicos tempora si fuerint nubila solus eris." Translated it says: "When you are lucky, many friends you have, once the sky turns cloudy, alone you remain." Unfortunately, the park itself is not well maintained.

In district V. at Vadász u. 29, where the "Glass House" is located there is a memorial room with a plaque to commemorate the deeds of **Carl Lutz,** the Swiss diplomat who created safe houses for the Jews under Swiss protection. The Glass House (Üvegház) was the headquarters of the Zionist youth movement. If you take Walking Tour 4: The Jewish District (p. 180), you will see the memorial honoring him.

Stolpersteine or **Stumble Stones** ★★★ in English was the inspiration of Cologne-based artist Gunter Demmig. He started making stone plaques with Holocaust victims' individual names on them and placing them in the pavement in front of the last-known address for the victim. They have already appeared in Italy, the Netherlands, and Austria, but as of April 2007, the first ones were placed in Budapest. Privately funded at 95€ each, the first three stones have been placed on **Ráday utca.** Each stone reads: "Here lived" followed by the person's name, date of birth, and fate. The first three are for Béla Rónai, an unemployed public official at Ráday u. 5; Oszkár Vidor Weisz, a textile dealer and shoe repair person at Ráday u. 25; and Imre Pollák, a spice dealer at Ráday u. 31. Throughout the summer of 2007, 50 more stones were placed throughout Hungary. One criterion for selecting those to be remembered is that they have no surviving relatives, thus keeping their memory alive when no one else is available to commemorate them. For more information, but in German only, see www.stolpersteine.com. I accidently came across the first one on Ráday utca after learning about these, but since then have seen them appearing on more streets. I have included two on the Jewish walking tour (see p. 180). It is heartwarming.

One of the newest monuments is sitting at Bethlen Gábor tér 2 by the Bethlen Square Synagogue. Inset from the sidewalk, wire fencing holds millions of small rocks in place; a small metal tree with metal leaves looks tired and weary. The plaque translates to "Without weapons on the field of bombs. For the memory of the Jewish laborers. 1939–1945."

OTHER SITES OF NOTE

Kazinczy utca Synagogue located in the middle of the historically Jewish VII District is the center of traditional Orthodox Jewish life. Enclosed by residential buildings there is the synagogue, prayer room, kosher restaurant, school, and nearby is the only mikveh of Budapest. Hours listed are Monday to Thursday 10am to 3:30pm, Friday and Sunday 10am to 12:30pm. Admission is 800 Ft.

Vasvári Pál utca Synagogue, VI. Vasvári Pál u. 5 just off of Király u (tram: Király u.), is operated by the Shas Chevra Lubavitch Shul and the Budapest Yeshiva. The synagogue entrance is through the courtyard.

Rumbach Synagogue, Rumbach u. off Dob u (no phone), was built in a romantic-Moorish style in 1872. It was closed for years due to it being so dilapidated. However, it reopened in 2006, though its interior and exterior condition is still in a devastated state. Their posted hours are Sunday to Thursday 10am to 5:30pm and Friday from 10am to 2:30pm, but each of those days they close for lunch from 1pm to 1:30pm. I have been told continually that it will be closed yet again for renovation, but it really will depend on them getting the money to do more of the work. No one knew when and for how long this would be; this "Nem tudom" (I don't know!) is a typical response in Hungary. My best advice is to stop by and check on the status when you are here, because I have gone during "open hours" and it has been closed.

The **Leo Frankel Synagogue,** II. Frankel Léo u. 49 (© **1/326-1445;** tram: 17), was built in 1928, but houses were built surrounding the shul to hide its appearance from outsiders passing by. The Germans used the shul as a stable during the Holocaust. It has recently been restored and is in use by members of the local Buda community. Suggested admission is by donation, which is gratefully accepted. Open Monday through Friday 9am to 1pm by prior arrangement. Services are Friday nights and Saturday mornings.

The Rabbinical Seminary at Gutenberg tér has been open since the early 1900s and was one of the few seminaries open during the Communist period. It houses a huge library of more than 150,000 priceless volumes of Jewish literature. You will need to make an appointment to visit, but they did not want their number published.

Gozsdu Udvar (Gojdu Courtyard) was a unique part of the Jewish District at one time connecting Dob u. 16 and Király u. 13 by six courtyards and seven attached buildings that were 240m (787 ft) long. The pavilion-structured houses served as a passageway between the two streets, with apartments on the top floors with 45 shops and workshops on the ground floor. It was this courtyard that served as a Jewish ghetto during the Holocaust. Thousands of Jews were locked in the courtyard by heavy gates. See "Walking Tour 4: The Jewish District" (p. 180).

BUDA
Museums
Budapesti Történeti Múzeum (Budapest History Museum) ★

This museum, also referred to as the Castle Museum, is easily overlooked since it is tucked in the back courtyard behind the palace. Once you approach it, there are no lavish signs advertising it either. If you are interested in the history of this great city as well as the whole Carpathian basin from medieval times, you will love this museum. When I went, I was not expecting much and was more than surprised at how enjoyable it was. The exhibit descriptions detail (in English) the palace's repeated construction and destruction.

What you should not miss is the third-floor exhibit where you will find historic maps of battle plans and weapons used in the liberation from the Turkish occupation. At the back of the main floor, you will find a statue area that has an outstanding collection of Roman and medieval-era pieces. The highlight is the lowest level; it is actually part of the old palace and hidden back there is a chapel. With the museum atop Castle Hill, the courtyard garden and tower (accessible only through the museum) have amazing views and there are benches to sit and relax with refreshments bought from the small stand.

I. In Buda Palace, Wing E., on Castle Hill. © **1/487-8887.** www.btm.hu. Admission 1,200 Ft adults, 600 Ft students and seniors. Photo 600 Ft; video 1,600 Ft. Audio-guided tours 850 Ft. Mar 20–Sept 15 daily 10am–6pm; Sept 16–Oct 31, closed Tues; Nov 1–Mar 19 10am–4pm, closed Tues. Bus: 16A from Moszkva tér or 16 from Deák tér to Castle Hill. Funicular: From Clark Ádám tér to Castle Hill.

Ludwig Múzeum (Ludwig Museum of Contemporary Art)

This museum is located in the Palace of Arts (Mûvészetek Palotája), which opened in 2005, overlooking the Danube. It has the most important collection of contemporary Hungarian and international art. The collection includes American, German, Russian, and French artists from the last 50 years and central European contemporary works from the 1990s. It includes several late Picassos, Andy Warhol's *Single Elvis,* as well as an eclectic mix of

Hungarian works by artists like Imre Bukta, Beáta Veszely, and Imre Bak. Like the Kunsthalle in Vienna, this museum is worth visiting for the various temporary exhibitions of contemporary works, mostly by alternative European artists. Art experts have told us that this museum uses its funding to bring exhibitions here, depleting their funds to add to the permanent collections. The last Sunday of every month, those under 26 years old get in for free. No justice in aging.

IX. Komor Marcell u. 1. ☎ **1/555-3444.** www.ludwigmuseum.hu. Admission for permanent collection 700 Ft for everyone; special exhibits vary considerably. Free admission on March 15, August 20, October 23. Tues–Sun 10am–8pm. Tram: 2.

Nemzeti Galéria (Hungarian National Gallery) ★ With a collection of more than 10,000 art objects, this museum is not for the cultural faint of heart. The works cover the period from the beginning of Hungary as a nation to the present day. I have yet to see the entire collection even with subsequent visits as it is so easy to succumb to sensory overload and not everything is labeled in English. In summer, you will get heat stroke without air-conditioning. Hungarian artists have produced some outstanding work, particularly the period for which they are most famous, the late 19th century. Permanent exhibitions include: medieval and Renaissance lapidariums, Gothic woodcarvings, Gothic winged altars, Renaissance and baroque art and the Hungarian celebrities Mihály Munkácsy, László Paál, Károly Ferenczy, and Pál Szinyei Merse. Some other pieces to look for are sculptures by Isván Ferenczy and Miklós Izsó. József Rippl-Rónai's canvases are premier examples of Hungarian post-Impressionism and Art Nouveau (see *Father and Uncle Piacsek Drinking Red Wine* and *My Grandmother*), while Tivadar Csontváry Kosztka's *Rousseau of the Danube* is considered by some critics to be a genius of early modern art.

I. In Buda Palace, Wings B, C, and D, on Castle Hill. ☎ **1/375-5567.** Admission to permanent collection 700 Ft for everyone; temporary exhibits vary. Dome 400 Ft. Photo 1,600 Ft; video 2,100 Ft. Tues–Sun 10am–6pm. Bus: 16A from Moszkva tér or 16 from Deák tér to Castle Hill. Funicular: From Clark Ádám tér to Castle Hill.

A Famous Church

Mátyás Templom (Matthias Church) ★★★ Originally founded by King Béla IV in the 13th century, this church is officially named the Church of Our Lady and is a symbol of Buda's Castle District. It is popularly referred to as Matthias Church after the 15th-century king Matthias Corvinus who added a royal oratory and was twice married here. The original church was built in stages that spanned from the 13th to the 15th century. Like other old churches in Budapest it has a history of destruction and reconstruction, always being refashioned in the architectural style in vogue at the time. Renovation has been an ongoing process as financial considerations allow and it is currently half-covered with scaffolding. When I went in to see how long this would continue, I was shocked to hear it was planned until 2012. Regardless, it is a church not to be missed and this one too has Zsolnay ceramic tiles. Do not miss the museum upstairs; often overlooked by travelers who do not realize it is there, it has an interesting history of the royal crown and a wonderful view of the church.

I. Szentháromság tér 2. ☎ **1/355-5657.** www.matyas-templom.hu. Admission 750 Ft adults, 500 Ft students. Photos free. Mon–Fri 9am–5pm; Sat 9am–2:30pm, but depends on weddings; Sun 1pm–5pm. Metro: Moszkva tér, then bus no. 10; or Deák tér, then bus 16. Funicular: From Clark Ádám tér to Castle Hill.

Spectacular Views

Gellért Hegy (Gellért Hill) ★★ Towering 235m (750 ft) above the Danube, Gellért Hegy offers the city's best panorama on a clear day (bus no. 27 from Móricz Zsigmond körtér to Búsuló Juhász-Citadella). Named for the Italian bishop Gellért, he assisted Hungary's first Christian king, Stephen I, in converting the Magyars to Catholicism. Gellért became a martyr when, according to legend, outraged vengeful pagans converted through the force and violent nature of Stephen's proselytism, rolled Gellért in a nail-studded barrel to his death from the side of the hill. An enormous statue now stands on the hill to celebrate his memory. On top of Gellért Hill you'll find the **Liberation Monument,** built in 1947 to commemorate the Red Army's liberation of Budapest from Nazi occupation. The 14m (45 ft) statue of the woman holding the palm leaf of victory can be seen from just about any viewpoint along the river. To her sides are statues representing progress and destruction. Following the first election in 1990, there was much discussion as to whether the statue should be removed since the Soviet troops were more occupiers than liberators. Also atop the hill is the **Citadella,** built by the Austrians shortly after they crushed the Hungarian uprising from 1848 to 1849. Views of the city from both vistas are excellent, but the Citadella is spectacular. Don't bother paying the extra to traipse up to the upper part; the view is not that much higher, so don't waste your money.

Halászbástya (Fisherman's Bastion) ★★ The neo-Romanesque Fisherman's Bastion, behind Matthias Church and the Hilton Hotel, has a spectacular panorama of the river and Pest beyond it. Built at the turn of the 20th century, it was included as part of the refurbishing of the church area. Local legend states that this stretch of medieval parapets was a protected area by the fishermen's guild, but the area was once a fish market area, so either could be true. The local city council imposed a fee of 420 Ft to pass through the turnstile allowing you to climb to the top lookout points. If you happen to be in the area after 6pm or 9pm in summer, it is no longer manned and you can go up for free. An overpriced cafe is open in the warm months, but don't let the tables intimidate you from going to the railing and looking at the view over the Danube to Pest, you can see (from left to right): Margaret Island and the Margaret Bridge, Parliament, St. Stephen's Basilica, the Chain Bridge with the Hungarian Academy of Sciences and the Gresham Palace behind it, the Vigadó Concert Hall, the Inner City Parish Church, the Erzsébet Bridge, and the Szabadság Bridge. To get here, take the no. 16A bus from Moszkva tér or bus no. 16 from Deák tér, or the funicular from Clark Ádám tér to Castle Hill.

ÓBUDA
Roman Ruins
Aquincum (Roman Ruins) ★★ When thinking of the conquests of the Roman empire, rarely does Hungary pop into anyone's mind, but if you enjoy Roman history or ruins, this is a must. One of the largest archaeological parks in the country, this area was the capital of the Lower Pannonian province in the 2nd century where the Romans flourished for more than 110 years. At the time it was an important city in the Roman empire, now named Óbuda. When you arrive by HÉV suburban train to the stop by the same name, you will see the ruined **Amphitheater of the Civilian Town** alongside the HÉV stop. It is open all the time, but it is often home to homeless people, so you may want to view it from the fence, rather than wander among the ruins. Just a little farther down the road is the **Aquincum** park with the **Aquincum Museum.** Don't be fooled by outside appearances; at first glance the park looks small, but once you enter you'll realize you need a good half-day here to do justice to the 2,000-year-old history that is still intact. Each section has its own map of the buildings in that section and the maps are in English. Chronoscopes have been installed to give the full effect of what the buildings originally looked like. There are shelters around the park that seem to be out of place,

but these house additional ruins that are being protected from the elements. The small museum has limited English explanations, but the visuals are still worth your time to view. There are many special events, some recreating Roman history during summer months.

III. Szentendrei út 139. ℂ **1/454-0438.** www.aquincum.hu. Admission 1,200 Ft adults, 450 Ft students, seniors 600 Ft, but over 70 free. Photo for garden free; photo for exhibitions 600 Ft; video for exhibitions 1,600 Ft. Apr 15–30 and Oct 1–31 10am–5pm; May 1–Sep 30 9am–6pm; closed Nov 1–Apr 14 and every Mon. HÉV: Aquincum (direction Szentendre from Batthyány tér).

BRIDGING PEST & BUDA

Széchenyi Lánchíd (The Chain Bridge) ★★ (Moments) Prior to the building of this bridge, people relied on a structure on the water that had to be dismantled when ships passed and that was easily wrecked in stormy weather. The Széchenyi Chain Bridge was named for the man who financed it in its original form, Count István Széchenyi. Széchenyi reportedly funded the bridge while his father was dying because he was not able to cross the river by ferry for medical assistance; bad weather delayed the ferry for 8 days, and his father died in the meantime. He came from one of the wealthiest families of the time and was intent on bringing Hungary into the modern times by funding a number of projects. He wanted not only to unite Buda with Pest for the first time, but also to unite the country as well. After successive trips to London to view bridge construction, he commissioned Tierney Clark to design the bridge. The bridge was an exact copy of the bridge Clark designed at Marlow for crossing the Thames. Ádám Clark, no relation to the designer, was hired as the chief engineer. He is responsible for the tunnel that runs under Castle Hill and the square at the foot of the bridge is named for him.

During the war with Austria in May 1849, the Austrians planned on blowing up the yet-to-be-completed bridge. Ádám Clark had the anchoring chambers flooded to foil their plans and the bridge was completed later that year. In January 1945, the Germans destroyed the bridge as well as all the others that were in existence by that time. The Széchenyi Chain Bridge was rebuilt and reopened in November 1949.

With its advantageous location in the city center, it is most beautiful at night when thousands of lights adorning it glitter like a chandelier until midnight. In summer, when festivals are held on it on weekends and traffic is diverted, it is a place to stroll while stopping at the booths set up by artists, craftspeople, vendors, and musicians who entertain the locals and tourists alike. At other times, there are pedestrian lanes on either side to take a walk across for a view of the Danube: a pleasant experience and an excellent photo opportunity from the center.

---

4 MORE MUSEUMS & SIGHTS

BUDA

Arany Sas (Golden Eagle) Pharmacy Museum If you have any interest in medicine, allopathic, or homeopathic, this small museum will fascinate you. The back area has all of the concoctions in lovely old bottles that were once used to create remedies. There is even a replica of the fireplace and cooking area to show how it was done. If old ceramics get your attention, then that is another reason to explore here. There are only four small rooms, but you will leave with tidbits of curious information. There is no set fee for photos, but a donation is accepted.

I. Tárnok u. 18. ⓒ **1/375-9772.** www.semmelweis.museum.hu. Admission 500 Ft adults, 250 Ft students and seniors. Mar–Oct Tues–Sun 10:30am–6pm; Nov–Feb Tues–Sun 10:30am–4pm. Bus: 16A from Moszkva tér or 16 from Deák tér to Castle Hill. Funicular: From Clark Ádám tér to Castle Hill.

Hadtörténeti Múzeum (Museum of the History of Warfare) Housed in a former barracks in the northwestern corner of the Castle District, this museum has a collection of many weapons from the days before the Turkish invasion to the 20th century. There is also a large display of uniforms, flags, models, weapons, maps, photographs, and 28,000 coins. All of the displays' distributive notes are in Hungarian only.

I. Tóth Árpád sétány 40. ⓒ **1/325-1600.** www.militaria.hu. Admission 700 Ft adults, 350 Ft students. Photo 600 Ft; video 1,200 Ft. Apr–Sept Tues–Sun 10am–6pm; Oct–Mar Tues–Sun 10am–4pm. Bus: 16A from Moszkva tér or 16 from Deák tér to Castle Hill. Funicular: From Clark Ádám tér to Castle Hill.

Kőzépkori Zsidó Imaház (Medieval Jewish Prayer House) (Finds) You could walk past this tiny medieval Sephardic synagogue without realizing it is here; the door is not well marked. This prayer house was built at the end of the 14th century and was excavated accidentally in 1964; no one knew it was here. What was found were Jewish decorations on the walls of a chapel from the 17th century. One picture shows a bow pointing to heaven with statements from Hanna's prayer: "The bows of the mighty men are broken, and they that stumbled are girded with strength." Another is a Star of David with Aaron's blessing: "The LORD bless thee, and keep thee: The LORD make his face shine upon thee, and be gracious unto thee," as translated in the King James Bible. In the entry chamber there is a medieval grave with headstones on display demonstrating the life and history of the early Jews in the area. For more information on Jewish history, see p. 12. The English-speaking caretaker will give you a free informal tour; he is more than pleased to have visitors. You can pretty much see the whole place from the entry; consider your admission fee a contribution to the museum.

I. Táncsics Mihály u. 26. No phone. Admission 500 Ft adults, 250 Ft students. Photos outside free. May–Oct Tues–Sun 10am–6pm. Bus: 16A from Moszkva tér or 16 from Deák tér to Castle Hill. Funicular: From Clark Ádám tér to Castle Hill.

Semmelweis Orvostörténeti Múzeum (Semmelweis Museum of Medical History) This museum, which traces the history of medicine from ancient times to the modern era, is located in the former home of Ignác Semmelweis, Hungary's leading 19th-century physician. Semmelweis is hailed as the "savior of mothers" for his role in identifying the cause of puerperal (childbed) fever and preventing it by advocating that physicians wash their hands between patients, an uncommon practice at the time. The museum, spread over four rooms, displays everything from early medical instruments to anatomical models to old medical textbooks. There's also a faithfully reconstructed 19th-century pharmacy. Descriptions are in Hungarian only, but many exhibits are self-explanatory.

I. Apród u. 1–3. ⓒ **1/375-3533.** www.semmelweis.museum.hu. Admission 700 Ft adults, 350 Ft students and seniors. Photo 600 Ft; video 1,500 Ft. Mar–Oct Tues–Sun 10:30am–6pm; Nov–Feb Tues–Sun 10:30am–4pm. Bus: 5 or 178A, or tram 19.

A Muslim Shrine

Gül Baba Türbéje (Tomb of Gül Baba) ★ (Finds) At the time of this writing, the tomb was closed for renovations with no future completion date available. However, the curious can still visit the area. Celebrating the conquest of Buda with festivities and dinner in 1541, the ill-fated Turkish dervish Gül Baba fell over dead. Gül Baba belonged to

Statues, Which Statues?

By now, most people have forgotten that the city was littered with statues to Lenin, Marx, Engels, and the other representations of the Communist times. If you have some recollection of them and are wondering where they have disappeared to, here is your answer. In the aftermath of 1989, they were not wanted any longer being constant reminders of difficult times. A plan was conceived for an outdoor museum, **Memento Park**, created in 1993 and expanded since then when funds allow.

Besides the 42 statues, you will find a lot of symbolism. As you enter the park, the statues are in three sections, each with a theme. Each section if viewed from above would be symbolic of an eternity symbol; Communism was meant to last all eternity. However, if you are standing at the front gate and follow the path forward, you will see a brick wall ahead of you. Communism ran into a brick wall. I fear that I was under the impression that the dry ugly grounds were from lack of care, but my guide explained this is a metaphor for the ugly realities of Communism.

The new exhibition hall created from an old army barrack has fascinating pictures of the past with English translations. A movie-viewing area continually shows an uncovered authentic training film for spies. It runs 50 minutes. I did not have time to watch it all, but was intrigued enough to return.

Located in the XXII district (extreme Southern Buda) on Balatoni út (© 1/424-7500; www.mementopark.hu), the park is a memorial to an era, to despotism, and to times of fear. The tiny museum gift kiosk sells Communist-era memorabilia, such as T-shirts with flamboyantly modern, humorous sayings, medals, and cassettes of Red Army marching songs. The park is open daily from 10am to dusk and admission is 1,500 Ft for adults or 1,000 Ft for students. To get to the park, take either bus no. 7E or 173E from Ferenciek tere to Kelen-földi pályaudvar, the end of the line. Buy round-trip tickets for 420 Ft for the

a group of Turkish religious who worked with horticulture, specifically on developing new species of roses. His tomb is located in the steep, twisting neighborhood of the Hill of Roses (Rózsadomb) District. The Turkish government maintains it as a Muslim shrine. The descriptions of the religious items and rugs on display are in Hungarian and Turkish, but an English-language pamphlet is available on request.

II. Mecset u. 14. © 1/326-0062. Tram: 4 or 6 to Margaret Buda hid; the most direct route to Gül Baba tér is via Mecset u., off Margaret u.

ÓBUDA

Varga Imre Gyűjtemény (Imre Varga Collection) ★★ (Finds) Imre Varga is Hungary's best-known contemporary sculptor. As you walk to the small museum, just off Óbuda's Fő tér, you will run into some ladies holding umbrellas regardless of the weather, one of his works on display outside. Inside the museum, a varied cross-section of Varga's work will have you alternating smiles with winces. At the back of the museum is a garden with more pieces; people are portrayed without embellished glory, while the museum's yellow Volán bus for a 10-minute ride to the park; ask the driver where to get off. The Volán bus is not a city bus; passes and transit tickets are not valid. The other options are to take bus 150 from Kosztolányi Dezső tér or take the convenient direct bus service from Deák tér for 3,950 Ft or 2,450 Ft for students (admission ticket to the park included). The timetable varies by season, but the 11am departure remains constant with an additional run at 3pm in July and August. Personally, the guided tour totally changed my opinion and appreciation for the park, so I highly recommend it. Tours on-site for those who come by public transport are 1,200 Ft.

Other statues have replaced those in this park, while others are in spaces not formerly graced with artwork. One statue that just about every tourist sees is *The Little Princess,* but without a plaque, it is often mistaken for a jester. It sits on the railing on Vigadó tér, a straight shot down to the river from Vörösmarty tér. You will see by her knees that she has been rubbed in admiration and luck for some time. The sculptor is László Marton, who also created the incredible statue of Attila József, the famous Hungarian poet, as he gazes toward the Danube by Parliament. Sculptor Imre Varga created the statue you will find on the tiny Vértanúk tér across from Parliament. He also created one of the pieces in the park. The man on the bridge is **Imre Nagy,** Hungary's prime minister during the '56 revolution, who tried to build a democratic Hungary by negotiating with the Soviets and gaining Western support. His place on the bridge is a metaphor for being caught in the middle. He was later taken prisoner by the Soviets and executed. Varga is also the artist who created the *Weeping Willow* in the courtyard of the Great Synagogue. And back again to Vigadó tér, you will find the fairly new *Girl with a Dog,* a playful statue of a child playing ball with her canine friend, by artist Dávid Raffay. All of these artists are contemporary, still living and working at their craft.

cats play in and out of the garden. For an example of the sculptor's work in a different public context, see the statue of Imre Nagy near Parliament. Have small currency ready: they rarely have change.

III. Laktanya u. 7. ✆ **1/250-0274.** Admission 500 Ft adults, 250 Ft students. Tues–Sun 10am–6pm. Train: HÉV suburban railroad from Batthyány tér to Árpád híd.

Victor Vasarely Museum   Often referred to as the father of op-art, Vasarely was born in Pécs, lived in Budapest, but left for Paris where he died in 1997. This museum was opened in 1987 after the artist donated 400 pieces of his work to the country. Downstairs you will find a number of his earlier graphic artist pieces and upstairs are the larger op-art works of colorful, geometric art. If this leaves you wanting more, there is also a museum with his work in Pécs, see chapter 14, p. 278.

III. Szentlélek tér 6. ✆ **1/388-7551.** www.vasarely.tvn.hu. Admission 800 Ft adults, 400 Ft students permanent collection; special exhibits variable. Photo 300 Ft; video 1,500 Ft. Tues–Sun 10am–5:30pm; call in advance, since the museum closes occasionally for private events. Train: HÉV suburban railroad from Batthyány tér to Árpád híd.

(Fun Facts   **Did You Know. . . ?**

- A network consisting of 10km (6¼ miles) of tunnels, built in the Middle Ages for military purposes, lies underneath Buda's Castle District.
- Budapest did not become a unified city until 1873, when Pest, Buda, and Óbuda merged. A bridge crossing the Danube prompted this momentous decision.
- Budapest is the site of the first underground metro line in continental Europe, which you can still ride today (the Yellow line). It was built for, you guessed it, the millennium celebration. So where was the very first metro built? London. The third was in Boston.
- The Swedish diplomat Raoul Wallenberg, stationed in Budapest, saved thousands of Jews from Nazi deportation by issuing fake passports and setting up safe houses, only to disappear himself into the Soviet gulag after the city's liberation. He was never heard from again. Petitions sent to the Soviet government requesting the opening of their secret records regarding Wallenberg's fate have fallen on deaf ears. Others who helped the Jews are discussed in Chapter 2, "Hungary and Budapest in Depth."
- The retreating Nazis blew up all of Budapest's bridges in the final days of World War II. They have all been reconstructed since then as close to their original designs as possible.
- The Red Army liberated Pest from Nazi occupation on January 18, 1945, but did not manage to liberate Buda until February 13.
- The longest "basket handle" bridge was opened in Dunaújváros, Hungary, in 2007. Being 308m (1,010 ft) long, beating the previous record holder, Osaka, Japan by 60m (197 ft).
- On St. Stephen's feast day and national holiday, Sunday, August 20, 2006, a major storm came from nowhere, destroyed trees and cars, and caused five deaths. On Sunday, August 19, 2007, another major storm whipped up the city, but a worse storm came through on Monday, August 20, 2007.
- If you ride either the 4 or 6 trams from beginning to end in either direction, you will have ridden the longest tram route in the world in the longest contiguous tram in the world.
- Matches that were safe and non-poisonous were invented in 1836 by Hungarian János Irinyi.
- The oversized "noodles" used in many Hungarian recipes are thought to date back to the 9th century, when fighters needed to cook a quick meal.

5 PARKS, GARDENS, & PLAYGROUNDS

Spending time in a park or any green space is a blissful escape for many of the city dwellers who cannot actually retreat from the city for some countryside getaway to recharge their mental batteries.

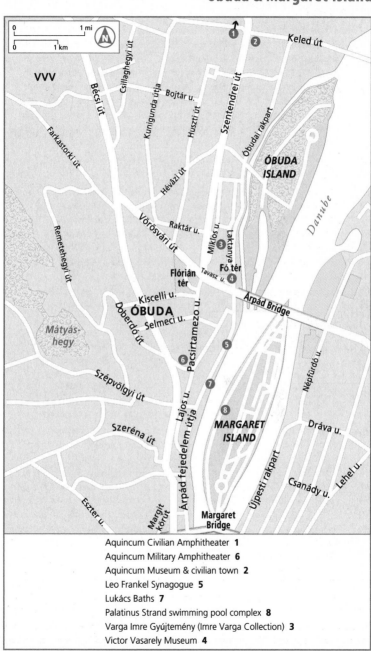

EXPLORING BUDAPEST

7

PARKS, GARDENS, & PLAYGROUNDS

Aquincum Civilian Amphitheater **1**

Aquincum Military Amphitheater **6**

Aquincum Museum & civilian town **2**

Leo Frankel Synagogue **5**

Lukács Baths **7**

Palatinus Strand swimming pool complex **8**

Varga Imre Gyújtemény (Imre Varga Collection) **3**

Victor Vasarely Museum **4**

Tips **Instant Picnic**

Before heading off on a hike, taking a leisurely stroll in a park, or going to Margaret Island, make the trip extra special and plan to have a picnic. Make your first
stop at **Duran Szendvics** VI. Bajcsy Zsilinszky út 7 (✆ **1/267-9624**) or V. Október
6 u. 15 (✆ **1/332-9348**). This Viennese chain has an extensive selection of more
than 20 varieties of artistically assembled open-faced sandwiches, which they
will box to go. You can buy bottled drinks or pick them up at one of the kiosks at
or near the park. Voila! Instant picnic with disposable waste, so there is nothing
to carry when you are done. Both locations are open weekdays from 8am to 6pm
and Saturday 8am to noon.

Popular **Margaret Island (Margit-sziget)** ★★★ has an interesting royalty-related
history going back to King Béla. He vowed that if he were successful in the Mongol
invasion from 1242 to 1244, his daughter Margaret would be brought up as a nun. Well
he was, so when she was 10, she was brought to the island to live a life of pious chastity.
On the island, there are the ruins attesting to the religious who lived here. You can walk
around what is left of the Dominican Convent where you'll find signs mentioning St.
Margaret, a 13th-century Franciscan church. The island was once called Rabbit Island
since it seemed to be infested with them. No bunny was able to leave without a bridge
connecting the island to shore at the time. The island has been open to the public since
1908, but visitors were charged a fee, double on Sunday. It was not until 1945 when it
was declared free for all. The long, narrow island is a leisurely escape from the hectic city.

In the summertime, you will find the large fountain plays classical music every 20
minutes and all of the selections are posted on a pole nearby. The flower gardens are well
kept, so it is not unusual to find crowds gathered on the lawn or benches surrounding it.

Connected to both Buda and Pest via the Margaret and Árpád bridges all but local
buses are banned from the island with few other exceptions. The island holds many
attractions including the Palatinus Strand open-air baths (p. 160), the Alfréd Hajós Sport
Pool, and the Open-Air Theater. In the warm season, there is a restaurant called the
Holdudvar, which serves good food at reasonable prices. It features outdoor movies and
is very popular with the university set.

Sunbathers line the steep embankments along the river, and bikes are available for rent
(see "By Bike," under "Getting Around" in chapter 4). There is a small petting zoo, many
walking trails, and lots of green areas for spreading a blanket out. Several snack vendors
and even clubs can fulfill your hunger or thirst needs. With what may seem like a near-
overload of options, Margaret Island remains a tranquil place for a city break within the
city. Margaret Island is best reached by tram no. 4 or 6, but construction on the bridge
will continue through 2012, closing the bridge to all traffic. You will need to walk over
the bridge from the last tram stop, Jászai Mari tér.

City Park (Városliget) ★★ sits behind Heroes' Square and is just as popular as Margaret Island for lazy walks, picnics in the grass, and the many attractions located in and
around the park. It was built in stages, but the first stage started in the mid-1800s. The
famous Hungarian poet, János Arany (Arany János u. fame), wrote a poem called "Song
of the City Park" in 1877. The park, along with Heroes' Square, has been privy to many
demonstrations as well as celebrations during its long history. The **Vajdahunyad Castle**

located by the lake is magical when lit at night. The lake is used for small boat rides in the summer. Near the lake, an area is flooded to provide a frozen surface for ice skating in winter (p. 162). The park also embraces **Animal Garden Boulevard (Állat-kerti körút),** where the zoo, the circus, and the amusement park are all found (see "Especially for Kids," below). You will also find Széchenyi Baths (p. 159) on one outer rim of the park. The **Transport Museum** is off at the southern end of City Park, which is considerably less crowded, but also less landscaped making it less attractive as a relaxation area. The nearby **Petőfi Csarnok** is the venue for a variety of popular cultural events, concerts, and the weekly flea market (p. 219). The Yellow metro line makes stops at Hősök tere (Heroes' Square), at the edge of the park, and at Széchenyi fürdő, in the middle of the park.

There are numerous parks and nature reserves in the **Buda Hills.** You can ride the Children's Railroad through the hills or take the János Hill chairlift to its highest point (p. 149).

The Buda Hills are an easy place to explore on your own; but depending on where you go, you may want to spot a bus or tram line for your return. Moszkva tér is the best place to start an excursion into the hills. Pick up tram no. 56 or bus no. 21, 22, or 28; get off when you see an area you like.

If you have time to saunter through Budapest, there are some well-maintained parks that are worth taking a seat in for a few moments rest. The Hungarian word for playground is *játszótér* (or *játszó kert*) or just *kert* for garden. **Karolyn kerts** ★★★ is a small enclosed park in the city, just a couple of blocks from the Hungarian National Museum. This is a perfect place to relax or for children to release some energy. It is bordered by Ferenczy István utca, Magyar utca, and Henszlmann Imre utca. Enter the park through a wrought-iron gate. Once inside, you'll find swings and seesaws, a sandbox with a slide, and a stretch of green grass on which to run. In the middle of all this is a fountain surrounded by flowers. This is a busy and popular park for mothers with their children and for seniors who like to sit and relax. It once belonged to the adjacent Károlyi mansion, which was the home of Mihály Károlyi, who served briefly as Hungarian prime minister in 1918. The mansion functions as the Petőfi Museum of Hungarian Literature (© **1/317-3611,** ext. 203; www.pim.hu). Its location in the Inner City makes it a convenient destination. Admission is 480 Ft and it is open Tuesday through Sunday 10am to 6pm.

---

6 ESPECIALLY FOR KIDS

Just because this section is geared toward children, you don't have to have children to visit the places mentioned here. Everyone has a child inside waiting for the chance to escape. When you are in a foreign country where no one knows you, it is a liberating opportunity to be playful, so let loose.

Directly behind the Mammut Shopping Mall in Buda's Széna tér is the **Millenáris Park** Zöld Péter playground where all the toys are based on a fairy tale. Besides the large wooden house to climb in, there are wooden toys, a giant fish, a smaller house, and a cable glider. Within the Millenáris Park is a fishpond and food court next to the Place of Miracles (see below). Parents can sit and watch their kids playing in this safe and creative playground from the shade of trees.

> ⓘ **Tips**   **City Guide for Children**
>
> A family from the Netherlands who moved to Budapest has created an outstanding children's guidebook with the cooperation of children from 12 schools adding their drawings to bring it alive. ***Benjamin in Budapest*** ★★★ is a phenomenal book for family outings; kids will love the chance to help plan the trip. It is available at most bookstores in the city including the children's bookstore Pagony (see p. 201), the Alexandra bookstore chain, and Tourinform offices. It will make a memorable souvenir.

Three attractions mentioned below are the zoo, the amusement park, and the circus. They are located in City Park (Városliget), along the famed Animal Garden Boulevard (Állatkerti körút). You could easily spend a whole child-oriented day here. In addition to the information below, see the information on the Palatinus Strand outdoor swimming-pool complex (p. 160) and horse and pony riding in the Buda Hills (p. 162). Also see the latter half of the section, "Parks, Gardens, & Playgrounds," above for the lowdown on the best of Budapest's playgrounds.

ART GALLERY

Carbora Labyrinth Playhouse (**Kids**)   Located at the Vim Design Art Gallery, this offers more than just child's play. Professional artists, musicians, and teachers provide quality learn-through-experience creative art projects and games from ancient to modern times. They incorporate music, art, literature, and history into various projects, so even children without knowledge of Hungarian will find some participatory activity to enjoy. Children are supervised, so parents can explore the gallery.

VI. Király u. 26. ⓒ **1/666-3100**. Saturday 10am–6pm. Tram: 4 or 6 Király.

MUSEUM

Természettudományi Múzeum (Museum of Natural History) (**Kids**)   During my days of discovery, visiting all the museums in Budapest, I found this museum delightful for children. It is child-friendly with a number of interactive modules to keep a youngster entertained and informed at the same time. Through the natural history of the Carpathian Basin and the exhibits, a child can learn about human development from the earliest times to present. The museum is ideally situated next to Orczy Kert (Orczy Garden), a large park featuring more than 100 different species of trees and a small lake. Until after World War II, the park belonged to the Hungarian Military School; the museum is in the more-modern building to the left of the old school.

VIII. Ludovika tér 2–6. ⓒ **1/210-1085**. www.nhmus.hu. Admission 600 Ft adults, 300 Ft students for permanent exhibits. Temporary exhibits variable rates. Photos 200 Ft. Wed–Mon 10am–6pm. Metro: Nagyvárad tér (Blue line).

FAMILY FUN IN CITY PARK

Fővárosi Állat és Növénykert Zoo and Botanical Gardens (**Kids**)   Opened in 1866, the zoo houses animals in some beautiful Art Nouveau- and national-style buildings designed by the best Hungarian architects of the time. It is located near the circus and the amusement park on City Park's famous Animal Garden Boulevard, a favorite spot for Hungarians for 140 years. The entrance is striking with two huge stone elephants flanking the gate. Parts of the zoo have been modernized several times attempting to create a contemporary and humane environment for their 2,000 animal residents. A polar bear exhibit has been built to show the frolicking of the bears when they are in the water or lazing on the ice. The elephant house has also been restructured giving the animals more space. It boasts the world's first test-tube rhino baby and triplet leopards. Two renovated greenhouses, the largest of their kind in central Europe, contain spectacular tropical plants. During the summer, the zoo hosts special concerts.

XIV. Állatkerti krt. 6–12. ℭ 1/273-4900. www.zoobudapest.com. Admission 1,850 Ft adults, 1,290 Ft children 14 and under and students with international student ID card, free for children 2 and under, family 5,290 Ft. Children 14 and under must be accompanied by a parent. Mon–Thurs 9am–5pm; Fri–Sun 9am–7pm; hours vary by month, verify on website. Metro: Hősök tere or Széchenyi fürdő (Yellow line).

Közlekedési Múzeum (Transport Museum) ★ (Kids) Located near the Petőfi Csarnok in the little-visited southeastern corner of City Park, this impressive museum, which celebrated its 100th anniversary in 1999, features large-scale 1:5 models of various kinds of historic vehicles, especially trains. The museum also exhibits vintage motorcycles and bicycles, early model cars, and antique horse buggies. A model train set runs every 15 minutes on the mezzanine level: follow the crowds. On weekends, a film on aviation history is shown at 11am. The gift shop features all sorts of transportation-related trinkets. An aviation exhibit is housed in the Petőfi Csarnok, an all-purpose community center nearby.

XIV. Városligeti krt. 11. ℭ 1/273-3840. www.kozlekedesimuzeum.hu. Admission 1,000 Ft adults, 500 Ft students and seniors for permanent collection; temporary exhibits variable rates. Photo 1,000 Ft; video 3,000 Ft. May–Sept Tues–Fri 10am–5pm, Sat–Sun 10am–6pm; Oct–Apr closes 1 hr. earlier. Trolleybus: 74 from Károly krt. (pick it up on Dohány u., across the street from Dohány Synagogue) or 7 or 173 from Blaha Lujza tér to Hungária krt.

Vidám Park (Amusement Park) ★★ This is a must if you're traveling with kids or are a child at heart. Some rides in particular aren't to be missed. The 100-year-old **Merry-Go-Round** *(Körhinta),* constructed almost entirely of wood, has been restored to its original grandeur, though it still creaks mightily as it spins. The riders must actively pump to keep the horses rocking, which is a sight in itself, and authentic Würlitzer music plays. The **Roller Coaster,** operating since 1926, has a wooden frame and is listed as a historic monument. You rush over nine waves before finishing the ride. The **Ikarus** will tickle your senses with its 30m (98 ft) height and 30kmph (18 mph) speed making for a titillating 3-minute ride.

XIV. Állatkerti krt. 14–16. ℭ 1/343-9810. www.vidampark.hu. Admission 15€ adults, 11€ children 100–140cm (39–55 in) tall. Admission includes most rides with the wristband provided, but five are extra fees. Oct–Nov Mon–Fri noon–6pm; Mar weekends only noon–6pm; Apr–May weekdays 11am–6pm, Sat–Sun 10am–6pm; June–Sept daily 10am–8pm Metro: Széchenyi fürdő.

A RAILROAD & CHAIRLIFT

Gyermekvasút (Children's Railroad) ★★★ (Kids) Built in the 1940s, this railroad is a throwback to Communist times when the Young Pioneers, the youth movement of the Communist Party, ran the operation. Today, it is only specially trained children learning and having fun under adult supervision. The scenery along this narrow-gauge rail journey is enchanting, especially in spring and fall. The youthful staff dresses in miniature versions of the official MÁV (Hungarian State Railways) uniforms, with all the appropriate paraphernalia. The train slowly winds 11km (6.8 miles) through the Buda Hills, providing numerous panoramas along the way.

To get to the Széchenyi-hegy terminus, take the no. 61 tram from Moszkva tér two stations to the cogwheel *(fogaskerekű vasút)* station (the stop is Városmajor, and it is across the street from the Hotel Budapest, on Szilágyi Erzsébet fasor in Buda). Take the cogwheel to the Széchenyi hegy terminus. One-way travel time on the railway is 45 minutes ending at Hűvösvölgy, where you can again take the no. 61 tram to get you back to Moszkva tér.

Call the Széchenyi hegy terminus. ✆ **1/395-5420.** www.gyermekvasut.com. One-way trip full line terminal to terminal 600 Ft adults, 300 Ft children 14 and under, free for children 5 and under; round trip 1,200 Ft adults, 600 Ft children 14 and under, free for children 5 and under, 3,000 Ft full day family ticket. Summer daily 10am–7pm; Winter Sep–Apr, Tues–Sun 9am–5pm. Trains are scheduled to run every hour or so, but check the website in English for exact timetables.

János-Hegy Libegő (János Hill Chairlift) ★★ (Kids) An old-fashioned chairlift, but only dating back to 1970, lifts you over the tree tops to János Hill covering 1,040m (3,412 ft) of forested area from as high as 262m (859 ft). From here you can take a steep 10- to 15-minute walk to Budapest's highest point. At the top is the neo-Romanesque *Erzsébet Kilátó* **(Lookout Tower)**, built in 1910. When I went there was no charge, but others have claimed there was a nominal fee to climb the tower. It is well worth it for the view. The tower is open daily from 8am to 5pm. You'll find a nondescript snack bar at the tower, but be careful of bees in the warm weather. You can ride the chair back down, hike back down to Dénes u. to catch the no. 22 bus, or, if you like, try the **Buda Triangle** above.

XII. Zugligeti út 97. ✆ **1/394-3764.** Chairlift trip one way 700 Ft or round trip 1,200 Ft adults, 400 Ft or 600 Ft children. Daily 10am–4pm; in summer to as late as 7pm, depending on demand. All year, depending on weather. Bus: 22 from Moszkva tér to Dénes u.

A CIRCUS

Nagy Cirkusz (Great Circus) (Kids) In Budapest, the circus is always in town, year-round. The building, which is the venue for the circus, is the only stone circus in central

---

(Kids) **The Buda Triangle**

Are you ready to head for the hills? No matter your age, you can enjoy the triple-transport triangular trip on the slopes of the Buda Hills. From Moszkva ter, hop on tram no. 61 for two stops to the **Cogwheel Railway (Fogaskereku)**, which clicks its way up a steep grade to the **Children's Train** on Szechenyi-hegy (hill). Uniformed children, true to the original model of the Soviet Pioneer Scouts, assist in ticketing and boarding the open-air cars. Enjoy the short ride across the wooded ridge. Get off at the fourth stop, János-hegy, where you will find the path to a terrace *bufe* (cafe) for refreshments, a playground, and toilet facilities. Nearby, the Erzsebet Lookout Tower, four stories high and on the highest point of Budapest (529m/1,736 ft), is worth the climb. There is no fee. When ready to return to the Danube area, take your seats on the gently descending **Chair Lift (Libego)**, and marvel at the spectacular views of the city. Just outside the exit, bus no. 22 will take you to Moszkva tér. The whole triangle can be done in reverse too. For those who may want more outdoor action, check with Tourinform (p. 28) for hiking trails atop the Buda Hills.

(Kids) Bábszínházak (Puppet Theaters)

Kids from around the world love **Hungarian puppet theater** ★. The shows are all in Hungarian, but with such standard fare as Hungarian versions of *Cinderella*, *Peter and the Wolf*, and local favorites *Misi Mókus*, *Marcipán cica*, and *János Vitéz*, no one seems to have trouble following the plot. The audience is an important part of the show: For instance, Hungarian children shriek "*Rossz farkas!*" ("Bad wolf!") at every appearance of the villain in *Peter and the Wolf*.

Budapest has two puppet theaters, with the season running from October to mid-June. Tickets are extremely cheap, usually in the 800-Ft-to-1,600-Ft range. The **Budapest Puppet Theater (Budapesti Bábszínház)** is at VI. Andrássy út 69 (① **1/321-5200**; www.budapest-babszinhaz.hu); the nearest metro station is Oktogon (Yellow line). The **Kolibri Puppet Theater (Kolibri Bábszínház)** is at VI. Jókai tér 10 (① **1/353-4633**; www.kolibriszinhaz.hu); Jókai tér is halfway between the Oktogon and Opera stations of the Yellow metro line. Shows start at various times throughout the day (days vary, so check in advance) with the first show usually at 10am and the last at 5pm, and tickets are available all day at the box offices.

Europe and seats 1,850. This is a traditional circus, with clowns, animals, jugglers, acrobats, and so on. In 2009, they celebrated their 120-year jubilee. When buying tickets, it's helpful to know that *porond* means "ring level" and *erkély* means "balcony." Check the website (it has an English link) to verify times, as the schedule has minor changes from year to year. The English pages are quite thorough and have a seating chart. The box office is open weekdays from 10am to 6pm, Saturday 9am to 7:30pm, and Sunday 9am to 6pm.

XIV. Állatkerti krt. 12a. ① **1/343-8300**. www.maciva.hu. 1,900 Ft–2,800 Ft adults, 1,500 Ft–2,200 Ft children, free for children 3 and under. Performances Wed–Fri 3pm; Sat 11am, 3pm, and 7pm; Sun 11am and 3pm. Metro: Hősök tere or Széchenyi fürdő (Yellow line).

7 FOR THE MUSIC LOVER

Museums in Budapest celebrate the contributions of great Hungarian musicians. The greatest composer of Hungarian music of the 19th century, and one of the country's most famous sons, is undoubtedly **Ferenc (Franz) Liszt** (1811–96). Although Liszt maintained a deep interest in Hungarian culture and musical traditions, as evidenced by his well-known *Hungarian Rhapsodies*, he is well known for creating the musical idiom known as the symphonic poem with his *Les Preludes* (1848). He served as the first president of Budapest's Academy of Music, which is named after him. To top it all off, Liszt was also one of the great virtuoso pianists of his century.

If Liszt was the towering figure of 19th-century Hungarian music, **Béla Bartók** (1881–1945) and **Zoltán Kodály** (1882–1967) were the giants of the early 20th century. The founders of Hungarian ethnomusicology, Bartók and Kodály traveled the back roads of the country in the early 1900s, systematically recording not only Hungarian and

Gypsy folk music, but also music of the whole Carpathian Basin region. Peasant folk music had been an important part of the region's rural culture for hundreds of years, but by the early 20th century, there were not many musicians playing and the music was in danger of being lost. In addition to saving a wealth of music from oblivion, Bartók and Kodály made some important discoveries in their research, noting both the differences and the interrelationships between Hungarian and other folk-music traditions (especially Gypsy music), which had fused considerably over time. Both men were composers, and the influence of the folk music they so cherished can easily be heard in their compositions. Kodály established the internationally acclaimed Kodály Method of musical education and lived to become the grand old man of Hungarian music, while Bartók died relatively young in the United States, an impoverished, embittered refugee from fascism.

Concerts are given at the museums below; see the Budapest's free bimonthly *Koncert Kalendárium,* available at most four- and five-star hotels, and tourist information centers, or online at www.koncertkalendarium.hu.

Bartók Béla Emlékház (Béla Bartók Memorial House) This little museum, high in the Buda Hills, occupies Béla Bartók's final Hungarian home and exhibits artifacts from Bartók's career as well as some of the composer's original furniture. The house has been decorated to reflect the time period and atmosphere in which the composer lived, and is run by the composer's heirs. The museum has undergone an extensive renovation extending the museum. Every year on September 26, the date of Bartók's death, the Bartók String Quartet performs. Concerts are also given on Friday evenings in spring and autumn, and sporadically on Sunday as well. Concerts are also offered on occasion, but they are only scheduled 3 months in advance and prices vary. Check the website for current details.

II. Csalán u. 29. © **1/394-2100.** www.bartokmuseum.hu. 1,000 Ft adults, 500 Ft students. Admission includes guided tour. Tues–Sun 10am–5pm. Closed first 2 weeks of Aug. Bus: 5 from Március 15 tér or Moszkva tér to Pasaréti tér (the last stop).

Institute for Musicology Primarily the archives for the Hungarian Folk Music and Folk Dance and the Bartók works, the small museum has a collection of musical instruments used by some of the great composers and musicians. They hold concerts here throughout the year, but not on a regular basis. Check their website for current information.

II. Táncsics u. 7. © **1/214-6770.** www.zti.hu. Admission by donation. Tues–Sun 10am–5pm. Bus: 16, Castle hill.

Károlyi Palace A renovated gem of inner Budapest, this palace is an intimate courtyard with a strong stay-a-while atmosphere while the Sándor Petőri Literary Museum occupies the bulk of the building. On a stage set up in the garden with seating capacity of 500, concerts of classical, jazz, and folk music fulfill the magic of a summer evening's entertainment. The upcoming schedule of events is only posted 1 month before the season, so call for current concert information.

V. Károlyi Mihály u. 16. © **1/317-3450.** www.pim.hu. Check performance schedule with Tourinform or website for dates/hours. Metro: Ferenciek tere or Kálvin tér (Blue line).

Kiscelli Museum Sitting at the top of Remetehegy (Hermit's Hill) in Óbuda, the Trinitarians first built this baroque castle as a monastery in the 18th century. What is left is an intriguing shell of a church hall, a bare courtyard, a baroque sculpture hall, and an enormous, mysterious crypt. During the summer months concerts are sporadically scheduled, which are worth attending just to see the building. Check the bimonthly *Koncert* or the other calendar resources given above for current offerings, if any. At **153** other times, the hall is host to an art gallery and special art exhibitions. The offerings are listed on their website.

III. Kiscelli út 108. (✆ **1/388-7817.** www.btmfk.iif.hu. 700 Ft adults, 350 Ft students. Photos 500 Ft; video 1,500 Ft. Tues–Sun 10am–6pm. Tram: 17 from Margit Bridge to Szent Margit Kórház.

Liszt Ferenc Emlékmúzeum (Ferenc Liszt Memorial Museum) Located in the apartment in which Liszt spent his last years, this modest museum features several of the composer's pianos, including a child's Bachmann piano and two Chickering & Sons grand pianos. Also noteworthy are the many portraits of Liszt done by the leading Austrian and Hungarian artists of his time and two busts by the Hungarian sculptor Alajos Stróbl. Concerts are performed here on Saturday at 11am.

VI. Vörösmarty u. 35. (✆ **1/322-9804.** 800 Ft adults, 250 Ft students with international ID. Photo 1,100 Ft; video 2,200 Ft. Mon–Fri 10am–6pm; Sat 9am–5pm. Closed first 3 weeks of Aug. Metro: Vörösmarty u. (Yellow line).

---

8 ORGANIZED TOURS: TRADITIONAL

BUS TOURS

There are plenty of options for sightseeing bus tours, but not all are created equal. The one that has gained my favor over the others is the **Budapest Sightseeing Hop-on Hop-off Bus Tour** (✆ 1/317-7767; wwwprogramcentral.hu). However, even this is not enough to distinguish it from some of the others who use the same hop-on hop-off information on the side of their buses. The one that I value the most runs 5,000 Ft per person, tickets are purchased on the bus and are good for 24 hours. What distinguishes this bus from the others, besides costing an extra 500 Ft to 1,000 Ft, is that you get two Danube riverboat rides. The boat-ride tickets are good until the end of the year in which you buy your bus ticket, so don't feel obligated to cruise the same night of your bus tour. The added bonus is a discount booklet for different things within the city. The office is located at the Meridien Hotel, Program Centrum Travel Agency Erzsébet Square 9–11. The first and earliest starting point is directly across the street.

Ibusz (✆ 06/40-428-794 (mobile phone only); www.ibusz.hu) has been around for a long time, but that does not always equal quality. They have 11 different boat and bus tours, ranging from basic city tours to special folklore-oriented tours. Unfortunately, the tours are pretty sterile and boring (if you want a bus tour, try one of the alternatives above). Ibusz operates April to October 10:30am to 5:30 pm and November to March 10:30am to 1:30pm. All buses are airconditioned during the summer, and all guides speak English. Their **Circle Sightseeing Tour** includes a 1-hour Danube river cruise for 16€. This is not a hop-on, hop-off tour. Tours can be booked at any Ibusz office and at most major hotels, or by calling Ibusz directly at the toll-free number above. All major credit cards are accepted.

---

9 ORGANIZED TOURS: UNTRADITIONAL

BIKE TOURS

Budapest Bike Budapest Bike was started in 2005 by six Hungarian cyclists. They offer the coolest bike tours downtown, starting at 10am daily for as few as one person.

The tour costs 5,000 Ft. It includes a tour guide, bike rental, helmet, map, a chain lock, and a drink. They also have tours outside of the city. If you are bound and determined to go it alone, they will rent you a bike for 6 hours for 2,000 Ft or for a full day at 3,000 Ft; a tandem will run you 3,000 Ft for 6 hours and 5,000 Ft for a full day. A helmet, chain lock, and insurance are all included in the rental. They also offer a guided evening program, called a pub crawl, which will take you to the hottest pubs in Budapest for a mere 5,000 Ft. Included in this tour is a guide for 4 hours, a minimum of four pubs, two beers, and a shot. A minimum group of four people is needed.

VII. Wesselényi u. 13 ✆ **06/30-944-5533** (mobile phone only). www.budapestbike.hu. Mar 15–Oct 15 daily 9am–6pm, from Oct 16–Mar 14 they have no scheduled hours, but will go in if called. Metro: Astoria (Red line) or Deák (all lines).

Yellow Zebra Bikes　Centrally and soon to be all over the city, Yellow Zebra Bikes offers bike rentals and guided bike tours, with optional helmets. Bike rentals cost 1,500 Ft for 1–5 hours or 4,000 for 24 hours. Guided tours may be your best option, setting you back 5,000 Ft for adults, 4,500 Ft for students with an ID card. The tour price includes the guide, a bike, optional helmets, baskets, and bungee cords. Just show up at the office before the tour leaves at 11am. In July and August, there is a second tour at 5:30pm.

V. Sütő u. 2 ✆ **1/266-8777**. www.yellowzebrabikes.com. High season daily 8:30am–8pm; Nov–Mar daily 10am–6pm. Metro: Deák (all lines). VI. Lázár u. 16. ✆ **1/269-3869**. Mon–Fri 9:30am–7pm; Sat–Sun 9:30am–4pm. Metro: Opera (Yellow line).

BOAT TOURS

If you venture down to the river, you will find a number of companies hawking their river cruises. Almost all are created equal, the only difference will be how many bridges they happen to go under. Let your wallet be your guide for choosing.

Legenda Tours ★★★　A private company founded in 1990 offers several boat tours on the Danube using panoramic boats. The daytime tour, called *Duna Bella*, operates daily starting at 11am with multiple choices thereafter during high season. Our 1-hour tour lasted 20 minutes longer and was excellent. Two drinks are included. They operate year-round with less daily offerings in off-season months. It is best to check their website for current times. The 2-hour ride includes a stop at Margaret Island, with a walk on the island. One- or 2-hour tickets on the *Duna Bella* charges adults 2,900 Ft or 3,900 Ft, students 2,900 Ft, and children 1,950 Ft. For the *Danube Legend*, a 1-hour evening tour, adults pay 4,900 Ft, students 3,700 Ft, and children 2,450 Ft. The nighttime tour departs daily at 8:15pm in high season. Their schedule is too complex to list here; visit their website for full details. All boats leave from the Vigadó tér port, Pier 7. Tickets are available through most major hotels, at the dock, and through the Legenda website.

V. Vigadó tér Pier 7. ✆ **1/317-2203**. www.legenda.hu. Full schedule on website. Tram: 2.

MAHART　The Hungarian state company operates 1-hour sightseeing cruises on the Danube. Boats depart from Vigadó tér (on the Pest waterfront, between the Erzsébet Bridge and the Chain Bridge, near the Budapest Marriott hotel), daily and hourly during the high season from May 1 to the end of September. From the end of September to November 1 and March 21 to the end of April, they are daily, but the frequency is less. Rates are 2,990 Ft for adults, 2,490 Ft for students with ISIC card, and 1,490 Ft for children 14 and under, free for children 2 and under. For something different, MAHART also offers evening cruises with or without dinner included from 7:30pm to 9:30pm. If this floats your boat, they sail daily during high season; in low season October through November, sailings are Friday, Saturday, and Sunday. Buffet dinner and cruise is 6,990 Ft for adults and 3,490 Ft for children 15 and under, children 5 and under are free. Cruise only 2,990 Ft for adults and 1,490 Ft for children 15 and under.

V. Belgrád rakpart. ✆ 1/484-4013. www.mahartpassnave.hu. Call for times and reservations. Tram: 2.

Operetta Ship If you are an opera buff, you may enjoy this unique candlelit boat tour that includes performers singing famous operas, operettas, Italian and Spanish songs, musicals, instrumental solos, along with Hungarian folklore. During the tours, you will hear excerpts from Strauss, Mozart, Lehar, Gershwin, Puccini, and others. For a live show in theater seating, tickets are 4,900 Ft for adults, and 4,000 Ft for children 11 and under. VIP tickets without dinner but table seating, sightseeing, and program are 7,900 Ft for adults, 6,000 Ft for children 11 and under. Finally, a VIP Dinner ticket will cost you 12,800 Ft for adults and 9,000 Ft for the children. Music sightseeing tours are guided in English, German, and Hungarian during breaks in the performance. This is more for the music enthusiast since you will not be paying much attention to both the sights and the singing; so you may have to choose one or the other.

Vigadó tér 9 at Március 15 tér. ✆ 06/20-332-9116 (mobile phone only). www.operetthajo.hu. Apr–Oct Mon, Wed, Fri, and Sun 8–10pm; additional show on New Year's Eve 8pm–2am. Tram: 2.

CAVE TOUR

Barlangaszat ★★★ **Kids** If you have a craving for caving, then this tour company will fill that hole in your life. They have been providing this tour since 1994. Spend 3 to 3½ hours traipsing through the second-longest cave of Hungary, the Pál-völgyi–Mátyás-hegyi cave system. Most of it is situated under Budapest. Following a professional caving guide, you will explore the natural untouched cave system. The guides explain the formation of the Budai Mountains, the cave formations, and fossils along the way. All the necessary equipment is provided with the tour: protective clothing, helmet, and headlamp. A changing room is available at the cave entrance. Crawling, scrambling, and hunkering down will be done many times during the tour, but no previous experience in caving is needed. Minimum age is 6 years, but no upper age limit. It is not recommended for those who are claustrophobic or unable to squeeze through tight places. Three English tours a week or a special tour for a minimum of five people are offered.

No office. ✆ 06/20-928-4969 (mobile phone only). www.caving.hu. 4,500 Ft. Meet at 3:45pm at Nyugati tér. Reservations mandatory by phone, Internet, or Yellow Zebra Bikes at V. Sütő u. 2 location only. Metro: Nyugati (Blue line).

INVISIBLE TOUR

Invisible Exhibition **Finds** Travel to a world of blindness, allowing your other senses to be awakened. Personally, I have had temporary blindness in my youth, so I have no need to familiarize myself again, but I can certainly advocate the experience for others. Within this tour guided in English you will experience among other things, a walk in the park, visiting a museum, or paying for a coffee all in pitch-black surroundings. Adult tickets are 1,450 Ft, but students and seniors pay 1,200 Ft. Family tickets are 4,000 Ft. For the most adventurous you can also have an invisible dinner on Thursdays where two dishes are 4,990 Ft or four dishes are 6,490 Ft. Not hungry? Try an invisible massage Tuesday to Saturday for 3,500 Ft for an hour.

Register at (✆ 20/771-4236 (mobile phone only). www.lathatatlan.hu. Located in the E-Klub block in Népliget Park. Metro: Népliget (Blue line) and the park is at the top of the stairs.

Chosen Tours   Operating since 1990, this tour explores Jewish life and heritage in Budapest. All the guides are from the Jewish community and speak excellent English. The Special City Tour is by coach lasting 3 hours with stops and adds the focus of the Jewish connections with the usual history. The **Jewish Heritage Tour** is 3 hours as a combined coach-and-walking tour taking you to Buda's extraordinary Jewish landmarks followed by a walk in Pest's Jewish quarter where you visit and enter all the highlights and the hidden treasures. Each group tour costs 10,000 Ft. The walking portion can be done separately at 7,000 Ft per person. To combine both 3-hour tours over 2 days, the cost is 16,000 Ft. For private tours for a minimum group of four, add 2,000 Ft to the rates above per person. Other tours are available with Jewish sights pointed out. A Jewish-focused tour is available to Szentendre, also.

No office. ✆ **1/355-2202**. chosentours@yahoo.com. Reservations mandatory.

SEGWAY TOUR

Segway Tour ★★★   How about a tour while riding a Segway? Take a Segway (a stand-up scooter) through the city getting an overview in a unique mode of transportation offered by Discover Budapest/Yellow Zebra. Reservations are necessary and they advise that you book 1 month ahead of time. You can combine a unique ride and a tour. Each of the tours begin with a 30- to 45-minute orientation session in the plaza and park next to their office, where you will practice on the Segway so you feel comfortable and ready to go out and conquer Budapest. The Segway is appropriate for virtually anyone 12 and older (riders must be a minimum of 12 years old). Unfortunately, pregnant women are not able to participate. Helmets are required to be worn at all times. An insurance damage and liability waiver will also be required for all riders.

VI. Lázár u. 16. ✆ **1/269-3843**. www.citysegwaytours.com. Apr–Oct 10am and 6:30pm; Nov–Mar 10am. 65€. Metro: Opera (Yellow line).

WALKING TOURS

Several companies offer walking tours of historic Budapest. Those in this section are the ones that I have personally experienced or have heard rave reviews about. For those of us who enjoy walking, but are not so enthralled with organized tours, see below for an option you will love.

Absolute Walking Tour is offered as part of the Discover Budapest/Yellow Zebra group (✆ **1/269-3843;** www.absolutetours.com). The tours are conducted by energetic, friendly, and knowledgeable guides who meet you at the pickup point outside the Evangelical Church on Deák tér (all metro lines) at 9:30am and 1:30pm from May 1 to September 30. From October through April, tours start daily at 10:30am only, from the same departure point above. No tours on December 24, 25, or January 1. Tickets are 4,000 Ft for adults, 3,500 Ft for students with ID, children 13–17 years 2,000 Ft, and 12 and below are free. Buy your ticket from the tour guide at the start of the tour. Tours last 3½ hours taking you throughout both central Pest and central Buda. Wear your best walking shoes and leave the heavy knapsack at your hotel. This company also offers other popular tours such as the **Pub Crawl** and **Hammer and Sickle,** call ahead for information and a reservation. Both offices offer an Internet cafe with Wi-Fi and terminals.

V. Suto u. 2. ✆ **30/211-8861** (mobile phone only). www.absolutetours.com), High season daily 8:30am–8pm; Nov–Mar daily 10am–6pm. Metro: Deák (all lines). VI. Lázár u. 16. ✆ **1/269-3869**. Mon–Fri 9:30am–7pm; Sat–Sun 9:30am–4pm. Metro: Opera (Yellow line).

Underguide Tours ★★★   May sound ominous, but relax. These tours are geared for those who don't want the usual and this is positively what you experience with their half- or full-day tour. These are fully organized around your desires, so when you meet your tour Underguide, he or she forms the tour based on your ideas and then takes you to off-the-beaten-path places he or she thinks you will like the best. It is fully customizable based on your interests and they strive to meet any requests. You can go it alone or with your own group, but never with strangers. If you book by Internet, you need to give them 1 day's notice, but by phone, the same day is possible. A 4-hour tour for one to four people will cost you 95€ and 25€ for each additional person, but children 3 and under are free. They now offer specialized tours such as the Budapest Delicatessen tour, eating Hungarian specialties along the way; the family tour; and a special tour for gay and lesbian travelers. This creative company is always evolving, so check their website for the latest.

℃ **06/30-908-1597** (mobile phone only). www.underguide.com . golocal@underguide.

Walker's Guide ★★★   For me, walking around the city is the perfect way to see things that I may otherwise miss, but I like doing it at my own pace, spending a bit more time in one place and less in another. This is why I was thrilled to find a tour where I can go at my own pace and only stop at sites that are of interest to me. What you do is rent a lightweight audio-player with a city guide full of thumbnail pictures and maps, and one larger map. Both maps have 90 numbered points of interest on them to correspond with the audio-player's 18 hours of entertaining descriptions. There are suggested routes, but everything is self-determined. At many points of interest, you can listen to a short lively description, but if it appeals to you, there are sub-menus for more information. In the back of the book, restaurant suggestions are offered along different routes as well as shopping stops, so it is a comprehensive package. The exceptional information and voice quality will hold the attention of the biggest space cadet. Short on time, but want to know more? I have been known to sit at home while listening to the audio-player and flipping through the pictures in the book. There is nothing boring about this tour. Rentals are available at some hotel receptions or partner offices listed on their website. Buda Castle or Inner City guides are 12€ for a full day or 20€ if returned by closing on the next day. The All Budapest guide is 14€ or 22€ for the next day return. Partner shop rentals require a credit card or cash deposit of 50€.

V. Báthory u. 24. ℃ **06/20-445-989** (mobile phone only). www.walkersguide.travel.

WINE TOUR

Taste Hungary   Co-owned by American Carolyn Bánfalvi, author of *A Food and Wine Lover's Companion to Hungary: with Budapest Restaurants and Trips to the Wine Country,* this boutique company offers wine and food tours throughout Hungary. They prefer all bookings to be made through their website.

℃ **06/20-453-6095** (mobile phone only). www.tastehungary.com.

Wine Time Hungary ★★★   You could travel to the wine regions on your own to sample Hungary's famous wines or you could take one of the wine tours offered by this new company. Each day's tour heads to a different part of the country, for example the fairy tale Lake Tour of North Balaton is currently on Thursday. The cost of 25,000 Ft includes transportation by air-conditioned vehicle, a trained guide, tours and tastings in four cellars of the region where four wines are tasted at each as the wine maker divulges some of its attributes. Snacks are provided, but lunch is on your own. If you don't have the time to travel even for a day, Wine Time also offers virtual tours or wine dinners right here in Budapest. A five-course dinner is carefully prepared with wines to accompany each course; be sure to visit their website with English, for times of events.

VII. Klauzál tér 13. fszt. 5. 🕐 **1/788–9645**. www.winetime.hu. Tram: 4 or 6, Király.

10 BUDAPEST'S MOST POPULAR THERMAL BATHS

The baths of Budapest have a long history, stretching back to Roman times. The thermal baths were popularized by the Turks who started building them in 1565 giving them a place to bathe in case of a siege on the city. Budapest and other parts of Hungary are built over hot springs making this a natural way of acquiring the mineral rich waters for bathing. Hungarians and other Europeans are great believers in the medicinal powers of thermal bathing with all of the thermals being medical clinics as well for the treatment of skin, muscular, and bone ailments. Even if you are not in need of the health benefits, time spent in thermal baths will lift your spirits. The Király's construction was started by Arslan, Pasha of Buda in 1565, but was completed by his successor. The Rudas, also built in the 16th century by the Turks, still functions today. Both are among the architectural achievements of the Turkish period. The Rudas boasts a 10m (33 ft) diameter dome, sustained by eight pillars with an octagonal pool. From 1936 until 2007, it was only for men. Today, women alone are allowed on Tuesday. In the late 19th and early 20th centuries—Budapest's "golden age"—several fabulous bathhouses were built: the extravagant and eclectic Széchenyi Baths in City Park, the largest spa complex in Europe; the secessionist-style Gellért Baths; and the solid neoclassical Lukács Baths. All of these bathhouses are still in use and are worthy of visiting. Most baths in Budapest have instituted a complicated new pricing system (dubbed the "refund system") that charges a flat fee, and then according to the time you have spent in the baths, you get tiny refunds, barely an incentive to leave early if you are enjoying your time. You receive a chip card upon entry; keep careful track of the card because if you lose it you are assumed to have stayed for the maximum time and you will not receive a refund. All of these bathhouses can be found on the same website, www.spasbudapest.com.

THE BEST & OTHER BATHHOUSES

Gellért Baths (Overrated)   Once one of Budapest's most spectacular bathhouses, the Gellért Baths are located in Buda's Hotel Gellért, the oldest Hungarian spa hotel and a secessionist-style hotel. Know that though the thermal and hotel share a building, the thermal area is owned by the city spa authority. The entire thermal area, both men's and women's sections, have been remodeled to their original glory. However, the cost of entry, which includes the two thermal pools and two swimming pools (one outdoors and only open in summer) would be better spent elsewhere. As an employee told me, it is too expensive for Hungarians, so it is frequented by foreigners who are staying at the hotel getting in for free. Once in the men's locker area, the staff is churlish, which I don't appreciate after parting with a hefty fee. If you go, enter the baths through the right side entrance of the hotel. Inside the lobby, the details are striking, especially the stained-glass windows, but pictures are not allowed. The unisex indoor pool has marble columns, majolica tiles, and stone lion heads spouting water. The two single-sex Turkish-style

thermal baths, off to either side of the pool, have had a total restoration. In the summer
months, the outdoor roof pool attracts a lot of attention for 10 minutes every hour on
the hour when the artificial wave machine is turned on.

XI. Kelenhegyi út 4. ☏ **1/466-6166.** Thermal baths and pools 3,800 Ft for day ticket, refund of 300 Ft
before 2 hours; powder massage 2,800 Ft for 15 min. Prices include a cabin. The extensive list of services
are posted in English at the cashier's desk. Apr 30–Sep 30 Mon–Fri 6am–7pm, Sat 6am–10pm, Sun 6am–
8pm; winter daily 6am–7pm. The last entrance an hour before closing. Tram: 47 or 49 from Deák tér to
Szent Gellért tér.

Király Baths ★★ This is one of the oldest baths in Hungary, dating back to around
1563, when the Turkish built the baths so they could bathe and be ready for battle. Other
legends say this was the way the Turks got the Hungarians to bathe. Regardless of the
reason, the Király Baths are still one of Budapest's most important architectural tributes
associated with Turkish rule. Bathing under the octagonal domed roof with sunlight fil-
tering through small round windows in the ceiling, gives the water a special glow. In late
afternoons in winter you can look at the night sky watching the stars hanging in the
distance. Either way, it is a relaxing experience. In addition to the thermal baths, there
are sauna and steam room facilities, but no swimming pools. If you so desire, you can get
a massage while you are there. Bathing suits are only required on Sunday, when you need
to bring a towel with you. Segregated days, men wear a cloth provided and towels are
furnished. Women can use the baths on Monday and Wednesday from 8am to 7pm.
Men are welcome on Tuesday, Thursday, Friday, and Saturday from 9am to 8pm. On
Sunday, they have a mixed day from 9am to 8pm. There is no longer a time restriction;
you can stay all day. You can enter up to 1 hour before closing, but it is not worth the
effort since everyone is required to head to the lockers ½ hour before closing time.

II. Fő u. 84. ☏ **1/202-3688.** All-day ticket 2,100 Ft, no refunds. Metro: Batthyány tér (Red line).

Rudas Baths ★★★ Near the Erzsébet Bridge, on the Buda side of the city, is the
second oldest of Budapest's classic Turkish baths, built in the 16th century. These baths are
for men only every day except Tuesday during the day or Friday night, and mixed with men
on weekends. Truly one of the most authentically beautiful, the centerpiece is an octagonal
pool under a 10m (33 ft) domed roof with some of the small window holes in the cupola
filled with stained glass, while others are open to the sky, allowing diffused light to stream
in. Along the sides, there are four corner pools of varying degrees of temperature. During
early mornings the crowd is predominantly composed of older men. You'll find the same
services and facilities here that you would at Király: thermal baths of varying degrees, a
sauna, and a steam bath, but in much more glorious surroundings.

I. Döbrentei tér 9. ☏ **1/356-1322.** All-day ticket 2,700 Ft, refund of 300 Ft before 2 hr; swimming pool
with locker 1,700 Ft. Weekdays 6am–8pm; weekends pool only 6am–5pm. Group bathing Fri 10pm–4am,
Sat 6am–7pm and 10pm–4am, Sun 6am–7pm. Bus: 7, not express stops right in front, first stop on the
Buda side.

Széchenyi Baths ★★★ One of the largest spa complexes in Europe, it was also the
first thermal on the Pest side first built in 1913 and expanded in 1927. Located in the
City Park, the Széchenyi Baths are the most popular with locals and travelers alike. From
the outside, you'd never believe its enormity, but once inside it is humongous with a
variety of 16 different pools, each with different water temperatures. One is a whirlpool
that spins you around. Crowds of bathers, including many families and tourists, visit the
palatial unisex outdoor swimming pool every month of the year, but due to its size, it
never feels overcrowded. Turkish-style thermal baths are segregated and are located off to

Tips **Thermal Bathing 101**

Thermal bathing is a social activity deep within the Hungarian culture and each bath has its own set of rules, which can change without notice. Bathhouse employees tend to be unfriendly holdovers of the old system, and still have a civil service position since most baths are owned by the city. Most do not speak English, and have little patience. Many foreigners find a trip to the baths stressful or intimidating in the beginning, but plunge forth, it is a cultural experience and they are not pinpointing you for their woes. Try to spot a resident and follow their example of what to do. Explore once inside and you'll find you will feel comfortable and confident within minutes. The best advice is to try to enjoy the foreignness of the experience, because after all, this is the reason you are here.

The most inhibiting part may well be when approaching the ticket window, with the long list of services and prices, often without English translations. Chances are you're coming to use one of the following facilities or services: *uszoda* (pool); *termál* (thermal pool); *fürdő* (bath); *gőzfürdő* (steam bath); massage; and/or sauna. There is no particular order in which people move from one facility to the next—do whatever feels most comfortable. Most of the thermals are also medical clinics, therefore, many services will not apply to you. Towel rental is *törülköző* or *lepedő*. Few places will provide a towel or sheet for drying off—if you don't want to rent one, bring your own. An entry ticket generally entitles you to a free locker in the locker room *(öltöző);* or, at some bathhouses, you can opt to pay an additional fee for a private cabin *(kabin).* Either way, an attendant will lock the door for you and give you a token on a string to keep getting back in. Hence, going in and out of the locker or cabin is going to irritate the workers.

Remember to pack a bathing suit and a bathing cap if you wish to swim in the pools so you won't have to rent vintage 1970 models. Lukács requires a

the sides of the pool. In warm weather, there is segregated nude sunbathing on the roof. If you like water, you will certainly want to spend the day here.

XIV. Állatkerti út 11–14, in City Park. ✆ 1/363-3210. Day ticket w/cabin 3,400 Ft or 3,000 Ft w/locker; refund of 300 Ft before 2 hr; massage 3,500 Ft for 30 min. Daily 6am–10pm, some pools close earlier on Sat–Sun. Metro: Széchenyi fürdő (Yellow line).

AN OUTDOOR POOL COMPLEX

Palatinus Strand ★★ **Kids** In the middle of Margaret Island is Budapest's best-located *strand* (literally "beach," but in reality a water park). The huge complex is fed by the island's thermal springs and consists of three thermal pools, an extra-large swimming pool, a smaller artificial wave pool, a water slide, a grassy area, and segregated nude-sunbathing decks on top of the building. Other facilities include ping-pong tables, pool tables, trampolines, and dozens of snack bars. The waters of the thermal pools are as relaxing as those at any of the other bathhouses (but the older ones offer a more memorable experience). Rates include either a locker or a cabin.

bathing cap for both sexes and for all thermals and pools. Long hair must be capped when bathing at the other facilities. In the single-sex baths—Rudas, Lukács, Gellért, and Király—men are provided with a loin cloth; bathing suits are frowned upon. Purity of the water is my guess, or they like the tush view. Who knows? You may want to bring your own towel with you into the bathing areas in a plastic grocery bag. Flip-flops are also a good idea. Shower before getting into a thermal or pool. Soap and shampoo are only allowed in the showers, but you should bring everything you will need from the locker or cabin to avoid multiple trips and having to hunt down the attendant to unlock the locker. Some of the waters are high in mineral content, so you will most likely want to shower well and shampoo your hair before leaving. Depending on the pool, you may find a strong sulfur smell, but remember it will do glorious things for your skin. If you can see without them, leave your glasses in your locker as they will get fogged up in the baths.

Generally, extra services (massage, pedicure) are received after a bath. Locker room attendants appreciate tips, especially if you plan on returning. A tip of 200 Ft is typical, unless you have repeatedly returned to the locker, then make it a bit more. Masseurs and manicurists expect a tip in the 500–700-Ft range. There are drinking fountains in the bath areas, and it's a good idea to drink plenty of water before, during, and after a bath. Bathing on an empty stomach can cause nausea and light-headedness for those unaccustomed to the baths. Some of the pools will show that you should not stay in the hot water for more than 10 minutes at a time. Most bathhouses have snack bars in the lobbies where you can pick up a cold juice or sandwich on your way in or out, but you must eat it there. Stay hydrated.

XIII. Margit-sziget. ☎ **1/340-4505.** Weekdays 2,100 Ft adults, 1,600 Ft children 13 and under; weekends 2,400 Ft adults, 1,800 Ft children; children 5 and under free. Prices include a locker. No refunds. May to mid-Aug daily 9am–8pm. Last entry at 6pm. Tram: 4 or 6 to Jászai Mari tér and then walk the bridge.

11 OUTDOOR ACTIVITIES & SPORTS

BIKING I have gone around and around with Gabor at one of the bike rental places about the safety of biking in Budapest due to crazed drivers and erratic-moving traffic. Later in the day he had me convinced I was wrong, I witnessed a man on a bike get hit by a car; obviously the car driver's fault. With that said, ride at your own risk, see "Getting Around," in chapter 4, "Getting to Know Budapest," or earlier in this chapter for some biking options.

GOLF You will not find much for the golfer in the city, which means you are in for a drive if you want to practice your drives. For information, contact the **Hungarian Golf**

Club, V. Bécsi út 5 (☎ **1/317-6025;** www.golfhungary.hu). The nearest course is located on Szentendre Island, 25 minutes north of Budapest by car. Call the course directly at ☎ **26/392-465.** For putting practice, the **19th Hole Golf Driving Range** is located at II. Adyliget, Feketefej u. 6 (☎ **1/354-1720**) or e-mail them at golfcentrum@golfcentrum.hu. Two golf stores have opened in Budapest, one on each side of the river. On the Pest side is **Golf Centrum** at VI. Nagymező u. 52 (☎ **1/354-1510**); or on the Buda side, **Swing** at II. Szilágyi Erzsébet fasor 121, floor I, no. 43 (☎ **1/275-0855**).

HORSEBACK RIDING   Riding remains a popular activity in Hungary, land of the widely feared Magyar horsemen of a bygone era. A good place to mount up is the **Petneházy Lovasiskola (Riding School),** at II. Feketefej u. 2 (☎ **1/397-1208**). Far, far out in the Buda Hills, the school is located in open country, with trails in the hills. Open riding with a guide is 3,500 Ft for 25 minutes. There are also pony rides for children at 2,500 Ft for 15 minutes, and the 30-minute horse-cart rides for 10 people is 25,000 Ft. The stable is open year-round, but only on Sunday from noon to 5pm. They will open Tuesday to Saturday, by appointment. Due to changes in transportation routes, it is not easy to reach via public transport.

The **Hungarian Equestrian Tourism Association,** located at IX. Ráday u. 8 (☎ **1/455-6183;** fax 1/456-0445; www.equi.hu), may be of interest to you if you are interested in horses or horseback riding. It seems all inquiries lead back to this office. Note, when this website opens, it shows a link in English, but changes to Hungarian instantly. Unless you are good at video games, you may have a problem.

ICE SKATING   Ice rinks in Budapest are very kid-friendly. The oldest, most popular, and largest in Europe is the ice rink in Városliget, on the lake next to Vajdahunyad Castle. Being an open-air facility, it is open only from mid-November till the middle of February. Hours are Monday through Friday 9am to 1pm and 4pm to 8pm; Saturday and Sunday 10am to 2pm and 4pm to 8pm. The fee is 500 Ft on Monday, 700 Ft Tuesday to Thursday, and 1,000 Ft Friday to Sunday. Skates rent for 800 Ft an hour. International visitors should also have their passports for ID when renting. Adults and children can rent in-line and ice skates at all rinks.

SQUASH   **City Squash and Fitness Courts (Országos Fallabda Központ),** at II. Marczibányi tér 13 (☎ **1/325-0082**), has four courts, which are an easy walk from Moszkva tér (Red metro line). The hourly rates vary during the day: 7am to 9am and 3pm to 5pm, 3,000 Ft; 9am to 3pm, 2,200 Ft; and 5pm to 10pm, 4,200 Ft for 1 hour of play. Racquets can be rented for 500 Ft; balls can be purchased. The courts are open weekdays 7am to midnight, weekends 8am to 10pm.

TENNIS   If you plan to play tennis in Budapest, you have to travel a bit for the courts. **Római Tennis Academy** at III. Királyok útja 105 (☎ **1/240-8616**) is open Monday to Friday with variable rates 7am to 11am 2,100 Ft; 11am to 4pm 1,600 Ft; 4pm to 8pm 3,000 Ft. On weekends, 7am to 1pm is 2,100 Ft and 1pm to 7 pm is 2,800 Ft. Rackets are rented for 500 Ft. Another is **Városmajor Tennis Academy** at XII Városmajor u. 63–69 (☎ **1/202-5337**). Open weekdays 7am to 10pm, weekends 8am to 7pm with fees running from 3,700 Ft to 5,400 Ft. Many luxury hotels, particularly those out of the city center, have tennis courts that non-guests can rent.

Strolling Around Budapest

Budapest is a walking city. There is nothing I like better than to wander around the streets to see what I can discover or rediscover. Every day brings a new discovery, even after so many years here. The walking tours included in this chapter are intended to give you a sense of the vibrancy that radiates from the city's history. On these walking tours, I have made a special effort to bring things to your attention that you may otherwise miss. In so saying, you can certainly choose parts of the tour that appeal to you most and hit those spots without doing the full tour. Many of the

city's top attractions such as the Buda Palace, Parliament, the National Gallery, and the National Museum are included on these tours, but dozens of minor sites—vintage pharmacies and quiet courtyards, market halls and medieval walls—are included as well. If you especially like to walk and discover, you should look at the longer and more comprehensive self-guided tours in chapter 7, "Exploring Budapest."

See chapter 3, "Suggested Budapest & Hungary Itineraries," for ways to incorporate these walking tours into a 1- or 2-day visit.

WALKING TOUR 1	THE MILLENNIUM TOUR

START:	Vörösmarty tér.
FINISH:	Mexikói út.
TIME:	2 to 3 hours (at a slow pace excluding restaurant or museum stops).
BEST TIMES:	Any time, but preferably mid-afternoon.
WORST TIMES:	Early morning.

When have you ever heard of a crowned monarch riding a subway? This tour will follow the historic metro line of the Millennium metro, where more than 110 years ago, the Austrian emperor and Hungarian king Ferenc József (Franz Josef) boarded the first subway in continental Europe. At the time, London was the only city in Europe to have a subway. It had just been completed ready for the 1896 millennium celebrations that would be held in Budapest. Galas and gatherings were planned all over the city, but the most important was held in Városliget. Andrássy út was the most direct link to the park; however, even then, it was a grand boulevard. Authorities had refused permission for a tram line that was either horse drawn or electrified, for fear of ruining the elegance of the street. It was not until 1893 that permission was given for the underground to be built to solve the logistics problem of moving huge gatherings of people from place to place. Bureaucracy being what it is they only had 20 months to complete the entire 3.7km (2.3 mile) long line. What helped their work was the fact that at the time, Andrássy was paved with wooden blocks making digging the tunnel that much easier. With a tight deadline, they built the metro to be ready in time. The white and burgundy tiles, the cast-iron pillars, and the wooden accessories create a distinctive atmosphere that is still maintained today. After Franz Josef completed the first ride, he agreed to allow it to be named after

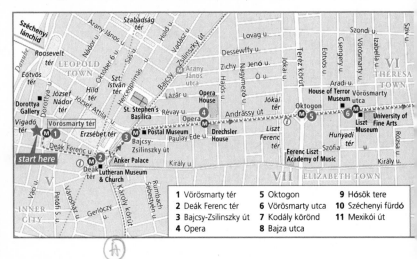

1 Vörösmarty tér   5 Oktogon   9 Hősök tere
2 Deák Ferenc tér   6 Vörösmarty utca   10 Széchenyi fürdő
3 Bajcsy-Zsilinszky út   7 Kodály körönd   11 Mexikói út
4 Opera   8 Bajza utca

him. The following tour is above ground, stopping at each of the metro's stops, so if you are so inclined, you can hop on the metro to skip from one stop to another, but if you do, you will be missing much above ground.

Begin at Vörösmarty tér, where the Yellow metro 1 line begins.

❶ Vörösmarty tér

In 1896, this square was named Gizella tér when it was not the hub of activity it is today. In the center is an enormous Carrara marble statue of the 19th-century poet, Mihály Vörösmarty. Vörösmarty wrote *Szózat,* the second-most important hymn in Hungarian history after the national anthem. This is the site of many holiday markets and celebrations.

The famous **Gerbeaud** coffeehouse (p. 119) is here as it was in 1858. The founder came from Switzerland with his pastry recipes to set up shop on this square. These recipes are still used today.

Today, this is where the **Christmas Market** is held and where the Spring Festival Parade starts from. In recent years, this square has had some major transformations with some old historic buildings being torn down to make way for the new and modern.

If you want to view a bit of art before we leave this square, the street to the left of Gerbeaud's has the **Dorottya Gallery.** The windows are so large there is no need to walk in to see everything they offer.

If you need a coffee and a pastry to fortify you, now is your chance to get them, though I consider them overpriced. From here, we go to Deák Ferenc tér past the statue and to the left.

❷ Deák Ferenc tér

Politico Ferenc Deák was named the "sage of the nation" for having worked on the Compromise of 1867 between Austria and Hungary when Austria refused to recognize Hungary's independence.

On one corner of the square is the Lutheran Museum and Church at Deák Ferenc tér 4. To the side of the church is a gold memorial tablet that states "Sándor Petőfi, the romantic poet, was educated here." The church gains attention through its plain structure and its lack of a spire. The original church did have a spire, but when the roof had to be reconstructed,

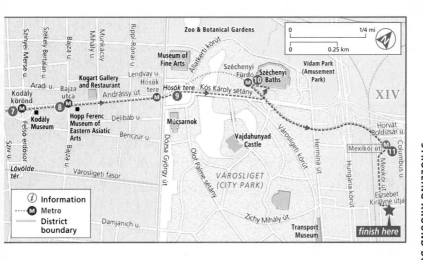

there was not enough money to stabilize it properly to hold the spire, so it was left off. The church is extremely simple inside even by Lutheran standards, according to my Lutheran friends. The church is only open for services or concerts; the concert schedule is posted outside.

The square has changed considerably since the first metro was built. This square is the only place where all three metros connect and in a few years four metros will connect here. In the station, if you descend the correct set of stairs among the number of ways to get down there, you will find the **Underground Railway Museum.** Outfitted like an old subway station, the museum features a beautifully preserved train from the European continent's first underground system, built in Budapest in 1896. Appropriately, the cost of admission is one transport ticket. If you wish to go in, the museum is small, so ½ hour is about all you need.

When you ascend again, you cannot help but notice the **Anker Palace** across the street from the Le Méridien Hotel. This impressive building was built at the turn of the 19th century. The towers and

bastion-looking architecture represent the romantic style. The antique marble columns on the second level and the triangle at the top give the building the name "palace." This square is the most frequented tourist destination.

On the other corner, is **Erzsébet tér.** This was where the National Theater was originally going to be constructed. However, with a political election and a change in power, the location was changed. The argument was that the final construction would block fresh air coming from the river to the inner city, so the idea was abandoned, but only after the underground parking had been built. Now you can find a serene fountain pond, attractive flower beds, and benches to relax on along the way.

Using the underground, you will cross under the street until you are in front of the Anker Palace and walk toward the basilica. You will see its steeple ahead of you.

❸ Bajcsy-Zsilinszky út

This is the start of Andrássy út. If you see a red mailbox, that is the **Post Office Museum** (p. 129), sitting at Andrássy út 3 on the first floor. The building was built for

Andreas Saxlehner; you can still see his initials in the ironwork. It is worth visiting the museum for the interior stained glass and frescoes created by Károly Lotz. The museum was originally the private home of Saxlehner, consisting of seven rooms. As you walk through the flat, you may notice his initials all over the flat as well as the building.

When you reach Andrássy út 9, you are in front of the former **Dutch Insurance Company** headquarters. What is not visible from the street level is the huge "drop" left on top after a 1990s' reconstruction for the board of directors. However, the view from the street is impressive. As you walk to the next stop, notice the architecture of the buildings and please be sure to look up. Most people miss some striking pieces by never looking above eye level. This will also distract you from looking at the designer shops along the way. Think of the money you are saving by looking up.

Continue on Andrássy to our next stop:
❹ Opera

When the metro was built, each station had an ornate entrance building covering it. They have long since been torn down, but this station still has the marble balustrade. The station does not take away from the glorious neo-Renaissance styled **Opera House** (p. 131 and p. 216). Built by Miklós Ybl, it was completed in 1884. Stop back for a tour or to buy tickets for a performance.

Across from the Opera House is a large building built by Ödön Lechner and Gyula Pártos in 1882. It was named the Drechsler House, because it once housed a large cafe by the same name on the street level and apartments occupied the upper floors. The building has a tainted history as six consecutive owners went bankrupt or committed suicide. The National Ballet Institute occupied the building for decades, but they abandoned it also.

For the movie *Munich,* the Paris scenes were filmed using the Opera house and the old Drechsler House, which was transformed by movie magic into a lamp store with a cafe on the left side of it.

On the opposite side of the street from the Opera House is the **Mûvész Confectionery** at Andrássy út 29 (p. 120). Although it has become touristy, it still has the old-fashioned feeling of the coffeehouse culture that is ingrained in Budapest. Try the chocolate orange cake; it is scrumptious.

Right before our next stop, you will cross the theater district of the city on Nagymező utca. It is here that you'll find the Thalia Theater, the New Theater, and the Moulin Rouge. Closely located to the Opera House, this is the most concentrated area of cultural events in the city.

If you have a snack attack and did not stop for a pastry, you are in luck. On the left is **Bombay Express,** a fast-food Indian restaurant with low prices and excellent quality food. If you walk a little farther, you will find Liszt Ferenc tér on one side of the street with the famous music academy of the same name at the very end of the tér. There is also a Tourinform office here in addition to a choice of more than 14 restaurants. The center park has been refurbished as a winding and undulating garden area with benches; it is quite charming with the humongous and commanding statue of Liszt in the center.

Opposite Liszt Ferenc tér is Jókai tér. In the back of the square is one of the two puppet theaters in the city (p. 151). Walking down Jókai, you will see a number of teahouses of various styles.

Walk down Andrássy to our next stop:
❺ Oktogon

When you come to the intersection of Andrássy út and the Nagykörút (large ring road), the buildings form an octagonal square providing its name. For 40-some years, this intersection was known as November 7 Square. It is one of the busiest intersections in the city. Sadly, over the years, it has become more commercialized now being home to what is supposed to be the world's largest Burger King on one corner and a T.G.I. Friday's on the opposite corner. The huge billboards and electric signs atop of the buildings for various companies have depleted the charm. After crossing through Oktogon, Andrássy starts to widen. It is this section of Andrássy, past Oktogon, that is a World Heritage site.

Now cross over the körut as we continue up Andrássy.

⑥ Vörösmarty utca

Don't confuse this with Vörösmarty tér, the pedestrian street. Notice how much wider the boulevard is from here on up to Heroes' Square. The street is lined with chestnut trees (chestnuts are often used in Hungarian pastries) giving a fresh feeling of leaving the city behind.

At this stop, you will find Franz Liszt's last home at Andrássy út 67 where he lived on and off in a first floor apartment for the last 5 years of his life. Today it is a museum displaying his pianos and other memorabilia dedicated to his life and work. During some months, there are free concerts on Saturday mornings, a tradition started when Liszt was alive. This building was where the Academy of Music originated with Liszt being a founding member.

Across the street almost in a different dimension is the House of Terror Museum at Andrássy út 60, the place where both the Nazis and Communists headquartered and tortured people. For more information, see chapter 7, p. 129.

The University of Fine Arts is located at Andrássy út 69–71. The central building was built in 1876 and refurbished in 1978. The exterior has sgraffito (decoration created by cutting away parts of a surface layer to expose a different-colored background) portraits of Bramante, Michelangelo, and Leonardo da Vinci. Students study here for 5 years in a selection of media to earn a master's of fine arts degree upon successful completion.

In the same building as the University of Fine Arts, you will also find the second puppet theater of Budapest at Andrássy út 69. Over 57 years old, this theater has presented puppet shows of high standards for adults and children alike, but only in Hungarian.

Continuing onward, we reach:

⑦ Kodály körönd

A *körönd* is a circle; here being a broad traffic circle where turns are not permitted, so the circle is cut into four pie slices to make turns. On each corner of the "pie" you will find a statue of someone famous. You will see **Szondy György**: he was the commander who with his troops stood firm against Ali Pasha and his Turkish troops when they invaded in 1552. **Bálint Balassi** was a poet who is considered the first to have brought poetry in the Hungarian language to world-class standards. He was a creator of new poetic forms. Combining love lyrics into the experiences of the fight against the Turkish conquerors, he has a close association with Szondy György. Next is **Zrinyi Miklós**, another defender of the nation from the Ottoman rule, but he did much of it from his castle in what is now part of Croatia. Well educated in languages and warfare, he was a strong commander who lost the backing of the Habsburgs and returned home in disgust. **Vak Bottyán** or "Blind Bottyán," the popular nickname of Bottyán János, fought for Buda against the Ottomans, but later for liberation from the Habsburgs.

The circle is named after **Zoltan Kodály**, who was one of the first persons to give special attention to folk music. He was one of the most significant contributors to early ethnomusicology, later becoming the mentor to Béla Bartók, another famous Hungarian musician. Although the Kodaly Method of teaching music is associated with him, he influenced it with his work, but did not actually create it. His former apartment at

Andrássy út 89 houses the museum dedicated to Kodály and his work. The building it is in has been undergoing renovations for more than a year, so if you see scaffolding, it still is not open yet.

Lofty mansions are situated on this ring; they were originally built for the Austro-Hungarian aristocracy. Peeking past the lavishly created wrought-iron gates, attached to stone pillars, you will notice that these frescoed beauties need a well-deserved makeover. Historical values not being the same to all, some of these lovelies nearby are being torn now to create new and modern apartment buildings in their place.

Continue straight onward to:

❽ Bajza utca

As you have walked to this stop, you may have noticed that the boulevard has widened even more and that the houses are changing in style. These personal palaces have a sense of serenity to them with personal parks spread between the entrance gates and the front doors of the houses. In this area, different countries have taken over the former private homes to create their embassies.

There is an interesting museum and also a private gallery/restaurant at this stop. On one side of the street is the **Kogart Gallery and Restaurant** at Andrássy út 112 (② **01/354-3820;** www.kogart.hu). The gallery has rotating exhibitions of Hungarian art upstairs and a fine restaurant downstairs.

At Andrássy út 103, you will find the **Hopp Ferenc Museum of Eastern Asiatic Arts.** Hopp was a business owner and a world traveler, which stimulated his collecting as well as being a patron of art. He bequeathed his entire collection of 4,000 pieces to the government to create a museum. If you need a rest, you can enter the Zen garden for free to relax. The museum is open Tuesday through Sunday from 10am to 5pm. Along this section of Andrássy, the house styles include Art Deco, baroque, and Communist-boring. However, this is the most desirable stretch of real estate in Budapest.

Continue down to:

❾ Hősök tere

Usually when people emerge from the metro station at this stop, they are in awe at the beauty of Heroes' Square with its arcade of statues (p. 130). It is even more stunning in the evening. Since you have been walking up to it, you have had the opportunity to see its glory get larger as you get closer.

On this square to the left is the Museum of Fine Arts (p. 126). If you are in this area at 11am or 2pm Tuesday to Friday or 11am on Saturday, I strongly encourage you to use this opportunity to take the free tour of one gallery by highly trained docents.

On the right of the square is the **Műcsarnok** (art hall) or just the Exhibition Hall. Prompted by the Hungarian National Fine Arts Association, it was founded in 1877. Originally, it was located at 69–71 Andrássy út where the University of Fine Arts is now located. As many other buildings were built specifically for the millennium celebrations so was the exhibition hall. Albert Schikedanz was the designer and the outside design is magnificent. Today the hall operates on the pattern of the German Kunsthalle: it is an institution run by artists, but does not maintain its own collection. Light enters through the roof by a three-bayed, semicircular apse. After a full renovation in 1995 the Műcsarnok opened to the public, displaying the work of leading Hungarian and international contemporary artists. It is open Tuesday to Sunday from 10am to 6pm and admission varies depending on the exhibit.

If you walk over the bridge behind the colonnade, on the right is a small pond area, usually empty until wintertime when it is filled with water to freeze for ice skating. You can rent skates here (p. 162) and partake in the action or you can just admire the view from the bridge. Once over the bridge, to the right, you will already have noticed the castle known as Vajdahunyad Castle (p. 129). It was originally built from cardboard for the millennium celebrations, but was so popular, it was rebuilt with more durable materials. Some call it a mishmash of styles, but it is intended to be this way, showing all of the different architectural styles of Hungary.

If you have time to visit the castle area, you will see small boats floating around the lake in the summer time. It is a popular place for celebrations and weddings.

Cross the street from the path that would lead to the castle and walk across the park to the:

⑩ Széchenyi fürdő

When you see pictures of men playing chess while floating in water, they are enjoying the thermal waters of the Széchenyi Baths. A bath existed here as early as 1881, but being a temporary one, it started to lose favor. Gyozo Czigler came up with the plans to create a more permanent structure in 1913 and it was expanded in 1927 with public bathing for men and women. By the middle of the 1960s, it was time to bring further improvements to the facility by adding a group thermal section and an outpatient clinic. All of the thermals treat muscular, bone, and some respiratory ailments. A fancy bath was installed, which is a whirling pool that twirls you around like an amusement ride. Effervescent

devices, neck showers, and water-beam back massages were added in the sitting bank areas. This is one of the largest spa complexes in Europe.

At one time, this was the last stop on the Millennium metro, but in 1973 that changed and one more stop was added.

From here, I suggest you hop on the metro for a ride to the end of the line, which is the next and last stop on this tour. If you want to see more of the park first, you could venture to the far end to visit the Transport Museum (p. 149) at Vajdahunyadvár with permanent exhibits that include History of the Railway, History of Urban Transport, and the History of Shipping and Road Traffic in Hungary in addition to others.

⑪ Mexikói út

Although there is nothing of note at this stop of a historic nature, it is the stop where one of my five most favorite restaurants in the city is located. If you ambled along on this tour, then I presume you will have built up an appetite and will appreciate this last stop. When you reach the top of the stairs of the metro station, turn right. You will see tram tracks and turn left after crossing them. At the end of the block is the **Trófea Grill Étterem** (see p. 114) at XIV. Erzsébet Királyné útja 5. This is the best all-you-can-eat restaurant in the city. There are others with the same name, but this is the only location I recommend. Enjoy!

Now that you are full and too tired to walk back, hop on the Millennium metro and enjoy the old-fashioned stations you will pass by on your way back.

WALKING TOUR 2   **THE CASTLE DISTRICT**

START:	Roosevelt tér, Pest side of Chain Bridge or alternatively take bus no. 16 from in front of the Le Méridien Hotel.
FINISH:	Tóth Árpád sétány, Castle District.
TIME:	3 to 4 hours (excluding museum visits).
BEST TIMES:	Tuesday through Sunday.
WORST TIME:	Monday, when museums are closed.

Castle Hill was not always the focal point of Hungarian rule and authority. The original capital was in Esztergom, where King Stephen was crowned and where the seat of the Hungarian Catholic Church is located. It was not until King Béla IV built a fortress on this hill that it become something more than a hill. During the reigns of Kings Charles

Robert and Louis the Great (1342–82), a castle was built. Holy Roman Emperor Sigismund of Luxembourg, who was also king of Hungary, built a large Gothic palace and strong fortifications against attack, making this the permanent seat of royal power. It was King Matthias who transformed the castle and decorated the hill with Italian Renaissance due to the influence of his Italian queen from Naples. This district has had its share of devastation, the last time being the 1945 Soviet bombing of Nazi forces. With each reconstruction, the prevailing style shifted from Gothic to baroque to Renaissance. Castle Hill, a UNESCO World Cultural Heritage site, consists of two parts: the Royal Palace (no longer a castle), and the associated Castle District, which is now a mostly reconstructed city reflecting a former time in history. The Royal Palace is home to a number of museums, including the Hungarian National Gallery and the Budapest Museum. The National Archives, the equivalent to the Hungarian Library of Congress, is an attached building in the back. The rest of the Castle District is a small tapered neighborhood with cobblestone streets and twisting alleys; with the exception of buses, most traffic is prohibited, making the streets pedestrian-friendly enhancing the tranquility and the old-world feel. Prime examples of every type of Hungarian architecture, from early Gothic to neo-Romanesque, can be seen. A leisurely walk in the Castle District will be a historical and memorable experience. When you see SZ on a sign followed by Roman numerals, it is indicating the century of the building. HELYÉN gives the name of the building that was on this site prior to the current building.

Views of Castle Hill can be seen from all points on the riverbank, but we will start from Pest's Roosevelt tér just past the Gresham Four Seasons Hotel and walk on the:

❶ Széchenyi Chain Bridge

Originally funded by Count Széchenyi after weather prevented his getting across the river to be with his dying father, the bridge was built in 1849. During World War II, the Nazis destroyed all of the bridges in the city to hold off the Allied forces. The bridge was rebuilt and in 1949 the opening ceremony was held 100 years to the day after its original inauguration.

Walk across the bridge. Arriving in Buda, you're now in:

❷ Clark Ádám tér

Ádám Clark was a Scottish engineer commissioned to build the bridge. After doing so, he stayed here with the Hungarian wife he met and married. This square was named for him.

From Clark Ádám tér, take the:

❸ Funicular (sikló)

The funicular, an almost-vertical elevator, will transport you up the 100m (328 ft)

long track to the entryway of the Royal Palace. It was originally put into service in 1870 to provide cheap transport to workers in the district, and it was run by a steam engine. It was destroyed during World War II and not rebuilt until 1986. The new funicular was built to be powered by electricity. At the time, it went up and down much faster than it does now making the trip in 1 to 2 minutes, but the public petitioned for it to be slowed down, so the view could be enjoyed longer. If you are feeling energetic, you can also walk up the steep stairs to Castle Hill or take the winding trail.

Whichever method of ascent you choose, when you arrive at the top, turn and look left at the statue of the:

❹ Turul

The oversized bird you see perched on the top of the wall looking out is often mistaken for an eagle, but it is in fact a *turul.* The *turul* is the Hungarian mythical bird that legends say appeared to Emese telling her she was pregnant with a great leader of the nation, Álmos, the future father of

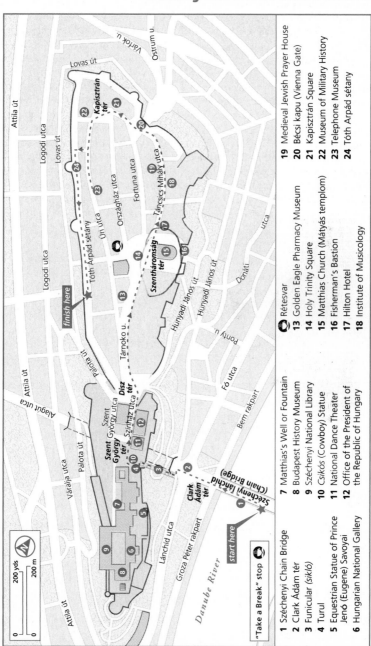

"Take a Break" stop

start here

finish here

1 Széchenyi Chain Bridge
2 Clark Ádám tér
3 Funicular *(sikló)*
4 Turul
5 Equestrian Statue of Prince Jenő (Eugene) Savoyai
6 Hungarian National Gallery
7 Matthias's Well or Fountain
8 Budapest History Museum
9 Széchenyi National Library
10 Csikós (Cowboy) Statue
11 National Dance Theater
12 Office of the President of the Republic of Hungary

Rétesvar
13 Golden Eagle Pharmacy Museum
14 Holy Trinity Square
15 Matthias Church (Mátyás templom)
16 Fisherman's Bastion
17 Hilton Hotel
18 Institute of Musicology
19 Medieval Jewish Prayer House
20 Bécsi kapu (Vienna Gate)
21 Kapisztrán Square
22 Museum of Military History
23 Telephone Museum
24 Tóth Árpád sétany

Árpád. It is supposed to be the largest bird statue in the world with a 15m (49 ft) wingspan. From here you enter:

The main courtyard of the palace. The entrance to the Hungarian National Gallery is located farther down the path, but first go down the nearby stairs to see the statue of the fisherboys and past them to the:

⑤ Equestrian Statue of Prince Jenő (Eugene) Savoyai

On September 11, 1697, Prince Eugene and his 50,000 men caught the Turks while they were crossing the river Tiza and annihilated the Ottoman army. You might want to visit the National Gallery now or return after the walking tour.

The first museum is the:

⑥ Hungarian National Gallery

This museum houses much of the greatest art ever produced by Hungarians. Be warned, it seems to go on forever and not much is in English, though it is worth a look. If you are an art lover, you will be in heaven. The most important era in Hungarian art was the 19th century and the artists of that period are Mihály Munkácsy, László Paál, Károly Ferenczy, Pál Szinyei Merse, Gyula Benczúr, and Károly Lotz. József Rippl-Rónai was a great Art Nouveau painter of the turn-of-the-20th-century period. You will also find pieces from medieval times, and the 18th, 19th, and 20th centuries as well.

Proceed through the courtyard to the:

⑦ Matthias's Well or Fountain

This is one of my favorite fountains in the city. Legend has it that King Matthias was on a hunting expedition when a fair maiden came across him by chance. She, Ilona, not knowing he was the king, fell in love instantly and him with her. He has the deer he has just killed, his hunting dogs, and his servants with him. This is probably the most photographed statue in the city.

If you continue around the fountain and into the large courtyard, directly in front of you is the:

⑧ Budapest History Museum

Boasting four floors, the museum offers exhibits containing pre-historic, ancient, Roman, pre-Hungarian and modern-day pieces. The highlights here are the Gothic rooms and statues that were uncovered by surprise when reconstruction and rebuilding of the Royal Palace was taking place. The rooms and all their contents, dating back as far as the 14th century, were buried for hundreds of years. From the downstairs, you can venture out on the grounds and you should do so to see some of the ancient architecture that has been preserved.

Next as we turn to leave the courtyard again, on our left we have the:

⑨ Széchenyi National Library

The library was started through the initiative of Ferenc Széchenyi, the father of István, who had the Chain Bridge named for him. It was founded in 1802. It now houses the world's greatest collection of "Hungarica," with some four million holdings. Any print matter that receives an ISBN number in Hungary has to have four copies sent here. It is the Hungarian Library of Congress.

Now proceed up the path, where you'll find the:

⑩ Csikós (Cowboy) Statue

The horse wrangler is taming a wild horse. This statue originally stood in front of the Riding School in the former Újvilág terrace. It was moved here after being repaired in 1983.

As you continue walking past the funicular, you will find the:

⑪ National Dance Theater

First built as a cloister and church by an order of Carmelites in 1736, this building was turned into a theater when the order disbanded in 1787. It was turned into a theater and today continues as the National Dance Theater.

Right next to the theater you will see:

⑫ Office of the President of the Republic of Hungary

The classicist palace next to the theater was ordered by Count Vincent Móric engaging the services of architects János Ámon and Mihály Pollack. It was the head office of the prime minister from 1887 to 1945. Now it is the Office of the President of the Republic of Hungary. Across from this in the grassy field, you can see the remains of a medieval church.

Before you leave here, a tour guide shared with me that behind the president's house is the most spectacular view from the entire hill. Let me know what you think. Continue walking away from the palace area, you will pass an open-air tourist area behind the wall, with crafts and folk goods for sale, but I don't recommend that you buy here here. Instead:

☕ TAKE A BREAK
The **Rétesvar** at Balta köz 4 (p. 121) has the best strudels I have eaten in Budapest. You can have a coffee or tea with a sumptuous pastry. They also have savory snacks. Sit on the bench in the köz and enjoy the rest. Difficult to find, look for the woman fountain statue and the köz is right behind her back.

Now that you are rested, we come to the:

⑬ Golden Eagle Pharmacy Museum (Arany Sas Patika- múzeum)

I love this museum. The Renaissance and baroque pharmacy relics displayed are really interesting, but what I like most is the display in the back room that shows how medications and remedies were created before the onslaught of modern-day medicines and drugs took over.

Just ahead on Tárnok utca is:

⑭ Holy Trinity Square (Szentháromság tér)

This central square of the Castle District is the highest point on the hill and where you'll find the Holy Trinity Column, or

Plague Column. At 14m (46 ft) high, it was under construction from 1710 to 1713. It was hoped that it would fend off another plague.

Sitting near it is the:

⑮ Matthias Church (Mátyás templom)

Officially called the Church of Our Lady, this symbol of the Castle District is universally known as Matthias Church because the Renaissance monarch, Matthias Corvinus, one of Hungary's most revered kings, was the major donor of the church and was married twice inside it. There's an ecclesiastical art collection on the second floor. Most people never notice the stairs and miss out. King Béla and his queen are buried here and you can see their tombs through the wrought-iron gates on the left side of the church. The church has frequent concerts. At different times, large parts of it are under scaffolding ruining the beauty of it. This is predicted to continue until 2012, but do go inside. It is worth it.

As we leave the church, to our left is the:

⑯ Fisherman's Bastion

This terraced area built in neo-Gothic and neo-Romanesque styles was built between 1895 and 1902. It has now been dominated by a restaurant where, during warm months, they force tourists to pay for the pleasant view by ordering a drink or food. However, if you go to the extreme left, you can go out on a parapet without having to make a purchase. The upper level costs 450 Ft for a higher view, but if you are around after 9pm, you can get up for free when the turnstile is turned down.

Walk around the church once again to come to the:

⑰ Hilton Hotel

The Castle District's only major name hotel, the Hilton, through the work of architect Béla Pintér, incorporated one wall of the old Jesuit cloister, built in late rococo and decorated in plaits along with the Gothic remains of a Dominican church dating back to the 13th century, into the modern hotel. The baroque facade of the 17th-century Jesuit college makes up the hotel's main entrance. The hotel has frequent art gallery shows in areas that demonstrate the melding of the old and the new. Admission is free. Summer concerts are held in the Dominican Courtyard.

Now we head a few feet away for a:

>  **LUNCH BREAK**
> If you would like some down-home Hungarian cooking, stop at the Fortuna passage, just across the street from the Hilton and a few doors down. Look for the A-frame sign that has ÖNKISZOLGÁLÓ VENDÉGLŐ. There is also a sign for garden shops. Turn into the passage, but pass the first door on the left, which goes to a more expensive restaurant, looking for the next door with a wooden sign that says ÖNKISZOLGÁLÓ VENDÉGLŐ. Open the door and go upstairs. You are in the main dining area, so walk to the back to get your cafeteria-style meal. It is only open weekdays from 11:30am to 2:30pm. The food is satisfying and inexpensive.

Because the entire length of each of the Castle District's north–south streets is worth seeing, the tour will now take you back and forth between the immediate area of Szentháromság tér and the northern end of the district. First, head down Táncsics Mihály utca, to Táncsics Mihály u. 7, to the:

⑱ Institute of Musicology
Built by Count György Erdődy in 1730, the building has the count's coat of arms over the ornamented door and the balcony. The building is now used by the Hungarian Academy of Sciences Department of Musicology; the museum portion was closed indefinitely as of 2007. If the museum is still closed when you visit, you can at least see the outside and the inner court. If it happens to have reopened, then you are in luck. The musical archives of the famous Hungarian composer Béla

Bartók are on display. This courtyard has a plaque stating that Táncsics Mihály u. 9, was once used as a prison. Two of the famous prisoners were Mihály Táncsics, the 19th-century champion of free press after whom the street is named, and Lajos Kossuth, the leader of the 1848–9 anti-Habsburg revolution. Buda's medieval Jewish community was centered on Táncsics utca. During excavation and reconstruction work in the 1960s, the remains of several synagogues were uncovered.

Continue walking down the street to Táncsics Mihály u. 26, where you'll find the:
⑲ Medieval Jewish Prayer House
This building dates from the 14th century. In the 15th and 16th centuries, the Jews of Buda thrived under Turkish rule. This building belonged to the Jewish Prefect. The synagogue was built in his home in the 16th century. The 1686 Christian reconquest of Buda was soon followed by a massacre of Jews. Many survivors fled Buda; this tiny Sephardic synagogue was turned into an apartment.

After exiting the synagogue, retrace your steps about 9m (30 ft) back on Táncsics Mihály utca, turn left onto Babits Mihály köz, and then turn left onto Babits Mihály sétány. This path will take you onto the top of the:
⑳ Bécsi kapu (Vienna Gate)
This is one of the main entrances to the Castle District. If you have come from or are going to Moszkva tér by bus, you will use this gateway. The enormous neo-Romanesque building towering above Bécsi kapu tér houses the National Archives. Bécsi kapu tér is also home to an attractive row of houses (nos. 5–8).

From here, it is a 1-minute walk to:
㉑ Kapisztrán Square
Named for a companion of the Turkish conqueror János Hunyadi, Kapisztrán Square is where you will see the ruins of a Gothic church, which was erected in 1276 honoring Magdalen. During the Turkish invasion it was alternately used by Catholics

and Protestants, only to become a Turkish djami. The church was destroyed during World War II, leaving only the base walls, the tower, and one window of the sanctuary left to memorialize it.

You don't have to venture far. On the northwest corner of the square is the:

㉒ Museum of Military History

On the northwest side of the square, you can't miss noticing the Museum of Military History (Hadtörténeti múzeum). Besides a large collection of flags, military uniforms, and other military memorabilia, it has a collection of items from Hungary's involvement in various wars. Admission is free.

Now take Úri utca back in the direction of the Royal Palace. In a corner of the courtyard of Úri u. 49, a vast former cloister, stands the small:

㉓ Telephone Museum

Sometimes the entrance to the courtyard changes from one side to the other, meaning it will be on the street parallel to Úri u. Press the bell for the attendant to open the door. The museum's prime attractions are the collection of old phones, the actual telephone exchange (7A1-type rotary system) that was in use in the city from 1928

to 1985, and the phone line cable system. I find it fascinating. Did you know a Hungarian invented the phone exchange system?

Walk back down Úri utca toward the tower and make the first left turn to bring you to the:

㉔ Tóth Arpád sétany

This promenade runs the length of the western rampart of the Castle District. This is a shady road with numerous benches. If you walk to the right, you will run into the Museum of Military History again, but it is worth the view over the wall to see the panorama of Buda's Rózsadomb (Rose Hill) district, Géllert Hill, and the small neighborhood of Krisztinaváros (Christine Town) situated just west of Castle Hill. Krisztinaváros is named after Princess Christine, the daughter of Maria Theresa, who interceded for buildings to be erected in this area. Walking away from the museum along the wall, you'll find your way to Korona Cukrászda, a pastry shop.

The walking tour ends here, where you can take the no. 16 bus down to Deák tér or if you go around the corner, the no. 16A bus will take you down to Moszkva tér.

WALKING TOUR 3	LEOPOLD TOWN & THERESA TOWN

START:	Kossuth tér, site of Parliament.
FINISH:	Művész Coffeehouse, near the Opera House.
TIME:	About 2 hours (excluding museum visits and the Opera House tour).
BEST TIMES:	Tuesday through Sunday. Note that if you want to visit the Parliament building, you should secure your ticket in advance in person. Tickets are not available online.
WORST TIME:	Monday, when museums are closed.

In 1790, the new region developing just to the north of the medieval town walls of Pest was dubbed Leopold Town (Lipótváros) in honor of the emperor, Leopold II. Over the next 100 years or so, the neighborhood developed into an integral part of Pest, housing numerous governmental and commercial buildings: Parliament, government ministries, courthouses, the Stock Exchange, and the National Bank were all built here. This tour will take you through the main squares of Leopold Town. You'll also walk briefly along the Danube and visit a historic market hall. Along the way, you can stop to admire some of Pest's most fabulous examples of Art Nouveau architecture, as well as the city's largest church.

Exiting the Kossuth tér metro (Red line), turn to the left at the top of the escalator and you'll find yourself on the southern end of:

❶ Kossuth tér

Walk toward Parliament where you will see the equestrian statue of Ferenc Rákóczi II the Transylvanian prince who led the revolt against the Habsburgs that turned into the War of Independence. At one time loyal to the Habsburgs, he grew disenchanted with their lack of interest in the Hungarian nobility. He was imprisoned for conspiring against them, but escaped and sought refuge in Poland. On the northern lawn, you will find a statue of Lajos Kossuth for whom the square is named. He was the political leader of the 1848 Hungarian War of Independence from the Habsburgs. Both men fought for the independence of Hungary and both were defeated in their efforts.

Sitting gloriously on your left is one of the most important symbols of Budapest, the neo-Gothic:

❷ House of Parliament

Work on the Parliament building began in 1884, but was not completed until 16 years later. The similarities to Westminster in London are due to them both having the same architect, Imre Steindl. Since 2000, besides its government functions, the Parliament building has also been home to the fabled Hungarian crown jewels. Many protests have been held in front of the building including the uprising in October 2006, when tapes were leaked that the prime minister had lied to the public about the state of the economy. Unfortunately, you can enter only on guided tours (the ¾-hour tour is worthwhile for the chance to go inside). It is a magnificent building inside as well as outside, being one of the largest Parliament buildings in the world. See p. 134 for tour times and information. Minor protests still occur in front sometimes disrupting the tour schedule.

Here, you have an option. If you are feeling fearless and are without children, go down the stairs behind the back of Parliament, and dodge the traffic on the busy two-lane road to the river embankment. Walk to your left toward the Chain Bridge. You will see dark bronzed shoes of various sizes and styles lined up along the river. This is a respectful remembrance of the Jews who were lined up along the river and shot by the Germans, during the last days of the Holocaust. The Germans knew they did not have time or access to continue sending train cars to detention camps.

When you return to Parliament and ascend the stairs again, head across the street to the eclectic-style building that now houses the:

❸ Ethnographical Museum

This museum boasts more than 150,000 objects in its collection. The From Ancient Times to Civilization exhibition contains many fascinating relics of Hungarian life. See p. 126 for more information.

Continue walking past the front of Parliament, and past the statue of 1848 revolutionary hero, Lajos Kossuth, mentioned earlier.

As you get to the corner with the Parliament Café turn left and continue through Vértanúk tere (Square of Martyrs). Here stands:

❹ Imre Varga's statue of Imre Nagy

The Nagy statue *Witnesses to Blood* was erected in 1996 portraying the former prime minister in a realistic manner of dress, but slimmer than he was in life crossing a symbolic bridge. Although he was a reformist Communist who was made prime minister with the backing of the Soviets, he attempted to create a solution for Hungarian independence. It was he who led the failed 1956 Hungarian Uprising. He was executed in 1958, 2 years after the Soviet-led invasion.

Now walk a few blocks down Nádor utca and turn left onto Zoltán utca. The massive yellow building on the right side of Zoltán utca is the former Stock Exchange, now headquarters of:

❺ Hungarian Television

There have been plans to move the television headquarters to a new building, but these plans constantly fail due to financial reasons. The significance of this building now is that this is where the riots of September 2006 started. Angry demonstrators

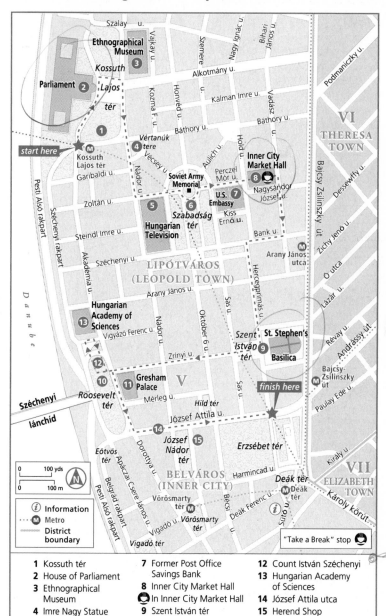

STROLLING AROUND BUDAPEST

8

LEOPOLD TOWN & THERESA TOWN

1 Kossuth tér
2 House of Parliament
3 Ethnographical Museum
4 Imre Nagy Statue
5 Hungarian TV
6 Freedom Square

7 Former Post Office Savings Bank
8 Inner City Market Hall
🍴 In Inner City Market Hall
9 Szent István tér
10 Roosevelt tér
11 The Gresham Palace

12 Count István Széchenyi
13 Hungarian Academy of Sciences
14 József Attila utca
15 Herend Shop

bombarded the stations' doors, destroyed equipment, and set fires inside, while setting cars on fire in front of the building.

The front of the television building is on:

⑥ **Freedom Square (Szabadság tér)**

Directly in front of you and barricaded is the Soviet Army Memorial, built in 1945 to honor the Soviet-led liberation of Budapest and topped by the last Soviet Star remaining in post-Communist Budapest. The monument has been vandalized several times, but after the riots occurred, the barriers were fortified. The American Embassy is at Szabadság tér 12, also surrounded by gates, barriers, and guards. The embassy is famous, but not for its architecture. During World War II, the Swiss governed over U.S. interests in Budapest. This was the official base of operations for Carl Lutz, the diplomat who saved thousands of Jews. Lutz later moved his safe house to 29 Vadász utca, the Glass House as it was called. On the wall of the embassy, if you can get close enough to see it, there is a plaque for Cardinal Mindszenty, who spent 15 years in internal exile within the embassy after being badly mistreated following the 1956 uprising.

Walk to the left of the U.S. Embassy to Hold utca and turn right onto Hold utca (Moon St.), formerly known as Rosenberg házaspár utca, for Ethel and Julius Rosenberg. Here you will find the spectacular and restored:

⑦ **Former Post Office Savings Bank (Posta Takarékpénztár)**

Stand across the street and look up for the best view, but if the trees are in bloom, you may have to risk standing in the street. One of the most unusual and one of my favorite buildings, it was designed by Ödön Lechner, the architect who in 1900, attempted to fuse Hungarian folk elements with the Art Nouveau style, which was popular at this time. I love the bees crawling up to the beehive as a metaphor for saving your money. At the top are

winged dragons and serpents, but you need binoculars to best view them.

⑧ **Inner City Market Hall (Belvárosi Vásárcsarnok)**

Built at the end of the 1800s, this is one of the five cavernous market halls around the city that all opened on the same day. It has been newly restored, but with limited light during parts of the day, so it seems cavelike at times. In this market, you will find fresh fruits, vegetables, and an assortment of spices. The bakery has some excellent selections of unusual and delicious varieties of bread.

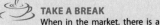

> **TAKE A BREAK**
> When in the market, there is a *lángos* stand in the side corner. Treat yourself to a Hungarian favorite snack, but don't be tempted to spoil it by getting the tourist variety like Mexican or Italian. Get the real thing with cheese, sour cream, and garlic juice.

Emerge from the Market Hall onto Vadász utca and turn right. Passing Nagysándor József utca, look right for a view of the colorful tiled roof of the former Post Office Savings Bank you recently passed. Turn right on Bank utca (the metro station you see on your left is Arany János utca; Blue line) and left on Hercegprímás utca. After a few blocks, you'll find yourself in:

⑨ **Szent István tér**

It would be impossible to miss the most famous church in Budapest, St. Stephen's Basilica. It is the largest church in the city and second largest in the country, after Esztergom's cathedral. With seating for 8,500 people, it can really pack them in. The first architect József Hild designed the neoclassical church, and construction started in 1851. However, he died before it was completed and Miklós Ybl reworked the plans creating a neo-Renaissance style, but he also died before it was completed. The third architect was József Krauser, who completed it in 1906. In the Szent Jobb Kápolna, behind the main altar to the left of the church, you can see an extraordinary and gruesome holy relic: Stephen's preserved right hand, but it will cost you 100 Ft to light up the box to get a good look. It is paraded around the city annually on St. Stephen's Day, August 20. Monday-night organ concerts are held in the church courtyard in summer. The square in front of the church has been completely refurbished and is now a restful place to spend some time. See p. 134 for more information.

Walk down Zrínyi utca, straight across the square from the church entrance. You may want to stop at the corner of Zrínyi utca and Nádor utca and walk into the building of the Central European University. The university is accredited in the U.S. through a N.Y. university. Returning now to the Danube, you'll find yourself emerging into:

⑩ **Roosevelt tér**

This square is pleasant and lies at the beginning of the famous Chain Bridge. Crossing the street to get to the grassy area can be dangerous to your health. When plans were made to destroy this park and cut the trees down to create a parking garage, a group of environmental activists chained themselves to the 100-year-old trees, defeating the plan to cut them down and transform the graceful park.

Surrounding the square are several important and attractive buildings, including:

⑪ **The Gresham Palace**

This Art Nouveau building was built in 1907 and is one of Budapest's best-known and most exclusive hotels: the Hotel Four Seasons Gresham Palace. During tediously detailed renovations, the hotel chain spared no expense to make sure every detail was as close to the original work as possible. It is absolutely magnificent inside. The staff is used to having travelers venture in to have a look around and they are proud of their hotel.

To your right, as you face the river, is the statue of the Greatest Hungarian:

⑫ **Count István Széchenyi**

Accompanying the statue of Széchenyi are four secondary figures representing the Great Hungarian's four areas of interest: Minerva (trade); Neptune (navigation); Vulcan (industry); and Ceres (agriculture).

Sitting behind the statue is the neo-Renaissance facade of the:

⑬ **Hungarian Academy of Sciences**

Széchenyi, being a patriot through and through, funded the Academy of Sciences just as he did with the Chain Bridge. After offering a tender for the design, the committee responsible rejected those of some of Hungary's most-famous architects of the day. The tender was re-opened and finally awarded to Freidrich August Stüler, the architect who designed the Stockholm National Museum and the Berlin National Gallery. Some Hungarians were upset that a foreigner was chosen to design a national building, but Stüler won out and the building was inaugurated in 1865. Guards prevent access beyond the academy's lobby, but it's worth sneaking a peek over their shoulder.

Turn left away from the river onto bustling:

⑭ **József Attila utca**

This street was named for the poet whose statue embellishes Kossuth tér. You're now walking along a portion of the Inner Ring (Kiskörút), which separates the Inner City (Belváros), on your right, from Leopold Town (Lipótváros), on your left.

At József nádor tér, you may want to stop in at the:

⑮ **Herend Shop**

Herend china is perhaps Hungary's most famous product, and this museum-like shop is definitely worth a look. If you miss out here, don't fret, there are others in the city.

If you pass this, you will arrive at Erzsébet tér and Deák to the right of it.

START:	Dohány Synagogue.
FINISH:	Wesselényi utca.
TIME:	About 2 hours (excluding museum visit).
BEST TIMES:	Sunday through Friday, before sunset.
WORST TIME:	Saturday, when the museum and most shops are closed.

Jews and their Jewish District in Pest have had a long and ultimately tragic history. There is an additional, although condensed, Jewish history within Budapest; see Chapter 2, "Hungary and Budapest in Depth" for more information. The impressive synagogues we will walk to on this tour will give you a sense of the vibrancy of the Jewish community prior to World War II. Under German occupation during the war, the district became a walled ghetto, with 220,000 Jews crowded inside; almost half perished during the war. Sadly, the neighborhood is now more or less in a state of decay. Buildings are either crumbling or are being bought by corporations to be destroyed and rebuilt into modern buildings that will house stores, restaurants, offices, and apartments. Much of the compacted neighborhood is rapidly changing, with history being ripped away, but there are still some impressive sights to see.

Halfway between the Astoria metro (Red line) and Deák tér (all metro lines) is the:

❶ Dohány Synagogue

This striking Byzantine building, Europe's largest synagogue and the world's second largest, was built in 1859. It was built before most of the other important buildings of Pest, including the Opera House (1884), and Parliament (1904), just to mention a few. It has a capacity of 2,964 seats (1,492 for men and 1,472 for women). Being a Neolog synagogue, it is still used by Budapest's Jewish community. Neolog is a combined form of Conservative and Reformed Judaism. See p. 134 for more details.

The small, free-standing brick wall inside the courtyard, to the left of the synagogue's entrance, is a piece of the original:

❷ Ghetto Wall

This brick wall is symbolic of the one that kept Budapest's Jews inside this district during World War II. This is not actually the wall, since the real one was built out of wood planks.

To the left of the wall, on the spot marked as the birthplace of Theodor Herzl, the founder of modern Zionism, is the:

❸ National Jewish Museum

On display are artifacts and art from the long history of Hungarian Jewry. Admission to the synagogue includes the museum and courtyard. The courtyard can be entered through the rear of the complex on Wesselényi utca. Between Wesselényi utca and the synagogue are many gravestones. Most of these are for the people who were held in the synagogue or surrounding area and died. By Jewish law, the dead need to be buried within 24 hours, yet another law is that the dead are not to be buried on synagogue grounds. Due to the circumstances during the war, one law had to give way to the other.

Inside the courtyard is the still-expanding:

❹ Holocaust Memorial

Designed by Imre Varga, a contemporary Hungarian sculptor, the memorial is in the form of a weeping willow tree and an inverted menorah with seven branches. An inscription above it is from the bible and reads, "Whose pain can be greater than mine?" Nearly 600,000 thin metal leaves are inscribed with the names of the Hungarian

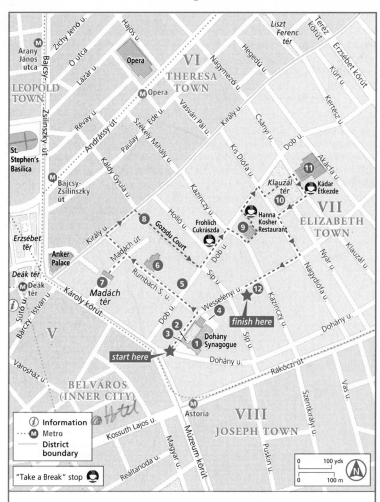

1 Dohány Synagogue

2 Ghetto Wall

3 National Jewish Museum

4 Holocaust Memorial

5 Memorial to Carl Lutz

6 Rumbach Synagogue

7 Madách tér

8 Connected Courtyards

🍵 Frohlich Cukrászda

9 Orthodox Kazinczy Synagogue

10 Klauzál tér

11 District Market Hall

🍵 Kádár Étkezde, or
Hanna Kosher Restaurant

12 Judaica Art Gallery

Jews killed in the Holocaust. A broken brick has the single word *Remember* on it. The courtyard behind the memorial is dedicated to the "righteous Gentiles" who saved thousands of Jewish lives in wartime Budapest. The more famous amongst them are Raoul Wallenberg from Sweden, Carl Lutz from Switzerland, and Angel Sanz Briz from Spain: all diplomats from their countries.

When you leave the synagogue, walk back up Wesselényi. Now turn left on Rumbach Sebestyén utca. On the corner of Dob, follow the cement wall around and you will see hiding under the tree near Dob utca 10, the unusual:

⑤ Memorial to Carl Lutz

Lutz was the Swiss consul who set up the safe house he declared as Swiss property. His heroic attempts are attributed with saving 62,000 of Budapest's Jews from the Nazi death camps. The inscription from the Talmud reads: "Saving one soul is the same as saving the whole world." The rest of the inscription states "In memory of those who in 1944 under the leadership of the Swiss Consul Carl Lutz (1895–1975) rescued thousands from National Socialist persecution." This somewhat abstract wall memorial is interesting but awkward; perhaps the artist, Tamás Szabó had a specific purpose when this was installed in 1991. However, when the tree in front of it is in full foliage, one can pass the monument without noticing it is there.

Continue on Rumbach Sebestyén utca, looking down to find some gold Stumbling Stones (see p. 136). At no. 7, you will see the gold Stumble Stones for Tyroler Gyula and Schreiber József. Half a block farther on Rumbach Sebestyén utca is the:

⑥ Rumbach Synagogue

Built in 1872 by the Vienna architect Otto Wagner, this handsome but decrepit yellow-and-rust-colored building is, in its own way, as impressive as the Dohány Synagogue. Be warned that this Orthodox synagogue occasionally closes for repairs. See p. 136 for more information.

Continue down Rumbach Sebestyén utca and make a left on Madách út to look at the giant archway of:

⑦ Madách tér

This is the area where the original old city was located in medieval times. Plans in the 1930s were to create a great boulevard similar in form and style to Andrássy út, but World War II put an end to that idea. Madách tér leads only to itself now. Looking through the arch on a clear day, you get an unusual view of Gellért Hill, crowned by the Liberation Monument.

Head back to Rumbach Sebestyén utca and proceed down that street. Take a right onto Király utca, which forms the northern border of the historic Jewish District. At Király u. 13, you will see what used to be a long series of:

⑧ Connected Courtyards

These historically significant courtyards once emerged onto Dob utca, back in the times of the Jewish District (which thrived in the 18th and 19th centuries) and until 2006. This kind of complex with residential buildings connected by a series of courtyards is typical of the Jewish District. Formed from the idea of Manó Gozsdu, a lawyer from the 19th century, the most famous is the Gozsdu Courtyard, with six interconnecting courtyards connecting seven buildings. During the war, these courtyards became ghettos with thousands of Jews locked within a courtyard.

 TAKE A BREAK
Frohlich Cukrászda, Dob u. 22, is the only functioning kosher *cukrászda* (sweet shop) left in the district. Here, you can find pastries, rolls, and ice cream. There are two unadorned tables to sit at while you eat. (Be aware that the shop is closed on Sat, and for 2 weeks at the end of August.)

Half a block to the left off Dob utca on Kazinczy u. 29 is the:

⑨ Orthodox Kazinczy Synagogue

Built in 1913 and still active, this synagogue is being slowly and beautifully restored. It has a well-maintained and lively courtyard in its center. There are a number of apartments in which members of the Orthodox community live. While hundreds of travelers visit the Dohány synagogue each day, far fewer make the trip here. Visiting times are based on luck. They have no set hours.

Go all the way through the courtyard, emerge onto Dob utca, turn right, and head into:

⑩ Klauzál tér

This is the district's largest square and its historic center. A dusty park and not completely renovated, but still an appealing playground fill the interior of the square.

At Klauzál tér 11, you'll find the:

⑪ District Market Hall (Vásárcsarnok)

One of the five great steel-girdered market halls built in Budapest in the 1890s and all opened on the same day. This one looks like it has had better days; age has not been kind. It now houses a Kaiser grocery store with small kiosks surrounding the perimeter as well as outside. The entrance area is filled with vendors selling fruits, vegetables, candies, shoes, and other surprises from time to time. On Saturdays, from early morning until 1pm, there is a farmers' market in the street.

☕ **TAKE A BREAK**
You have two lunch options in Klauzál tér and its immediate vicinity, each with a markedly different character. **Hanna Kosher Restaurant,** back at the Kazinczy Synagogue, is one of the city's two kosher restaurants. It's open daily for lunch and offers a limited selection. Wash your hands at the sink on the way in. Men should keep their heads covered inside. (**Note:** Meals can't be purchased on Sat—they have to be prepaid the day before, though they can be eaten on Sat.) **Kádár Étkezde,** at Klauzál tér 9, is a simple local lunchroom with bargain prices (Tues–Sat 11:30am–3:30pm) serving a regular clientele ranging from young paint-spattered workers to elderly Jews and the occasional tourist.

Now head back out on Nagydiófa utca to Wesselényi utca, where you can end the walking tour at Wesselényi u. 13, the:

⑫ Judaica Art Gallery

Here you'll find Jewish-oriented books, both new and secondhand (some are in English). Clothing, ceramics, art, and religious articles are also for sale.

STROLLING AROUND BUDAPEST

8

TABÁN & WATERTOWN (VÍZIVÁROS)

WALKING TOUR 5   **TABÁN & WATERTOWN (VÍZIVÁROS)**

START:	The Pest side of the Erzsébet Bridge.
FINISH:	The Buda side of the Margaret (Margít) Bridge.
TIME:	About 2 to 3 hours (excluding museum visits).
BEST TIME:	Any time except a hot summer day.
WORST TIME:	In the hot summer sun.

This tour will take you through a narrow, twisting neighborhood along the Buda side of the Danube. Tabán, the area between Gellért Hill and Castle Hill, was once a vibrant but very poor workers' neighborhood. The neighborhood was razed in the early 20th century for sanitary reasons; only a handful of Tabán buildings still stand below the green expanse of parks where the rest of Tabán once was. The neighborhood directly beneath Castle Hill, opposite the Inner City of Pest, has been called Víziváros (Watertown) since the Middle Ages. Historically home to fishermen who made a living on the Danube, Víziváros was surrounded by walls in Turkish times. The neighborhood still retains a quiet integrity; above busy Fő utca (Main St.), which runs one street up from and parallel to the river along the length of Watertown, you'll wander along aged, peaceful lanes. This walk includes lots of stairs and small hills.

Begin the walking tour on the Pest side of the:

❶ Erzsébet Bridge

The nearest metro stations are Ferenciek tere (Blue line) and Vörösmarty tér (Yellow line). The Erzsébet was named for the much-loved queen of Hungary. The bridge was completed in 1903 and sits at the most narrow part of the Danube. All of the city's bridges were destroyed by the Germans in World War II. The bridge you are walking over was reconstructed from 1961 to 1964. The bridge starts at Marcius 15 tér at one of the oldest churches in Pest, the Inner City Parish Church, which dates to the 12th century. Cross the bridge on the right side with the flow of traffic. In order to do this, you'll need to be in front of the church; there's a staircase opposite, leading up to the bridge.

You are walking toward Gellért Hill with the statue of Bishop Gellért. Remember he was killed by the vengeful 11th-century pagans, who were forced with cruelty to convert to Christianity. Bishop Gellért was an Italian bishop, who assisted King Stephen's crusade and suffered by being put to death in a spike-embedded barrel and rolled in the river far below.

Upon reaching Buda, going down the steps you will pass the statue of Queen Erzsébet, for whom the bridge was named. There is a tablet here to commemorate the anti-fascist revolutionaries who destroyed the statue of Gyula Gömbös, which was located here. Gömbös was a leading Hungarian fascist politician between the wars. You're now at the bottom of the historic Tabán District. Walk away from the bridge, toward the yellow church, whose steeple is visible above the trees. Your first stop here in Buda is the:

❷ Tabán Parish Church

Tabáni plébánia templom is a baroque church with one steeple. It was dedicated to St. Catherine of Alexandria, built between 1728 and 1740 to replace a medieval church, which, during the Turkish occupation, was known as the Mustafa Mosque. Inside, you'll find a copy of a 12th-century carving called the *Tabán Christ*. The original is in the Budapest History Museum (inside the Buda Palace; p. 137).

When you leave the church, you will see in front of and above you the southern end of the Buda Palace. Watertown is the long, narrow strip of Buda that lies on a slope between Castle Hill and the Danube. Continue now down Apród út. The rust-and-white building at Apród út 1–3 is the:

❸ Semmelweis Medical History Museum

Named for Ignác Semmelweis (1818–65), the obstetrician and "savior of mothers" was born and is buried in this house. He was the first to discover that puerperal fever could be prevented by hand-washing with chlorinated lime solution. The exhibition follows the history of healing and medicines, has exhibits related to a variety of medical fields, and contains furnishings from the 19th-century Szentlélek Pharmacy. Open 10:30am to 5:30pm Tuesday to Sunday.

Proceed down the street to:

❹ Ybl Miklós tér

This narrow square on the Danube is named for one of Europe's leading architects and Hungarian son, born in Székesfehérvár. The interesting building at the square's southern end is the former Várkert (Castle Garden) Kiosk; it's now a casino. The patio ceiling is covered with sgraffito, a decoration created by carving into a coating of glaze to reveal the color below. Directly across the street from Miklós Ybl's statue is the Várkert Bazaar. Once a beautiful place that went into ruin, it is now designated for gentrifying. The goal was to have it completed by 2010, but there has been a problem with finding investors.

Walk the length of the old Bazaar to Lánchíd utca (Chain Bridge St.), so named because it leads into Clark Ádám tér, the Buda head of the Chain Bridge. Walking away from the river, take the steep set of stairs on your left up to quiet, canyonlike:

❺ Öntőház utca

In summer, the terrace gardens of these residential buildings thrive. Flowers, small trees and shrubs, ivy, and grape vines are cultivated with care.

1 Erzsébet Bridge
2 Tabán Parish Church
3 Semmelweis Medical History Museum
4 Ybl Miklós tér
5 Öntóház utca
6 Clark Ádám tér
7 Funicular (sikló)
8 The Tunnel
9 Fó utca (Main St.)
10 Hunyadi János út
11 Institut Français
 French Institute/ Le Jardin de Paris
12 Capuchin Church
13 Corvin tér
14 Iskola utca (School St.)
15 Bem rakpart
16 Szilágyi Dezsó tér
17 Batthyány tér
18 St. Anne's Church
19 The Vásárcsarnok (Market Hall)
20 St. Elizabeth's Church
21 Nagy Imre tér
22 Király Baths
23 Chapel of St. Florian
24 Öntödei (Foundry) Museum
25 Bem József tér
26 The Buda Side of the Margaret Bridge

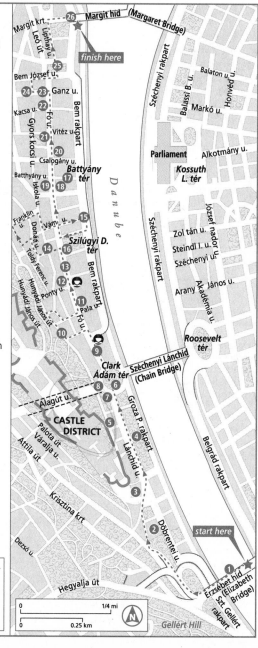

Overpass or Bridge
Tunnel
Medieval Wall
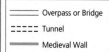 "Take a Break" stop

| 0 | | 1/4 mi |
| 0 | 0.25 km | |

Turn right, winding back down to Lánchíd utca toward:

❻ Clark Ádám tér

This is a busy traffic circle named for the Scottish engineer who supervised the building of the Chain Bridge in 1848 and 1849. Clark fell in love with a Hungarian woman, married and stayed in Budapest until his death at the very early age of 55 years old. Clark Ádám tér was one of the few streets named after a foreigner that was not renamed during Communism. A hotel has been planned for this small space for years, but has yet to materialize.

Immediately to your left is the:

❼ Funicular (sikló)

The funicular opened for business on March 2, 1870. It was destroyed in World War II, but reopened in 1986. It climbs a length of 95m (312 ft) at a grade of 48% using two cars, one for each direction at 3m (10 ft) per second. It carries passengers to the Buda Palace. In front of the funicular is the Zero Kilometer Stone, the marker from which all highway distances to and from Budapest are measured. The original marker was at the threshold of the Royal Palace, but changed to its current location in 1849.

Straight across the square from the Chain Bridge is:

❽ The Tunnel

Built between 1853 and 1857, the tunnel connects Watertown with Christina Town (Krisztinaváros) on the other side of Castle Hill. The old joke is that the tunnel was built so that the precious Chain Bridge could be placed inside when it rained. Just across the street from the tunnel, a set of stairs marks the beginning of the long climb up to Castle Hill. Adam Clark was also the builder of this project.

Passing straight through the square, you'll find yourself at the head of Watertown's:

❾ Fő utca (Main St.)

You'll be either on or near this long, straight street for the remainder of this walking tour.

Now head left on Jégverem utca (Ice House St.). Proceed up the stairs to the next street:

❿ Hunyadi János út

Notice the absurdly tall, narrow doorway of Hunyadi János út 9.

At the intersection with Szalag utca, turn right, then right again on Szőnyeg utca, back toward Fő utca. Bear left on Pala utca. Crossing Kapucinus utca, continue down the steps. Here are the rooftops you viewed from a distance a short while ago. Emerge onto Fő utca, where you'll see the site of the monstrous:

⓫ Institut Français

Note also the reconstructed remains of a medieval house across the street from this French cultural center.

 TAKE A BREAK Stop for a coffee and snack at the **French Institute** or have lunch or an early dinner at **Le Jardin de Paris,** I. Fő u. 20, a delightful French bistro.

Across the street from Horgásztanya is the former:

⓬ Capuchin Church

This church dates back to medieval times; it was built by the Capuchin order of monks. When it was refurbished, it was built into the hillside and in romantic style. Note the Turkish door and window frames on the church's southern wall.

Just past this church is:

⓭ Corvin tér

Several interesting buildings, including the home of the Hungarian Heritage House that houses the Hungarian Folk Ensemble, the Folks Arts Department, and the Folklore Documentation Center are at no. 8 on this square. If the timing is right, you might hear a rehearsal through the open windows. Note the row of very old baroque houses at the top of the square. If you look up, you can see the spires of Fisherman's Bastian from here.

Head above Corvin tér to:

⑭ Iskola utca (School St.)

Turn right on Iskola utca and left up the Donáti *lépcső* (stairs) to Donáti utca; a clay frieze of two horsemen adorns the residential building to the left, opposite the stair landing. Turn right and walk to the next set of stairs, Toldy *lépcső*. Turn left up the stairs and right onto Toldy Ferenc utca, a residential street lined with old-fashioned gas lampposts. This street is so tranquil that the only other travelers are likely to be following this very walking tour. Notice the gorgeous brick secondary school on your right (Toldy Ferenc Gimnázium); a plaque notes "ITT TANÍTOTT ANTALL JÓZSEF" ("József Antall (first post-Communist prime minister) taught here").

Now turn right on Iskola utca, then left onto Vám utca. Cross Fő utca, heading to the:

⑮ Bem rakpart

This is the Danube embankment. In pleasant weather, it can be a gentle walk along the river's edge, but below the wall to the river is a highway, which can distract any relaxing thoughts. Directly across the river is Parliament; the view is rewarding during the day, but exceptional at night. The next bridge on your left is the Margaret Bridge, where this walking tour will end.

Turn right now and you'll immediately find yourself in:

⑯ Szilágyi Dezső tér

The architect, Samu Pecz, who designed this church, used the same type of brick that was used in the Great Market, but in a neo-Gothic style for this Calvinist Church. It dates from the end of the 19th century. Composer Béla Bartók lived at Szilágyi Dezső tér, 4 in the 1920s. The Danube bank near this square is the site of a piece of Hungary's darkest history: here, the Arrow Cross (Nyilas), the Hungarian Nazis, massacred thousands of Jews in 1944 and 1945, during the last bitter winter of World War II. Many were tied

together into small groups and thrown **187** alive into the freezing river.

Returning now to Fő utca, turn right and continue on toward Watertown's main square, Batthyány tér. You may want to stop in at the Herend Village Pottery shop at Bem rakpart 37, on the ground floor of the housing block. You'll find several attractions along:

⑰ Batthyány tér

One of this area's principal sights is the 18th-century:

⑱ St. Anne's Church

One of Budapest's finest baroque churches, St. Anne's was started by Kristóf Hamon in 1740, but completed by Mátyás Nepauer in 1761. It was almost destroyed in the early 1950s because the Hungarian dictator Mátyás Rákosi (known as "Stalin's most loyal disciple") thought that when Stalin visited him at his office in Parliament, he would be loath to look across the Danube at a Buda skyline dominated by churches. Fortunately, Rákosi's demented plan was never realized. It has been threatened by floods, earthquakes, and even the construction of the metro, but it still survives.

Also on the square is:

⑲ The Vásárcsarnok (Market Hall)

One of the markets built in 1897 to improve sanitation of meats and vegetables, this building now houses a grocery store that really drains the charm from the building. The interior is worth a look. Two doors down is the former White Cross Inn with a mix of rococo and baroque ironwork on the balconies. Joseph II (1780–90) stayed here twice as did the legendary womanizer, Casanova. This is where the ground-floor nightclub acquired its name. To the left of the back gate is where tradesmen enter the market hall.

Continue along Fő utca. The next church on your right is:

⑳ St. Elizabeth's Church

This church has a fine baroque interior if you can ever get in to see it. As with most churches here, when there is no mass, you can only enter the foyer and peek in the glass windows to the church's interior. The frescoes date from the 19th century.

Continue along Fő utca. You're now approaching the northern border of Watertown where the streets get larger, such as Batthyány utca and Csalogány utca, which bisect Fő utca. You can no longer see Castle Hill. The next square is:

㉑ Nagy Imre tér

A small park hidden behind a Total gas station, this square is named for the reform Communist leader who played a leading, if slightly reluctant, role in the 1956 Hungarian Revolution. The prison-like building on the corner is the Military Court of Justice, where Nagy was secretly tried and condemned to death in 1958, thus providing Hungary with yet another martyr. Nagy's reburial in June 1989 was a moment of great national unity, and a statue of Nagy was later erected near Parliament (p. 131). The main entrance to the Military Court of Justice is on Fő utca.

Two blocks farther up Fő utca, at Fő u. 82–86, are the:

㉒ Király Baths

This 16th-century bathhouse is one of the city's major positive reminders of Turkish rule. Most people walk right past it even when purposefully looking for it since, from the street, it does not look like much at all. Inside, the gorgeous interior dome over the baths has holes in the ceiling that let in rays of light. You won't get to see it unless you pay the entry fee and use the thermal's waters. The baths are open on different days for men and women (p. 159).

Next door, at the corner of Fő utca and Ganz utca, is the baroque:

㉓ Chapel of St. Florian

A baker had this chapel commissioned in the 18th century. Due to flooding before the protective wall was built on the river, the church had to be lifted 1.4m (4½ ft) in 1938. The contemporary painter Jenő Medveczky painted all of the frescoes. Now it is home to the Greek Orthodox community in Buda.

Turn left on Ganz utca, passing through the small park between the baths and the church. At the end of Ganz utca is the:

㉔ Öntödei (Foundry) Museum

This museum is housed inside the original structure of the famed Abraham Ganz Foundry (started in 1845). From the exterior, painted a creamy yellow with a rusty-red trim, it's hard to imagine the vast barnlike interior. The collection of antique cast-iron stoves is the highlight of the exhibits.

Turn right onto Bem József utca, a street with several small fishing and army-navy-type supply stores, and head back down toward the Danube. You'll find yourself in:

㉕ Bem József tér

Józef Bem was of Polish origin, and a hero in the War of Independence of 1848. He commanded the Hungarian troops against the Habsburgs. On October 23, 1956, the square hosted a rally in support of the reform efforts in Poland. The rally, and the subsequent march across the Margaret Bridge to Parliament, marked the beginning of the famous 1956 Hungarian Uprising.

Turn left onto Lipthay utca, which is parallel to the river. Always remember to admire the buildings as you make your way to the end of the tour at:

㉖ The Buda Side of the Margaret Bridge

Here, you can walk the bridge to Jászai Mari tér for the no. 4 or 6 tram or head to Buda's Moszkva tér (Red metro line).

Budapest Shopping

The world of fashion and commercialization has bombarded the capital with a silent invasion. Each week, COMING SOON signs appear on storefront windows promising yet more pieces of globalized fashion, but you can rest assured they're not for the average Hungarian. From designer labels like Louis Vuitton and Gucci, to brand-names like Nike, and stylish secondhand shops, Budapest offers an array of shopping experiences with each passing year trying to outguess the economy.

As is the global trend, megastores are forcing out the small business owner at a rapid rate. Still, buyer beware: quality and value do not always go hand in hand with a hefty or bargain price tag. A number of fashion-driven, retro-loving, or economically suppressed shoppers are still ferreting out the smaller shops where they can claim the prize of a bargain. To add to the mix, secondhand clothing stores have started to pop up like mushrooms after a good rain.

Shopping vocabulary to know:

Nyitva-tartas	Opening hours.
Nyitva	Open.
Zarva	Closed.
Akció	Sale going on.

% Without a number, means there's a sale with multiple discounts.

Vásárló utca is an underground 'street' of shops off Váci utca near Haris köz—you'll recognize it by the escalator going down to it. I don't recommend you go down there, especially at night. It's easy to get trapped by unsavory types, particularly business ladies who may have brawny friends at the top of the escalator to convince you to use unwanted services.

FOLKLORE Travelers seeking folklore objects do not have far to look. The first place to look is the second floor of the **Nagyvasarcsarnok (Great market)** for a wide selection of popular items that include pillowcases, embroidered tablecloths, pottery, porcelain, intricately painted and carved eggs, dolls, dresses, skirts, and sheepskin vests. The vendors have become jaded with tourists, so don't bargain as much as they used to. Antiques shops, running along **Falk Miksa utca** in downtown Budapest, feature a broad selection of vintage furniture, ceramics, carpets, jewelry, and accessories, but over the years, it has become more expensive with less bargaining going on for tourists.

Transylvania, once part of Hungary before the Trianon Treaty after World War I, still comprises mostly ethnic Hungarians amongst the population. Women come to Budapest with bags full of handmade craftwork selling their goods to Hungarians and tourists alike. Their prices are generally quite reasonable, and bargaining is customary. Keep your eyes open for these vendors, who sell on the street or in the metro plazas—they are unmistakable in their characteristic black boots and dark-red skirts, with red or white kerchiefs tied around their heads. If they spot the police, they may disappear fast, but often return when the coast is clear again.

PORCELAIN A popular Hungarian item is porcelain, particularly from the country's two best-known producers, Herend and Zsolnay. Although both brands are available in the West, you'll find a better selection, but not lower prices, in Hungary. Collectors have told me they now have to hunt with a keen eye for substantial bargains, more so than in the past. The Zsolnay factory has declared bankruptcy, so the government had to take receivership. Although they are trying to sell it, it is unclear how this will change demand or availability.

HUNGARIAN FOOD Typical Hungarian foods make great gifts. Hungarian salami is world famous. Connoisseurs generally agree that Pick Salami, produced in the southeastern city of Szeged, is the best brand. Herz Salami, produced locally in Budapest, is also a very popular product (though not as popular as Pick). You should be aware that some people have reported difficulty in clearing U.S. Customs with salami; bring it home at your own risk. Another typical Hungarian food product is chestnut paste *(gesztenye púré)*, available in a tin or block wrapped in foil; it's used primarily as a pastry filling but can also top desserts and ice cream. Paprika paste *(pirosarany)* is another product that's tough to find outside Hungary. It usually comes in a bright-red tube. Three types are available: hot *(csípős)*, deli-style *(csemege)*, and sweet *(édes)*. Powdered paprika also comes in the same three varieties as the paste. All of these items can be purchased at grocery stores *(élelmiszer)*, delicatessens *(csemege)*, and usually any convenience store. In the great market, you will find the powdered version in little decorated cloth bags, making it ready for gift giving. If spice is your thing, saffron is very cheap. Stock up and thrill others with the yellow powder. Another product to look for is Szamos-brand marzipan. **Szamos Confectioners**, a recently reestablished family business that was originally founded in 1935, is also said to make the best ice cream in the country. They're based in Szentendre, with a shop in Budapest at

V. Párisi u. 3 (© **1/317-3643**). See chapter 2, p. 23, "Hungarian Eats & Treats" for more food information.

WINES Illustrious local traditional wines and spirits have matured. The sweet white Tokaji Aszú, Tokaji Eszenzia, and Tokaji Szamorodni, and the mouth-tingling Egri Bikavér, Villányi Cuvée, Szekszárdi Bikavér, and Kékfrankos are the most representative. The infamous palinka is a strong fruit brandy that is a Hungarian treasure. Unless you indulge in an expensive brand, you may get a bottle that seems to have had the fruit waved over the top without ever really touching the drink. If someone offers you schnapps, you are getting palinka; chances are it is homemade and usually much better than the less-expensive commercial brands. Visit the House of Hungarian Palinka (p. 212) to learn about the different types and qualities. Every European culture has its herbal digestive drink that they swear will cure what ails you. For the Germans it is Jagermeister; for Hungarians, it is the black spirit made of 40 different herbs—Unicum—the trademark product of Zwack. It is a bitter liqueur and an acquired taste. In the last couple of years, they tried their hand at a carbonated version called *Unicum Next* to lure the youth market; it has been successful.

MARKETS If you love markets, you're in for a treat. There are numerous markets here: flea markets *(használtáru piac)*, filled not only with every conceivable kind of junk and the occasional relic of communism, but also with great quantities of mostly low-quality new items like clothing and shoes; and food markets *(vásárcsarnok, csarnok, or piac)*, which sell row after row of succulent, but limited varieties of fruits and vegetables, much of it freshly picked and driven in from the surrounding countryside.

1 THE SHOPPING SCENE

MAIN SHOPPING STREETS The hub of the tourist-packed capital is the first pedestrian shopping street in Budapest, **Váci utca**. It runs from the stately Vörösmarty tér in the center of Pest, across Kossuth Lajos utca, all the way to Vámház körút. This area is for both Hungarian elite and travelers alike to stroll. Váci utca as well as the bisecting pedestrian streets and courtyards are filled with boutiques and shops packed with mostly upscale items waiting to be given a new home. Váci utca was formerly known throughout the country as *the* street for good bookshops. Sadly, only one remains, but don't fret. We have other bookstore recommendations to follow that will satisfy your needs. The street is now largely occupied by Euro-fashion chain stores that flood every major city with their European-style prices. There are an overwhelming number of folklore/souvenir shops, which might be good for window-shopping, but unless we have recommended them below, you may be paying more than you should for that souvenir. This area is home to many cafes and bars, but it, like Castle Hill, is notorious for tourist traps.

Another popular shopping area for travelers is the **Castle District** in Buda, with its abundance of overpriced folk-art boutiques and art galleries. This is where tour buses drop off travelers with minimal time to shop, thus forcing them into impulsive buying.

Most Hungarians like to browse or people-watch in these two neighborhoods, but tend to do their serious shopping elsewhere. One of the favorite shopping streets is Pest's **Outer Ring (Nagykörút),** which extends into **West End Center,** a shopping mall located just behind the Nyugati Railway Station. Another bustling shopping street is Pest's **Kossuth Lajos utca,** off the Erzsébet Bridge, and its continuation, **Rákóczi út,** which extends all the way out to Keleti Railway Station. **Király utca** has gentrified and is becoming known for its intimate home decor boutiques. **Andrássy út,** from Deák tér to Oktogon, is an example of contradiction. There are now over a dozen empty storefronts at any given time, yet the elite designer shops still want to make their mark here. No bargains to be found, but you can drool over the gurus of fashion like Emporio Armani, Ermenegildo Zegna, Gucci, Louis Vuitton, Burberry, and Fidji Couture, which features Dior, Versace, and Lanvin. For youthful fashion, the likes of Nike and Adidas are represented here also. Andrássy út is also where evenings come alive, with numerous cafes and restaurants. If you shop until you drop, **Liszt Ferenc tér** and **Nagymező utca**, both run off Andrássy út and are intermingled with a plethora of cafes and restaurants. For more purchase power, check out the revitalized **Ráday utca** with its offering of a few tiny shops with unique ceramic, glass, and other bric-a-brac, which may be exactly what you are missing for your souvenir list. You can often pay by credit card in the most popular shopping areas.

HOURS This is the general rule used in this chapter: Stores are open Monday through Friday from 10am to 6pm and Saturday from 10am to 2pm. Otherwise, when a store waivers from the rule, I have their hours in the listing. The high-end designer stores are open Saturdays until 6pm. Most independent shops are closed on Sunday, except for those on Váci utca. Shopping malls are open on weekends, sometimes as late as 9pm, but this is always subject to economic changes.

TAXES & REFUNDS If you reside outside of the European Union, refunds on the 25% **value-added tax (VAT),** which is built into all prices, are available for most consumer goods purchases of more than 45,000 Ft purchased in one store, in one day (look for stores with the "Tax-Free" logo in the window.) The refund process, however, is elaborate and confusing. In most shops, the salesperson has to provide you with the necessary documents: the store receipt, a separate receipt indicating the VAT amount on your purchase, the VAT reclaims form, and the mailing envelope. The salesperson should also be able to help you fill out the paperwork. Use a separate claim form for each applicable purchase. If you are departing Hungary by plane, you can collect your refund at **Magyar Pénzváltó** in **Ferihegy Airport 1** or **OTP Bank** at **Ferihegy Airport 2**. You have to do this right after checking in but *before* you pass security control. Otherwise, hold on to the full packet until you leave Hungary and get your forms certified by Customs when you land. Then, mail in your envelope and wait forever for your refund. Two wrinkles: you must get your forms certified by Customs within 90 days of the purchase showing that it is leaving the country; and you must mail in your forms within 183 days of the date of export certification on the refund claim form. I have never found this to offer any significant savings after they deduct the service charge for the transaction. Unless you are making grandiose purchases, you may want to save your time and energy for other things. For further information, contact **Global Refund (Innova-Invest Pénzügyi Rt.)** at IV. Ferenciek tere 10, 1053 Budapest (*©* **1/411-0157;** fax 1/411-0159; www.global refund.com).

SHIPPING & CUSTOMS You can ship a box to yourself from any post office, but the rules on packing boxes are as strict as they are arcane. The Hungarian postal authorities prefer that you use one of their official shipping boxes, for sale at all post offices. They're quite flimsy, however, and have been known to break open in transit, probably before leaving the city. The Hungarian post does not have a five-star rating for service, but they do rank four stars for misappropriating packages coming and going from the country.

Very few shops will organize shipping for you. Exceptions to this rule include most Herend and Zsolnay porcelain shops, Ajka crystal shops, and certain art galleries, which employ the services of a packing-and-shipping company, Touristpost. Touristpost offers three kinds of delivery: express, air mail, and surface. The service is not available directly to the public, but functions only through participating contracted shops. You need to consider whether the cost of shipping will still save you money by purchasing your fine porcelain and crystal in Hungary than at home.

Hungarian customs regulations do not limit the export of noncommercial quantities of most goods, except collectibles. However, the export of some perishable food is regulated, but allowed if acceptable to the receiving country. The limit on wine and spirits is not limited at export if shipped, but may be limited by Customs at your destination. Shipping wine can be prohibitively expensive. For more on customs, see p. 32.

2 SHOPPING A TO Z

ANTIQUES

Just about everywhere a traveler will venture, one will find shops carrying antique artifacts from keys to heirloom furniture; Budapest antiques shops have something to please every shopping buff.

Maria Theresa approved the establishment of pawn shops in 1773 with the goal of preventing predatory lending of money. These pawn shops have evolved into today's antiques stores. Many of them still function as a pawn shop as well as an antiques store, selling what people have not returned to claim. During the Communist times, art collecting or trading was illegal, so couldn't be done openly. Dealers and collectors made their covert deals around the pawnbroker shops on Falk Miksa utca. When the laws changed, newsagents, grocers, and repair shops changed hands and became antiques shops.

Nevertheless, when shopping for antiques, you should know that Hungary forbids the export of items that are designated "cultural treasures." All antiques more than 50 years old need to follow a process. First, the antique must be shown to an expert for valuation purposes. To receive the valuation certificate, you will need to present the object, or a minimum of five photographs of it, and the charge of valuation is a percentage of the item's price. After you have the valuation certificate, you must then receive a permit issued by the appropriate official government office: For paintings, it is the Hungarian National Gallery; for furniture, the Museum of Applied Arts; and all other objects, the Cultural Inheritance Office. The entire process can take up to 4 weeks to complete.

The most celebrated street for art and antiques is **Falk Miksa utca** where more than 20 shops and galleries are filled to the brim with collectables of all varieties; some shops specialize in particular items, while others are generalists. As you stroll through the city, you will no doubt find other isolated antiques shops as well. Please see the note above about opening hours.

The **Ecseri Flea Market** (see "Markets," later in this chapter) also deserves mention here, as numerous private antiques dealers operate booths at this one-of-a-kind open-air market. As with all flea markets, the quality and selection are never consistent, so it is just luck of timing in finding a real bargain. Take your chances for the fun of it; it may be your lucky day.

Anna Antiques   Carefully packed from wall-to-wall, this beautiful shop presents a nice selection of furniture and pottery while also excelling in hand-embroidered textiles. Take your time and find out more about the objects on display from the charming shop owner. V. Falk Miksa u. 18–20. ☎ 1/302-5461. Tram: 4 or 6 Jászai Mari tér.

Antikvitás   As plain and simple as its name, this bite-sized shop is manageable for a casual browse through without sensory overload. It is clean, well organized, and well lit. What more could you ask for? V. Váci u. 75. No phone. Tram: 47 or 49 Fővám tér.

Bardoni Eurostyle Antiques   With its stay-a-while atmosphere, the store is decorated as a chic but congested living room. Bardoni carries characteristic Art Nouveau, Bauhaus, and Art Deco furniture and decorative items. V. Falk Miksa u. 12. ☎ 1/269-0090. Tram: 4 or 6 Jászai Mari tér.

BÁV (Bizományi Kereskedőház és Záloghitel Rt   Although it no longer has a monopoly on the sale of antiques, this state-owned trading house continues to control the lion's share of the antiques market in Hungary. BÁV people will tell you where to take an item for valuation, however, once it is purchased, they will only refund 60% of the paid price if their "permission to export" is denied, so it is best to take photographs first and then only purchase the item after receiving "permission to export" certificates. V. Bécsi u. 1. ☎ 1/429-2090. Metro: Vörösmarty tér (Yellow line). V. Ferenciek tere 10. ☎ 1/318-3733. Metro: Ferenciek (Blue line). II. Franken Leo u. 13. ☎ 1/315-6588. Tram: 4 or 6 Jászai Mari tér.

Dunaparti Auction House and Gallery   One of the largest galleries with a wide range of antiques, paintings, porcelains, furniture, rugs, and lamps with something for collectors and souvenir hunters as well. Hours are Monday through Friday 10am to 6pm and Saturday from 10am to 4pm. V. Váci ut 36. ☎ 1/267-3539. Metro: Vörösmarty (Yellow line).

Empire Antique Gallery   A family-owned treasure chest operating shops in Lima, Peru, and Ecuador, this gallery is located in the lush environment of the Budapest Marriott

Hotel's foyer, so call the hotel to be connected. Showcased are valuable porcelain, jewelry, silverware, numismatic medals, and paintings. V. Apáczai Csere János u. 4. ⓒ **1/486-5000.** Metro: Deák tér (all lines).

Mihálka Gallery   In this centrally located cramped gallery you'll find a wide array of 18th- and 19th-century vintage furniture, paintings, objets d'art, and interior decorative items. V. Markó u. 3. ⓒ **1/30-951-4652** (mobile phone only). Tram: 2 Szalay.

Pintér Antik Diszkont   This shop stocks a widespread selection of vintage furniture, porcelain, and decorative items in its daedal interior, a small post-bomb shelter salon, while the **Pintér Szonja Contemporary Gallery** is located within the antiques shop, which also displays groundbreaking contemporary Hungarian artworks. V. Falk Miksa u. 10. ⓒ **1/311-3030.** Tram: 4 or 6 Jászai Mari tér.

ART GALLERIES

Budapest is home to a developing, yet often economically turbulent art gallery scene. Many galleries open, seem to generate public enthusiasm, then just as quickly are vacant storefronts. Uniquely, some art galleries are also auction houses, and vice versa, but dedicated art galleries are trying their hand at independence. Many galleries are antique and contemporary hybrid ventures that feature anything from fine art to vintage books. A new generation of Hungarian collectors has developed, and significant interest from European and international collectors has really fueled the development of the Hungarian modern-art market. The market for antiques has also been on the rise as long-forgotten objects from the Communist era have been removed from storage and are once again entering the market. Contemporary artists have made less headway in the past, but in the last few years they are starting to get recognized and rewarded for their efforts.

Export rules apply to all works of art as well as antiques that are considered Hungarian cultural treasures, although that list has become less expensive than it once was. Before completing a purchase, confirm that you'll be allowed to take the work out of the country; gallery proprietors should have the requisite documentation on hand. See the information above about documentation needed.

The new galleries are breaking with tradition regarding their opening hours. Some are open daily, while others are closed on Monday, like museums. Still others are open until early evening on Saturday, really deviating from all norms. Two areas of concentration are the Inner City of Pest and Buda's Castle District. However, breaking out of the crowd means breaking out of the neighborhood too. If you want to power browse in a concentrated area, then head to the art and antiques area of Budapest along Falk Miksa, from Jászai Mari tér down to the parliament. A host of art galleries and antiques shops can be found along this route.

ACB   A contemporary art-oriented gallery, it hosts frequently changing exhibitions of Hungarian and international artists. The gallery also features the eclectic, dynamic paintings, digital prints, photos, and videos collected by the founders, now described as the **Irokéz Collection.** It is open Tuesday through Friday 2pm to 6pm or by appointment. VI. Király u. 76. ⓒ **1/413-7608.** www.acbgaleria.hu. Tram: 4 or 6 to Király.

Art Factory Gallery and Studio (Finds)   I discover and rediscover this gallery and studio. Although they are compact, you can arrange to visit the studio and the artists while they are working and view the gallery at the same time. The artists' work is varied and exceptional. Meeting the artist really gives a new dimension to the work. Even hanging on your wall at home, it will speak of a memorable experience. Organized and run by an American, Dianne Brown, you can contact her via e-mail for a studio tour; however, the gallery itself is in a public building with open hours noted above, so you can view it without prior contact. See later in this section, "Contemporary Hungarian Art Lights the Spark" for more information. XIII. Váci út 152–156 (ABB Building). www.budapest artfactory.com. Metro: Forgách u. (Blue line).

Csók István Galéria One of my favorites for browsing, this gallery has it all and sells it all too. There is a fine collection of paintings, ceramics, glassware, and other artful objects by Hungarian artists who are trying to break into the art scene. Open daily from 10am to 8pm. V. Váci u. 25. ✆ 1/318-5826. www.kepcsarnok.hu. Metro: Vörösmarty tér (Yellow line).

Dorottya Gallery Albeit oppressively austere and small to some, this one-room gallery is associated with the Ernst Museum and compiles excellent contemporary installations, photographs, and media art. You don't even need to go in; you can see it all from the windows. It is open Monday through Saturday 10am to 6pm. V. Dorottya u. 8. ✆ 1/266-0223. Metro: Vörösmarty tér (Yellow line).

Ernst Gallery The gallery features fine and applied arts from Hungary and around Europe. The Ernst Gallery, the poshest gallery in town, is run by a dynamic duo of Austrian-born Ernst Wastl and his Greek-born wife, Eleni Korani. They put together exhibitions, discover "unknown" Hungarian artists, and whatever they put their hands onto ends up being the talk of the town. The gallery also exhibits and sells fine furniture and a wealthy collection of rarities including vintage art books, posters, and other curiosities. V. Irányi u. 27. ✆ 1/266-4016 or ✆ 1/266-4017. www.ernstgaleria.hu. Metro: Ferenciek tér (Blue line).

Godot Gallery Located beside the cafe of the same name, Godot opened its door to the arty crowd in 1999 in order to present a new, dynamic space for contemporary Hungarian art. Exhibitions follow distinctly different themes, which makes it a gallery worth returning to. It is closed on weekends. VII. Madách út 8. ✆ 1/322-5272. www.godot.hu. Metro: Deák tér (all lines).

kArton Gallery Run by the art institution kArton, kArton and its sister **raktArt Gallery** feature a colorful segment of contemporary visual art: underappreciated genres like comics, illustrations, and cartoons. The opening hours are out of sync with other galleries' hours, Monday through Friday 1pm to 6pm and Saturday by appointment. V. Alkotmány u. 18. ✆ 1/472-0000. www.karton.hu. Metro: Ferenciek tere (Blue line).

Kieselbach Gallery and Auction House Established and directed by art historian Tamás Kieselbach in 1994, the Kieselbach Gallery functions as a gallery and auction house. It also puts on museum-type shows that present artworks from private collections at biannual non-selling exhibitions. The gallery specializes in paintings by Hungarian artists dating from the 19th and 20th centuries, which are becoming short in supply. Most are now off the market. The gallery has a reputation for the documentation and display of artworks previously unknown to the public. V. Szent István körút 5. ✆ 1/269-3148. Tram: 4 or 6 Jászai Mari tér.

Koller Gallery This is the oldest private gallery in Hungary. Since 1953, it has been representing internationally known sculptors and artists. I. Táncsics Mihály u. 5. ✆ 1/356-9208. www.kollergallery.hu. No convenient public transportation.

Liget Gallery Curator and art critic, Tibor Várnagy, has run this gallery since 1983. The Liget (meaning grove) gallery in the City Park features nonprofit exhibitions and an

Contemporary Hungarian Art Lights the Spark

Sometimes a foreigner can make a difference in the country they adopt as a home, and this is what Dianne C. Brown has done. After moving here in 1994 when her husband was transferred to Budapest, Dianne founded the **Friends of the Fine Arts Museum,** the first museum Friends program in Hungary. At the time, the museum was a place for research, but not an amicable place for visitors. Many of the holdings of the museum were shipped to Germany during the war, and returned at the end of the war with the help of repatriated Hungarians who raised money and awareness of the importance of the pieces. The newly founded Friends organization sponsored events such as Open Day, allowing a behind-the-scenes look at the holdings which were not on display and how paintings were restored. Dianne continued to work with the organization for 6 years acting as its first president and continuing as a member of the board.

With her 16-year commitment to working with Hungarian art, she has been inspirational in renewing interest in the country's contemporary artists and their work. Dianne founded the **Sparks Gallery**; she opened the **Art Factory** in 2005 and continues as its director.

The Art Factory was created with the mission of highlighting some of Hungary's most promising young artists while promoting their work abroad and establishing their place in the international art world. To achieve this, the Art Factory participated in several international art fairs. In 2007, Sparks Gallery and the Art Factory were combined to create the Art Factory Gallery. Up to this point, the most important period of Hungarian art was from the late 19th and early 20th century, but with all of those pieces off the market, new interest has developed in contemporary pieces. Gallery manager, Virag Major, and gallery

open, easygoing artistic space for performances, film screenings, and concerts. Highlights are the socially conscious artwork of local talents. Open Wednesday through Monday 2pm to 6pm. XIV. Ajtósi Dürer sor 5. ⓒ 1/351-4924. www.c3.hu/~ligal. Metro: Hősök tere (Yellow line).

Stúdió Gallery The frequently changing exhibitions in this gallery feature the works of Hungarian art students. If you're looking for the zest of the newest artsy trend, don't miss out on this studio. Open Tuesday, Thursday and Friday 10am to 6pm; Wednesday noon to 8pm and Saturday noon to 4pm. VII. Rottenbiller u. 35. ⓒ 1/342-5380. http://studio.c3hu/studio_galeria/galeria_english/index.html. Bus: 74 Rottenbiller.

Vam Design ★★★ Adding to the appeal of an interior design store, where various pieces of home decor are offered, Vam took over the apartment building behind the store. What is unique is that the apartment courtyard and each apartment in the multistory building is an art gallery. Walk from apartment to apartment to view works of art hanging in the otherwise empty apartments. According to their literature, "This is a unique presentation of the arts of 120 years of human history." Such famous artists as Frank Lloyd Wright are included in the offerings. The feeling of voyeurism lurking in the rooms curator, Delia Vekony, oversee a rigorous exhibition schedule in several venues, including galleries, institutions, and museums abroad.

The studio is located in a Socialist-era industrial complex near the center of Budapest: a tremendously large space where artists can develop their style and their career simultaneously. While the artists work in all media and styles, the common thread is a distinctly Eastern European emotional expressionism. Artists-in-residence are Zsolt Bodoni, Dora Juhasz, Marta Kucsora, and Sandor Szasz, and are often joined by visiting artists. Their work can be viewed at the Gresham Four Seasons Hotel, which has purchased work from the studio's artistic pool.

In addition to the Art Factory Gallery's vast studio and exhibition space, the facility also houses a newly built micro-gallery for photography, video, and works on paper. You'll also find a smart-sized gallery and photo gallery at this location, but viewing is by appointment only along with a studio tour. Contact artfactorybudapest@gmail.com for information about current exhibitions or arranging a studio tour.

The **Art Factory Gallery** itself is located in public space in the mezzanine of the ABB Office Building, XIII. Váci út 152–156 (just past the Arpad Bridge). Admission is free when the building is open, which is Sunday through Friday 10am to 6pm and Saturday 11am to 2pm. Since this is a public space, the gallery is unattended, but the studio is nearby, making a tour convenient if arranged ahead.

makes it especially intriguing. The store is open regular shop hours described above, but the gallery is open daily 10am to 6pm. VI. Király u. 26. © 1/666-3100. Tram: 4 or 6 Király.

Várfok Gallery An art dealer by the name of Károly Szalóky has an ambitious plan to transform Várfok utca in the Castle District into a street of contemporary Hungarian art galleries. He has already opened two new galleries on the street, **Spiritusz** and **XO Gallery.** The main gallery, Várfok, features a fine mix of old and novel Hungarian artwork. Open Tuesday through Saturday 11am to 6pm. I. Várfok u. 14. © 1/213-5155. Metro: Moszkva tér (Red line) and then walk three blocks.

Virag Judit Gallery and Auction House Established and directed by art historian Judit Virág and her husband, István Törö, this gallery also functions as an auction house. This is the second-oldest gallery in the city after the change in government, having opened in 1997. Similar to its main competitor, the Kieselbach Gallery, it also puts on museum-type shows presenting artworks from private collections. Paintings by 19th- and 20th-century Hungarian artists are found here, a gallery that regularly produces record-setting prices for artists. Auctions are held twice a year. V. Falk Miksa u. 30. © 1/312-2071. www.viragjuditgaleria.hu. Tram: 4 or 6 Jászai Mari tér.

Kenderkó Serving and boosting creative ideas, this store features wooden boxes and other wooden pieces for collage as well as the tools needed for carving. It also has a selection of fiber art supplies. VII. Ertzsébet krt. 10–12. ✆ **1/351-9620.** Tram: 4 or 6 Királyi.

Képesbolt ★★★ (**Finds**) This is the absolute best place to buy your postcards and other stationery items. They have an extensive selection of postcards for 30 Ft apiece, large panoramic ones for 60 Ft. Postage is expensive, so you may want to buy them for the photos. You can also choose from an extensive selection of calendars and other paper good items. Their rather strange hours are Monday to Friday 8:45am to 6:30pm and Saturday 9:30am to 2pm. VIII. Deák Ferenc tér 6. No phone. Metro: Deák tér (All lines) corner of Bajcsy-Zsilinszky út.

Művészellátó Szakáruház Like to scrapbook while you travel to organize as you go? This store will most likely have some unique items for your collection. From scrapbook supplies to oil paints, it has it all and a helpful staff. Perhaps you can fill a sketchbook with pencil drawings while you are here. There are two convenient locations in the city. VIII. Üllői út 36. ✆ **1/212-1938.** Metro: Üllői (Blue line), and VI. Nagymező u. 45–47, ✆ **1/311-7040.** Metro: Opera (Yellow line).

Pátria Nyomda For the painter within needing acrylic or oil paints or for the child on your souvenir shopping list, this shop carries it all. Your child will be the first on their block to have a Hungarian pencil case for school. Closed weekends. VI. Nagymező u. 37. ✆ **1/463-0440.** www.patria.hu. Trolleybus: 78 Zichy Jenő u.

BEAUTY & HEALTH

Before you happen to have the need for an aspirin, but realize you forgot to pack it, it is best to know that anything remotely related to medication from pain relievers to stomach upset remedies, can only be purchased in a pharmacy. Conversely, personal products for ladies, and condoms can be found everywhere.

Bio-ABC ★★★ Bio-ABC started as a little hole-in-the-wall health food store, but due to popular demand and the closure of all of the Bio chain stores, this one has flourished. It is now like a health supermarket with everything from organic produce to soy cheeses, and vitamins, plus everything in between. The staff speaks limited English, but they are always willing to try to be of assistance. V. Múzeum krt. 19. ✆ **1/317-3043.** Metro: Astoria (Red line) or Kálvin tér (Blue line).

DM Forget to pack your toothbrush? Need shampoo? Head over to a DM store. A mainstream brand of cosmetics, perfumery, and personal essentials, DM operates more than 150 outlets around the country. It carries more than your ordinary drugstore-type store, but no medicines other than herbal remedies. You can find quick birthday gifts like cheap CDs, home decor, and even munchies for your favorite pet. They are all over the city, but you will find many on the ring road, the route of the nos. 4 or 6 tram lines.

Ilcsi Beautifying Herbs Everyone wants beautiful skin; some have it and some know how to "create" it. Mrs. Daniel Molnár and son, Ferenc Molnár, are creators of Ilcsi. More than 130 products made from 65 to 70 herbs, fruits, vegetables, and water, build the base of this enterprise, one that strengthens the legend of the beauty of Hungarians. Try the tomato suntan lotion to block those nasty rays, but still get a perfect tan. Only licensed beauty salons are allowed to carry their products. They are listed at **www.ilcsi.com.** One option is Health Island (*Egészségsziget*). Open Monday, Wednesday, and

Friday 1pm to 8pm, and Tuesday and Thursday 9am to 2pm. VII. Dohány u. 16–18.
(C) 1/352-0675. www.kozmetikati.hu. Metro: Astoria (Red line) or Bus: 74.

Lagos African Market and Hair Braiding ★★★ (Finds) As the name implies, this little shop is owned and operated by a couple from Lagos. They provide hair-braiding services for all hair types, but more importantly, they offer grooming and hair care products of particular interest to those of African descent. Hours are Monday to Friday 10am to 7pm and Saturday 10am to 6pm. The second location has the same hours. VII. Akácfa u 10. (C) 1/321-6325. VIII. Neszinhaz u. 42–44. (C) 1/215–2916. Metro: Blaha Lujza tér (Red line).

Long-Time Liner If you want to return home a bit more glamorous than when you left, then this cosmetic salon will provide you with permanent make-up. Trained professionals can provide permanent eyeliner, augment your existing eyebrows to make them look lush, or do lip contouring all with a microprocessor. V. Váci u. 8, félem 1 (in courtyard). (C) 1/318-4951. Metro: Vörösmarty tér (Yellow line).

Lush ★★★ Lush creates outstanding, environmentally friendly soaps, lotions, creams, and more out of purely organic materials such as pine, lavender, orange, avocado, or banana. Take a long, relaxing balmy bubble bath in French Kiss or Blue Skies aroma bars. The citrusy shower gel Slammer will open your eyes, but my favorite is Pied de Pepper for tired dry feet when researching this book. Hours are Monday to Wednesday 10am to 7pm, Tuesday and Friday 10am to 8pm, Saturday and Sunday 11am to 6pm. Other Lush stores can be found at Kristóf tér 3 as well as in MOM Park and Árkád shopping malls. V. Szent István krt. 1. (C) 1/472-0530. www.lush.hu. Tram: 4 or 6 to Jászai Mari tér.

Masculin ★★★ Beauty treatments abound for women in every city, but what about men? Now men can be pampered in masculine privacy in a men's emporium of revolutionary procedures to maintain youthful and supple looks. Popular choices start with manicures and pedicures, but continue with a number of other treatments to make you feel regenerated. Monday to Friday 9am to 9pm, or weekends from 2pm to 6pm. XIII. Pozsonyi u 12. (C) 1/786-4642. www.masculin.hu. Tram: 4 or 6 Jászai Mari tér.

Orange Optika Szalon ★★★ Record, film, and recycling buffs will love the sunglasses offered at this unique shop for Tipton Eyeglasses. All their sunglasses and frames for eyewear are made from recycled LP records with strips of old 16mm or 35mm film in the side arms. Prices are for all budgets, but the high end offers movie frames from famous international films. They started in Seattle, Washington, but are now headquartered here in Budapest for manufacturing. The store is open 10am to 7pm weekdays with usual Saturday hours of 10am to 2pm. VI. Király u. 38. (C) 1/243-2931. www.orangeoptika.hu. Tram: 4 or 6 Király u.

Rossmann As ubiquitous as the DM stores above, they basically carry the same merchandise, so it is just a matter of which one is closer when your need arises. Outlets are all over the city and are recognizable by their signs with the name in red letters on a white background. There are many along the nos. 4 or 6 tram lines.

BOOKSTORES

There is never a moment when we are without a book, so browsing in a bookstore is an avocation. If you are time limited, want a book fast, but don't want to splurge on a new book, Bookstation, Red Bus, and Treehugger Dan's are the best for used English-language books.

Bestsellers Bestsellers is Budapest's first English-language bookstore (opened in 1992). With its spacious and bright interior, the shop is popular with the expat crowd and English-speaking travelers who need the latest best-selling title before returning home. The store has a wide selection of fiction, science fiction, travel, and children's books, including books on Hungary. Half of the store is devoted to French-language books. A large range of newspapers and magazines is also available. Open Monday through Friday 9am to 6:30pm, Saturday 10am to 5pm, and Sunday 10am to 4pm. V. Október 6 u. 11. ℂ 1/312-1295. www.bestsellers.hu. Metro: Arany János utca (Blue line).

Bookstation ★★★ (**Kids**) This is a great store. It's a bit difficult to find, but worth the effort. The staff will happily check their in-stock inventory for a book by title, author, or subject. The focus is fiction, nonfiction, cookbooks, and many other genres, including a large selection of children's books, all in English. It is located in an *udvar* (courtyard). Cross the street from Keleti Station and about a half a block up, look for the Thököly udvar sign on the top of the building. Walk into the courtyard and the store is at the back. Hours are Monday to Saturday 10am to 7pm. XIII. Katona József u. 13.–ℂ 1/413-1158. www,bookstation.hu. Metro: Nyugati (Blue line).

Central European University Bookstore ★ This store features books covering a wide variety of disciplines. The selection of books on central and eastern European politics and history is particularly notable since the Central European University Press publishes a great variety of books on all topics central European. It is associated with the university, but they also have a selection of fiction. In addition, they are in association with **Pendragon Books**. V. Zrinyi u. 12. ℂ 1/327-3096. Metro: Kossuth tér (Red line) or Arany János u. (Blue line). XIII. Pozsonyi út 21–23. ℂ 1/340–4426. Tram: Jászai Mari tér.

Honterus Antikvárium és Aukciós Ház Kft. Located near the Központi Antikvárium, across the street from the Hungarian National Museum (Nemzeti Múzeum), this shop has more prints and maps on display than any other *antikvárium* in town, which is suitable; the shop was named after János Honter, a renowned Transylvanian map master. There's a shelf of mostly arcane, outdated English-language academic books as well as a stack of *National Geographic* magazines. V. Múzeum krt. 35. ℂ 1/267-2642. www. honterus.hu. Metro: Astoria (Red line) or Kálvin tér (Blue line).

Írók Boltja ★ *Írók Boltja* means "Writers' Bookshop," and this shop is truly a literary center with a rich history, first-rate literary events, and inspired window displays, making it a Mecca for writers, readers, and curious bystanders. In the first half of the 20th century the store was the Japanese Coffee House, a popular literary coffeeshop, then it became the Spark Bookstore around 1955, during the Communist era. The shop's name was changed around 1958, and was state run until 1991, when 14 employees became the co-owners during the privatization of state-owned business. It is now practically an institution, and Hungarian authors such as Péter Nádas, Péter Eszterházy, and Nobel Prize–winner Imre Kertész have read here. Events are in Hungarian. VI. Andrássy út 45. ℂ 1/322-1645. Metro: Oktogon (Yellow line).

Központi Antikvárium Central Antikvárium is the city's oldest and largest old-and-rare book store. Indeed, it is said to be the largest of its type in all of central Europe. Opened in 1885 across the street from the Hungarian National Museum on "Antikvárium Row" (Múzeum krt. was the Antikvárium u. during the pre–World War I era, home to 37 different shops at that time), this shop has books, prints, maps, and a shelf of assorted really junky and dusty knickknacks. The staff is fluent in English but can be abrupt with English speakers. V. Múzeum krt. 13–15. ℂ 1/317-3514. Metro: Astoria (Red line) or Kálvin tér (Blue line).

Libri Studium Könyvesbolt This is one of the few bookstores left on Váci utca, which was formerly home to dozens of bookstores. This is a good option for those in search of English-language books published by Corvina about Budapest or Hungary. Coffee-table books, guidebooks, fiction and poetry in translation, and scholarly works are available. There's also a good selection of maps, including the hard-to-find Cartographia trail map of the Buda Hills *(A Budai Hegység)*. Libri is a chain; if you miss this one, you are bound to find others all over the city. They have the good taste to stock this book besides. Hours are Monday through Friday 10am to 7pm, weekends from 10am to 3pm. V. Váci u. 22. ℂ 1/318-5680. Metro: Vörösmarty tér (Yellow line) or Ferenciek tere (Blue line).

Litea: Literature & Tea Bookshop   Situated in the Fortuna courtyard, opposite the Hilton Hotel, this bookshop/tea house stocks a wide range of books on Hungary, CDs and cassettes of the works of Hungarian composers, and cards, maps, and other quality souvenirs for serious enthusiasts of Hungarian culture. Take your time browsing, order a cup of tea, sit, and have a closer look at the books that interest you. This calm, no-obligation-to-buy atmosphere along with friendly staff is a rare find. I. Hess András tér 4. ℂ 1/375-6987. Bus: 16a from Moszkva tér or 16 from Deák tér; funicular: from Clark Ádám tér to Castle Hill.

Pagony Children's Bookstore ★★★ (Kids)   A bookstore devoted to children in my opinion is an exceptional idea. Not only will kids find books here, mostly in Hungarian, but some English titles too. They will also discover toys, presents, CDs, and DVDs. The children's reading area with the huge tree, lots of pillows, and other child-safe items, make this an ideal place for kids to unwind. What better memory of their trip and something to show off to their friends than a Hungarian alphabet book? It just might inspire a future linguist. They also carry the children's guidebook *Benjamin in Budapest*. Weekdays, they stay open until 7pm and Saturday 10am to 2pm. XIII. Pozsonyi út 26. ℂ 1/239-0285. Tram: 4 or 6 Jászai Mari tér.

Red Bus Bookstore ★★★   This is a paperback sanctuary with a large selection of classical literature, thrillers, and fiction by more British authors than the other bookstores, but authors published in English are here too. For as narrow as this shop is, they have stuffed an incredible 5,000 plus books into it, forcing the serious browser to spend considerable time here, especially since it doesn't have a computerized inventory. Nevertheless, the staff is helpful. It is open Monday through Friday 11am to 6pm and Saturday 10am to 2pm. V. Semmelweis u. 14. ℂ 1/337-7453. Metro: Astoria (Red line) or Deák tér (all lines).

Treehugger Dan's Bookstore Café ★★   Treehugger Dan's is another tiny giant of a bookstore and now at two locations. Run by an American expat, these wisps of a store are loaded to the rafters with more than 4,000 books, all in English. The extensive collection includes a vast travel guide selection, including Frommer's. How can you not love this place? Have a cup of fairtrade organic coffee or tea while shopping and receive a free hour of Wi-Fi Internet service besides. Dan has a computerized inventory and the staff is helpful finding particular items. He will also do a book exchange if you want to lighten your load of that last novel you just finished. Two locations below: Open Monday through Friday 10am to 7pm and Saturday 10am to 5pm; or Monday through Friday 10am to 6:30pm and weekends 10am to 4pm, respectively. VI. Csengery u. 48. ℂ 1/322-0774 and VI. Lazar u. 16 (in Yellow Zebra Bike Rentals office) ℂ 1/269-3843. www.treehugger.hu. Metro: Oktogon (Yellow line), Opera (Yellow line).

COINS

Nuismatica Érembolt   A coin collector's haven, this conveniently located store sits on the corner of this famous square offering a wide selection in a clean well-lit shop with normal weekday hours. It is closed weekends. V. Vörösmarty tér 6. ℭ **1/3374908.** Metro: Vörösmarty (Yellow line).

COMPUTER REPAIR

ExPatTech ★★★ (Finds) With the advancements in reducing the weight of laptops and especially with the popularity of netbooks, many travelers no longer leave them at home. However, when something goes wrong on the road, you need reliable service with reasonable repair costs. The owner is expat Texan, Alec Dean, and he and his staff can solve your problems with either PC or Apple computers. Either they can come to your accommodation or you can bring your computer into their shop. They have saved my technological life a number of times and I can attest to their honesty and fairness in pricing. Need a laptop, but did not bring one? They also rent laptops. IX. Ráday u. 32. ℭ **1/215-1143.** www.expattech.com. Metro: Kálvin tér (Blue line); Trams 47 or 49 Kálvin tér.

DEPARTMENT STORES & MALLS

As everywhere else in the world, Budapest has a lion's share of seen-one-seen-most-of-them-style malls, which, like in many other places, is putting a strain on the financial health of small independent stores. Although they are immensely popular with Budapesters, the locals also lament the closing of local shops that were once their only shopping opportunity. Due to high rents in malls in conjunction with a fragile economy, you may just find a number of empty stores from time to time. I am listing only the most popular malls, although there are others.

Arena Plaza This is the newest and largest mall in central Europe, after opening late in 2007 with a number of delays. You'll find a big Tesco inside, and many famous fashion brands (Peek & Cloppenburg, Terranova, Zara, H&M, Springfield, Mexx, Marks & Spencer, Mango, Lacoste, Retro and much more). They have the only IMAX cinema in Hungary. Open Monday to Saturday 10am to 9pm, Sunday 10am to 7pm. VIII. Kerepesi út 9. ℭ **1/880-7000.** www.arenaplaza.hu. Metro: Keleti (Red line) and then a 10-minute walk.

Árkád The spacious, but not immense mall is German owned and contains some of the trendiest stores including Marks & Spencer, C&A, Mexx, Nike, and Zara. The large circular cafe/restaurant section in the heart of the mall tends to rapidly fill up in the afternoon. X Örs vezér tere 25. ℭ **1/433-1400.** Metro: Örs Vezér tér (Red line).

Asia Center Built in the proximity of the Polus Center, the Asia Center opened its doors in 2003 to myriad Asian-produced products from clothing to furniture, replacing a huge outdoor Asian market that had been popular for years. Open daily from 10am to 7pm. XV. Szentmihályi út 167–169. ℭ **1/688-8888.** www.asiacenter.hu. Bus: 73 (red-lettered) or Polus mall shuttle departing from Keleti train station.

Duna Plaza This was the first mall built and boasts 120 different shops, a nine-screen Hollywood Multiplex, snack bars and pubs, and a bowling alley. Duna Plaza is open weekdays 10am to 9pm and weekends 10am to 7pm. The entertainment complex closes later than the rest of the mall. XII. Váci út 178. ℭ **1/465-1600.** Metro: Gyöngyösi (Blue line).

Mammut Mammut is really a two-part mall, with Mammut I and Mammut II connected by a glass passageway connecting the two wings. The mall was extended in 2001, and thus comprises more than 300 shops, although when you see the immense open courtyard in one wing, you'll wonder where they are hiding all the stores. Along corridors, you will see parts of mammoth remains found while excavating the mall, hence its name. This is the mall where the bowling alley is filled with English speakers, an expat hang-out. At the back of the mall, on the outside ramp, you will find the Fény utca market selling produce and flowers. See Markets below. Open Monday to Saturday 10am to 9pm, Sunday 10am to 6pm. II. Lövőház u. 2–6. ⓒ **1/345-8020.** Metro: Moszkva tér (Red line).

MOM Park   Located near the Budapest Congress Center, MOM Park is a spacious, sophisticated new conglomerate. Home to one of three Palace Cinemas where you can catch a movie in English and with air conditioning during the summer heat. Open Monday to Saturday 10am to 8pm, Sunday 10am to 6pm. Cinema is open after shops close. XII. Alkotás utca 53. ⓒ **1/487-5500.** Metro: Moszkva tér (Red line) and then tram: 61 to Csörsz u.

WestEnd City Center   This behemoth mall opened in 2000 right behind Nyugati Railway Station, giving it the auspicious title of being the largest mall in central Europe. This changed with the construction of yet more malls. It has generated much concern about the future of downtown shops and boutiques, and has led to the demise of numerous small businesses in the immediate area of the Outer Ring boulevard. Within its 400 or so shops, however, it has a rich selection of stores. There is a fountain on the ground floor that reaches one story up that was donated from Canada. Take a breather from shopping and relax on the open-air garden roof terrace with a cafe in the summer and an ice-skating rink in the winter, and lovely statues all year-around. Open Monday to Saturday 10am to 9pm, Sunday 10am to 6pm. VI. Váci út 1–3. ⓒ **1/238-7777.** www.westend.hu. Metro: Nyugati (Blue line).

FASHION FOR WOMEN & MEN

I have listed some options assuming that you'll discover new ones on your own, but to start you off, I suggest you begin on **Haris köz**, an alleyway that is actually just a small street that starts at Váci utca. There is a large and diverse selection of fashionable shops there. For discount clothes, see "Markets," later in this chapter.

Alessandro & Co.   This store offers made-to-measure suits characterized by taste and quality of the finest Italian tradition. Casual wear, dress shirts, neckwear, shoes, and accessories are also available. I. Lánchíd u. 5. ⓒ **1/201-5526.** On the Buda side, just off the Chain Bridge. Metro: Batthyány tér (Red line).

Bagaria ★★★ (Finds)   I don't carry one, but if these handbags and purses make me take notice of them, they will certainly attract your attention and then attract others' attention to you. Venconi, a Hungarian designer, makes up 50% of the collection, while the rest are Italian designs. The colors and styles are bright, exciting, and original. The shop is back in the courtyard at this address, so don't miss it. They are open Monday through Saturday 10am–6pm. V. Váci utca 10. ⓒ **1/318-5768.** www.bagaria.hu. Metro: Vörösmarty tér (Yellow line).

Bolt Design Workshop ★★★ (Finds)   Recycled leather jackets are made into purses; what was once a rubber tire, is now a backpack. Twenty artists are represented here who recycle what could have found its way into a landfill. They turn it into creative clothes, jewelry, and accessories, being one of the favorite shops of the 20-something generation, but those who are older are welcomed also. VII. Kertész u. 42–44. No phone. www.bolt muhely.hu. Mon–Fri 11am–7pm, Sat 11am–5pm. Tram: 4 or 6 Király.

Chantal Boutique   If shoes are your thing, don't pound the pavement looking until you see the offerings at this shoe boutique, where you are sure to find some innovative designs. End of season offerings are steeply discounted. V. Haris köz 2. ℂ **1/318-3812.** Metro: Vörösmarty tér (Yellow line).

Eventuell ★★★ (**Finds**)   A young American friend came upon this store and has made this her store of choice on each visit to the city. Among the unusual textiles used in clothing, she swears by the felt jacket she purchased. It looks terrific. The scarves and other clothes, jewelry, and home accessories are unique. V. Nyálry Pál u. 7. ℂ **1/318-6926.** www. eventuell.hu. Metro: Ferenciek tere (Blue line).

Iguana   Looking for some sparkling oversize grandma glasses or perhaps crazy '60s or '70s cult accessories? A shrine for retro rats, the shop stocks rows of peace jackets, trousers, bags, and jewelry. Listen to or purchase some of their all-star euphoric secondhand CDs. Don't confuse this store with the restaurant of the same name. No nachos here. VIII. Krúdy Gyula u. 9. No phone. www.iguanaretro.hu. Metro: Kálvin tér (Blue line). Tram: 4 or 6.

Intuita Art Gallery ★★★   You will also find this gallery listed under home decor below, because they have two locations with the same name, but very different products. This shop is filled with textiles; clothing, scarves, handbags, hats, and jewelry all made by Hungarian designers filling the shelves and racks. Notice the artistic wood walls and shelves while you are there. The owner handcrafted them himself and they are superb. This is at the end of the pedestrian street closer to the Nagyvasarcsarnok great market. V. Váci u. 61. ℂ **1/337-1248.** Tram: 47 or 49 Fövám tér.

Katalin Hampel ★★★   This Hungarian designer has her own unique designs blending traditional Hungarian clothing with a modern flair. Katalin Hampel designs women's clothing marked by delicate precision of handmade embroidery creating a new chic style. V. Váci u. 8 in the back of the courtyard. ℂ **1/318-9741.** www.hampelkati.com. Metro: Vörösmarty tér (Yellow line).

Katti Zoób   Celebrated Hungarian fashion-designer Zoób's high-end couture ranges from slick, eccentric, yet harmonious businesswomen's outfits to smart and naughty on-the-go wear and accessories. The shop, located in the capacious MOM Park, is open Monday through Saturday 10am to 8pm and Sunday 10am to 6pm. V. Szent István körút 17. ℂ **1/312-1865.** www.kattizoob.hu.Tram: 4 or 6.

Látomás ★★★   Run by 25 suave, creative designers since 1998, the shop is a fashion statement to the young Hungarians who want to break the molds of the past and cast their own impression on the fashion world. The colors and designs to spice up your life and your wardrobe can be found in their collection of chic and unique hats, handbags, clothing, jewelry, and accessories, not just for the younger woman. Browse through their saucy selection to find some fashion bargains. Their first store is around the corner from Dohány Synagogue, open Monday to Friday 11am to 7:30pm and Saturday 11am to 4:30pm. For men and women, they opened a second store open Monday to Friday noon to 8pm, Saturday noon to 6pm, and Sunday 2pm to 6pm. VII. Dohány u. 16–18. ℂ **1/267-2158.** www.latomas.hu. Metro: Astoria (Red line). VII. Király u. 39. ℂ **1/786-6659.** Tram: 4 or 6 Király.

Monana ★★★ (**Finds**)   Most of the goodies sold here are made by people with disabilities, so profits are funneled back not only for their livelihoods, but their continued work as well. There are different types of jewelry, ragdolls, and various sorts of bric-a-brac, utilitarian or purely decorative. With a purchase here, you will be helping an underfunded group of people to have a purpose. In addition to normal weekday hours, Saturdays they stay open until 5pm. Note that the sign outside may still have the old name, Maota. VI. Hajós u. 26A. No phone. Metro: Opera (Yellow line).

Budapest's Youthful Designers

WAMP (**WA**sárnapi **M**űvész **P**iac) is the Hungarian designers association that follows the example of the London and New York markets. Their main objective is to establish a regular forum for design and applied-art products. Secondly, they want to create a more intense relationship between artists and potential buyers through interaction. Success has come for many artists in this organization when they have improved their craft through interactions with buyers or direct feedback from visitors.

Not every artist or craftsperson can get into WAMP; first a portfolio of their work is presented, it is judged for quality of workmanship, design, and unique appeal and only after it passes, can one register. The artist is then entered in the WAMP database and is allowed to sell at their sponsored functions.

The number of Hungarian designers associated with WAMP is quickly growing with more than 1,000 artists exhibiting and selling their products after 3 years of the organization's existence. Artists are realizing the uniqueness of the sponsored events as a seal of approval of their work. A wide range of design objects, such as jewelry, textiles, clothing, ceramics, glassware, children's toys, games, and cake design are routinely presented. WAMP opens its market, usually on the first Sunday of the month. During the warm months, it is held at Erzsébet tér (a former bus station) across from Le Méridien Hotel from 11am to 8pm. During the winter, the locations change and increase for the holiday season, so check their website (**www.wamp.hu**) for current information.

For information about youthful Hungarian designer shops, pick up a free copy of the seasonal *Budapest Navigator* at Tourinform.

Náray Tamás   Situated in the posh Ybl Palace, across from the Central Kávéház, this elegant and spacious shop sells the creations of one of Hungary's most celebrated designers, Tamás Náray. The clothes are tasteful, but expensive. VI. Hajós u. 17. ✆ **1/266-2473**. www.naraycompany.hu. Metro: Opera (Yellow line).

Oltozo ★★   Young Hungarian designers for women do not lack imagination when set free in the wild world of fashion. This is apparent in this store that serves as a consortium outlet for a number of talents waiting to make their break in the big time. If you like a design, but want modifications, they are happy to do it for you. Just a look in the window will tell you they manifest the "unusual" in a multitude of ways. They are located right next door to Monana above, sharing the same address, but are only open weekdays noon to 6pm. VI. Hajós u. 26A. No phone. Metro: Opera (Yellow line).

Retrock   A group of young contemporary designers display their modern, exclusive, entrancing clothes and accessories for women and men in a nostalgic atmosphere of the last century. I call this a den of discovery for those fashion aficionados who like living on the edge. Being very popular with the college crowd they are open longer hours, Monday to Friday 10:30am to 7:30pm and Saturday 10:30am to 3:30pm. V. Ferenczy István u. 28. ✆ **1/318-1007**. www.retrock.com. Metro: Astoria (Red line).

Tisza Cipő A former Soviet-era brand, Tisza Shoes has been smartly resuscitated into a retro-athletic shoe brand that shot up on the must-have shoe list in Hungary and is steadily moving into the international market. It is now enjoying its laid-back high-end segment market position. VII. Károly krt. 1. ℂ **1/266-3055.** www.tiszacipo.hu. Metro: Astoria (Red line).

Vakondgyár With the Hungarian youth fashion market in mind, this T-shirt boutique chain features outrageous shirts designed by a whimsical young artist. Starting with the mole figure, the cute key character that gave the brand its name, the shirts' self-indulgent designs include fanciful insects, goofy Hungarian cartoon characters, and other New Age logo-like creations in a cacophony of color. VI. Terez krt. 54 and VIII. József krt. 19. No phone. www.vakondgyar.hu. Tram: 4 or 6.

V50 Design Art Studio ★ Fashion designer Valeria Fazekas has an eye for clothes that are both eye-catching and elegant. Her hats are works of art. Prices are reasonable, and she now accepts credit cards. She has a second shop at V. Belgrád rakpart 16, where she can often be found working late into the night in the upstairs studio, but that shop is closed weekends. V. Váci u. 50. ℂ **1/337-5320.** Metro: Ferenciek tere (Blue line), Trams 47 or 49 Fővám tér.

Za-Za Za-Za offers the imaginative creations of the hot young Hungarian designers of Magenta Clothing Company, who brag that they have a new line every 2 weeks. I cannot attest to this, but their display of clothes did get my attention. They have a store in all of the malls with longer hours. V. Váci u. 1–3. ℂ **1/267-0280.** www.mgnt.hu. Metro: Vörösmarty tér (Yellow line).

FOLK CRAFTS

Hungary's famous folkloric objects are the most popular souvenirs among foreign visitors. The mushrooming number of folk-art shops (*Népművészeti Háziipar*) has a diverse selection of handmade goods. Popular items include pillowcases, embroidered tablecloths, runners, wine cozies, pottery, porcelain, dolls, intricately painted or carved eggs, dresses, skirts, and sheepskin vests. One shop that has a wide selection and helpful staff is **Folkart Craftman's House** (ℂ 1/318-5143) on the side street, Régiposta u. 12 right off of Váci utca and open daily 10am to 7pm. An outstanding private shop on Váci utca is **Vali Folklór,** in the courtyard of Váci u. 23 (ℂ 1/337-6301) open Monday to Saturday 10am to 8pm and Sunday noon to 8pm. A soft-spoken man named Bálint Ács, who travels the villages of Hungary and neighboring countries in search of authentic folk items, Communist-era badges, pins, and medals, runs this cluttered shop. His sales staff does not speak English, so don't try to ask questions.

Holló Folkart Gallery is an unusual gallery selling handcrafted reproductions of folk-art pieces from various regions of the country. V. Vitkovics Mihály u. 12. ℂ 1/317-8103. Metro: Astoria (Red line) or Ferenciek tere (Blue line).

FOR KIDS

Baby Planet Babaáruház This store carries everything for the baby from clothes to booties. They also have car seats, strollers, feeding supplies, playtime diversions, and gift ideas for the little ones. IV. Aradi u.16. ℂ **1/272-1230.** www.babyplanet.hu. Metro: Újpestvároskapu (Blue line).

Kenguru Kuckó Providing a holistic supply of mandatory kids' gear, this shop has an extensive selection of clothing, toys, books, and accessories. Choose and schedule one of

> **Fun Facts** **Penning a Name in History**
>
> **László József Biró** was born in Budapest, Hungary, in 1899. In the 1930s he worked as a journalist, and he noticed the ink printed on newspapers dried immediately. He tried using this ink in fountain pens, but it clogged the nib. Working with his brother, a chemist, they invented a roller-ball fit at the bottom of the pen to pull the ink from the cartridge, thus inventing the ballpoint pen. They patented it in Paris in 1938, after escaping anti-Jewish laws in Hungary. They later sold the patent to Marcel Bich, and the pen is now known as the Bic pen. Biró also invented the automatic gearbox for automobiles.

their entertaining children's events for the weekend. Open weekdays only 10am to 6pm. II. Margit krt. 34. ✆ 1/212-4780. www.kengurugold.hu. Metro: Nyugati Pályaudvar (Blue line).

Kis Herceg Gyermekdivat (Little Prince Children's Fashion) Infant and children's clothes and shoes are sold here. You'll find everything from swimsuits to ski jackets in bright sunny colors and adorable prints. VI. Andrássy u. 55. ✆ 1/342-9268. Metro: Oktogon (Yellow line).

Pagony Children's Bookstore ★★★ See p. 201. XIII. Pozsonyi út 26. ✆ 1/239-0285. Tram: 4 or 6 Jászai Mari tér.

GIFTS & HOME DECOR

Artizan Art & Design (Finds) Quirky, comical, and fresh-styled art framed or ready to be framed, handbags, T-shirts and other fun and funny designs are all the work of one artist, Marcus Goldson, an expat from Kenya via England. IX. Ráday u. 20. ✆ 30/322-3853. Metro: Kelvin tér. (Blue line) or trams 47 or 49.

BomoArt This jam-packed tiny shop stocks unique handmade paper "artworks" of boxes, stationery, and diaries. Seductive nature-inspired decorative accessories further stimulate visitors to let loose their inner creator. V. Régiposta u. 14. ✆ 1/318-7280. www. bomoart.hu. Metro: Deák tér (all lines).

Demko Feder Here you'll find bedding, furniture, and home comforts, all in natural materials. Demko Feder's line of pure wool and non-allergenic bedding is sure to please the most temperamental sleeper. XIII. Hegedüs Gyula u. 8. ✆ 1/329-3792. Metro: Nyugati (Blue line).

Goa Love Featuring furnishings for the home in the spirit of Provence, this charming interior decorating and design shop specializes in singular wedding presents and Japan ceramics. They keep expanding their space with multiple stores side by side. Right next door is Goa Home. VII. Király u. 19. ✆ 1/352-8449. Metro: Deák tér (all lines) or Tram: 4 or 6 Király.

Hephaistos Háza Having contacts with many of the interior designers in Hungary as well as abroad, this shop either has what you want or can get it for you. They have stores or outlets throughout the world. V. Molnár u. 27. ✆ 1/266-1550. Tram 2: Szabadság tér.

Intuita Art Gallery (Finds) This innovative, little 6-year-old shop features unusual ceramic ware, leather-crafted books, sculpted glasses, and leather game boards with ceramic pieces featuring Aquincum designs. The enameled jewelry pieces are also pieces of art to wear. Their sister shop features mainly clothing items from Hungarian designers at Váci u. 61. Hours for both stores are daily 10am to 6pm. V. Váci u. 67. ⊙ **1/266-5864.** Tram: 47 or 49 Fövám tér.

Roomba Home Culture Created by talented brothers Oszkár and Bence Vági, this novel furniture and design shop offers sizzling trendy yet reasonably priced designs, decorations, and accessories. V. Arany János u. 29. ⊙ **30/689-2072** (mobile phone only). Metro: Arany János u. (Blue line).

Sós Antikvárium This small store has a splendid, extensive selection of prints and antique maps that would dress up any wall adding a sophisticated air to a room. Hours are Monday through Saturday 11am to 6pm. V. Váci u. 73. ⊙ **1/266-3204.** www.sosantik varium.hu. Tram: 47 or 49 Fövám tér.

JEWELRY
Varga Design In this shop, you'll find a wide and individualized handcrafted selection of jewelry by Miklos Varga, who after perfecting gold jewelry turned to silver and semiprecious stones. Each design is available in a complete set of necklace, earrings, and other pieces. Open Monday through Saturday 10am to 6pm V. Harias köz 6. ⊙ **1/318-4089.** www.vargadesign.hu. Metro: Vörösmarty tér (Yellow line).

MARKETS
Markets in Budapest are very crowded, bustling places. Beware of pickpockets; carry your valuables under your clothing in a money belt rather than in a wallet (see "Safety," on p. 42 in chapter 3, "Planning Your Trip to Budapest").

Open Markets (Piac)
Ecseri Flea Market According to locals you can find anything at this busy flea market—from the glorious to the kitsch, old soda siphons to antique violins, and more. Well, if you're not prone to sensory overload, you can see for yourself. Row after row of wooden tables overflow with old dishes, toys, linens, old watches, paintings, and bric-a-brac. From the tiny cubicles in the narrow corridors, serious dealers market their wares: Herend and Zsolnay porcelain, Bulgarian and Russian icons, silverware, furniture, clocks, rugs, prewar dolls and stuffed animals, antique clothing, and jewelry. Due to all the tourist attention, mostly weekend shoppers, the prices have increased severely. Some bargains can still be made, but sellers are less willing to seriously barter with tourists. Haggle over the price, but in some instances, you will not budge the seller too far from the original price. Antiques buyers: Be aware that you'll need permission from the Museum of Applied Arts to take your purchases out of the country (p. 128). Only cash is accepted for purchases. I personally think it is difficult to get to and not worth the effort. Unless you have plenty of time in the city, you're much better off spending it elsewhere. The market runs weekdays 8am to 4pm, Saturday 6am to 3pm, and Sunday 8am to 1pm. XVII. Nagykörösi út ⊙ **1/280-8840.** Bus: 54 from Boráros tér.

PECSA Flea Market Located in the area of the open-air stage at Petőfi Csarnok, this market is little known by travelers. In the midst of the enchanting Városliget (City Park), it features a wide array of offerings, most of which many have classified as junk, but then again one man's junk is another man's treasure. Selections include vintage bric-a-brac, antique jewelry, books, clothing, and electronic equipment. This place is where you can find a bargain, where few tourists have ventured to date. Open on weekends from 7am to 2pm, but the earliest bird gets the goodies. XIV. Zichy Mihály út 14. ⊙ **1/363-3730.** www. pecsa.hu. A short walk in the park from Hősök tere (Heroes' Square; Yellow line).

There are five vintage market halls *(vásárcsarnok)* in Budapest. These vast cavernous spaces, architectural wonders of steel and glass, were built in the 1890s in the ambitious grandiose style of the time. Three are still in use as markets and provide a measure of local color you certainly won't find in the grocery store. Hungarian produce in season is sensational, and you'll seldom go wrong with a kilo of strawberries, a cup of raspberries, or a couple of peaches.

The **Központi Vásárcsarnok (Central Market Hall)**, IX. Vámház krt. 1–3 (℡ **1/217-6067;** Metro: Kálvin tér on Blue line or Tram: 47 or 49), is the largest and most spectacular market hall. Located on the Inner Ring (Kiskörút), just on the Pest side of the Szabadság Bridge, it was impeccably reconstructed in 1995. This bright, three-level market hall is a pleasure to visit. Fresh produce, meat, and cheese vendors dominate the space. Keep your eyes open for inexpensive saffron and dried mushrooms. We have had French guests who found truffles for less than 10€. The mezzanine level features folk-art booths, coffee and drink bars, and fast-food booths. The basement level houses fishmongers, pickled goods, a complete selection of spices, and Asian import foods, along with a large grocery store. Open Monday 6am to 5pm, Tuesday through Friday 6am to 6pm, and Saturday 6am to 2pm.

The restored **Belvárosi Vásárcsarnok (Inner City Market Hall)**, V. Hold u. 13 (℡ **1/476-3952;** Metro: Kossuth tér on Red line or Arany János utca on Blue line), is located in central Pest in the heart of the Lipótváros (Leopold Town), behind the Hungarian National Bank at Szabadság tér. It houses a large supermarket and several cheesy discount clothing shops, in addition to a handful of independent fruit-and-vegetable vendors. Open Monday 6:30am to 5pm, Tuesday through Friday 6:30am to 6pm, and Saturday 6:30am to 2pm.

The **Rákóczi tér Vásárcsarnok**, VIII. Rákóczi tér 7–9 (℡ **1/313-8442;** Tram: 4 or 6 to Rákóczi tér), was badly damaged by fire in 1988 but was restored to its original splendor and reopened in 1991. There's only a small area of private vendors; the rest of the hall is filled with retail booths. Open Monday 6am to 4pm, Tuesday through Friday 6am to 6pm, and Saturday 6am to 1pm.

In addition to these three large classic market halls, Budapest has a number of neighborhood produce markets. The **Fehérvári úti Vásárcsarnok**, at XI. Kőrösi J. u. 7–9 (℡ **1/385-6563**), in front of the Buda Skála department store, is the latest classic food market in Budapest to be renovated. Some of the charm is lost, but such is progress. Just a block from the Móricz Zsigmond körtér transportation hub, it's open Monday 6:30am to 5pm, Tuesday through Friday 6:30am to 6pm, and Saturday 6:30am to 1pm. To get there take tram no. 47 from Deák tér to Fehérvári út, or any tram or bus to Móricz Zsigmond körtér.

The **Fény utca Piac** is on the Buda side behind the Mammut Mall at II. Fény utca (Metro: Moszkva tér on Red line or Tram: 4 or 6 Széna tér). It is attached to the back of the Mammut shopping mall. Open Monday 6am to 5pm, Tuesday through Friday 6am to 6pm, and Saturday 6:30am to 1pm.

Lehel tér Piac (VI. Lehel tér; ℡ **1/288-6898;** Metro: Lehel tér on Blue line), is another neighborhood market, whose reconstruction was completed in 2003, making it look like a beached ship. The market features a changeable selection of fresh food and meats, cheap Hungarian trademark products as well as rinky-dink kiosks for clothing, kitchen appliances, and flowers. Shops continually open and close depending on the current economy. Open weekdays 6am to 6pm and Saturday 6am to 2pm.

Akt.Records Once known as Afrofilia, this cozy shop in the heart of Budapest stocks an impressive collection of minimal, hip-hop, electro, jazz, and folklore records. VI. Lovag u. 17. ✆ 1/269-3134. www.aktrecords.hu. Tram: 4 or 6 Oktogon.

Fonó Budai Zenéház The Fonó Budai Zenéház entertainment complex is your source for Hungarian folk music. The complex features a folk-music store and an auditorium for live folk performances *(táncház)*. It's open Monday and Tuesday 2pm to 5pm, Wednesday through Friday 2pm to 10pm, and Saturday 7pm to 10pm. It has a summer camp for children and Argentine tango on Monday in July, otherwise it is closed July and August. XI. Sztregova u. 3. ✆ 1/206-5300. Tram: 49 from Deák tér (five stops past Móricz Zsigmond körtér).

Hungaroton The factory outlet of the Hungarian record company of the same name, this is definitely *the* place for classical-music buffs looking for Hungarian composers' recordings by contemporary Hungarian artists such as Zoltán Kocsis, Dezső Ránki, and András Schiff. Reasonable CD prices keep the Hungarian music alive. Open Monday through Friday 8am to 3:30pm. VII. Rottenbiller u. 47. ✆ 1/322-8839. www.hungaroton.hu. Bus: 74 Rottenbiller.

Liszt Ferenc Zeneműbolt (Ferenc Liszt Music Shop) Budapest's musical crowd frequents this shop, located near both the opera house and the Ferenc Liszt Academy of Music. Sheet music, scores, records, tapes, CDs, and books are available. The store carries an excellent selection of classical music, composed and performed by Hungarian artists. It has expanded the collections to include jazz recordings. Saturday they close at 1pm. It is associated with the Libra Bookstore chain. VI. Andrássy út 45. ✆ 1/322-4091. Metro: Oktogon (Yellow line).

Wave On a small side street off Bajcsy-Zsilinszky út, directly across the street from the rear of St. Stephen's Basilica, Wave is a popular spot among young Hungarians looking for acid rock, rap, techno, and world music. VI. Révay u. 4. ✆ 1/331-0718. Metro: Arany János u. (Blue line).

NEWSPAPERS & MAGAZINES

Newsagent (Finds) When you cannot live without a news fix from home, this newsagent can fill the bill with newspapers from around the world shipped in daily. There is also a wide selection of magazines in English to fill anyone's need. VI. Fővám tér 6. ✆ 1/266-3146. Daily 8am–8pm. Tram: 47 or 49 Fővám tér.

PORCELAIN, POTTERY & CRYSTAL

Ajka Crystal Hungary's renowned crystal producer from the Lake Balaton region sells fine stemware and other crystal at great prices. Founded by Bernát Neumann in 1878, the company was privatized by FOTEX Rt. in 1990. Showcased are the company's brilliant, yet simple crystal glasses, chalices, and crystal artwork. Note that the Ajka Crystal Company has gone into bankruptcy with an unknown future as of this writing. V. József Attila u. 7. ✆ 1/317-8133. Metro: Deák tér (all lines).

Herend Shop Hand-painted Herend porcelain, first produced in 1826 in the town of Herend near Veszprém in western Hungary, is world renowned. This shop, the oldest and largest Herend shop in Budapest, has the widest selection in the capital. They can arrange shipping through Touristpost. The one store is located on a quiet street just a few minutes' walk from Vörösmarty tér. Note that there are other stores that sell Herend, but

> **(Fun Facts** **A Cube by Any Other Name**
>
> The inventor of the **Rubik's Cube** is a Hungarian professor of architecture and a sculptor, Ernő Rubik. He created the cube in 1974 and originally named it "MagicCube." It was bought by Ideal Toy Co. in 1980 when it was first exported from Hungary and they changed the name. With six faces, there are 43,252,003,274,489,856,000 possible combinations, but only one solution. The first international "speed cubing" contest was held in Hungary in 1982. International contests include solving the cube with one hand or while blindfolded.

are not Herend stores. József nádor tér 11. ℂ **1/317-2622;** VI. Andrássy u. 16. ℂ **1/374-0006;** I. Szentháromság u. 5. ℂ **1/225-1051.** www.herend.hu.

Herend Village Pottery Some find the formal Herend porcelain styles stuffy or overly decorative. An alternative is the casually designed pottery, but know that this is not associated with the Herend porcelain company. The *majolika* (village pottery) is a hand-painted folklore-inspired way of making pottery. Choose from a wide variety of colors and patterns or have custom pieces made with names added, such as for a baby's first plate. All pieces are dishwasher and oven safe. Prices are reasonable here and reorders are welcome. The owners are very knowledgeable and eager to assist, but not pushy. Upon a visit, the owner claimed that this is the *only* store in Budapest that carries every Herend design, all 65 of them, whereas the other stores only have samples of different styles. You are on your own to decide; personally, I don't care for Herend. Open Tuesday through Friday 9am to 5pm and Saturday 9am to noon. II. Bem rakpart 37. ℂ **1/356-7899.** www.herendimajolika.hu. Metro: Batthyány tér (Red line).

Zsolnay Markabolt This is the other famous porcelain made in Hungary. Take note if you are a collector that the company has gone bankrupt and is in receivership, which may cause dramatic changes in prices. The factory will still operate under government ownership until a buyer is found. This store is open Monday to Saturday from 10am to 6pm. XIII. Pozsonyi út 11. No phone. Tram: 4 or 6 Jászai Mari tér.

TOYS

Apróságok Boltja (Small Fry Shop) **Kids** While many toy stores have been driven out of business, this store has survived. It specializes in wooden toys, but also carries games, puppets, and other toys for young children. VII. Erzsébet krt. 23. No phone. Tram: 4 or 6 Wesselényi u.

Toys Anno Part museum, part specialty shop, Toys Anno might be of more interest to toy collectors than to kids. This itsy-bitsy shop sells exact replicas of antique toys from around the world. The tin toys are exceptional, especially the monkeys on bicycles, Ferris wheels, Soviet rockets, old-fashioned dolls, and puzzles. Items are behind glass and tagged with serial numbers. Although you have to request prices and ask to see the toys that interest you, the clerk is more than happy to oblige. They close at 1pm on Saturdays. VI. Teréz krt. 54. ℂ **1/302-6234.** www.jatekanno.hu. Metro: Nyugati pu. (Blue line).

WINES & SPIRITS

Wine store hours are Monday to Friday 10am to 6pm and Saturday 10am to 3pm, unless noted otherwise in the description.

A Magyar Pálinka Háza (The House of Hungarian Pálinka)   Locals say that good palinka (a traditional form of brandy) should warm the stomach and not burn the throat, a common side effect of strong brandy. This shop offers the finest selection of palinka distilled from everything from plums, pears, apples, and walnuts to honey paprika. Watch out for the after-drink kick effect. Unfortunately, you cannot taste before buying. VIII. Rákcozi u. 17. ⓒ 1/338-4219. www.magyarpalinkahaza.hu. Metro: Blaha Lujza tér (Red line); Bus: 7.

Bortársaság (Budapest Wine Society)   Truly among the experts in wine, the Wine Society operates four shops in Budapest. Founded by Tom Howells and Attila Tálos, each shop sells wines produced by more than 50 local winegrowers. Drop in for free samples on Saturday at the Batthyány utca location—a much larger store with a wider selection. Open Monday to Friday 10am to 8pm, Saturday 10am to 6pm. I. Batthyány u. 59. ⓒ 1/212-0262. www.bortarsasag.hu. Metro: Batthyány tér (Red line).

In Vino Veritas ★★   Like a wine supermarket, this store carries a vast assortment of wines and wine accessories from all over the country. You will notice its logo in many restaurant wine lists as the supplier of the wine and the list. The gentleman who runs this store speaks English well. Hours are weekdays 9am to 8pm and Saturday 10am to 6pm. VII. Dohány u. 58–62. ⓒ 1/341-0646 or ⓒ 1/341-3174. www.borkereskedes.hu. Metro: Blaha Lujza tér (Red line).

La Boutique des Vins   Sophisticated, classy, and welcoming, this wine shop is a cut above the others. This is a great place to learn about and purchase Hungarian wines. The longtime manager of the shop, Ferenc Hering, speaks very good English and is extremely well versed in his merchandise. Try the excellent Villány reds (some from the shop's own vineyard) or the fine whites from the Balaton region. You can pick up a fine bottle for as little as 1,500 Ft to 15,000 Ft. A wide range of Hungary's famous Tokaj dessert wines, in the general price range of 5,000 Ft to 25,000 Ft, is also available. Shipping can be arranged, but at a steep price. Hours as above, except during summer; they are closed on Saturday. V. József Attila u. 12 (behind the Jaguar dealership). ⓒ 1/317-5919 or ⓒ 1/266-4397. www.malantinszky.hu. Metro: Deák tér (any line).

Pántlika Borház ★★   Not only does this store carry a vast selection of wines from all over Hungary, but the owner's knowledge of them is just as impressive. His English is good and he is willing to help you make the right choice of wine for any occasion. Also in the store, you will find a nice selection of wine glasses, decanters, and other vino enthusiast accessories. For an extra 500 Ft, you can have a custom label put on any bottle of wine. Open weekdays 10am to 6pm. V. Király Pál u. 10. ⓒ 70/409-2569 (mobile phone only). Metro: Kálvin tér (Blue line).

Présház   This tasteful wine store—named after the press room, or the room where the grapes are rammed to extract the sweet nectar—shares the same courtyard as Bagaria (p. 203). It offers more than 300 types of Hungarian wine and has a knowledgeable staff who is fluent in English. You can have your order delivered within Budapest if you purchase a crate for free, but within Europe it is 50€. Wine taste and shop Monday to Saturday 10am to 6pm. V. Váci u. 10. ⓒ 1/266-1100. www.preshaz.hu. Metro: Vörösmarty tér (Yellow line).

Unicum   Unicum is a beloved digestive bittersweet liqueur that is said to cure all ills, especially aching stomachs. Made with more than 40 herbs and spices, Unicum is the trademark product of Zwack, the best-known spirit brand in Hungary. With its memorable bomb-shaped bottle, emergency-cross logo, and unforgettable taste, it has to be

Unicum. Try it at the Zwack Museum on a tour given Monday through Friday 10am to 6pm at a cost of 1,700 Ft per adult. Child tickets are 950 Ft without the tasting session. Best to e-mail ahead (museum@zsackunicum.hu) or call when you arrive. If you don't get there, it is available in all grocery stores. IX. Soroksári út 26, entrance on Dandár u. ⓒ 1/476-2383. Tram: 2 Haller u.

ASSORTED FOODSTUFFS

Culinaris Missing a taste of home while traveling and cannot find it in the markets? Self-catering and need ingredients? Well then, you'll not want to miss a visit to **Culinaris.** It stocks everything from American Cheerios to Australian Vegemite. Its goal is to be the prime location for food from around the world. Two stores are on the Pest side and one on the Buda side. Both the Perc u. 8 and the Balassi u. 7 (ⓒ 1/373-0028) locations are open Monday through Saturday 9am to 8pm. While the Hunyadi store is open Monday noon to 7pm, Tuesday through Saturday 9am to 7pm. In July and August, this store closes at 4pm on Saturday. www.culinaris.hu. III. Perc u. 8 ⓒ 1/345-0780, V. Balassi u. 7. ⓒ 1/373-0028 and VI. Hunyadi tér 3. ⓒ 1/341-7001.

Supermarkets Buying snacks for the day or doing self-catering, you may need a supermarket. There are plenty around the city, but the prevalent chains are Kaiser, Spar, Plus (all the same company), Smatch, Match, and CIB. Many Match stores are now open 24 hours. There are nonstop shops in every neighborhood for picking up essentials like a soft drink or cookies. Just about every mall and the great market have a supermarket. Here are a few locations for starters. Kaiser at VII. Blaha Lujza tér 1, Match on the corner of Rákóczi tér and Erzsébet körút in the VII district, which is open 24 hours. Rothchilds at Oktogon is open 24 hours.

T. Nagy Tamás Sajtkereskedése (Thomas T. Nagy's Cheese Shop) Opened in 1994, this shop deals exclusively in cheese, selling more than 300 types of hard and soft cheeses, including Hungarian, as well as imported French, Italian, Dutch, and English varieties. They supplement these with a selection of olives as well. Open Monday through Friday 9am to 6pm and Saturday 9am to 1pm. V. Gerlóczy u. 3. ⓒ 1/317-4268. www.tnagytamas.hu. Metro: Deák tér (all lines).

Budapest After Dark

Budapest is definitely a cosmopolitan city with a tremendous variety of cultural events all throughout the year. There is no event that is unaffordable to the average tourist if you don't have your heart set on a particular section of a theater, but even then, seats are bargains as compared to New York, San Francisco, or London. At the opera house, one of Europe's finest, tickets generally range from 600 Ft for the nosebleed balcony to 16,000 Ft for the ultra-luxurious royal box once used by the Habsburgs, depending on the performance. Almost all the city's theaters and concert halls, with the exception of those hosting internationally touring rock groups, offer tickets within an affordable 2,000 Ft to 10,000 Ft range. Of course, higher-priced seats are available at the same venue if you want a closer view. In some cases, it is wise to choose performances based on the venue. For example, you may not particularly be a fan of ballet, but if that is all that is offered during your stay, you may want to consider less expensive tickets just to see the opera house up close and personal. You won't regret it: its splendor is superlative and it can be better appreciated with any performance than just a tour.

The opera, ballet, and theater seasons run from September through May with some sporadic events in June, but most theaters and halls also host performances during the summer festivals. Bear in mind that none of them are air-conditioned and heat rises. If you are sitting in a balcony on a hot evening, you may be miserable. A number of the better-known churches and stunning halls offer concerts exclusively in the summer. While classical music is ingrained into the culture in Budapest, the country, jazz, blues, rock, disco, and every other variation you left at home is here also. Stylish and unique new clubs and bars open and close regularly. The bar and club scene starts late and lasts until morning, sometimes until the last patron leaves. Only the bars in residential areas have strict closing times. Restaurants and bars in these areas in the summer have to bring in their tables at 10pm by district law in consideration of the neighbors. So whether you have dancing feet or a taste for opera, whatever your entertainment preference, Budapest nights offer plenty to choose from.

PROGRAM LISTINGS For the most up-to-date information, go to www.jegymester.hu and click on the English link. This site includes information for the opera house as well as the major theaters in the city. A complete schedule of mainstream performing arts is found in the free bimonthly **Koncert Kalendárium,** available at any of the Tourinform offices, or you can check it online at www.koncertkalendarium.hu; there is a link for English. **Funzine** (see "Fast Facts: Budapest," in chapter 15, "Getting to Know Budapest") also has events calendars; the weekly **Budapest Times** includes cultural listings. **Where,** a free monthly tourist booklet, highlights different topics each month, but includes some entertainment listings. Our latest addition for the city scene is **Time Out**, an internationally known magazine that focuses on a particular city's culture and entertainment scene in greater depth. Pick up a free copy at Tourinform offices or pay 450 Ft at newsstands. All of the publications mentioned above are in English.

TICKET OFFICES If you are looking for the easy way out, you can look at ticket availability online for purchasing opera, ballet, theater, or concert tickets for a number of different venues at www.jegymester.hu. It shows how many tickets are available with a seating chart to help you decide how much you want to spend for what seat. Its secure server allows you to make your purchase online. You can also prepurchase special museum exhibitions on this site, but it may require you to print an e-ticket. If you don't have Internet access, you can save time by going to the **Cultur-Comfort Ticket Office (Cultur-Comfort Központi Jegyiroda),** VI. Paulay Ede u. 31 (*C* **1/322-0000).** The office is open Monday through Friday 9am to 6pm. It is easier than going to the individual box offices. They sell tickets to just about everything, from theater and operettas to sports events and rock concerts. Schedules are posted for a variety of choices and they will show you a seating chart. If none of the cashiers speaks English, find a helpful customer who can translate for you. For last-minute tickets or performances that are looking like they are sold out, try the venue box office for no-show

tickets about 30 minutes before the performance. For **opera and ballet,** go to the **Hungarian State Opera Ticket Office (Magyar Állami Opera Jegyiroda),** VI. Andrássy út 22 (*C* **1/353-0170),** open Monday through Friday 11am to 5pm. Try **Concert & Media,** XI. Üllői út 11–13 (*C* **1/455-9000;** www.jegyelado.hu), for classical performances as well as pop, jazz, and rock concerts. For just about everything from rock and jazz concerts to opera, ballet performances, and theater tickets, try **Ticket Express,** VI. Andrássy út 18 (*C* **30/303-0999** mobile phone only; www.tex.hu), open Monday through Friday from 10am to 6pm. You do have the option to buy online and print your own tickets if you have access to a printer.

Note: For cheaper tickets, look online at one of the sites above and then try going to the actual box office of the venue. Some of the ticket agencies only carry the higher-end price range of tickets. You may also find that agencies charge a commission (usually about 4% or higher), especially for hit shows or international performers.

1 THE PERFORMING ARTS

The major symphony orchestras in Budapest are the Budapest Festival Orchestra, the Philharmonic Society Orchestra, the Hungarian State Symphony Orchestra, the Budapest Symphony Orchestra, and the Hungarian Railway Workers' (MÁV) Symphony Orchestra. The major chamber orchestras include the Hungarian Chamber Orchestra, the Ferenc Liszt Chamber Orchestra, the Budapest String Players, and the Hungarian Virtuosi. Major choirs include the Budapest Chorus, the Hungarian State Choir, the Hungarian Radio and Television Choir, the Budapest Madrigal Choir, and the University Choir.

Budapest is now on the touring route of dozens of major European ensembles and virtuosos. Keep your eyes open for well-known touring artists.

Note: Most Budapesters tend to dress more formally than casually when attending performances. However, the location of your seat determines your dress code. If you are on the lower level, you should dress from smart casual to more semiformal. In the upper regions, you can get away with jeans and a sweater. In wintertime, you are expected to check your coat and any bags. There is no getting around this, so don't annoy the attendant by trying to argue the point. The usherette will not seat you.

Budapesti Operettszínház (Budapest Operetta Theatre) What is known as the Operetta Theatre was designed by the famous Viennese architects, Fellner and Helmer, in 1894. When it was built, the giant stage of the auditorium faced two levels of intimate boxes arranged in a semicircle. A dance floor was included to provide a space adequately large enough for the waltz, polka, mazurka, and the galop. Between 1999 and 2001, the theater was fully restored. The 100-year-old chandelier presides above the auditorium. The original lamp statues and supporting columns blend in with the newly added colored glass windows, mirrors, and the period-style furnishings of the snack counter. The original ornamentation was restored, a row of boxes in the circle was rebuilt, and the most advanced European stage machinery was installed. Today the theater not only boasts having 917 seats, but it also has air-conditioning in the auditorium. A highlight among Art Nouveau style buildings, the Operetta Theatre hosts exquisite banquettes and balls—among which is the opulent Operetta Ball. Performances of *Romeo and Juliet* are among the rotating standards. The off season is mid-July to mid-August. The box office is open Monday through Friday 10am to 2:30pm and 3pm to 7pm and Saturday 1pm to 7pm. VI. Nagymező u. 17. ✆ **1/312-4866**. www.operettszinhaz.hu. Tickets 1,300 Ft–15,000 Ft. Metro: Opera or Oktogon (Yellow line).

Magyar Állami Operaház (Hungarian State Opera House) One of the most important buildings in Budapest, this opera house was designed by famous Hungarian architect Miklós Ybl. He was also the designer of the basilica and the original Parliament (now the Italian Institute). The opera house was completed in 1884 and is considered one of the most beautiful in Europe. When standing outside, on the first level, you can see the muses of opera: Erato, Thalia, Melpomene, and Terpsichore. There are also statues of Franz Liszt and Hungary's father of opera, Ferenc Erkel. The second level has statues of famous composers. The lobby is adorned with Bertalan Székely's frescoes; the ceiling frescoes in the concert hall itself are by Károly Lotz. Hungarians are great opera fans and many tickets are sold as season tickets. Regardless, if you don't wait until the last minute, often you will have a wide range of seats from which to choose. The season runs from mid-September to mid-June. During the regular season, there are often matinees on Saturday and Sunday at 11am. Regular performances start at 7pm, not the customary 8pm starting time. Summer visitors, however, can take in approximately eight performances (both opera and ballet) during the Summer Operafest in July or August. Seating capacity is 1,289. The box office is open weekdays from 11am until the beginning of the performance, or to 5pm when there is no performance. Sunday from 10am to 1pm and 4pm until the beginning of the performance. **Guided tours** of the opera house are offered daily at 3pm and 4pm; the cost is 2,800 Ft or 1,400 Ft with international student ID. VI. Andrássy út 22. ✆ **1/353-0170**. www.opera.hu. Tickets 300 Ft–16,900 Ft. Metro: Opera (Yellow line).

CLASSICAL MUSIC

Bartók Béla Emlékház (Béla Bartók Memorial House) This charming little hall is in Béla Bartók's last Budapest residence, and in addition to hosting concerts and exhibitions, it is the site of a Bartók museum (p. 152). Concerts are organized and performed from the end of September through December independently of the museum. The museum rents out its concert hall for performing musical artists. Getting to the English pages on its website (www.bartokmuseum.hu) can sometimes be an exercise in frustration. Your best bet is to check the schedule information in the bimonthly *Koncert*

Tips **Bistros: For the Sophisticated Night Owl**

Hopefully, you will not have difficulty finding a watering hole at 2am, with many pubs and clubs open until, yawn, 5am. However, district by district, they are trying to change the laws forcing restaurants, pubs, and bars to close early, meaning by 10pm, to control "happy" customers' noise as they leave the establishments. The lesser popular districts have been successful, but it may be a domino effect in the future. With that in mind, if you're looking for a late-night cocktail but want to avoid the typical bar and club scene, **Paris, Texas** (p. 224) on the popular Ráday utca, is a pleasant place to sit down and talk or eat after a concert, but their food comes from the **Pink Cadillac** (p. 112). For a summer alternative check out *Funzine* for the *kerts* or garden pubs that are currently open. For more information on *kerts*, see p. 225.

Kalendárium or the other calendar resources given above. Open Tuesday through Sunday 10am to 5pm, but closed the first 2 weeks in August. Ticket prices depend on the performance. II. Csalán út 29. **℃ 1/394-2100.** Bus: 5 from Március 15 tér or Moszkva tér to Pasaréti tér (the last stop).

Matthias Church In my opinion, this is one of the most beautiful churches in Budapest, an icon in the center of the historic Castle District. This church is a neo-Gothic classic, named after Matthias Corvinus, the Renaissance king who was married here. King Béla and his queen are buried here. Much to the dismay of many, the church is undergoing major renovations, which will last incredibly until 2012 if the schedule is kept. Much of it is under scaffolding at all times. However, the church is a key location for excellent organ recitals, sacred music concerts for a cappella choir, orchestras, and folk concerts at times throughout the year. Ticket prices vary widely based on the offering, so the prices here are just a guideline. The ticket office is open Wednesday through Sunday 1pm to 5:30pm. I. Szentháromság tér 2. **℃ 1/355-5657.** Tickets 1,000 Ft–7,000 Ft. Bus: 16 from Deák across from the Le Meridian Hotel or 16A bus from Moszkva tér (Metro: Red line).

Óbudai Társaskör (Óbuda Social Circle) In an island within Óbuda's residences, a building dating back to the turn of the century has been restored to its original appeal. Temporary exhibitions, music workshops, and theatrical performances on the open-air stage during the summertime all elevate this tiny venue to compete with its larger rivals. Since 1995, it has hosted *Art Salon in Óbuda* where art in many forms, such as music, literature, and the visual arts, coexist to be available for those interested in a particular subject or period in history, a school of art or, occasionally, a taste in gastronomy. Proudly, it is also home to the Budapest Ragtime Band, it's a prominent venue of the Budapest Spring Festival, and also presents up-to-par chamber music concerts. Ticket prices vary considerably from program to program, but each has its own set price. The box office is open daily 10am to 6pm. III. Korona u. 7. **℃ 1/250-0288.** www.obudaitarsaskor. hu. Tickets from 1,500 Ft–to over 3,000 Ft. Tram: 1 from Árpád Híd (Metro: Blue line) over the bridge to Szentlélek tér or the HÉV to Árpád-híd.

Palace of Arts ★★ The Palace of Arts' National Concert Hall and Festival Theater concert and performing arts venues opened in 2005. For the first few years, the locals either loved the building or they hated it, but all have come to at least accepting it. Originally scheduled to be at Deák tér, a change in government after an election turned the original space into underground parking and a park. The Palace of Arts was awarded the FIABCI Prix d'Excellence 2006 in the specialized category, which is the equivalent of an Academy Award for construction and real estate development. The main concert hall is the finest contemporary classical music venue in Budapest; it now hosts concerts from celebrated orchestras from around the world. The scheduled events run the gamut along with the admission prices, but they are not only for classical music; the website has been beautifully created to be user friendly. IX. Komor Marcell u. 1. 📞 1/555-3001. www.mupa.hu. Tram: 2 from downtown toward the Lágymányos bridge.

Pesti Vigadó (Pest Concert Hall) Located right in the middle of the famed riverside Danube Promenade (Dunakorzó), the Vigadó is one of the city's oldest concert halls, dating to 1864. It is a magnificent building from the outside and I cannot wait to see the inside after the remodel, but that wait will be longer than anticipated. The remodel was planned for completion by 2006, but like most things in Hungary, scheduled times can vary by years. As of this writing, it has not yet reopened, so we suggest you stroll by for a look at the exterior at bare minimum. It is close to the Little Princess statue, a tourist icon, so you cannot miss the theater. Chances are it will not reopen during the life of this edition. V. Vigadó tér 2. 📞 1/318-9903. www.vigado.hu. Metro: Vörösmarty tér (Yellow line).

Saint Michael's Church in the City This church is the venue for summer concerts. Built in 1765, with the original frescoes still intact, it has one of the oldest organs in Budapest dating to 1893. Summer concerts are held on Friday and Saturday nights in the coolness of the church. There is another concert series in October also. Tickets can be purchased at the church shop or at Libri Bookstores. V. Váci u. 67–68. No phone. Daily 10am–6pm for visits. No transport nearby.

Stefánia Palace Cultural Center The eclectic-style 19th-century palace hosts a number of entertainment options by renting out its space to different groups for events. This was the cultural center during the Communist times for the armed forces. I would recommend checking one of the event calendars in the English papers for current ticket prices since they vary considerably from event to event depending on who is sponsoring it, but during the last 4 years, I have not seen much offered for English speakers, and it is off the beaten track. XIV. Stefánia u. 34. 📞 1/273-4132. Bus: 7 or 73 to Stefánia u.

Zeneakadémia (Ferenc Liszt Academy of Music) Unfortunately, the academy closed after the Autumn Festival in 2009 for extensive renovations and will not be reopened for at least 2 years. Once known as the Royal National Hungarian Academy of Music, the academy has five buildings around the city, but the primary one is at this location. With a seating capacity of 1,000, it is Budapest's leading center of musical education and students come from around the world to study here. The academy was built in 1907 in its present form; the building's interior is decorated in lavish Art Nouveau style. VI. Liszt Ferenc tér 8. 📞 1/462-4600. Metro: Oktogon (Yellow line).

FOLK PERFORMANCES

Budai Vigadó (Buda Concert Hall) The Budai Vigadó is the home stage of the Hungarian State Folk Ensemble (Állami Népi Együttes Székháza). The ensemble is the oldest in the country, having started in 1951 with the goal of keeping Hungarian traditional dance and music alive. The group has toured more than 44 countries and consists of 30 dancers, a Gypsy orchestra of 14, and a 5-member folk orchestra. Tickets can be reserved by telephone. The box office is open 10am to 6pm daily. Performances usually start at 8pm on Tuesday, Thursday, and Sunday. I. Corvin tér 8. 📞 1/317-1377. www.hungarianfolk.hu. Tickets

The Millennium City Center

The **Millennium City Center** is situated on what was the last large available parcel of riverfront land in Budapest. On the 10 hectares (25 acres) of land, the plans have been to build a convention center in the southern section to include a 10,000-seat center for hosting conventions and sporting events, a casino, and a medicinal and recreational spa. A multifunctional exhibition hall will be adjacent to the Convention Complex while two international hotels will be built on the north side.

With the opening of the **Palace of Arts** ★★ in early 2005, the latest cultural complex created in the Hungarian capital includes a **National Concert Hall,** the **Ludwig Museum of Contemporary Art,** and the smaller **Festival Theater.** To reach this center, take tram no. 2, a scenic route that begins at Jászai Mari tér.

3,600 Ft–6,200 Ft adults; 3,300 Ft–5,600 Ft students. Bus: 86 till Szilágyi Dezső tér or tram 19 till Halász u. stop.

Hungarian Heritage House   In the same building as Budai Vigadó, the Heritage House is composed of three divisions: the Hungarian State Folk Ensemble, the Folklore Documentation Centre, and the Folk Arts Department. Revival of folk dance for stage performances did not come about until the beginning of the 1970s; they reproduce the dances in the precise manner and interpretation they were originally intended. I. Corvin tér 8. (*©* **1/225-6056.** www.heritagehouse.hu. Tickets 1,100 Ft–6,000 Ft. Bus: 86 till Szilágyi Dezső tér or tram 19 till Halász u. stop.

Petőfi Csarnok   Located in the tree-lined surroundings of the Városliget (City Park), this old-style no-frills hall has stages used for some of the best folk performances in the city. The venue hosts folk dance events, various national folk performances, and festivals in addition to jazz, blues, pop, and rock concerts; exhibitions; workshops; and a weekend-only flee market. The main folk event is the annual Csángó Bál, which presents the colorful culture of this small, Moldavian-born community, and is a must-see event for folk dance and tradition seekers. The box office is open weekdays 2pm to 7pm and Saturday 9am to 2pm. XIV. Zichy Mihály út 14. (*©* **1/363-3730.** www.pecsa.hu. Tickets 800 Ft–9,900 Ft. Metro: Hősök tere (Yellow line).

THEATER & DANCE

Budapest has a varied and vivacious theater season from September through June, but the majority of plays are in Hungarian only. The **Merlin Theater,** V. Gerlóczy u. 4 (*©* **1/317-9338** or *©* **1/318-9844**; www.merlinszinhaz.hu), used to be the mainstay for English speakers, but the options are slim and rare. Located on a quiet street in the heart of the Inner City, the Merlin now programs less than 20% English-language shows. During the unusual times when they do have an English show, tickets cost 1,000 Ft to 2,500 Ft; the box office is open weekdays 11am to 7pm. Take the metro to Astoria (Red line) or Deák tér (all lines).

For international or Hungarian dance, music, or theater of the contemporary sort, the **Trafó House of Contemporary Art,** IX. Liliom u. 41 (*©* **1/215-1600** or *©* **1/456-2040**; www.trafo.hu) is the place to go. Having opened in 1998, this venue has offered a wide range of events that are extremely different and experimental, definitely not for the traditional thinker. Regardless, there have been performances I could have seen repeatedly and those where I wanted to demand a refund, but it all equalizes in the end. If you happen to be here for any length of time, they now have three, five, and seven performance tickets priced at 6,000 Ft, 8,000 Ft, and 10,000 Ft. The beauty is that you can get two tickets for the same performance deducted from your season ticket, to take a friend along. Prepare to get there early and stand close to the theater doors. With open seating, it is like a herd of cattle stampeding through. We especially recommend some of the dance works of the French-Hungarian **Compagnie Pál Frenák** (www.ciefrenak.hu); their men on ropes were unbelievably well done. Tickets cost 1,500 Ft to 2,000 Ft; the box office is open Monday through Friday from 2pm to 8pm and weekends 5pm to 8pm. Reserve or purchase tickets in advance on the website. Take tram nos. 4 or 6 or the metro to Ferenc Körut (Blue line).

One theater company that has been brought to my attention is the **Katona József Theater** at V. Petőfi Sándor u. 6. (© 1/765-0174; www.katonaj.hu). As a public theater, its main support is provided by the City of Budapest. An independent company was created here in 1982, after seceding of the National Theatre of Budapest. The troupe has extensive international connections, which are enhanced by its being a founding member of the Union of European Theatres. The company regularly embarks on international tours and to date has performed in more than 60 cities of the world. The productions as well as the artists have received numerous national and international awards. Depending on how vulnerable you are to nose bleeds, the prices range from 2,900 Ft up in the high altitude section to a pricey 14,400 for primo seating.

For musical productions, especially those by Andrew Lloyd Webber, go to the **Madách Theater,** VII. Erzsébet krt. 29–33 (© 1/478-2041; www.madachszinhaz.hu). However, I find it disconcerting to hear these show tunes I know redefined to a Hungarian translation, so brace yourself for the experience. The theater was built in 1961 on the site of the famous Royal Orpheum Theater and has been restored to its former elegance. Its hit production since spring 2003 is *The Phantom of the Opera.* The theater has a love affair with the plays by Tim Rice and Andrew Lloyd Webber. *Cats* anyone? You will find many of the plays rotating for years with a few other American classics thrown into the mix. Ticket prices are 900 Ft to 9,000 Ft, but if you value your legs, do not sit in the balcony where leg room is nonexistent. The box office is open daily from 3pm to 7pm; performances are usually at 7pm. Take tram nos. 4 or 6 to Wesselényi utca.

Affectionately called the wedding cake, the very ornate and striking theater is the **Vígszínház (Comedy Theatre of Budapest),** XIII. Szent István krt. 14 (© 1/329-2340; www.vigszinhaz.hu). Here again you will find productions in Hungarian only, usually by Hungarians, but at times there will be international playwrights. The Vígszínház operates in the traditional repertory system, which is incredible to most foreigners; almost every evening a different performance is given with the technical staff having to build and strike down the sets each day. The theater has a repertoire of actors who appear in numerous shows over the course of the month, having to learn the roles for each show. The repertory comprises 10 to 12 plays on the stages of the Víg's 1,100 seats. With a show almost every night, the theater stages numerous plays that pull in delighted audiences. The box office is open daily 11am to 7pm. Depending on the performance ticket prices are 900 Ft to 5,000 Ft. Take the metro to Nyugati pu. (Blue line).

An important venue in the world of contemporary performing arts in Budapest is the **MU Theatre,** XI. Körösy József u. 17 (© 1/209-4014; www.mu.hu). Offering the work of contemporary choreographers and young dancers, this venue has similar events as the

Trafó above. The box office is open Monday through Thursday 6pm to the beginning of the performance, and Friday through Sunday from 1pm until the start of the performance. Tickets run the gamut from 1,000 Ft to 2,000 Ft. Take tram no. 6 to Moricz Zsigmond körtér.

The first children's and family theater in Budapest, the **Kolibri Pince** (Hummingbird Cellar), VI. Andrássy út 77 (℃ **1/351-3348**), is a small theater with seating for 60. It offers entertainment for all age groups, but children are its main focus. The repertoire includes adaptations and story-musicals as well as one-man shows and small theater pieces. Other theater locations include the **Kolibri Fészek** (Hummingbird Nest), VI. Andrássy út 74, a room-theater where 50 to 70 children view the show sitting on pillows and chairs. The largest is the **Kolibri Színház** (Hummingbird Theater), VI. Jókai tér 10, with a stage where puppet performances are usually held seating 220. Metro: Oktogon (Yellow line). Tickets cost 800 Ft to 1,600 Ft depending on theater and performance.

2 DANCE CLUBS

Budapest has a hot club scene, but what is offered at any given time is apt to change often depending on the current trend. To find out what is happening when you are ready to explore the nightlife, it is best to pick up a copy of *Funzine*, the English-language guide, published every 2 weeks for up-to-date information. Other English-language publications published monthly are *Time Out* and *Where* magazines. The *Budapest Times* (www.budapesttimes.hu) also lists highlights; however, they are less likely to list the bar scene venues unless a well-known name is performing. For online only access, *XPatloop* found at www.xpatloop.com keeps we foreigners who live here in the circle, but we will let you share the information. Club opening hours vary, but most don't start to vibrate the walls until around 11pm and stay lively until closing time, which could be as late as 5am. There are no laws stating when traditional bars or clubs have to close, but those with outside seating may be restricted by district laws to move things inside after 10pm or 11pm in consideration of the neighbors.

Barokko Club and Lounge   Still one of the hotspots on Liszt Ferenc tér, where seeing and being seen is of the utmost importance for those in their 20s and 30s when it really matters. Don't be fooled by the restaurant above, the club itself rocks. Open Sunday through Tuesday noon to 2am and Wednesday through Saturday noon to 3am. VI. Liszt Ferenc tér 5. ℃ **1/322-0700.** www.barokko.hu. Metro: Oktogon (Yellow line).

Cactus Juice Pub   If you miss that Old West feeling, head here for a large drink selection with more than 50 whisky blends and a real party atmosphere. After the dinner time is over, the tables are pushed back to clear the floor for fun. Open Monday through Thursday noon to 2am and Friday and Saturday noon to 4am for those in their 20s, 30s, and pushing it a little older. VI. Jókai tér 5. ℃ **1/302-2116.** www.cactusjuice.hu. Metro: Oktogon (Yellow line).

E-Klub   Meeting Hungarian guys or the young fashionable ladies is not a problem at this huge and hedonistic disco oozing with popularity. At one time, it was the "E" building of Polytechnic University, hence the name. It has since moved to its current location and has been remodeled a number of times. It offers different special events for the party animals around the city. Guys have to pay 1,200 Ft for entry, but the ladies are always free. Drinks are cheap. Open for those in their teens to 20s on Friday and Saturday 10pm to 5am. X. Népligeti u. 2. ℃ **1/263-1614.** www.e-klub.hu. Metro: Népliget (Blue line).

Fat Mo's Music Club ★★   A restaurant with an American Prohibition speakeasy theme, it has live jazz, blues, and R&B concerts that start at 9pm, but the dancing doesn't begin until 11pm. Open Monday through Wednesday noon to 2am, Thursday and Friday noon to 4am, Saturday 6pm to 4am, and Sunday 6pm to 2am. The music crowd includes those in their 30s. V. Nyári Pál u. 11. ✆ **1/267-3199.** Metro: Kálvin tér (Blue line).

School Club Közgáz   Touted as the biggest and most famous of the university pubs, this party place is located in the basement of Corvinus University. The disco floors are packed solid during weekends. Cheap drinks, all mix music, and the chance to test your singing with a karaoke tune, all add up for a ton of fun. Open Tuesday to Thursday for college parties, Friday and Saturday 10pm to 5am for all. Crowd: 20s and 30s. IX. Fővám tér 8. ✆ **1/215-4359.** Cover: 1,000 Ft for men, free for women. Metro: Kálvin tér (Blue line) or tram 2.

3 LIVE MUSIC

A38 Boat ★★   This is a former Ukrainian stone-carrying ship anchored at the Buda-side foot of the Petőfi Bridge. On the lower deck, you can get your fill of the city's best range of jazz, world, electronic, hip-hop, and rock music bands. The terrace is open only in the summer while the concert hall downstairs is open year-round. Open daily 11am to 4am, with crowds generally in their 20s and 30s. XI. Pázmány Péter sétány. ✆ **1/464-3940.** www.a38.hu. Cover varies for different events. Tram: 4 or 6 to the Buda side of Petőfi bridge.

Columbus Jazz Klub   Discover the world of music on the Columbus ship without leaving port. Besides being a restaurant, this is where bands of the Society of Hungarian Jazz Artists and other guests take to the stage nightly at 8pm. Concerts last for 2¾ hours for those who have reserved seats. All ages are welcome. V. Vigadó tér dock 4. ✆ **1/266-9013.** www.columbuspub.hu. Reservation recommended. Admission 800 Ft. Metro: Vörösmarty tér (Yellow line).

Gödör Club   Located right in the middle of the city, Gödör (Pothole) was built in/under a park, where the main bus station used to be until an election changed the administration, who then moved the bus station elsewhere. This versatile space is sometimes an art gallery and sometimes a music lounge or outdoor movie theater. Outside of the summer months, events seem to be sporadic. You are bound to be at Deák, so you may want to check it out to see if there is anything going on. The park is a popular hangout for skateboarders in the evening and other alterative-lifestyle youth. Prices depend on the event. V. Erzsébet tér. ✆ **20/201-3868** (mobile phone only). www.godorklub.hu. Metro: Deák (all lines).

Lámpás Student Pub   Like the name suggests, this is a young people's pub only open during the school year to chill out after those tedious classes and exams. Owned by the Spinoza Étterem below, it is no surprise that they share an address, but this pub is down in the cellar entrance to the left of the restaurant. VII. Dob u. 15. ✆ **1/413-7488.** www.spinozahaz.hu. Open Sept–May daily 5pm–2am. Bus: 74 to Dohány Synagogue.

Living Room ★★   A real hotspot for the 20s and 30s crowd, this club has two halls with different music. It plays Hungarian and international songs from the current list of hits. It is very popular with the university set, especially on students' nights. Open Wednesday through Saturday 10pm to 5am. V. Kossuth Lajos u. 17. ✆ **30/992-9932** (mobile phone only). www.livingroom.hu. Cover varies for different events. Metro: Astoria (Red line).

Old Man's Music Pub ★★ Old Man's offers the best jazz and blues in Hungary. Hobo and his blues band are regulars here. Hobo was a friend of Alan Ginsberg and he broke new ground in Hungary by writing his master's thesis on rock 'n' roll in the 1960s. The pub has an ever-changing menu of music from rock to blues and jazz in between. If you are in the neighborhood, see the list of current entertainment posted inside the door. This pub created its own Hard Rock version of Hungarian music artists. Be cautioned, it is downstairs with only one visible exit and it gets very crowded. Music is daily, but only from 9pm to 11pm. No music in August. Open daily 8pm till the crowd leaves, usually around 5am. Crowd: 30s and up. Akácfa u. 13. ℂ 1/322-7645. www.oldmans.hu. Metro: Blaha Lujza tér (Red line).

Piaf Named after the French torch chanteuse, Piaf is infamous for its very late-night, after-hours parties. Some have said that you need a woman on your arm to gain entrance beyond the bouncer at the door, while others say they have heard people banging on the other side of the door to get out. Decked out like a brothel in red velvet furnishings and low lights, part of its mystique is what happens once you are in and if you can survive the experience. On the downstairs dance floor, the spinning of oldies can get pretty heated, and the crowd can be quite wild. Open Friday and Saturday 10pm to 7am. Crowd: varied. VI. Nagymező u. 25. ℂ 1/312-3823. Metro: Oktogon or Opera (Yellow line).

Spinoza Étterem ★★ (Finds A restaurant is in front, but in back there is a small cabaret where nightly music performances are offered from Klezmer to classical. Monthly programs are posted in the window or you can check the website. Friday evening offerings are a dinner with Klezmer concert. For a small venue, they always have something musical happening. VII. Dob u. 15. ℂ 1/413-7488. www.spinozahaz.hu. Performances range 2,000 Ft–5,000 Ft with dinner. Bus: 74 to Dohány Synagogue.

Trafó Bar Tango Associated with the dance venue by the same name and location, this club is housed in the basement. Trafó has a reputation for hosting the best of the best in alternative artists, from reggae to classic Indian music. The dance floor is not a reason to come here, but the small bar area is only the way station before heading to the relaxed, easygoing lounge where you can chill out with friends. Open daily 6pm to 4am or later depending on performances. Crowd: varied. IX. Liliom u. 41. ℂ 1/456-2049. www.trafo.hu. Cover: 500 Ft–2,000 Ft. Metro: Ferenc krt. (Blue line); tram: 4 or 6 Üllöi út.

---

4 PUBS & CAFE BARS

Balettcipő The "Ballet Shoe" is a cheerful coffeehouse/bar on the street to the side of the opera house. We found it the best when it first opened since we did not have to share the space. When weather does not permit outdoor seating, the place fills quickly with a local crowd. The cafe-style menu is widely eclectic in offerings, but the food is good regardless of what you choose. We love the Greek mural inside. Open daily 10am to midnight. VI. Hajós u. 14. ℂ 1/269-3114. www.balettcipo.hu. Metro: Opera (Yellow line).

Café Aloe This sizzling comfortable cellar offers powerful, yet remarkably cheap drinks prepared by attentive bar staff. This place is known among locals as the temple of good, inexpensive cocktails. Open daily 5pm to 2am. VI. Zichy Jenő u. 37. ℂ 1/269-4536. Metro: Nyugati pu. (Blue line).

Café Bobek Named for a communist rabbit, this is a cute little cafe bar where you can go for a quiet drink with friends. It also offers free Wi-Fi. Open Monday through

Bar Warning

The Longford Irish Pub, V. Fehérhajó u. 5 (📞 **1/267-2766**), has been reportedly gouging both tourists and Hungarians alike. Due to numerous complaints sent to the Budapest Times, the paper did an "undercover" investigation and reported their findings in the June 18–24, 2007, issue. What they reported was that the bill received at the end of the meal was illegible and incomplete in details, thus allowing the bar to include higher-priced items or items that had not been ordered at all. Although this practice has been reported at some restaurants in the Castle District, this is the first experience with an establishment in Pest. See p. 89 for other U.S. Embassy warnings.

Thursday 8am to 1am, Friday 8am to 3am, Saturday 11am to 3am, and Sunday 11am to 1am. VII. Kazinczy u. 51. 📞 **1/329-0729.** www.bobek.hu. Tram: 4 or 6 Király u.

Fregatt This was the first English-style pub in Hungary, though depending on the day you go, it could be overcrowded or dead. Locals make up the better half of the clientele, but English-speaking expats manage to find it also. Although the name refers to a ship theme, it does not deliver on that count, but the atmosphere is amicable and that is what matters. Guinness stout is on draft. Live jazz is offered on various nights, but it starts and ends early. Open Sunday through Friday 4pm to 1am and Saturday 5pm to 1am. V. Molnár u. 26. 📞 **1/318-9997.** Metro: Ferenciek tere (Blue line); tram: 2, 47, or 49.

Irish Cat Pub This was the first Irish-style pub in Budapest; there's Guinness on tap along with other beer favorites in addition to the great selection of whiskies. It's a popular meeting place for expats and travelers. It serves food and has special events, especially around March 17. Open Thursday to Saturday 4pm to 4am. V. Múzeum krt. 41. 📞 **1/266-4085.** www.irishcat.hu. Metro: Kálvin tér (Blue line).

Janis Pub Named after the legendary Janis Joplin, this easygoing pub has an Irish theme with Guinness, a selection of alcohol, live music on occasion by local talent, and Janis Joplin artifacts for you fans out there. Open daily 4pm to 2am. V. Királyi Pál u. 8. 📞 **1/266-2619.** www.janispub.hu. Metro: Kálvin tér or Ferenciek tere (Blue line).

Kuplung Located in a former motorcycle repair shop, Kuplung (meaning clutch) packs a lively, young crowd in its gardenlike interior. In the squatters-pub atmosphere you will find table football (*csocsó*) fans spinning away on one of the many tables, while loud groovy sounds fill this vast hangar. Cheap drinks might just make you "clutch" onto your chair, but clutch your purse instead. Bag theft happens. Look carefully for the sign on the building or you won't find it easily, so take note of the address before venturing out. Open daily 4pm to 2am. VI. Király u. 46. 📞 **061/30-986-8856.** Tram: 4 or 6 to Király u.

Paris, Texas Paris, Texas has the distinction of being the first nightlife spot with the foresight to have opened up on the now-buzzing Ráday utca, the partial pedestrian-only street now lined with bars and cafes. The clientele runs the gamut during tourist season, but other times it is mainly student-aged who linger into the morning. This is a cozy place to drink and talk, but any food ordered comes from the Pink Cadillac nearby. The walls of three adjacent rooms are lined with old photographs, providing a window into the local culture of the 1910s and 1920s. In summer there is limited outdoor seating. It

(Finds) Budapest's Underground Courtyard Parties

One of the strangest things I have come across is the underground nightlife scene in Budapest. Entrepreneurs take over the space of an abandoned building or courtyard and create a pub there until they are evicted or the building is torn down. Often found inside dark **abandoned building courtyards** not visible from the street, these squatters' pubs, ruins pubs, or *kerts* (gardens) as they are known here, are mysterious and exciting to visit. If you were merely strolling by, you would have no idea of the party scene shaking the interior walls, just a few feet away behind what on the outside is a dilapidated facade or an overly abused door.

How do these parties get started? Here is the generic explanation I have been able to filter out, but I am still searching for the full story. Organizers seek out properties that are in a bureaucratic quagmire; usually they are buildings with no tenants, and the ownership of the property is questionable, making renovations impossible. As in all real estate deals, location is the prime ingredient for success. They peruse the notices for abandoned properties ripe for squatting. These are the places that have fallen from the radar of the bureaucratic. Add this situation to a bit of rebelliousness and the desire to make money, and before you know it, a star is born on the party scene. However, to stay undercover, these party places are generally advertized by word of mouth only, so you have to ask around to find the current hotspots. When the wrecking ball is looming above, the party is over and then it is on to the next spot.

One *kert* success story is the bustling bar known as **Szimpla Kert** (p. 226). Colorful paintings hung on the walled-up doors, a bar and jukebox occupied the empty courtyard, and paper lanterns and strange sculptures were hung from above. The party was eventually shut down, but the "Szimpla Kert" party moved on to other venues with a dark cloud hanging over it waiting for the swansong to announce the end of a decade. However, that did not happen. Szimpla Kert is still going strong and is more vibrant than ever before. With an actual roof covering it now, it is no longer the *kert* of days past, but still a hot, hotspot to be with the in crowd.

Although Budapest's courtyards seem to disappear one after the other, one or two open in the summer months somewhere in the city, with the seventh, eighth, and ninth districts currently the popular areas of choice, perhaps due to the number of vacated buildings.

is open Monday through Friday 10am to 3am, Saturday and Sunday 1pm to 3am. IX. Ráday u. 22. (✆) **1/218-0570.** Metro: Kálvin tér (Blue line).

Picasso Point   This cafe-bar is a warm spot to hang out. It offers a limited selection of pizzas and sandwiches. Others find pleasure in the basement party-arena during their short evening hours. Open Monday to Wednesday 11am to midnight, Thursday 11am to 2am, Friday 11am to 4am, Saturday 4pm to 4am, and Sunday 4pm to midnight. VI. Hajós u. 31. (✆) **1/312-1727.** Metro: Nyugati pu. (Blue line).

Pótkulcs   A bohemian bar, Pótkulcs (Spare Key) draws an artsy-looking crowd of travelers and locals alike. My students took me here my first year and I believe the bar's motto: "Pótkulcs is difficult to find and hard to leave." Beyond the rusty metal entrance, this large pub is filled with rickety chairs, couches, and tables—a great place to socialize. The friendly yet crazy-looking chef prepares tasty and ample meals. Presenting the local artists-to-be, the pub features an eclectic mix of temporary art exhibitions and unique concerts. Open Sunday through Wednesday 5pm to 1:30am and Thursday through Saturday 5pm to 2:30am. VI. Csengery u. 65/b. ✆ 1/269-1050. www.potkulcs.hu. Metro: Nyugati pu. (Blue line).

Szilvuplé   This is a lounge, cafe, restaurant, and bar all rolled into one large party place. Szilvuplé's attractiveness lies in its steady, calm, welcoming atmosphere. The secession-style indoor design, colorful cocktail bar, attentive staff, moderate prices, and talented DJs set the tone with rock and indie music; it also features karaoke nights and dance lessons during the week. Open Thursday through Saturday 6pm to 4am and Sunday through Wednesday 6pm to 2am. VI. Ó u. 33. ✆ 20/992–5115 (mobile phone only). www.szilvuple.hu. Metro: Opera (Yellow line).

Szimpla Kert ★★   For cultural experiences, you cannot pass up Szimpla Kert. It is a beer garden, alternative culture Mecca. Located in an abandoned apartment courtyard that has not seen the wrecking ball, Szimpla Kert mixes junkyard aesthetics with such modernisms as Wi-Fi, a daytime cafe, and evenings of live music and indie film screenings. Dimly lit, couch-packed, with little open to the sky rooms off the courtyard, it is a relaxing, pleasant place to unwind. Check in your reality at the door. Open weekdays 10am to 2am and weekends noon to 2am. VII. Kertész u. 48. ✆ 1/321-9119. www.simpla.hu. Metro: Oktogon (Yellow line); tram: 4 or 6 to Király u.

Szóda   When I need a Wi-Fi and caffeine fix at the same time, this is my favorite hangout. Redesigned a few times, it seems to look the same each time, with retro-futuristic leather bench seats and '50s style chairs. The windows are filled with empty old-fashioned clear glass spritzer soda bottles. The underground bar and dance floor is shelter for the whacky all-night dance-rats. Supposedly open daily 8am to 5am, but their hours vary by whim. VII. Wesselényi u. 18. ✆ 1/461-0007. www.szoda.com. Tram: 4 or 6 to Wesselényi u.

5 HUNGARIAN FOLK-DANCE HOUSES

Hungarian folk music has many styles, sounds, and instruments with some music associated with dances, while others are autonomous. Hand in hand with national identity, folk music has had a revival via the *táncház* (dance house). An evening of folk music and folk dancing can be a wonderful cultural experience during your stay here. The events in a neighborhood community center certainly come with a higher recommendation than those offered as tourist events. When an American choreography student was studying here, she pointed out that many of the dances were male-centered with the ladies as window dressing. Perhaps some are, but others are definitely mixed equally. Listed below are a few of the best-known dance houses. The offering is dance instruction for an hour and then several hours of dancing accompanied by a live band. You just might hear some of Hungary's best folk musicians in these simple dance houses. If you have two left feet, just come to watch and listen. Every festival has some folk dancing included, so if you

The Budapest Klezmer Music Scene

The word **klezmer** is derived from two Hebrew words, *clay* and *zimmer*, denoting a vessel of music or song with the idea being that an instrument personifies human characteristics such as joyous laughter or mournful crying. Originally it was part of the Eastern European Yiddish culture.

Klezmer musicians were wanderers who went from village to village playing traditional songs, folk songs, dances, and solemn hymns before prayer time. Rarely did they read music; there was no one in the *shtetl* to teach them. They had to travel in order to make a living, earning little money as they played. Typically, a group consisted of three to six musicians playing various instruments: trumpets, bugles, flutes, clarinets, fifes, violins, cellos, and drums.

The music of the *klezmorim*, the players of *klezmer*, was influenced by other cultures as the Jewish people traveled throughout Central and Eastern Europe. Thus the music has strong Middle Eastern influences, which are heard in Jewish liturgical music with other influences coming from Romania, Russia, and the Ukraine.

In the late 1800s, the clarinet gained popularity as the most important instrument of *klezmer* replacing the violin. Brass instruments were introduced at the end of the 19th century.

When Jews immigrated en masse to the U.S. between 1880 and 1920, it happened to be the time that commercial recording devices were being developed. Those recordings of *klezmer* produced between 1912 and 1940 survived as the primary source material for the current revival of *klezmer* music. *Klezmer* fell out of favor after World War II with Jews assimilating into mainstream society; however, in the 1970s, it was discovered yet again.

Today, it is more popular than ever and is played by bands around the world. The popular bands are touring the world as well as recording CDs. The Budapest Klezmer Band, organized in 1990, was responsible for the revival of *klezmer* in Hungary, and it is the first *klezmer* band to form in Hungary since World War II.

The Budapest Klezmer Band is just one of many *klezmer* bands that have come into existence over the years, getting their start in Budapest. *Klezmer* no longer has a strictly Jewish fan base or a Budapest one either. Due to this, when they do land back in Budapest, they are playing at larger venues than in years past, to sell-out audiences. This makes it difficult to point the direction for finding a *klezmer* concert. The locations of the past are not as reliable as they once were. Therefore, I direct you to the website of two of the popular bands to check their concert schedules for the time of your visit. The **Budapest Klezmer Band's** schedule is on their website at www.budapestklezmer.hu and the **Chagall Klezmer Band** at www.chagallband.hu. Both have an English-language link. Alternatives are to look for listings for performances by the **Pannonia Klezmer Band, Sabbathsong, Klezmer Band,** or **Klezmereszek.** A few of these groups play at **Spinoza Étterem** (p. 223) or contact the Fonó Music Hall at XI. Sztregova u. 3. (© **1/206-5300;** www.fono.hu). It produces many of the *klezmer* CDs. Lastly, you can check with Tourinform for concert information. If you happen to be here at the end of August to the beginning of September, you will find *klezmer* concerts at the annual Jewish Festival.

are too inhibited to try these places, try to arrange your trip around some festival time. Most dance houses are open from September to June and are closed for the summer.

Authentic folk-music workshops are held at least once a week at several locations around the city. The leading Hungarian folk band is **Muzsikás,** the name given to musicians playing traditional folk music in Hungarian villages. They have toured the U.S., playing to great acclaim, so may not always be available at a Budapest *tánchoz.* Music is Every Thursday (Sept–May only) from 8pm to midnight for 700 Ft, there's music at the **Marczibányi Square Cultural House (Marczibányi tér Művelődési Ház,** II. Marczibányi tér 5/a (✆ 1/212-2820). Take the Red line metro to Moszkva tér. Also try the **Municipal Cultural House (Fővárosi Művelődési Ház),** at XI. Fehérvári út 47 (✆ 1/203-3868). At the **Kalamajka Dance House,** Belvárosi Ifjúsági Művelődési Ház, V. Molnár u. 9 (✆ 1/371-5928), reachable by M3 Ferenciek tere, is the biggest weekend dance, with dancing and instruction on the second floor, while jam sessions and serious palinka drinking take place on the fourth. The Kalamajka band is led by Béla Halmos, who started the dance-house movement in the 1970s. Usually traditional villagers give guest performances. Open Saturday from 8pm to 1am for 700 Ft, you can dance until you drop.

An important heritage-preserving center, the **Almássy Square Culture Center (Almássy téri Művelődési Központ),** VII. Almássy tér 6 (✆ 1/352-1572), from 6pm to 10pm hosts folk dances to the music of the electric Greeks Sirtos in the main hall. Upstairs is a bit crazier with the small fanatic band of Magyar dancers who twirl to the Kalotaszeg sounds of the Berkó Band until midnight. A short walk from Blaha Lujza tér (Blue line or tram nos. 4 or 6) gets you to this folk center. Entrance fees vary from 700 Ft to 1,500 Ft.

Most people who come to a *tánchoz* evening do so to learn the folk dances and the music that accompanies them, not for touristy reasons. However, this does not mean that tourists are not welcome to learn the dances or sit and observe while hearing musicians practicing and partake in a local scene at next to no expense. You have the opportunity to become part of the program instead of merely watching others perform.

Every Monday, Friday, and Saturday from May to mid-October at 8:30pm, the more touristy Folklór Centrum presents a program of Hungarian dancing accompanied by a Gypsy orchestra at the Municipal Cultural House. This performance is one of the best of its kind in Budapest.

6 GAY & LESBIAN BARS

The bar scene regardless of orientation is volatile, most likely due to the low wages of the local working stiffs regardless of their profession. There is not much discretionary income to spend in bars. Gay bars open and close in the blink of an eye. The gay bar scene in Budapest is largely male-oriented though progress is being made for women. Ladies are welcomed at most of the bars and there is a once-a-month PURE Party for lesbians. The dates and venues change, so for reliable and up-to-date information, if you find your way to one of the bars, there is a monthly gay magazine available. Although it is in Hungarian, there are resource pages in English in the back with current events. Alternatively visit **www.budapestgaycity.net, www.gayguide.net**, or subscribe to the free Yahoo **Gay Budapest Information** group by sending an e-mail to gaybudapestinfo-subscribe@yahoo groups.com.

While I have your attention, if you are reading this section, chances are you will be interested in the gay-owned/friendly restaurants. They are all in the "Where to Dine" chapter, so look for Amstel River Café, Club 93 Café, and Café Eklektika.

Action Bar   This is a well-hidden bar and can easily be overlooked. It is only one of two exclusively gay male bars in the city. The hanging sidewalk sign is usually not even close to the entrance. Look for a large yellow *A* sign and this is the entrance to this dark, often-crowded basement bar. Most of the group consists of other tourists with a few locals mixed in, but exclusively men. You will receive a drink card that obligates you to drink the minimum of 1,000 Ft or pay the difference when you leave. Make sure the bartender marks your card with every drink you order. There is a hefty fine for "lost" cards. Highlights are the spicy strip shows and go-go shows on Fridays at 12:30am and 1:45am (extra entry fee of 700 Ft), the busy dark video rooms, and the sizzling hot atmosphere, but it is empty until 11pm. Open daily 9pm to 4am. V. Magyar u. 42. ℂ **1/266-9148.** www.action.gay.hu. Metro: Kálvin tér (Blue line).

AlterEgo   Another club that made its way to the gay scene in 2007 and lives on; this is regaled as a hip jumping club for the younger set, but older folks of both genders are welcome too for their different events. Besides karaoke, it has guest singers and transvestite shows. Open Friday and Saturday 10pm until the sun rises again. The cover is 1,500 Ft, without a drink, but no minimum consumption required. VI. Dessewffy u. 33. ℂ **06/70-345-4302** (mobile phone only). Metro: Oktogon (Yellow line).

Árkádia   In the city center, this small, intimate sometimes packed bar with a popular backroom is the perfect place to meet, dance, or get cozy with an attractive stranger. There is no cover or minimum consumption charge, but this place attracts the rent boys. There are no entry or spending requirements here. Open daily 5pm to 5am. V. Türr István u. 5. No phone. www.arkadiagaybar.hu. Metro: Vörösmarty tér (Yellow line).

Café Smile   The owner speaks decent English, so if no one else, you can speak with him. This is another small bar, but seems to have lasted the test of time for now. There is a minimum consumption of 1,000 Ft, but no entry fee. Reports have been that it is a pleasant relaxed place, not loud, good for chatting. VII Nagydiófa u. 17. ℂ **06/30-403-1372** (mobile phone only). www.cafesmile.hu. Metro: Blaha Lujza (Red line).

Capella   Although labeled a gay club, with a cross-dressing bar staff, this club draws a large non-gay crowd. It offers cabaret-style shows and extravagant drag shows, which are a draw for the curious heterosexuals at midnight and 1am. There are three levels to the bar. Some have reported that the cover charge changes sporadically and some customers have been overcharged, so proceed with caution and count your change carefully. Entrance will run you 1,500 Ft on Friday and Saturday, and 500 Ft on other nights, but if there is a special event, it can be as high as 3,500 Ft. Open daily 10pm to 5am. V. Belgrád rkp. 23. ℂ **1/328-6231.** Metro: Ferenciek tere (Blue line).

CoXx Club   Once known as Chaos, this is a modern, metallic bar only for gay men who like to sizzle in the underground shelter. The entry level has an overpriced Internet café and a small art gallery, where you will be greeted and given your consumption card. In the winter, coat check is mandatory. Nothing happens here until midnight at the earliest. The later the better. Open daily 9pm to 5am. VII. Dohány u. 38. ℂ **1/344-4884.** www.coxx.hu. Minimum consumption 1,000 Ft. Metro: Astoria or Blaha Lujza tér (Red line).

Funny Carrot   Hey, I don't make up these names and why someone would open up another bar with the same address as another is beyond me. This bar shares the same address as the Habrolo Bisztro below, but the hours here are daily 7pm to 6am. There is no minimum consumption or entry fee. V. Szep u. 1/b. ℰ **06/20-942-9419** (mobile phone only). Metro: Astoria (Red line).

Habrolo Bisztro   This is a small gay bar where locals hang out, so you can practice your Hungarian skills here. The staff from the former Angyal's bar has been here since its opening in 2006. **The Funny Carrot** is at the same address. Drinking hours are daily 7pm to 4am. There is no minimum consumption or entry fee. V. Szep u. 1/b. ℰ **06/20-211-6701** (mobile phone only). Metro: Astoria (Red line).

Le Café M   Once upon a time it was the Mystery Bar, which was the first gay bar in the city. Then it changed its name for unknown reasons; maybe the tax man was after them. It is a very tiny, but friendly place that draws a large foreign clientele making it a great place to strike up a conversation and meet new people. Open Monday through Friday 4pm to 4am and Saturday and Sunday 6pm to 4am. No entry or consumption fees. V. Nagysándor József u. 3. ℰ **1/312-1436.** www.lecafem.com. Metro: Arany János u. (Blue line).

7 MORE ENTERTAINMENT

CASINOS   Budapest has a couple dozen respectable casinos. Many are located in luxury hotels: **Las Vegas Casino,** in the Atrium Hyatt Hotel, V. Roosevelt tér 2 (ℰ **1/317-6022;** www.lasvegascasino.hu); and **Orfeum Casino,** in the Hotel Béke Radisson, VI. Teréz krt. 43 (ℰ **1/301-1600**). Formal dress is required. Other popular casinos include: **Grand Casino Budapest,** V. Deák Ferenc u. 13 (ℰ **1/483-0170**), **Tropicana Casino,** V. Vigadó u. 2 (ℰ **1/327-7250;** www.tropicanacasino.hu), and the most elegant **Várkert Casino** on the Danube side, Ybl Miklós tér 9 (ℰ **1/202-4244;** www.varkert.hu). There are a number of smaller independent casinos around the city, but we do not recommend patronizing them.

MOVIES   There is no longer a wide selection of movie theaters showing movies in their original language. Movies labeled *szinkronizált, m.b.,* or *magyarul beszél* mean that the movie has been dubbed into Hungarian; *feliratos* means subtitled. Tickets cost around 1,500 Ft to 2,100 Ft. **MOM Park**, XII. Alkotás u. 53 (ℰ **1/487-5500**), multiplex provides the option of seeing movies in their original language even if the movie itself was dubbed, but this is one of the more expensive theaters. Check listings at **www.palacecinemas.hu.** To reach MOM Park, take tram no. 61 from Moszkva tér to Csörsz u.

The art cinemas where English-language movies are only sometimes found are **Corvin,** VIII. köz 1 (ℰ **1/459-5050;** tram nos. 4 or 6 to Ferenc krt.); **Európa,** VII. Rákóczi út 82 (ℰ **1/322-5419;** no. 7 bus to Berzsenyi u.); **Hunnia,** VII. Erzsébet krt. 26 (ℰ **1/322-3471;** tram nos. 4 or 6 to Wesselényi u.); **Művész,** VI. Teréz krt. 30 (ℰ **1/332-6726;** tram nos. 4 or 6 to Oktogon); **Puskin,** V. Kossuth L. u. 18 (ℰ **1/429-6080;** metro to Astoria, Red line); and **Uránia,** VIII. Rákócxi út 2 (ℰ **1/318-8955;** metro to Blaha Lujza tér, Red line).

Going to a movie at one of the cinemas above can be a cultural experience in itself. Some theaters are smaller than most people's living rooms. Seats are assigned in all of the theaters. *Jobb* means right and *Bal* means left. First, find the sign to see if that theater uses right and left as you face the seats or as you are facing the stage; it is not a uniform custom. Then find your row number *Sor,* and finally your numbered "chair" *Szék.* If you do not sit in your assigned seat, you may find an upset Hungarian hovering over you telling you that the seat is theirs. As a throwback to earlier times, you will find a half-empty theater with people insisting they have to sit in their assigned seat when better seats are freely available. If popcorn is sold in the theater, don't expect any butter or other topping. As much as the Hungarian diet is made up of fats, they don't use any for their movie munchies.

The Danube Bend

The Danube Bend (Dunakanyar), a string of small riverside towns just north of Budapest, is a popular excursion spot for both Hungarians and international travelers. The name "Danube Bend" is actually a misnomer. It should be the Danube twist, turn, and twist again. The river doesn't actually change direction at the designated bend. The Danube enters Hungary from the northwest flowing southeasterly forming the border with Hungary's northern neighbor, Slovakia. Just after Esztergom, about 53km by train (32 miles) north of Budapest, the river changes abruptly to the south. This is the start of the Danube Bend region. From here the river then sharply twists north again just before Visegrád, then goes south

yet again before reaching Vác. From Vác, it flows more or less directly south, through Budapest on toward the country's borders with Serbia and Croatia. When looking at it on a map, it looks like a long snake after a seizure.

The small, but historic towns along the snaking Bend, in particular, Szentendre, Vác, Visegrád, and Esztergom, are easy day trips from Budapest since they're all within a half-hour to a couple of hours from the city. The natural beauty of the area, where forested hills loom over the river, makes it a welcome haven for those weary of the city. Travelers with more time in Budapest can easily make a long weekend out of a visit to the Bend, but I suggest a Budapest base with half-day or day trips.

1 RAILING THROUGH THE DANUBE BEND

GETTING THERE

BY BOAT   From April to September, boats run between Budapest and the towns of the Danube Bend. A leisurely boat ride through the countryside is one of the highlights of a boat excursion. All boats depart from Budapest's Vigadó tér boat landing, which is located in Pest between Erzsébet Bridge and Szabadság Bridge, stopping to pick up passengers 5 minutes later at Buda's Batthyány tér landing, which is also a Red line metro stop, before it continues up the river.

Schedules and towns served are complicated and change sometimes due to water levels of the river, so contact **Mahart,** the state shipping company, at the Vigadó tér landing (© 1/318-1704; www.mahartpassnave.hu; click on the British flag) for information. You can also get MAHART information from Tourinform.

One-way prices by riverboat are 1,490 Ft to Vác, 1,590 Ft to Visegrád, and 1,990 Ft to Esztergom. Trips to Szentendre cost 2,235 Ft roundtrip. Children 5 and under ride for free, children 15 and under receive a 50% discount, and students receive a 25% discount with the ISIC card.

The approximate travel time by boat from Budapest is 2 hours to Szentendre, 3½ hours to Visegrád, and 5 hours to Esztergom. If time is tight, consider the train or bus (both of which are also considerably cheaper).

BY TRAIN   For information and details on traveling by Budapest rail, see p. 36.

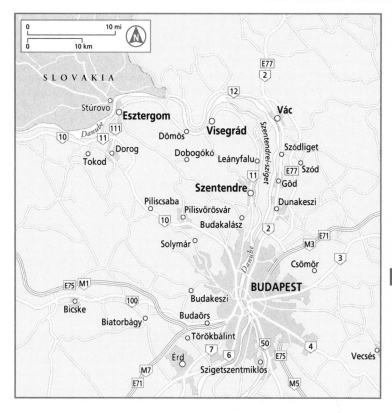

To Szentendre The HÉV suburban railroad connects Budapest's Batthyány tér Station with Szentendre. On the Pest side, you can catch the HÉV from the Margit Híd, Budai Híd Fő stop on tram nos. 4 or 6. Trains leave daily, year-round, every 20 minutes or so from 4am to 11:30pm. The one-way fare is 600 Ft each way. If you have a valid Budapest public transportation pass, the supplemental ticket is 265 Ft each way. The trip is 45 minutes.

To Vác An incredible 85 trains leave from Nyugati Station during the week and 58 on weekends giving you plenty of freedom on time of day to go. However, shoot for the train that leaves 7 minutes after the hour, since the trip is only 25 minutes. Other trains can take 45 minutes to 1½ hours for unknown reasons. The one-way fare is 560 Ft each way. All of the trains are locals, so no reservation is needed.

To Visegrád There's no direct train service to Visegrád. Instead you can take one of 28 daily trains departing from Nyugati Station for Nagymaros-Visegrád (trip time: 40 minutes to 1 hour). From Nagymaros, take a ferry across the river to Visegrád. The ferry dock (RÉV © **26/398-344**) is a 5-minute walk from the train station. A ferry leaves every hour throughout the day. The train ticket to Nagymaros costs 955 Ft; the ferryboat ticket to Visegrád costs 250 Ft for adults and 125 Ft for students.

To Esztergom   One train every hour makes the run daily between Budapest's Nyugati Station and Esztergom (trip time: 1½ hours); InterCity trains are not available on this route. Train tickets cost 955 Ft each way.

BY BUS   Approximately 30 buses travel the same route to Szentendre, Visegrád, and Esztergom, departing from Budapest's **Árpád híd bus station** (© 1/329-1450; at the Blue line metro station of the same name). Some are only on specific days of the week, while others are daily. Buses charge by mileage ranges. Depending on the bus, the number of stops, and the day of the week, it could be a pleasant or excruciatingly long ride. The one-way fare to Szentendre is 475 Ft; the trip takes about 45 minutes. The fare to Visegrád is 750 Ft, and the trip takes anywhere from 1¼ to 3 hours. To Esztergom, take the bus that travels via a town called Dorog; it costs 1,050 Ft and takes from 1¼ hours to 2 hours depending on the day of the week or bus selected. Keep in mind, of course, that all travel by bus is subject to traffic delays, especially during rush hour.

BY CAR   From Budapest, Route 11 hugs the west bank of the Danube, taking you to Szentendre, Vác, Visegrád, and Esztergom. Alternatively, you could head "overland" to Esztergom by Route 10, switching to Route 111 at Dorog.

2 SZENTENDRE ★★★

21km (13 miles) N of Budapest

Szentendre (pronounced *Sen*-ten-dreh, St. Andrew), 21km (13 miles) north of Budapest, has been populated since the Stone Age by Illyrians, the Celtic Eraviscus tribe, Romans, Lombards, Avars, and naturally, Hungarians. Serbians settled here in the 17th century, embellishing the town with their unique characteristics. Szentendre, counts half a dozen Serbian churches among its rich collection of historical buildings.

Since the turn of the 20th century, Szentendre has been home to an artists' colony, where today, about 100 artists live and work, referred to as "The City of Artists." The town boasts of its selection of 48 museums and monuments, but few people come here to visit the museums, distracted perhaps by the shopping opportunities. It could also be that the times and hours posted are just a loose guide. Museums do not have stable hours, even when posted on the door; there is oftentimes a sign stating that the museum is closed for "technical reasons," but no future reopening date is given. Think of a museum as icing on the cake; if it is open, take the opportunity to visit it.

The town is an extremely popular destination, with buses pouring tourists into the streets for a few hours of exploring. This is sometimes a turn-off for other visitors, but the town really is a treasure. To appreciate its rich flavor, we recommend you look beyond the touristy shops and wander the streets looking at the architecture, the galleries, and the churches, if only from the outside. Dare to wander off the main streets to find hidden shops, beautiful old homes, and quiet green spaces. Almost all the streets are cobblestones, so choose comfortable footwear.

At the top of the hill, you'll find the Roman Catholic churchyard, with views of the red-tile rooftops. One surprise from here is the winged blue man on a rooftop a couple of blocks away; I could not find anyone to tell me what its purpose was other than frivolity. If you take the steps down from the courtyard, you will come across, in my opinion, the best *lángos* vendor (see below) in Hungary. If you wander down the hill on the side streets, the palinka shop has been known to give a free sample in hopes of making a sale. Szentendre is too small for you to get lost in and too beautiful for a less-than-thorough

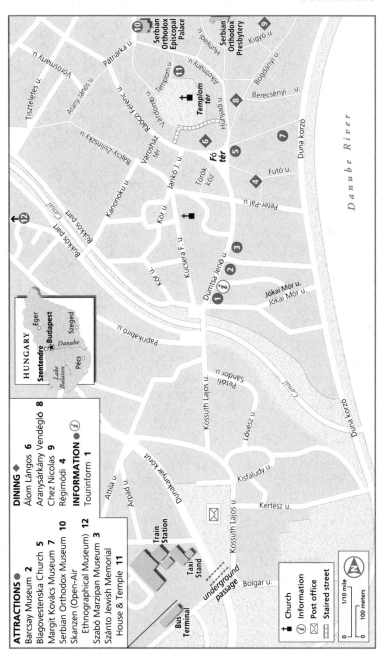

THE DANUBE BEND **11** **SZENTENDRE**

ATTRACTIONS ●
Barcsay Museum **2**
Blagovestenska Church **5**
Margit Kovács Museum **7**
Serbian Orthodox Museum **10**
Skanzen (Open-Air
Ethnographical Museum) **12**
Szabó Marzipan Museum **3**
Szánto Jewish Memorial
House & Temple **11**

DINING ◆
Álom Lángos **6**
Aranysárkány Vendéglő **8**
Chez Nicolas **9**
Régimódi **4**

INFORMATION ● ⓘ
Tourinform **1**

✝ Church
ⓘ Information
⊠ Post office
▦ Stairred street

HUNGARY
Eger
Budapest
Szeged
Danube
Szentendre
Pécs
Lake
Balaton

exploration, so make the most of a day, but don't miss walking along the Danube for a blissful view of the river and the tree-lined bank on the other side.

ESSENTIALS

For information on getting to Szentendre, see above. One of Szentendre's information offices, **Tourinform,** is at Dumtsa Jenő u. 22 (*©* **26/317-965**), with maps of Szentendre (and the region), as well as concert and exhibition schedules. The office can also provide hotel information. It is open April through August, Monday to Friday from 9am to 5:30pm, weekends 10am to 5:30pm. In September to November it's open Monday to Friday from 9:30am to 4:30pm, weekends 10am to 4pm. December through March, the hours are the same as autumn, but they open half an hour later weekdays. To get here, just follow the flow of pedestrian traffic into town on Kossuth Lajos utca. Like all things in this town, the office marches to the beat of its own drummer, not always keeping with the schedule it gives. If you arrive by boat, you may find the **Ibusz** office sooner, located on the corner of Bogdányi út and Gőzhajó utca (*©* **26/310-181**). This office is open April to October, Monday through Friday from 10am to 6pm and weekends 10am to 3pm. From November to March, it's open weekdays only, 10am to 5pm. They close for lunch from 1pm to 1:30pm daily.

WHERE TO STAY

Róz Panzió ★, located at Pannónia utca 6/b (*©* **26/311-737;** fax 26/310-979; www. hotelrozszentendre.hu), has 10 units and a garden overlooking the Danube where you can eat breakfast when weather permits. Rooms are 50€ for a double during off season, 55€ in high season; breakfast is included. With its new website, you can book online and view videos. Parking is available.

EXPLORING THE MUSEUMS & CHURCHES

Barcsay Museum ★   The conservative socialist dictates of the day restricted the work of artist Jenő Barcsay (1900–1988). Nevertheless, in his anatomical drawings, etchings, and charcoal and ink drawings, Barcsay's genius shines through. I particularly like his pastel drawings of Szentendre street scenes.

Dumtsa Jenő u. 10. *©* **26/310-244.** Admission 600 Ft (free for E.U. citizens). Wed–Sun 10am–6pm.

Blagovestenska Church ★   The Blagovestenska Church at Fő tér 4 is the only one of the town's several Serbian Orthodox churches that you can be fairly sure to find open. The tiny church, dating from 1752, was built on the site of a wooden church from the Serbian migration of 1690. A rococo iconostasis features paintings by Mihailo Zivkovic; notice the eyes of all the icons are upon you.

Fő tér 4. No phone. Admission 300 Ft. Tues–Sun 10am–5pm.

Margit Kovács Museum ★★   This expansive museum features the work of Hungary's best-known ceramic artist, Margit Kovács, who died in 1977. It displays the breadth of Kovács' talents. Many appreciate her sculptures of elderly women and her folk-art interpretations of village life. When the museum is full, people are required to wait outside before entering.

Vastagh György u. 1. *©* **26/310-244.** Admission 1,000 Ft. Tues–Sun 10am–6pm. Walk east from Fő tér on Görög utca.

Serbian Orthodox Museum ★★   The Serbian Orthodox Museum is housed next door to a Serbian Orthodox Church (services are at 10am Sunday) in one of the buildings of the former episcopate, just north of Fő tér. The collection here—one of the most exten- sive of its kind in predominantly Catholic Hungary—features exceptional 16th- through 19th-century icons, liturgical vessels, scrolls in Arabic from the Ottoman period, and other types of ecclesiastical art. Informative labels are in Hungarian and English. Have small bills with you for the entrance fee; they rarely can break large bills. Entrance to the museum entitles you to visit the church, but a museum attendant unlocks the door for you and waits for you to leave again.

Pátriárka u. 5. (© 26/312-399. Admission 600 Ft. May–Sept Tues–Sun 10am–6pm; Oct–Apr Tues–Sun 10am–5pm. Walk north from Fő tér on Alkotmány utca.

Szabó Marzipan Museum ★★ (Kids)   Interestingly, this is the most widely known museum in this village, claiming to be the only museum of its type in the world. Who could pass up this chance to see the 1.5m (5 ft) long Hungarian Parliament made entirely in marzipan? Kids will love the Disney characters and the 1.8m (6 ft) Michael Jackson made of white chocolate. What they can create in marzipan and chocolate is amazing. For a coffee or pastry, their cafe is right next door.

Dumsta Jeno u. 12. (© 26/311-931. Admission 400 Ft. May–Sept daily 10am–7pm; Oct–Apr daily 10am–6pm.

Szántó Jewish Memorial House and Temple ★★★ (Moments)   This is the first temple built in Hungary after World War II as a memorial to those from this area who died in the Holocaust. It is probably the smallest Jewish temple in the world. It was dedicated on May 17, 1998, by Professor József Sweitzer, the chief rabbi of Hungary. Men are given a yamaka to wear when entering.

Albotmány u. 4. No phone. Donations accepted. Tues–Sun 11am–5pm.

SIGHTS OUTSIDE TOWN

Skanzen (Open-Air Ethnographical Museum) ★★ (Kids)   About 3km (2 miles) northwest of Szentendre is one of Hungary's better *skanzens,* or reproduction peasant villages. This ambitious *skanzen,* the largest in the country, represents rural life from all regions of the country. There are several reconstructed 18th- and 19th-century villages, with thatch-roofed houses, blacksmith and weaving shops, working mills, and churches. You can purchase a guidebook in English at the gate.

Szentendre's bus station is behind the HÉV terminal. Take the bus from bay 7 (fare is 170 Ft) and get off at the Szabadság-forrás stop. The bus will not stop automatically, so you must press the stop request button. A more convenient way is to go to the boat landing and take a taxi. If you're driving, follow Route 10N. Turn left on Sztaravodai út.

Sztaravodai út. (© 26/502-500. www.skanzen.hu. Admission 1,200 Ft regular, 1,600 Ft for festivals; student ticket 600 Ft regular, 800 Ft for festivals. Outdoor exhibitions Apr–Oct Tues–Sun 9am–5pm. See directions above.

WHERE TO DINE

Aranysárkány Vendéglő (Golden Dragon Inn) ★ HUNGARIAN   Located just east of Fő tér on Hunyadi utca, which leads into Alkotmány utca, the Golden Dragon is always filled to capacity. The crowd includes a large percentage of Hungarians, definitely a good sign in a heavily visited town like Szentendre.

Long wooden tables set with sterling cutlery provide a relaxed, but tasteful atmosphere in this air-conditioned restaurant. You can choose from such enticing offerings as alpine lamb, roast leg of goose, Székely-style stuffed cabbage (the Székely are a Hungarian ethnic group native to Transylvania), spinach cream, and venison steak. Vegetarians can order

(Finds) Best Lángos Ever

If you get a snack attack, you will find the best *lángos* in Hungary here in Szentendre at **Álom Lángos** ★★★ at Fő tér 8 (© **06/20-970-7827** mobile phone), an unassuming little stand. Sometimes the long waiting lines are attesting to this fact, since most will be Hungarians in the know. *Lángos* is the Hungarian version of fried dough with toppings (see "Hungarian Eats & Treats" in chapter 2, p. 23). When standing in Fő tér, there are yellow signs near an alley with LÁNGOS written on them. Halfway up the alley is a gate for the small shed where, for very little money, you can have the Hungarian favorite snack: *lángos* with sour cream, ham, and shredded cheese. Garlic and hot sauces are on the counter for you to add. For me, this is worth a trip to Szentendre alone. The stand is only open March through November Tuesday through Saturday 10am to 6pm and a *lángos* will cost you 300 Ft to 500 Ft.

the vegetable plate, a respectable presentation of grilled and steamed vegetables in season. Various traditional Hungarian beers are on draft, and the wine list features selections from 22 regions of the country.

Alkotmány u. 1/a. © **26/301-479.** www.aranysarkany.hu. Reservations recommended. Main courses 2,400 Ft–4,000 Ft; special tourist menus 3,300 Ft. AE, MC, V. Daily noon–10pm.

Chez Nicolas ★★★ FRENCH/HUNGARIAN Set away from the bustle of the square, this charming restaurant has intimate romantic dining with an outdoor terrace looking out to the river. For an even more romantic experience, request the single balcony table. You can choose from Hungarian or French dishes. The owner, Tamás Horváth, will be happy to explain the ingredients of each dish in his excellent English. We recommend the Pork Brasso with choice chunks of pork cooked in paprika, oil, and potatoes. This restaurant is a favorite of local residents.

Kígyó utca 10. © **26/311-288.** Reservations recommended. Main courses 1,700 Ft–3,800 Ft. MC, V. Tues–Sun noon–10pm.

Régimódi ★★ HUNGARIAN If you walk directly south from Fő tér, you'll find this excellent choice for dining. An elegant restaurant in a former private home, Régimódi is furnished with antique Hungarian carpets and chandeliers. Original artworks decorate the walls. Limited terrace dining is available and in the summer, you will appreciate the outside seating. The menu offers a wide range of Hungarian specialties, with an emphasis on game dishes. There are also numerous salad options, with specials each day on the board. Whatever you choose, the portions are hearty. There's an extensive wine list. It does get crowded with tour groups.

Futó u. 3. © **26/311-105.** Reservations recommended. Main courses 2,000 Ft–4,550 Ft. Three set menus from 2,200–2,800 Ft. DC, MC, V. Daily 9am–10pm.

SHOPPING

Blue Land Folklor ★★★ (Finds) The lady who owns and runs this store is a wealth of information on Hungarian folklore. She is really chatty and will give you the history of everything she sells that has some folk significance. I sometimes wonder if these stories are true or just good selling, but either way, they are entertaining. What is certain is that this store carries authentic Hungarian products, not Chinese imports, plus decorated eggs from 38 different regions of Hungary, including some from the ethnic Hungarian areas prior to the Trianon Treaty's loss of land. They are all labeled, and custom boxing is provided to ensure safe transport back home.

Alkotmány u. 8. ✆ **26/313-610.** Daily 10am–5pm.

Ecclesia Galéria ★★★ (Finds) If you like ceramic dishes, plates, bowls, or wall hangings, you will love this tiny hidden shop tucked away in a small alley and to the left. Having spotted the alley for years, it took a curious friend who was visiting to get me to view it. The works of Katalin Kovács are simply, but beautifully rendered in delightful, sometimes whimsical designs on all types of ceramics. Well worth a look.

Alkotmány u. 8. ✆ **06/26-314-576** (mobile phone only). Daily 10am–5pm.

Handpets ★★★ (Kids) Being a teacher, formerly elementary and now university, I cannot pass up sharing this information. If you want to find a unique shop while in Hungary, this is it. Handpets are the most creative hand puppets I have ever seen. They are made for three or five fingers and for child or adult hands. Designed by Kati Szili, they are handmade of high-quality material and are sure to delight children of all ages. This is the only exclusive shop where the entire collection is available, although limited designs and poor imitations are sold elsewhere.

Dumsta Jeno u. 15. ✆ **30/954-2584** (mobile phone only). www.handpets.hu. Daily 10am–5pm.

Old Goat Art Gallery ★★★ (Finds) Featuring the work of artist Győry Eszter, you will find the versatility of the work incredible both in style and medium. She has prints, ceramics, stained glass, postcards, magnets, and small treasures to remember your trip. The artist has works on permanent display throughout the U.S. and Hungary, with a number of awards to her credit.

Dumsta Jeno u. 15. ✆ **06/30-523-9184.** www.gyory.com. Daily 11am–5pm.

3 VÁC ★★★

34km (21 miles) N of Budapest

Just past Szentendre along the Danube, sits this historic town full of trees and intriguing little streets to explore. It dates back 9 centuries, but I have to admit, that it took me 6 years and the writing of the last edition of this book to explore this little beauty. According to legend, there was a monk hermit, Laszlo, who lived in the forest in what is now known as Vác. He prophesied that Prince Géza would win the battle against King Solomon. The prince and the monk came upon a wondrous sight, a deer with candles on its horns. After seeing this, Géza decided to establish a church on this site making it a bishopric, Vác.

ESSENTIALS

For information on getting to **Vác,** see earlier in this chapter. When you leave the train station, you will find that there is only one street leading away from it. Don't be disheartened by the mundane architecture of the shops that fill the street, thinking you got off at the wrong station. Walk straight down Széchenyi utca for about 15 minutes until you run into Március 15 tér, where you will find a number of interesting buildings with history to share. **Tourinform** is located at Március 15 tér 17 (*C* **27/316-160;** www. tourinformvac.hu). As they say, opening hours are "flexible" depending on tourist season. Claims are that the hours are 9am to 5pm weekdays, 10am to 2pm Saturday. My bet is that the tourism people close early when the season is over, although officially the hours are year-round. I don't cover places to stay since the town is small and conveniently located to Budapest. If you have a desire to stay overnight, check with Tourinform for information on accommodations.

EXPLORING THE TOWN

The beauty of this city is that you can see quite a bit for very little money at all. Starting with the main square at **Március 15 tér ★★★**, the center promenade was completely renovated in 2006 according to the design of architect László Sáros, an Ybl Miklós (architectural) Award winner. The huge square is a pleasant area with places to sit and relax by the peaceful fountain, and glass flooring. The square was an important commerce center way back to the Middle Ages. The dominant building on the square now is **White Friar's Church ★★** at Március 15 tér 24. It was built in the 18th century by the Dominican order of priests. Decorated in baroque-rococo style, the inside is highly ornate in bright colors. However, the statues are white, reflecting the white habits that Dominicans wear. What makes this church extra special is what was found underneath it. In 1995, when doing reconstruction work, workers found a secret crypt with several mummies inside. Final excavations found that walling up the entrance created an ideal climate to maintain the integrity of 262 coffins and their inhabitants. The exhibition is available to view at the **Memento Mori ★★★** (*C* **27/500-750**) in the cellar of the house at Március 15 tér 19. The museum is open Tuesday through Sunday 10am to 6pm, but closed in winter. Admission is 1,000 Ft, 500 Ft for students. On the side of the church is a statue of **St. Hedwig** with a three-stage fountain at her feet. St. Hedwig is the patron saint of the Danube and Vác is at the heart of it. St. Hedwig was born in 1373, the third and youngest daughter of the Hungarian-Polish king Louis the Great. She had a passion for helping the poor, the ill, the orphaned, and the widowed.

As you approach Március 15 tér 20, you will see the medieval building was once a private residence, renovated in baroque style and from 1170 operated as a hotel. The front is an eclectic style and the **Wine Museum** was established here in September 2006. It is open 10am to 5pm Monday through Friday. But what caught my attention was the **Chocloteria** in the same building. Operating as a cafe, it has a large selection of chocolates, pastries, coffees, and teas. It is open Monday through Thursday 9am to 8:30pm, Friday through Saturday 9am to 9:30pm, and Sunday 10am to 8:30pm. The building also houses a public gallery free to the public. Outside is the **Bell Pavilion** with a glockenspiel that plays every hour.

Walking down the square first you will come to **City Hall** located at Március 15 tér 11, considered the best baroque building in Vác. Above the front door is a wrought-iron balcony. On the frontage is a coat of arms of the town. Three statues sit above this with the Greek goddess of Justice in the center with two reclining women on either side; one holds the nation while the other holds the family crest of an important family. Strolling farther you will see the **Hospital of Mercy** and the **Greek Catholic Chapel** at Március 15 tér 7–9. The small chapel is worth a peek; although you cannot enter it, you can view it through the glass windows. Next at Március 15 tér 6, you will find the **András Chazár Education Institute for Deaf-Mutes.** This was the first school of its kind in Hungary, established in 1802. Before that, the building housed a bishopric palace, a school for religious orders, a cloister, and then a girls' school. Across from this you will find the former **Palace of the Great Provost** at Március 15 tér 4, a medieval house that was rebuilt in baroque style in the second half of the 18th century. The front is decorated with ionic offsets, and a triangular frontal piece at the top. It houses the clerical art collection of the former owner. If you continue down the square you will come to the **Vienna Town Gate,** a modern stone structure closing off the square.

Leave the square to find other treasures in this small town. The **Triumphal Arch** ★★, the oldest baroque arch in Europe outside of France, sits at Köztáraság utca.

The **Cathedral of the Assumption** on Konstantin tér has an elegant facade designed by Isidore Canevale. It is the only building in Hungary that was inspired by Parisian revolutionary architecture. The interior is decorated with the paintings of F. A. Maulbertsch. At Géza Király tér is the **Franciscan or "Brown" Church** next to the castle, the oldest building in Vác, which faces the Danube waterfront park. The synagogue on Eötvös utca is a special building in the town. It was built by Abbis Cacciari, an Italian architect, in 1864 in romantic style. It was renovated in 2006.

A walk along the Danube will be a delightful peaceful time. The entire riverside is lined with trees and an extremely wide promenade; it boasts separate winding walking paths intertwined with resting areas, all along the side of sidewalks next to the street for a different stroll under the chestnut trees. Garden patches are dotted here and there where the flowers add color and beauty to the large boulevard. For children, there are a number of play areas that include swings and playhouses, where they can work off extra energy.

WHERE TO DINE

Desszert Szalon ★★★ (Finds)   As you face the Tourinform office, if you turn right and go all the way down the square, you will find award-winning pastries created by Mihályi László. The visual presentation is as delightful as the taste of the sweets. Truly some of the best pastry I have eaten in Hungary was at this shop.

Köztársaság út 21. No phone. Coffee 260 Ft–380 Ft; pastries 520 Ft–580 Ft. No credit cards. Mon–Thurs 9am–8pm, Fri–Sun 9am–9pm.

Főtéri Cukrászda ★★   Formerly the Nosztalgia pastry shop, the change of ownership has increased the quality of the goods. The selection of desserts is mouth-watering. Located right on the square, this is a place to people-watch or relax at a table by the fountain in good weather. Inside is decorated like an old-fashioned cafe with old pictures on walls covered with flocked wallpaper. Sit outside when weather permits to enjoy the square.

Széchenyi u. 2. (℗ **30/742–9229** (mobile phone only). Coffee 420 Ft–580 Ft; pastries 220 Ft–280 Ft. No credit cards. Daily 9am–9pm.

Mosolytár Kávéház ★★★ (Finds)   According to my student who lives in Vác, this name means something like "container for smiles." It is named for characters created by a famous Hungarian children's author, Sajdik Ferenc, whose art is featured from floor to ceiling and all for sale. He has written a series of books with "Pom-Pom," a tiny pompom-like creature that gets into many adventures. His style is far beyond children's illustration, so it is more like a gallery of fine art. In the second room, additional artists are displayed. Tables and chairs painted in primary colors, smaller than adult size, are filled with big people reliving the smaller person within.

Eszterházy u. 10. (℗ **20/947-8058.** Coffee 240 Ft–590 Ft. MC, V. Daily 10am–10pm.

Vácz Remete Pince ★★★ HUNGARIAN CONTEMPORARY On a warm sunny autumn day, my friend and I sat on the terrace outside this restaurant next to the hill-sloped garden filled with flowers. The menu was plentiful with choices and the food was creatively presented in a beautiful manner. Many Budapest restaurants could take a lesson. Be warned though that the portions are huge. Peeking inside, the two large rooms are decorated in dark wood furniture, with artificial greenery around the arched door-ways, giving them a cozy, homey feel.

Fürdő lépcső 3. (**©** **27/302-199.** Reservations recommended in summer. Main courses 1,390 Ft–2,690 Ft. MC, V. Daily noon–10pm.

---

4 VISEGRÁD ★

45km (28 miles) NW of Budapest

Halfway between Szentendre and Esztergom, Visegrád (pronounced *Vee*-sheh-grod) is a sparsely populated, sleepy riverside village, which makes its history all the more fascinat-ing and hard to believe. The Romans built a fort here, which was still standing when Slovak settlers gave the town its present name in the 9th or 10th century. It means "High Castle." After the Mongol invasion (1241–42), construction began on both the present ruined hilltop citadel and the former riverside palace. Eventually, Visegrád boasted one of the finest royal palaces ever built in Hungary. Only one king, Charles Robert (1307–42), actually used it as his primary residence, but monarchs from Béla IV in the 13th century through Matthias Corvinus in the late 15th century spent time in Visegrád and contributed to its development. Corvinus expanded the palace into a great Renaissance center known throughout Europe.

ESSENTIALS

For information on getting to **Visegrád,** see "Railing through the Danube Bend," earlier in this chapter. **Visegrád Tours,** RÉV u. 15 (**©** **26/398-160**; www.visegrad.org), is located across the road from the RÉV ferryboat landing. It is open daily 8am to 5:30pm; from November through March, but they conduct business from the associated hotel next door. The lively time is summer when there are historical recreations, but other times of the year are fine for a sedate vacation experience.

WHERE TO STAY

Good accommodations can be found at **Honti Panzió and Hotel,** Fő utca 66 (**©** **26/398-120**). Double rooms cost 50€ for the *panzio* and 65€ in the hotel, both with multi-night packages. All rates include breakfast and VAT, but not the 300 Ft tax per person per night; parking is provided.

EXPLORING THE PALACE & THE CITADEL

Once covering much of the area where the boat landing and Fő utca (Main Street) are now found, are the excavated remnants and restoration of parts of the **King Matthias Museum** ★★, at Fő u. 27 (**©** **26/398-026**; www.visegradmuzeum.hu). It consists of the 14th- and 15th-century palace that covers an area more than 500m (1,640 ft) in length and 150m (492 ft) in width at the foot of the hill. The terraced palace complex consists of three large units: the northern Matthias Palace, the Chapel, and the southern Beatrice Palace. The tower of the lower castle, known as **Solomon's Tower,** was built in the 13th century. Entrance to the palace is 1,040 Ft and 620 Ft for the tower. Students

An Annual Festival

Each summer on the second weekend in July, Visegrád hosts the **International Palace Tournament** ★★, an authentic medieval festival replete with dueling knights on horseback, medieval music, and dance. If you cannot make it to this fabulous event, you can enjoy a tournament on a smaller scale combined with a medieval dinner at 6pm on Thursday in July and August. For more information, contact Visegrád Tours at ℂ **26/398-160.**

receive a 50% discount. Both are open Tuesday to Sunday from 9am to 5pm, but the tower is closed from October 1 to April 30. The buried ruins of the palace, having achieved a near-mythical status, were not discovered until the 21st century.

The **Cloud Castle (Fellegvár)** ★★★ (ℂ **26/598-082**), a mountaintop citadel above Visegrád, affords one of the finest views you'll find over the Danube. Admission to the citadel is 900 Ft. It is open daily from 9:30am to 5:30pm from March 15 to October 14. The "City Bus," a van taxi that awaits passengers outside Visegrád Tours, takes people up the steep hill for a steep fare of 2,500 Ft apiece or 4,000 Ft for a round trip, if you stay a maximum of 30 minutes, otherwise, it is again 2,500 Ft. Note that it is not a casual walk to the citadel; consider it a day hike and pack accordingly with bottled water.

WHERE TO DINE

Nagyvillám Vadászcsárda (Big Lightning Hunter's Inn) HUNGARIAN   This restaurant is set on a hilltop featuring one of the finest views of the Danube bend, Fekete-hegy, infusing a leafy, countryside dinner with an elegant and warm atmosphere. Although vegetarians may struggle with a menu consisting mainly of meat and game dishes, it is nevertheless an extensive menu combining Mediterranean influences with Hungarian recipes using 12 varieties of wild forest mushrooms. If you can, reserve a window table to maximize the glorious view and make this a unique dining experience.

Fekete-hegy. ℂ **26/398-070.** Main courses 1,750 Ft–4,900 Ft. MC, V. Daily noon–11pm; winter hours it is suggested that you call.

Renaissance Restaurant ★★ ⓚ HUNGARIAN   This restaurant specializes in authentic medieval cuisine. Food is served in clay crockery without silverware, only a wooden spoon. Guests are offered Burger King–like paper crowns to wear. The decor and the lyre music enhance the fun, albeit openly kitschy atmosphere. This is perhaps the only restaurant in the whole country where you won't find something on the menu spiced with paprika, since the spice wasn't around in medieval Hungary. If you're big on the medieval theme, come for dinner on a Thursday (July and August), when a six-course "Royal Feast" (not so vegetarian-friendly) is served, following a 45-minute duel between knights. It is available for groups of not less than 30 people. However, if you call, they will include you in a group if one is scheduled. It's open daily, from noon to 10pm. Tickets for this special evening are handled by Visegrád Tours (p. 242). The duel gets underway at 6pm sharp.

Fő u. 11 (across the street from the MAHART boat landing). ℂ **26/398-081.** Set menu 4,500 Ft. V. Daily noon–10pm.

5 ESZTERGOM ★

53km (32 miles) NW of Budapest

Formerly a Roman settlement, **Esztergom** (pronounced *Ess*-tair-gome), was the seat of the Hungarian kingdom for 300 years. Hungary's first king, István I (Stephen I) renamed from Vajk by German priests, received the crown from the pope in A.D. 1000. He converted Hungary to Catholicism, and Esztergom became the country's center of the early church. Although its glory days are long gone due to invasions from the Mongols and later the Turks, it was rebuilt once again in the 18th and 19th centuries. This quiet town remains the seat of the archbishop primate, known as the "Hungarian Rome."

From Esztergom west all the way to the Austrian border, the Danube marks the border between Hungary and Slovakia, with an international ferry crossing at Esztergom. There's little to entice anyone to stay overnight here with Budapest so close, so I strongly recommend making this a day trip returning to Budapest at the end of the day.

ESSENTIALS

The station is on the outskirts of town, while the tourist information center is in the city center. The primary reason to take the trip at all is the cathedral, so just take bus nos. 1 or 6 to the Baszilika stop and walk up to the church. Buses depart from outside the train station and you can buy your ticket on the bus. Bus no. 6 tickets cost 100 Ft, but on our return to the station, when we were much closer, the ticket on bus no. 1 was 165 Ft. We realized they are two different companies.

EXPLORING THE TOWN

Balassa Bálint Múzeum   Sure to please history or royalty buffs, this small museum is loaded with historical tidbits of Esztergom, where royals reigned for centuries. They have a well-written handout in English to self-guide you through the exhibits.

Pázmány Péter u. 13. ✆ **33/412-584.** Admission 500 Ft adults, 250 students. Tues–Sun 9am–5pm.

Castle Museum   This museum is next door to the cathedral on the left, in the reconstructed Royal Palace. The palace, vacated by Hungarian royalty in the 13th century, was used thereafter by the archbishop. Although it was one of only two fortresses in Hungary that was able to withstand the Mongol onslaught in 1241 and 1242, it fell into disrepair under the Turkish occupation. The museum has an extensive collection of weapons, coins, pottery, stove tiles, and fragments of old stone columns; unfortunately, the descriptions are in Hungarian only. Outside the palace, sections of the fortified walls have been reconstructed. Besides the museum, entrance includes the waxworks and gemstone exhibits. Behind the museum, you can enjoy a panoramic view of the Danube overlooking Slovakia.

Szent István tér. ✆ **33/415-986.** Admission 840 Ft adults, 1,560 Ft family ticket, 1,560 Ft photo, 3,140 Ft video; special exhibits 550 Ft–1,000 Ft. Summer Tues–Sun 10am–6pm; winter Tues–Sun 9am–5pm.

Esztergom Cathedral ★★ **(Kids)**   This massive, neoclassical cathedral on Szent István tér on Castle Hill, is the largest church in Hungary. In good weather, it is a 3.5km (2 mile) walk, otherwise bus nos. 1 or 6. The cathedral is Esztergom's most popular attraction and one of Hungary's most impressive buildings. Built in the last century, it was to replace the original cathedral ruined during the Turkish occupation. The blue and red marble coloring in the church and chapel is striking, and it claims the world's largest

altarpiece painted on one continuous piece of canvas. The crypt, built in old Egyptian
style with a magnificent statue of an angel, is also the last resting place of bishops. The
cathedral **treasury** *(kincstár)* ★ contains a dazzling array of ecclesiastical jewels and gold
works. If you brave the ascent of the cupola, you're rewarded with unparalleled views of
Esztergom and the surrounding Hungarian and Slovakian countryside. There is a warning for the cupola that if you're agoraphobic, you should not risk it. Actually, it should
be if you're claustrophobic, as the staircase and walking areas are extremely narrow. If you
happen to be in town during the first week of August, don't miss out on one of the classical guitar concerts performed in the cathedral; the acoustics are said to be sublime. The
concerts are part of Esztergom's annual **International Guitar Festival** ★★.

Szent István tér. (*33/411-895.* Cathedral admission free; treasury 700 Ft adults, 350 Ft children; cupola
400 Ft; crypt 200 Ft. Cathedral summer daily 8am–7pm, winter daily 8am–4pm; treasury and crypt summer daily 9am–4pm, winter Tues–Sun noon–4pm, cupola summer daily 9am–4pm, closed in winter.

Keresztény Múzeum (Christian Museum) This museum, in the neoclassical
former primate's palace, houses Hungary's largest collection of religious art and the largest collection of medieval art outside the National Gallery in Budapest. The Lord's Coffin of Garamszentbenedek is probably the museum's most famous piece; the ornately
carved, gilded coffin on wheels was originally used in Easter celebrations.

To get to the museum, leave the basilica by the museum downward path and follow
it to the right. You will come to a souvenir shop. Turn right on that street, Mindszenty
József u. When you get to the next church, the museum is beyond it to the right. Don't
be fooled by the other building under renovation.

Mindszenty József tér 2. (*33/413-880.* www.keresztenymuzeum.hu. Admission 600 Ft adults; 300 Ft
children. Thurs–Sun Nov 1–Jan 1 and Mar 15–Apr 30 11am–3pm; Thurs–Sun May 1–Oct 31 10am–5pm.
Closed Jan and Feb.

WHERE TO DINE

Padlizsán Étterem ★★★ HUNGARIAN Creative specialties abound at this
homey restaurant behind the basilica. In warm weather, enjoy the view of the basilica
above the hill. Four of us dined here and each was impressed with our selection. At the
time, the service was scattered, but most likely due to a wedding inside.

Pazmány Peter u. 21. (*33/311-212.* Main courses 1,850 Ft–3,800 Ft. No credit cards. Mon–Thurs noon–
10pm, Fri–Sun noon–11pm.

For a few other cafes and snack stops you can try the limited selections on the main
square, **Széchenyi tér**.

The Lake Balaton Region & Sopron

First settled in the Iron Age, the Balaton region has been a recreation spot since at least Roman times. From the 18th century onward, the upper classes erected spas and villas along the shoreline. Not until the post-World War II communist era did the lake open up to a wider tourist base. Many large hotels along the lake are former trade union resorts built under the previous regime.

Lake Balaton may not be the Mediterranean, but it is the largest freshwater lake in Europe. For many years, it has attracted German and British tourists in droves as well as other European sun worshipers in smaller numbers, filling the lake's beaches. With each passing year, though, the love affair with the lake fades while the beauty of the Croatian beaches infiltrate the tourism market as the leading water-based destination in the region. Hungary has instituted a fierce marketing campaign to redevelop the lake's regional favor with tourists, since many of the small towns depend on tourism for their survival. Companies have developed watersports and wellness centers to revitalize the area with new offerings, but in spite of their efforts, foreign tourism is shrinking. In the past, the Balaton region was a Mecca for East Germans, before the wall came down, making German a common second language. English speakers who ventured here for vacations and reported back claimed to be inhibited by the inability to communicate in English. Natually, Hungarians are proud of their resort and will defend this spot as one of the best in Europe; many city dwellers own summer homes here. With that said, there are still many other places to see and enjoy, even if you are not a sun or water person. I do caution you to check the quality of the lake's waters near the time of your planned trip. Some years, the water level has been too low to support the many watersports it has become famous for and, at other times, there have been outbreaks of algae covering the water's surface in many tourist areas.

For the best of times, pick up a free copy of the ***Balaton Funzine*** available at Tourinform offices throughout the lake resorts. The seasonal Balaton issues are bilingual Hungarian/English and have all the latest information to enrich a visit to the lake region. Throughout the long summer, swimmers, windsurfers, sailboats, kayaks, and cruisers fill the warm and silky smooth lake. It is 80km (50 miles) long and 15km (9 miles) wide at its broadest stretch. Around the lake's 197km (122 miles) of shoreline, vacationers cast their reels for pike; play tennis, soccer, and volleyball; ride horses; and hike in the hills.

On the south shore, **Siófok** was established as a resort in 1891. It is considered one of the most important tourist centers in the region, and is frequented mostly by the youthful generation or those who love to party. Beachside hotels overflow all summer long with party people playing disco music that pulsates into the early morning hours. My students have warned me about having people stop here if they are post-college age. Even for some of them, it is too rowdy to be enjoyable. The most popular venue is the **Coca-Cola House** where there is nonstop music and dancing until dawn from the last week in June to the last week in August, making it the popular choice for the party animal that really doesn't care about the water adventures. According to my students, Budapest youth take the train to Siófok, party until the very wee hours, and then return to Budapest on the first train the next morning.

On a positive note, the town itself has an open-air exhibition with sculptures and monuments on public squares including the work of the contemporary Hungarian sculptor, Imre Varga (p. 142), who was born here in 1923.

For those of us who are post college and post party until the morning light, and families, the better choice may be the graceful north shore, and it's the region we cover in this section. *Note:* Here and there you will find little villages neatly tucked away in the rolling countryside, where the grapes of the popular Balaton wines ripen in the strong sun. Due to the needs of tourism, the area is becoming more and more commercialized with the small food vendors being pushed aside by modern restaurants.

The best way to see the area is to move westward along the coast, passing from one lakeside settlement to the next, and making the occasional forays inland into the rolling hills of the Balaton wine country.

You'll discover the **Tihany Peninsula,** a protected area whose 12 sq. km (4¾ sq. miles) jut out into the lake like a protruding nose. The city of **Keszthely,** sitting at the lake's western edge, marks the end of the northern shore area.

An annual cultural event called the **Valley of Arts**(Muvészetek Völgye) is held on the northern side of the lake, near **Kapolcs,** attracting thousands of local and international artists and travelers. It was started as a local project by a handful of Hungarian contemporary artists who settled down in Kapolcs, the center of six little adjacent villages in the gorgeous Káli valley. The 10-day-long arts event includes film, music, theater, visual art exhibits, and literature readings, and is held at the end of July, running through the beginning of August. Visit www.kapolcs.hu for information on exact dates from year to year. For general information on programs and services of just about any area of Balaton, see www.balaton-tourism.hu.

Balaton has an airport called FlyBalaton; however, in 2009 it was closed due to lack of airlines utilizing the airport. Ryanair was the major carrier, but it pulled out, leaving Lufthansa's minimal weekend flights from limited German destinations. The airport is closed indefinitely.

1 EXPLORING THE LAKE BALATON REGION

ESSENTIALS
Getting There & Getting Around

BY TRAIN   From Budapest, trains to the various towns along the lake depart from Déli Station (p. 250). A few express trains run from Keleti Station (p. 276) and hook around the southern shore to Keszthely only. All towns on the lake are within 1½ to 4 hours of Budapest by a *gyors* (fast) train, though the trip will take much longer on a *sebes* (local). The *sebes* trains are interminably slow, stopping at each village along the lake. Unless you're going to one of these little villages (sometimes a good idea, though we cover only the major towns in this section), try to get on a *gyors*. The number of trains to Balaton destinations is at their peak from the end of June to the end of August, then decrease in number for the "winter schedule."

BY CAR   From Budapest, take the M7 motorway south through Székesfehérvár until you hit the lake. Route 71 circles the lake. Driving directly to the lake from Budapest will

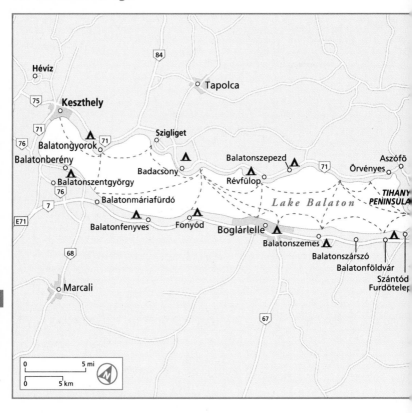

take approximately 1½ hours depending on where along the lake you are planning to visit and, of course, traffic. During the summer season, traffic can be congested.

If you are planning to settle in one area, a car is not needed. If you're planning to visit different points on Lake Balaton for more than a day or two, you should consider renting a car, to give yourself much greater mobility. The various towns differ enough from one another that you may want to keep driving until you find a place that really sparks your interest. Without a car, this is obviously more difficult. Also, wherever you go in the region, you'll find that private rooms are both cheaper and easier to get if you travel a few miles off the lake.

BY BOAT & FERRY   Passenger and car ferries on Lake Balaton allow you to travel across the lake as well as between towns on the same shore. The boat routes are extensive, and the rates are cheap, but they are considerably slower than surface transportation. All major towns have docks with departures and arrivals. A single ferry (*komp*) running between Tihany and Szántód lets you transport a car across the width of the lake. Children aged 3 and under travel free, and those 13 and under get half-price tickets.

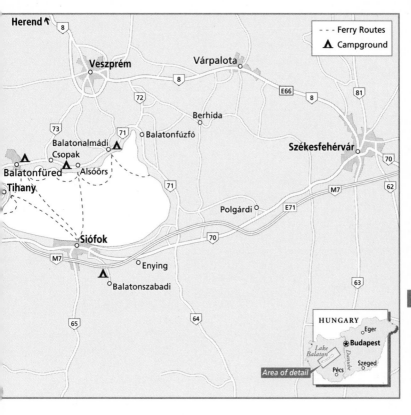

All boat and ferry schedule information and rates are listed in English at www.balatonihajozas.hu/en/menetrend.htm. The **Balaton Shipping** office in Siófok (© **84/310-050**) and local tourist offices all along the lake also have schedules and other information.

BY BUS   Once at the lake, you might find that buses are the best way of getting around locally. Buses will be indispensable, of course, for those who have taken the train to the lake, if you take private-room lodging a few miles away from the lake.

WHERE TO STAY

Hotel prices are unusually high in the Lake Balaton region, because many are transforming into health spas to attract tourism. Many local families rent out a room or two in summer as **private rooms**, I especially recommend private rooms as the lodging of choice in this area if you're not worried about communication issues. Most are clean and will give you the opportunity to get to know the local population. You can reserve a room through a local tourist office (addresses are listed under each town) or you can just look for the ever-present SZOBA KIADÓ (or ZIMMER FREI) signs (meaning vacancy) hanging on most front gates in the region. Note the language of the sign will be a clue as to which languages they speak. When you take a room without using a tourist agency as the intermediary, prices are generally negotiable. In the height of the season, you shouldn't have to pay more than 10,000 Ft for a double room within reasonable proximity of the lake. Many budget travelers pitch their tents in **lakeside campgrounds** all around the lake. Campgrounds are generally quite inexpensive, and their locations are well marked on maps. All the campgrounds have working facilities, but are probably not as clean as many people are accustomed to.

2 EN ROUTE TO LAKE BALATON: VESZPRÉM ★★

116km (72 miles) SW of Budapest

Just 16km (10 miles) from Lake Balaton, **Veszprém** (pronounced *Vess*-praym) surely ranks as one of Hungary's most charming and vibrant small cities, and it's the ideal starting point for a rail tour of Lake Balaton's northern shore. History and modern living are delightfully combined in this little city. The self-contained and well-preserved 18th-century baroque Castle District spills effortlessly into a typically modern city center, distinguished by lively wide-open, pedestrian-only plazas.

The history of Veszprém, like the scenic Bakony countryside that surrounds it, is full of peaks and valleys. According to local legend, Veszprém was founded on seven hills, like Rome. The seven hills are: Várhegy (Castle Hill), Benedek-hegy (St. Benedict Hill), Jeruzsálem-hegy (Jerusalem Hill), Temetőhegy (Cemetery Hill), Gulyadomb (Herd Hill), Kálvária-domb (Calvary Hill), and Cserhát (no translation).

King Stephen (István) I defeated the armies of his chief opponent, Koppány, near Veszprém in an effort to make Hungary a Christian nation. Hence, Veszprém became the seat of the first Episcopal See in 1009. This was the favorite city of King Stephen's queen, Gizella. The city is often called the City of Queens. It was completely destroyed during the course of the long Turkish occupation, the Habsburg-Turkish battles, and the subsequent Hungarian–Austrian independence skirmishes. The reconstruction of Veszprém commenced in the early 18th century, though the castle itself, blown up by the Austrians in 1702, was never rebuilt. The baroque character of that era today attracts thousands of visitors who pass through each year.

ESSENTIALS

GETTING THERE Fifteen trains depart daily from Budapest's Déli Station and five from Keleti Station, for Veszprém. Only six of them are so-called direct (but still require a connection) taking as little as 1 hour and 45 minutes. It's 2½ hours or a longer trip if you don't plan wisely. Tickets cost 2,350 Ft for a direct train, while on other trains the fare is 2,150 Ft to 2,350 Ft. If you're driving take the M7 to the lake, then take Route 71 to Route 72 leading into the city.

VISITOR INFORMATION **Tourinform,** Vár u. 4 (© **88/404-548**), is open in summer, weekdays from 9am to 6pm and weekends 10am to 4pm; in winter, weekdays 9am to 5pm, and closed weekends. **Ibusz**, Rákoczi u. 6 (© **88/565-540**), is open Monday through Friday from 8:30am to 4:30pm. Both offices provide information, sell city maps, and help with hotel and private-room bookings.

Most of Veszprém's main sights are clustered along Vár utca, the street that runs the length of the city's small, but charming Castle District.

Housed inside the 18th-century cannon's house, the **Queen Gizella Museum (Gizella Kiralyne Muzeum),** Vár u. 35 (no phone), has a fine collection of religious (Roman Catholic) art. Admission is 300 Ft for adults and 150 Ft for students. It is open daily from 10am to 5pm, May 1 through October 15.

At Vár u. 18, the vaulted **Gizella Chapel (Gizella-kápolna),** named for King Stephen I's wife, was unearthed during the construction of the adjoining Bishop's Palace in the 18th century. Today, it houses a modest collection of ecclesiastical art, but is best known for the 13th-century frescoes that, in various states of restoration, decorate its walls. Admission is 200 Ft for adults, 100 Ft for students. It is open Tuesday through Sunday 10am to 5pm from May 1 through October 31.

For a view of the surrounding Bakony region, climb the steps to the narrow observation deck at the top of the **Fire Tower (Tuztorony)** at the beginning of Vár u. The tower is famous for the enchanting melody it plays every hour on the hour. Although the foundations of the tower are medieval, the structure itself was built in the early 19th century. Enter via the courtyard of Vár u. 9, behind Óváros tér. Admission is 300 Ft for adults, 250 Ft for students. It is open daily from 10am to 6pm, March 15 through September 30.

In addition to Roman relics uncovered in the surrounding area, the **Laczkó Dezső Museum** (© 88/564-310), near Megyeház tér, features local folk exhibits (art, costumes, tools, utensils, and a detailed look at the prehistoric times of the area). There are also exhibits about the highwaymen of the region, celebrated figures from 19th-century Bakony who share some characteristics with the legendary outlaws of the American West. Admission is 700 Ft for adults and 350 Ft for children. From mid-March through mid-October, it is open 10am to 6pm, otherwise noon to 4pm. To get to the museum, walk directly south from Szabadság tér, where the old and new towns converge.

The **Veszprém Zoo (Kittenberger Kálmán Növény és Vadaspark)** is located at Kittenberger u. 15 (© **88/566-140;** www.veszpzoo.hu). It's open daily in summer 9am to 6pm until September 30, and in winter daily from 9am to 4:30pm until the end of February. Admission is 1,400 Ft for adults, 960 Ft for children. The zoo is set in a small wooded valley at the edge of the city center and boasts 550 animals from 130 species. The zoo's latest addition is a state-of-the-art Chimpanzee House where you will find other simians as well.

WHERE TO STAY

You'll pay some 2,500 Ft for a double room in a private home in Veszprém, and you can find a list of accommodations at www.veszpreminfo.hu. The room price usually does not include breakfast. You can book a private room through either of the tourist offices mentioned on p. 250.

Péter-Pál Panzió ★★ (© **88/328-091;** www.peterpal.hu), is conveniently located on Dózsa György u. 3; it's a 5-minute walk from the center of town. Don't be put off by the grungy building facade. Inside are 20 tidy but smallish rooms with a shower-only bathroom, and a TV. Insist on a room in the rear of the building, as the pension sits close to the busy road. The rate is 9,160 Ft for a double on an upper floor or 10,560 Ft for one leading to the garden. Breakfast is an additional 800 Ft per day. Call ahead for reservations.

Herend: Home of Hungary's Finest Porcelain

About 16km (10 miles) west of Veszprém lies the sleepy village of Herend. What distinguishes this village from other villages in the area is the presence of the Herend porcelain factory, where Hungary's finest porcelain has been made since 1826.

Herend porcelain began to establish its international reputation as far back as 1851, when a dinner set was displayed at the Great Exhibition in London. Artists hand paint every piece, from tableware to decorative accessories. Patterns include delicate flowers, butterflies, and birds.

The **Porcelanium Visitors Center** features the newly expanded **Herend Museum** (© 88/261-801; www.museum.herend.com), which displays a dazzling collection of Herend porcelain. Both the minimanufactory and museum are open daily from April 14 to October 25, 9:30am to 4:30pm and Tuesday through Saturday from October 27 to April 11, 9:30am to 3:30pm. Museum admission only is 500 Ft for adults, 200 Ft for students. Minimanufactory and museum admission is 1,700 Ft for adults, 600 Ft for students or a family pass for two adults and two children at 3,600 Ft. The Porcelanium Visitors Center also has a coffeehouse and upscale restaurant. Food is, naturally, served on Herend china.

At the **Viktória Brand Shop**, you might find patterns that are unavailable in Budapest's Herend Shop. This factory store is open Monday to Friday, April 14 to October 25, 9:30am to 6pm. Saturday hours are 9:30am to 5:00pm and Sunday 9:30am to 4:30pm. October 27 to April 11 hours are Monday to Friday, 9:30am to 5pm and Saturday 9:30am to 2pm. Herend is easily accessible via bus from the Veszprém bus station—the destination "Herend" is indicated on the front of the bus you want. The ride takes 15 minutes and costs 350 Ft; the bus leaves every 15 minutes.

Hotel Veszprém (© 88/424-677; www.hotelveszprem.hu) is located just in the middle of the town located near one of the main roads, so traffic is consistently busy for most of the day. Double rooms are 9,600 Ft, but without a television is 600 Ft less. They have 73 rooms with a variation in size. Some have shared bathrooms.

Hotel Villa Medici ★★ (©/fax 88/590-070; www.villamedici.hu), at Kittenberger u. 11, is a modern, full-service hotel set in a small gorge on the edge of the city, next to Veszprém's zoo-park. There are 24 double rooms and two suites; each has a bathroom with shower and the usual hotel amenities. Rates are 28,500 Ft for a double room and 36,200 Ft for a suite. Breakfast is included. The hotel also features two restaurants, a pub, a wine cellar, a sauna, and a small indoor swimming pool. Check the website for package deals. The reception staff speaks English and will make tour arrangements for you. Major credit cards are accepted. Take bus no. 4 from the train station to the stop in front of Veszprém Hotel, and then change to bus nos. 3, 5, or 10. These buses will take you as far as the bridge overlooking the gorge. You can walk from there.

Veszprém does not have many dining options, but you should be able to find a satisfying meal at the following places:

Cserhát Étterem ★ (𝒞 **88/425-441**), housed in the huge structure at Kossuth u. 6, is an old-style *önkiszólgáló* (self-service cafeteria). You'll find this very popular cafeteria behind some clothing stores; go up the winding staircase inside the building. Hearty traditional meals are available for less than 500 Ft. The menu changes daily; you'll find it posted on a bulletin board on the wall inside the restaurant upstairs. It is open Monday through Friday from 10am to 6pm and Saturday 10am to 3pm.

Recommended for its exquisite view of the castle, **Oliva Étterem** at Buhim u. 14-16 (𝒞 **88/561-900**; www.oliva.hu) offers daily specials for 650 Ft–1,150 Ft. Open Monday to Thursday 11:30am to 11pm, Friday and Saturday 11am to midnight. During the summer, they offer live jazz music in the garden.

For something more upscale, **Villa Medici Étterem** (in the hotel of the same name), at Kittenberger u. 11 (𝒞 **88/590-072**), is *the* place. It's expensive for Hungary but worth it. Main courses here are between 3,500 Ft and 5,500 Ft. Villa Medici serves Hungarian/Continental cuisine daily from noon to 11pm.

---

3 KESZTHELY ★★

187km (117 miles) SW of Budapest

KESZTHELY

Keszthely (pronounced *Kest*-hay), which sits at the western edge of Lake Balaton, is one of the largest towns on the lake, and is easily reached by rail from both Budapest and other lake towns. Although Keszthely was largely destroyed during the Turkish wars, the town was rebuilt in the 18th century by the Festetics, an aristocratic family that made Keszthely their home during World War II. The town's main sites all date from the days of the wealthy Festetics clan.

Essentials

GETTING THERE Eleven daily trains depart Budapest's Déli Station and 10 from Keleti Station for Keszthely; additional InterCity (IC) trains also make the journey daily, but are much longer. If the only city you plan to visit on Lake Balaton is Keszthely, take the IC. They are no longer as quick as in the past, but they are air-conditioned and cleaner (trip time: 3½ hours). A reserved seat is required at the time of booking. The trip costs 3,650 Ft to 4,760 Ft, depending on time of day and the train. Other trains can take up to 5 hours.

If you're heading to Keszthely station out of Szigliget, you can hop on any of the 12 daily trains in normal hours or others in the wee hours. Make sure, however, to consult a timetable before leaving, as there's no direct service and where you choose to transfer can seriously affect your journey time from a very reasonable 47 minutes to a ridiculous 2½ hours. Tickets cost 560 Ft.

The train station is on the southeastern edge of the town, but it's a scenic walk that takes about 10 minutes. You can also take a taxi from the main square to the station for less than 900 Ft.

For information, stop in at **Tourinform**, at Kossuth u. 28 ((C)/fax **83/331-4144;** www.keszthely.hu), in the city's former town hall. From the train station, walk up Mártírok utca, then turn right onto Kossuth utca, and walk north until you get to the city's main square (Fő tér). It's open daily from July 1 to August 31 from 9am to 7pm. The rest of the year, its scheduled hours of Monday to Friday from 9am to 5pm are at the discretion of the employees after determining the need during any particular week.

Top Attractions & Special Moments

The highlight of a visit to Keszthely is the splendid **Festetics Mansion** ★, at Szabadság u. 1 ((C) **83/314-194;** www.helikonkastely), in the center of the city, a short walk north of the Tourinform office. The baroque 18th-century mansion (with 19th-century additions) was the home of the Festetics family for generations. Part of the mansion (16 rooms in total) is now open as a museum. The main attraction is the ornate **Helikon library** featuring magnificent floor-to-ceiling oak bookcases, which were hand carved by a local master, János Kerbl. In a second building, the museum also features hunting gear and trophies of a bygone era. The museum is open July and August daily 9am to 6pm; the rest of the year it is open Tuesday through Sunday from 10am to 5pm. Admission is 1,800 Ft for adults and 900 Ft for students. A combination ticket for the Festetics Museum, Carriage Museum, and the Museum of Hunting is available for 3,200 Ft for adults and 1,600 Ft for students.

The mansion's opulent concert hall, the Mirror Gallery, is the site of **classical music concerts** almost every night throughout the summer (just two or three times a month from September to May). Concerts usually start at 8pm; tickets, ranging all the way from 1,000 Ft to 5,000 Ft apiece, are available at the door or earlier in the day at the museum cashier.

Another Keszthely museum worth a visit is the **Balaton Museum** ★, on the opposite side of the town center from the Festetics Mansion, at Múzeum u. 2 ((C) **83/331-2351;** www.freeweb.hu/bmuseum). This museum features exhibits on the geological, archaeological, and natural history of the Balaton region. It's open from May through October Tuesday through Sunday from 10am to 6pm, and November through April, Tuesday through Saturday from 9am to 5pm. Admission is 500 Ft, and students pay 250 Ft.

Located down the hill from Fő tér (Main Square), off Bem utca, is Keszthely's **open-air market.** The major selling days are Wednesday and Saturday. While dawn to 1pm, is the busiest time, some vendors stay open later into the afternoon. You'll find fruit and vegetables, spices, preserves, and honey, as well as household appliances, handmade baskets, and children's clothing.

Where to Stay & Dine

The center of Keszthely's summer scene, just like that of every other settlement on Lake Balaton, is down by the water on the "strand." Keszthely's **beachfront** is dominated by several large hotels. Regardless of whether or not you're a guest, you can rent windsurfers, boats, and other water-related equipment from these hotels.

A good hotel bet is the 232-room **Danubius Hotel Helikon** ((C) **83/388-9600;** www.danubiusgroup.com). The small but comfortable guest rooms offer balconies overlooking Lake Balaton and have all the necessary amenities. The resort also has an indoor swimming pool, sauna, massage parlor, and outdoor sun deck. Rates run from 17,000 Ft to 30,000 Ft for a double, including breakfast. Numerous special packages and off-season rates are available from its website.

Oázis Reform Restaurant, at Rákóczi tér 3 (© **83/331-1023**), is a self-service salad bar featuring adequate (if uninspired) vegetarian fare. There are cold and hot options and you can combine any salads you want. Go at lunchtime, when the food is freshest. Oázis is open Monday through Friday, 10am to 4pm. All food items cost 2,000 Ft per kilogram.

4 BADACSONY & SZIGLIGET ★

Badacsony is 160km (99 miles) SW of Budapest. Szigliget is 175km (108 miles) SW of Budapest.

Nestled in one of the most picturesque corners of Lake Balaton is Badacsony, an area that includes four villages noted for their beautiful vistas and some of the best wines of Hungary. The Badacsony area is dotted with wine cellars, and the tradition of viticulture and winegrowing dates back to the Celtic and Roman times. Other than wine tasting, Badacsony boasts walking trails where you can study the diverse basalt forms and the former quarry walls. You'll also find a 4km (2.5 mile) long circular trail, starting from the Kisfaludy House on the southern side of Badacsony Hill. Contact **Botanikai tanösvény Badacsony** (© **87/555-260;** www.bfnpi.hu) for guided tours.

One of the better-known vintners in Hungary is **Huba Szeremley,** founder of the Pannonian Wine Guild and whose Badacsony wines won one-third of the 2001 international competitions awarded to Hungarian wines. The best way to find out about Szeremley's regular wine tastings is to visit his restaurant, **Szent Orbán Borház és Étterem,** Badacsonytomaj, Kisfaludy S. u. 5 (© **87/431-382;** www.szeremley.com). It is open Friday to Sunday from noon to 10pm.

The **Borbarátok Panzió** ★★, Badacsonytomaj, Római út 78 (© **87/471-000;** www.borbaratok.hu), is a family-owned and -operated restaurant and hotel. It serves traditional Hungarian fare and also offers a wide variety of programs including wine tasting, harvest, fishing, and walking tours. During the summer months, different music programs are offered each night of the week. Main courses at the restaurant run from 1,040 Ft to 3,400 Ft. The restaurant is open daily 11:30am to 11pm in high season, and daily 11:30am to 10pm in low season. Room rates are based on per person, per night. Two beds 6,000 Ft, one double 8,500 Ft, extra bed 4,000 Ft. The Nepun apartment for four people is 19,500 Ft per day. Taxes are included.

SZIGLIGET

Halfway between the Tihany peninsula and Keszthely is the tiny village of Szigliget (pronounced *Sig*-lee-get), a picturesque Hungarian lake village with some magnificent castle ruins and an easy stopover point for rail travelers.

Essentials

GETTING THERE   Five daily trains that require at least one change of train along the way leave from Veszprém's rail station getting you to **Badacsonytördemic-Szigliget Station.** The trip can take as little as 3½ hours or as much as 4½ hours depending on the train you catch and how many connections you need to make (there is no direct train service). InterCity trains (you must make a reservation!) are available for at least part of the route, but, in this case, won't get you to Szigliget any faster than some of the *gyors* trains because you have to make a number of connections.

It is a 20-minute bus ride to Szigliget from the train station. Each arriving train is met by a bus, which stops on the platform right outside the station building. The destination of the buses is Tapolca, and you get off the bus at the stop near the beach in Szigliget village center (the village itself is tiny and easily traversed on foot).

VISITOR INFORMATION   **Natur Tourist** 97 Bt. ((C) **87/461-197**), in the village on Strand 1, will assist in booking private rooms. They are open daily from 9:30am to 6pm. There are also ZIMMER FREI signs along the roads.

Top Attractions & Special Moments

Szigliget is marked by the fantastically preserved ruins of the 13th-century **Szigliget Castle,** which stand above the town on **Várhegy (Castle Hill).** In the days of the Turkish invasions, the Hungarian Balaton fleet, protected by the high castle, called Szigliget home. You can hike up to the ruins for a splendid view of the lake and the surrounding countryside; look for the path behind the white 18th-century church, which stands on the highest spot in the village.

If you really enjoy **hiking**, you might take a local bus from Szigliget (the bus station is in the village center) to the nondescript nearby village of **Hegymagas,** about 4.8km (3 miles) to the north along the Szigliget–Tapolca bus route. The town's name means Tall Hill, and from here you can hike up **Szent György-hegy (St. George Hill).** This marvelous vineyard-covered hill has several hiking trails, the most strenuous of which goes up and over the rocky summit.

The lively **beach** at Szigliget provides a striking contrast to the quiet village. In summer, buses from neighboring towns drop off hordes of beachgoers. The beach area is crowded with fried-food and beer stands, ice-cream vendors, a swing set, and a volleyball court.

Szigliget is also home to the **Eszterházy Wine Cellar,** ((C) **06/20-414-4853** mobile phone only; www.eszterhazypince.hu/en) the largest wine cellar in the region.After a hike in the hills or a day in the sun, a little wine tasting just might be in order. Natur Tourist (p. 256) can provide you with the best directions, as getting here can be a bit confusing. Tours of the cellar are offered only for organized groups; others can drop in and sample the wares. The hours are by prior arrangement. Charges are based on services requested.

Where to Stay

Szőlőskert Panzió ((C) **87/461-264**) on Vadrózsa utca, might be the best option for a stay, given its close proximity to the beach, which is just 387m (1,270 ft) away. Situated on the hillside amid lush terraces of grapes, the pension is open only in summer. A double is 9,500 Ft and includes breakfast.

SIDE EXCURSION TO SÜMEG

If you are staying in either Keszthely or Hévíz and have lots of time, you may want to take an excursion to the small town of Sümeg, a half-hour drive north of Balaton. The main attraction here is the **Fortress of Sümeg** ((C) **87/550-166**; www.sumegvar.hu). Hours change with the season from year to year, so call ahead. Originally constructed in the 13th century, it was subsequently rebuilt 300 years later. The fortress fended off the Turks, but was set ablaze in the 18th century by the Habsburgs. Today, perched high on the hilltop, the fortress hosts performances that take you to the Middle Ages, with horse shows, folk dances, and reenactments of knightly tournaments with period weaponry. At the foot of the hill is the **Hotel Kapitány** at Tóth Tivadar u. 19 ((C) **87/550-166;** www. hotelkapitany.hu), a hotel and wellness center which includes saunas, fitness areas, and

Kids An Excursion to the Thermal Lake in Hévíz

If you think the water of Lake Balaton is warm, just wait until you jump into the lake at **Hévíz** ★★ Kids (pronounced *Hay*-veez), a resort town about 8km (5 miles) northwest of Keszthely. Here, you'll find the largest thermal lake in Europe and the second largest in the world (the largest is in New Zealand), covering 16,723 sq. m (180,005 sq. ft).

The lake's water temperature seldom dips below 85°F (29°C), even in the most bitter spell of winter. Consequently, people swim in the lake year-round. Hévíz has been one of Hungary's leading spa resorts for more than 100 years, and it retains a distinct 19th-century atmosphere.

While the lakeside area is suitable for ambling, no visit to Hévíz would be complete without a swim. An enclosed causeway leads out into the center of the lake where locker rooms and the requisite services, including massage, float rental, and a *palacsinta* (crepe) bar, are housed. **Note:** There is no shallow water in the lake, so take care.

Hévíz is an easy 15 minutes by bus from Keszthely (there's no train service), which costs 210 Ft. Buses (labeled "Hévíz") depart every 10 minutes during the day from the bus station adjacent to the train station. The entrance to the lake is just opposite the bus station. You'll see a whimsical wooden facade and the words "*tó fürdó*" (Bathing Lake). They have a complicated pricing structure, but 2,100 Ft will buy you 3 hours, 2,950 Ft for 5 hours, and 3,700 for all day. Entry includes the use of a locker. You are given a "watch" to keep track of your time. If you exceed your time limit, it is 10 Ft a minute thereafter.

massage. The complex also includes a Turkish bath, restaurants, and a conference room. Note that the town is also known for Austrian painter, F. A. Maulbertsch's beautiful 18th-century frescos, located in the baroque **Church of the Ascension,** at Szent Imre tér.

GETTING THERE   Some local hotels and travel agencies offer day trips to Sümeg, including a medieval dinner and show, for an average of 10,000 Ft.

5 LAKE BALATON'S SOUTHERN SHORE

If you're in that youthful energy category of spending long days in the sand and surf and then want to follow it up by spending long nights being the party animal, then the town of Siófok at the southern shore of Lake Balaton is where it is at. After all, a million Hungarian students can't be wrong. Or could they?

Siófok, located at the lake's southeastern end, is known as the capital of Lake Balaton; it is also the largest resort town on the lake. Siófok's railway station was completed in 1863, thus 1863 is considered to be the year of Siófok's birth as a holiday resort, with Budapest now connected by rail to the resort town. In 1865, Siófok, a settlement of not more than 200 houses with 1,500 inhabitants was permitted to attain the status of market-town. As the saying goes, the rest is history. It started to become overrun with holiday-makers during the summer season.

Siófok is the star attraction for the young, active crowd of mostly students and teenagers who flood the town's beaches from sunrise to sunset and then move en masse to the town's discos until the sun rises yet again. Large, modern, expensive hotels line the shore and more are being developed. If you are looking for a quiet beach experience, you will not find it here, but you will find windsurfing, tennis, and boating. English will be at a premium; although many younger Hungarians may speak English to some degree, they are not as tempted to indulge when surrounded by their fellow native speakers. Some older people may speak some German, learned in the communist times. This could be an isolating experience and difficult within the town itself once you leave the hotel.

While this city is no cultural capital, the architecture of some of the older buildings is impressive. Note the old railway station, and the many villas around the **Gold Coast** (Aranypart). You will also find some important contemporary buildings, notably the Evangelical Church, designed by one of Hungary's most appreciated architects, **Imre Makovecz**—who is known for his use of wood and light in his structures that dot the country. Most of the wood used for the building was imported from Finland.

Siófok has also partaken in the major marketing campaign that includes all of the popular resorts of Lake Balaton. It is trying to bring back the throngs of visitors that have abandoned the lake for the rediscovered beaches along Croatia's coastline. Due to the development of tourism infrastructure, the prices have made this destination less of a bargain during high season, but the weakening global economy and the fact that "wellness centers" have been popping up like unwanted gophers in a well-groomed yard, has put a noose around their neck, so look for bargains if you go to this area. Remember that their published rates are at an unrealistically high level. Ironically, Siófok is being rejuvenated by constructing new wellness centers that cater to rejuvenation procedures, and by the allure of the warm-water springs of Hungarian fame. These facilities will be 365-day operations in an attempt to stimulate the economy of the region as an all-year-round attraction.

For more information on the southern shore, contact **Tourinform** (☎/fax **84/315-355;** www.siofokportal.com) or pick up the *Balaton Funzine* free at any Tourinform office.

Where to Stay

Siófok is wall to wall with mostly Hungarian tourists during the summer months. You will find a wide variety of lodging options including large hotels and resorts from the Gold Coast to the east of the center of town, and from the **Silver Coast** (Ezüstpart) to the west. Additional accommodations can be found on the city's website at www.siofok portal.com.

Pampering is always at the top of my list of things to do in a resort area. Shop around, you have plenty of choices, but one suggestion is the **Hotel Azúr** ★★, Vitorlás u. 11 (☎ **84/501-400;** www.hotelazur.hu), one of the more comfortable, plush, and welcoming hotel and wellness centers in town, however, competition has been springing up on a regular basis. It has 222 air-conditioned rooms, many with balconies. The pools are large, and it has a fitness room, sauna, massage club, Finnish saunas, beauty salon, and thermal pools. The whole complex is extremely tasteful. Rates are 104€–202€ for a double room depending on the time of the year. Breakfast and all taxes are included.

The **Hotel Residence** ★, Erkel Ferenc u. 49 (☎ **84/506-840;** www.hotel-residence. hu) with its 56 rooms also has an extensive list of services, including massages, gyms, baths, and aromatherapy. It is located 150m (492 ft) from the beach. Rates fluctuate greatly throughout the year running 28,640 Ft–40,640 Ft for a double room with break-fast included. The hotel has a good-size indoor swimming pool, a sauna, a massage club, Finnish saunas, a beauty salon, and thermal pools.

Where to Dine

Try the **Sándor Restaurant** (© **84/312-829;** www.sandorrestaurant.hu), on Erkel F. u. 30, popular with locals for large portions of contemporary Hungarian food. If you're looking for more traditional Hungarian fare with live Gypsy music, try the **Csárdás Restaurant,** at Fő u. 105 (© **84/310-642**). The menu contains Hungarian fish and meat dishes, but they also have international and vegetarian options as well.

6 SOPRON

216km (134 miles) NW of Budapest

The gem of the northwestern border of Hungary is the city of **Sopron**. At the base of the Austrian Alps, it is only 60km (37 miles) from Vienna, 80km (49 miles) from Bratislava, and 220km (136 miles) from Budapest. It is filled with history and is the link between Hungary and its neighbors to the west.

At one time it was another province of those ubiquitous Romans; they called the city Scarbantia. Hungarians claimed the land during the 9th century after the Romans had abandoned the territory. The city walls were fortified and a castle was built. It wasn't until the 11th century that the city received its Hungarian name, after a castle steward named Suprun.

During the Ottoman invasion in 1529, the Turks ravaged the city, but did not settle here. This caused those from other parts of the country to flee here away from where the Turks did settle, thereby increasing the importance and population of Sopron. Jumping ahead to 1676, fire ruined the city destroying all of the medieval buildings only to be replaced over decades with the baroque buildings you see today.

Good times did not last for long for the good people of Sopron. In 1703, when they refused to be part of the revolt planned by Francis II Rákócz, the Hungarian aristocrat who wanted to break from Habsburg rule, the armies of István Bocskai infiltrated and ruined the city.

During World War II the city was bombed a few times, but after the war, with the demise of the Austro-Hungarian empire, four western counties that were part of Hungary were awarded to Austria through the Treaties of St. Germain (1919) and Trianon (1920). Due to local unrest, Sopron and eight other villages surrounding it, held a public election in 1921 and decided to be part of Hungary instead of Austria. Due to this, Sopron is referred to as "The most faithful city of Hungary." Memorializing this decision, found on the south side of the **Firewatch Tower** (p. 263) stands the "Gate of Faith." Once being part of the Austro-Hungarian empire, the German name of the city is Ödenburg. This is also the reason you may be surprised to find that the street signs are bilingual: Hungarian on top and German underneath.

Sopron is a city to savor at a slow pace, not one to try to rush through. Like a fine wine, you need to let it sit on your tongue to allow all of the senses to appreciate it. Walking the narrow streets within the city, you will find not only pleasant architecture, but often whimsical wall art popping out from the side of businesses.

12

Sopron has a long history, but in more modern times, it played a pivotal role in ripping a hole in the Iron Curtain. Just outside of Sopron in a countryside meadow that held little significance, there was a barbed-wire fence erected in 1948 barring entry into Austria. It was at this spot on August 19, 1989 that the "**Pan-European Picnic**" was organized. Flyers were spread by Hungarian organizers stating that on this date, a picnic was going to form, during which time a hole would be made in the barbed wire fence. Droves of people arrived from East German to Sopron; Hungary was an acceptable vacation destination for them during communist times. Dressed as peace demonstrators, they congregated.

Hungarian Prime Minister Miklós Nemeth received word of what was planned, but made the decision to allow the East Germans the ability to reach freedom through this area of Hungary. **Arpad Bella** was the Hungarian guard in charge at the border on this day. He too received a word that something was afoot, but complete details were not available at the time, nor was he instructed as to what action he and the other guards were to take. Prime Minister Nemeth later stated that he intentionally did not give instructions in the hopes that Bella would do the right thing. Bella suddenly found he and the other guards were faced with hundreds of people, including a number of women and children. With only seconds to implement a plan, his choice was to let the people through the hole in the fence, which was being held open by the Austrian guards on the other side of the border. Those who made it through, were warmly greeted and welcomed to Austria and their freedom. Exhausted with emotions, some people continued running well beyond the border not yet comprehending that they were now safe. Others fell on the Austrian soil for a cathartic cry, followed by the realization that they had been liberated. One popular story is that a student did not believe this simple movement through the wire was all it took, so he crept through the fence repeatedly simulating a more dangerous getaway.

On the Austro–Hungarian border, a small section of the famed barbed-wire fence celebrating the event is in evidence. Hungary's western border finally opened on September 11, 1989, allowing about 50,000 East German refugees to have a free access way to Austria. This lasted until October 7, without any Soviet intervention. West Germany and its communist East were border free by November 1989 when the Berlin Wall that segregated them came falling down.

Commemorating the 20th anniversary, on August 19, 2009, German Chancellor Angela Merkel, Hungarian President Laszlo Solyom and former Prime Minister Miklós Nemeth assembled with hundreds of survivors of this escape along with their families. They dedicated a statue as a marker to remember this historical event. The open-air exhibition is open all year. Tours can be arranged in Sopron or through the hotels.

Wine lovers should be aware that Sopron is a significant wine-producing region in Hungary and is amongst the few to make both red and white wines. Red wines use the Kékfrankos (Blue Frankos) grapes, a late-ripening, and dark-skinned grape rich in tannin, yet with a spicy quality. Traminer or Gewürztraminer grapes are used for the white varieties. These grapes are pink to red in skin color, usually producing a semi-dry wine. There are only a couple of wineries that offer tours, but this often changes, so it is best to check with Tourinform for the latest tour information at the time of your visit.

Just as all of Hungary is well known for its thermal baths with much of the country sitting on natural springs with differing water compositions lending themselves to healing properties, Sopron is no exception. There are two thermal baths famous for their water's chemical make-up. See p. 264 for more information.

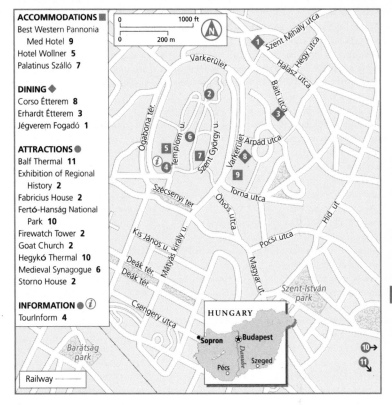

ACCOMMODATIONS ■
Best Western Pannonia
   Med Hotel **9**
Hotel Wollner **5**
Palatinus Szálló **7**

DINING ◆
Corso Étterem **8**
Erhardt Étterem **3**
Jégverem Fogadó **1**

ATTRACTIONS ●
Balf Thermal **11**
Exhibition of Regional
   History **2**
Fabricius House **2**
Fertő-Hanság National
   Park **10**
Firewatch Tower **2**
Goat Church **2**
Hegykő Thermal **10**
Medieval Synagogue **6**
Storno House **2**

INFORMATION ● *(i)*
TourInform **4**

HUNGARY

•Sopron   ☆ Budapest

Pécs   Szeged

Railway

ESSENTIALS
Getting There

BY TRAIN   Trains from Budapest are frequent, but not all are created equal. Trains leave from both Déli and Keleti Stations with the trip taking from 2½ to 4 hours. Only 7 out of 24 trains are direct connections. Train tickets cost 3,950 Ft to 5,880 Ft depending on the time of day. Direct trains require reservations at an additional cost of 520 Ft. Like most destinations in Hungary, Budapest is the hub, so from most other cities, you will have to return to Budapest before heading to Sopron. From Vienna, there is a train approximately every 2 hours; however, rates are not available. The Sopron train station is conveniently located close to the city center, only a 15-minute walk away.

VISITOR INFORMATION   **Tourinform**, Liszt Ferenc u. 1 (© **99/517-560**; www.sopron. hu), is open in summer Monday to Friday 9am to 5pm, Saturday 10am to 4pm, Sunday 10am to 2pm. Winter hours run from mid-September to April. They are Monday to Friday 9am to 5pm, Saturday 9am to noon.

All three hotels listed are located in the city center and rates include taxes and breakfast, but not the local tax of 1½€ per person/per night. With the city being small, it is easy to walk to all of the sights. Many are located on Fő tér. Buses will only be needed if you travel to the thermals or the forest outside of Sopron.

If you envision a dental vacation is in your future, head to the **Best Western Pannonia Med Hotel** at Várkerület 75 (© **99/513-652**; fax 99/340–766. ww.pannoniahotel.com). The hotel was built in a classic style at the end of the 19th century and sports 62 rooms. Owned by a dentist, there is a dental clinic on the second floor with a full range of dental services available. The hotel accommodates both smokers and nonsmokers on separate floors with comfort and classic rooms, the latter are furnished with antiques. For families, there are apartments with four beds. All rooms are of a size inviting a relaxed stay. Classic rooms are 80€–100€, comfort 110€–140€, apartments 120€–155€.

Set on a cozy cobblestone street is **Hotel Wollner** ★★ Templom u. 20. (© **99/ 524-400**; fax 99/524-401, www.wollner.hu). Formerly a baroque palace dating 300 years, the 18 rooms are spacious with sleigh beds and mattresses to hug your body making for a delicious night's sleep. An inner courtyard with tables and chairs is where smokers have to congregate as all rooms are nonsmoking. At the back of the hotel, one floor up from the entrance is a lush green relaxation garden with chairs and tables. Double rooms are 80€–90€, triples are 100€–110€. The hotel has its own restaurant and a small bar.

Palatinus Szálló ★ Új u. 23. (© **99/523-816**; fax 99/523-817, www. palatinussopron. hu) sits on a triangle just off an inner courtyard walkway close to the Fire Tower. It offers 30 plain, simple, but extremely clean smallish comfortable rooms. Standard doubles are old fashioned, not having been remodeled. The superior doubles are more fresh and attractive. Rooms run from 30€–72€ for a double to an apartment for four people. All rooms are nonsmoking. Parking is available for eight cars at 4½€ per day.

WHERE TO DINE

The **Corso Étterem** (**Value**) Várkerület 73 (© **99/340-990**) is open Monday to Saturday 11am–10pm, Sunday 11am–4pm. Tucked away in a courtyard, you have to walk up the ramp to find this little hideaway dining venue. We attempted to dine here on a Sunday, but every table both inside and on their terrace was full. Looking over people's shoulders as we hunted for a table, we noticed the generous portions. This and a peak at the menu prices (all under 980 Ft) made it obvious why they were filled to capacity. Note that they do not speak English and the menu is only translated into German.

Erhardt Étterem ★★★ is at Balfi u. 10. (© **99/506-711**). Serving times are Monday to Thursday 11:30am–11pm, Friday and Saturday 11:30am–midnight, Sunday 11:30am–10pm. The foundation of the building may date back to the 16th century, but the food and service are very modern. Weather permitting, sit in the garden courtyard area surrounded by historic wall fortifications. Inside the restaurant are delightful sectioned rooms for intimacy and privacy when dining. I highly recommend the turkey medallions stuffed with French plums and bacon, served with Princess potatoes. Not only did both of our dinners look like models from a gourmet magazine, the flavors would please the fussiest of chefs. They also offer wine tastings of Sopron wines in their wine cellar for small to large groups.

Jégverem Fogadó is conveniently located at Jégverem u. 1 (© **99/510-113**; www. jegverem.hu). An outer courtyard dining area is partially covered with a red tiled overhang along the perimeter. Inside, dining is pleasantly old fashioned. If you dine here, I suggest you avoid a starter as the meals are so humongous, you will have plenty of left- **263** overs. My layered potatoes with sausage also had two extra large pork cutlets on top and were served in a baking pan that could normally serve four. As good as it was, I could barely put a dent in it. Opening hours are Monday to Thursday 11am–11pm, Friday and Saturday 11am–midnight, and Sunday 11am–10pm.

EXPLORING THE CITY

Sopron is compact, making it easily accessible to see the majority of sights on foot and as you will see, many of them are on the same square. Unless noted, all museums share the same phone number (© **99/311-327**); they are all closed on Mondays.

Fabricius House on Fő tér 6 transcends to the days of the Roman settlers. Within the building you will find three exhibits. Artifacts from the Roman town of Scarbantia, what is now Sopron, are located in the cellar. Included are head stones, altar stones, and sar-cophagi amongst other uncovered treasures. On two floors at the back of the building is "Three-thousand years on the amber road," which provides information about life and culture of the Illyrian, Celtic, and Romans who were settlers here moving forward to the conquering Hungarians and to modern times. Interior design of the 17th and 18th cen-tury is on exhibit on the street level and continues to the next floor up. Hours are April to September 10am–6pm and October to March 10am–2pm. Admission is 700 Ft for adults and 350 Ft for children 16 and under.

Firewatch Tower on Fő tér (no number) is the symbol of the city. Built upon the ancient Roman wall, it served as the north tower of the city from the 13th century onward. After the great fire of 1676, it was refurbished with a baroque roof and balcony added on. The foundation was damaged in 1893, so a wide main port was used to add stability. If you brave the 200 spiral stairs, your reward is a spectacular view of the city. Open April, September, October 10am–6pm; May to August 10am–8pm. Entrance is 700 Ft for adults and 350 Ft for children 16 and under.

Goat Church sits on Fő tér (no number, but it cannot be missed). Franciscans built the church when they arrived in the area in 1280. It is considered an excellent example of Hungarian Gothic architecture. This Franciscan order was dissolved by József II in 1787. The church was later acquired by the Benedictine monks. It has been the site of many coronations and parliamentary sessions. The sanctuary still holds much visual appeal, but the rest of the church is in dire need of repair. On the south side through the church is the **Chapter House**, which served as a prayer house with an adjacent burial chapel. The Gothic religious art reveals the seven major sins within the leaf ornaments where there are hidden figures of human heads with animal bodies. Church hours are January 10 to April 15 8am–6pm; April 16 to September 30 8am–9pm. Chapter House hours are April to September 10am–noon and 1pm–6pm daily. October to March 10am–noon and 1pm–3pm daily. Free admission to both.

Medieval Synagogue (Új u. 22) was built in the 14th century, although Jews are believed to have settled here in the 13th century. There is a tympanum decorating the main door with two side consoles that date back to 1300. Inside is rich with motifs of grapes and leaves. Behind the main prayer room is the separate women's prayer room. Next to the synagogue are the remains of the ritual bath. There was once a school and refuge for travelers next door. Jews were forced to leave the area in 1526, causing the synagogue to fall into ruin. Open April to September 10am–6pm. Admission is 700 Ft.

Storno House and the Exhibition of Regional History are two separate exhibits, but are located at the same address at Fő tér 8. **Storno House** provided accommodations for King Matthias in 1482–83 when he attacked Vienna. Franz Liszt held two concerts here in 1840 and 1881. The Storno family, originally from Switzerland, acquired the building in 1872. Ferenc Storno was a chimney sweep, too poor to receive education for his artistic talents. After living and working in Sopron, his talents were discovered and became his legacy. On the street level of Storno House is the **Exhibition of Regional History** featuring the complete history of the Sopron area. Hours are the same for both museums, April to September 10am–6pm and October to March 2pm–6pm. Admission to Storno House is 1,000 Ft for adults, 500 Ft for children, photo ticket 200 Ft; Exhibition admission is 600 Ft for adults, 300 Ft for children 16 and under.

EXPLORING THE ENVIRONS

Thermals

Two of the most famous thermals in the area are just outside of Sopron. **Balf Thermal** (Fürdő sor 8. *✆* **99/314-060**) is only 6km (3.7 miles) outside the city. With the high hydrogen sulfide content of the water, it is used as a curative for rheumatic and a range of motion diseases of the limbs. Medicinal baths and thermal areas are open Monday to Friday 7am–5pm and weekends 9am–5pm. Local buses leave Sopron plaza regularly with Balf as the destination. Tickets cost 500 Ft, purchasable from the driver. **Hegykő Thermal**, located in the village of Hegykl[da], is part of the Fertő-Hanság National Park and the Fertő/Neusiedlersee, a World Heritage Cultural Landscape. The hours are the same as Balf Thermal. Located 20km (12.5 miles) outside of Sopron, it is easily reached by public bus that shows Fertőd as the final destination. Bus tickets are 500 Ft.

Fertő-Hanság National Park at Rév-Kócsagvár Pf 4, Sarród (*✆* **99/537-620**; www. ferto-hansag.hu) is located outside of Sopron, but it is adjacent to the Austrian Neusiedler National Park. Both are World Heritage Sites. This park is Hungary's seventh World Heritage Site, being so-named in 2001. Crossing the border of the two countries is the world's second-largest steppe lake, which covers a total of 315 sq. km (122 sq. miles), with only 75 sq. km (30 sq. miles), on the Hungarian side. Separated into three zones for environmental protection, the tourist zone has walking and biking trails. The park is known not only for the beauty of the forest, but also as a sanctuary for distinctive plant and animal life. It is said the air here has added oxygen coming from the Alps. Guided tours are available from April to December. Contact Sopron Tourinform (p. 261) for more information.

Fertőd

If you need a castle fix, the **Eszterházy Castle,** Bartók Béla 2 (no phone), should fit the bill. It is the third-largest historical building complex in Hungary. Referred to as the "Hungarian Versailles," this baroque-style complex was the home of Miklós Esterházy the "Glorious." Reconstruction started in 1763 and was completed in 1766. Miklós and his wife, Countess Margit Cziráky, rebuilt what was once a 20-room hunting lodge belonging to József Esterházy. The owner's death, compounded by World War II, brought decrepitude to the complex. On the exterior, the baroque style is exemplified with all of its ornamental glory present. Music lovers will appreciate that Joseph Haydn was in service to the family from 1766 to 1790, composing a number of his most famous pieces within these rooms. Tours through a portion of the interior are available, but you will not have access to all of the 126 rooms, which is most likely a good thing. You can freely walk the gardens and the grounds afterward. Open March 15 to October 31 Tuesday to Sunday 10am to 6pm; November 2 to March 14 Friday to Sunday 10am to 4pm. For more information about tours, contact Sopron Tourinform (p. 261).

13

Northeastern Hungary: Traveling into the Hills

Northeast of the Danube Bend is Hungary's hilliest region with the country's highest mountain, Matra Hill rising to 998m (3,274 ft). It also contains the country's smallest village, where the first Hungarian-language bible was written, and the oldest railway from the 19th century. Here you can visit the preserved medieval village of Hollókő; see remnants of the country's Turkish heritage in Eger, also known for its regional wines and the region of the famous Tokaji aszú wines; and explore the 23km (14 mile) cave system in Aggtelek.

1 HOLLÓKŐ: A PRESERVED PALÓC VILLAGE ★

102km (63 miles) NE of Budapest

The village of Hollókő (pronounced *Ho*-low-koo, meaning raven stone) is one of the most charming spots in Hungary hidden in the Cserhát hills. Legend has it that the lord of a castle kidnapped a beautiful maiden, whose nurse was a witch. The nurse made a pact with the devil for the girl's return. The devil's servants disguised themselves as ravens who took the stones of the castle away. The castle of Hollókő was built on top of the rock. Village history dates back to the 13th century; after the invasion by the Mongols, the castle was built on Szár Hill. This UNESCO World Heritage Site is a perfectly preserved, but still vibrant Palóc village with only 400 residents. The rural Palóc people speak an unusual Hungarian dialect, and have some of the more colorful folk customs and costumes (used for holidays only). They have been able to preserve some of their folkways partly due to their isolation. If you're in Hungary at Easter time, consider spending the holiday in Hollókő. Hollókő's traditional Easter celebration features townspeople in traditional dress and masses in the town church. When you see people in traditional dress, they are genuine, not a troupe of actors. You will sharpen your acting skills, since you will find less English speakers here than in larger cities. The websites below have no English links.

ESSENTIALS

GETTING THERE It is difficult to reach without a car. There is only one direct bus to Hollókő, which departs from Budapest's central bus station, **Stadionok Bus Station** (② 1/382-0888). It departs weekends only at 8:30am and takes about 2½ hours to reach the town if there is no traffic, but be warned, it could take as much as 3½. They don't stop for bathroom breaks either. The one-way fare is 1,750 Ft. Alternatively, you can take a bus from Árpád híd bus station in Budapest (② 1/412-2597) to Szécsény or Pásztó, where you switch to a local bus to Hollókő; there are four daily, but the trip will be longer. If you're **driving** from Budapest, take the motorway M3 as far as Hatvan, then along the main road turn off onto Route 21 in the direction of Salgótarján until you come to the junction for Hollókő. From here, it is a 17km (11 mile) drive.

VISITOR INFORMATION The best information office is the **Foundation of Hollókő,** at Kossuth Lajos út 68 (✆ **32/579-010;** www.holloko.hu). It's open in summer Monday to Friday 8am to 8pm and weekends 10am to 6pm; in winter, it's open Monday to Friday 8am to 5pm and weekends 10am to 4pm. You can also get information through **Nograd Tourist** in Salgótarján (✆ **32/310-660**) or through **Tourinform** in Szécsény, at Ady Endre u. 12 (✆ **32/370-777;** www.szecseny.hu).

SEASONAL EVENTS

At Easter, everyone in the village puts on ornamented folk clothes and during the 2-day celebration (Easter Monday is a holiday), the old Easter traditions of the village are revived. Folklore programs fill the day with displays of folk articles for purchase, artisans' presentations, food specialties, and games for children. On the last weekend in July, folk groups of Nógrád county and from other countries gather to perform on the open-air stage of the village for the **Palóc Szőttes Festival** ★. On the second Sunday of October for the **Vintage Parade,** the young people of the village walk along the main street in ornamented folk clothes, demonstrating that grape picking is over, celebrating that there will be wine in the next year, too.

EXPLORING THE VILLAGE

A one-street town, Hollókő is idyllically set in a quiet, green valley, with **hiking trails** all around. A restored 14th-century castle is perched on a hilltop over the village. In the village itself you can admire the 14th-century wooden towered church and the sturdy, traditional peasant architecture (normally seen only in stylized open-air *skanzen* museums, such as the one near Szentendre, p. 234), and observe the elderly women at work on their embroidery (samples are for sale). You can also visit the **Village Museum** at Kossuth Lajos u. 82, where exhibits detail everyday Palóc life starting in the early 20th century. Official hours are Tuesday through Sunday from 10am to 4pm, but it is closed in winter. Like everything else in town, though, the museum's hours are up to the whims of the caretakers. Entry is 620 Ft.

WHERE TO STAY

If you miss the only direct bus back to Budapest, you'll need a place to stay. In Hollókő, traditionally furnished thatch-roofed **peasant houses** are available for rent on a nightly or longer basis. You can rent a **room in a shared house** (with shared facilities), or rent an **entire house.** The prices vary depending on the size of the room or house and the number of people, but 9,000 Ft for a double room is average. Standard **private rooms** are also available in Hollókő. All accommodations can be booked in advance through the tourist offices in Hollókő or Salgótarján (see "Essentials," above). If you arrive without reservations (which is not advised), the address and phone number of a room finder are posted on the door of the Foundation of Hollókő.

WHERE TO DINE

Dining options are limited in tiny Hollókő. The **Vár Étterem** (✆ **32/379-029**) at Kossuth Lajos u. 95 serves decent Hungarian food at very low prices. Try a dish prepared with the "treasure of the local forests," porcini mushrooms. There is indoor and outdoor seating. The menu is available in English, and the waiters are patient. The restaurant is open daily noon to 8pm, except Christmas Day.

126km (78 miles) NE of Budapest

Eger (pronounced *Egg*-air) is the third-most visited city in the country and the most visited of Northern Hungary. It is a small baroque valley city between the Matra and Bükk mountains. Eger's fame is based on three things: its castle, its wine, and the brave struggle of its 16th-century women. When the Turkish army attacked in 1552, there were only 500 equestrians and an equal number of soldiers inside the fortress. The battle against 80,000 Turks was a little imbalanced to say the least. Those in the fortress, including the girls and women, stood up to the Turks to defend themselves and were remarkably victorious. The exuberant triumph is documented with golden letters in Hungarian history. Today, you can visit the exhibitions of the István Dobó Fortress Museum within the walls of the castle.

From the fortress, you can see a number of church towers defining Eger as a once-important church center for centuries, starting with an archbishopric since 1804. But alas, the Turks eventually succeeded in occupying the town, and the minaret, 40m (131 ft) high with 14 sides, is a reminder of their 100 years of rule from 1596. The view from the top will delight you with a vista of the town's surroundings.

Today Eger's landscape presents a harmonious blend of old and new. The ruined castle, one of Hungary's proudest symbols, dominates the skyline. Eger is convincingly known as the city of baroque. In its historic city center many beautiful and valuable baroque and late-baroque buildings fill each street. If you wander beyond the confines of the old section, you'll find a small modern city.

One of the most widely known and prestigious wines produced in this city is the claret, **Eger Bull's Blood**. Its distinctive traits are spiciness, fieriness, and relatively high acidity. In the Valley of the Beautiful Women, the most important outer part of town, wine producers are always ready to receive travelers to offer and sell them wine. Many wineries are out of town, making them difficult to access without a car.

If you don't want to rent a car, but want to enjoy the wines of the region, another option may be one of the festivals. Festivals include: Eger Spring Festival, an art festival of all mediums in late March to early April; the Feast of Eger Bikavér, a wine and food extravaganza in July; Wine Tasting, when wine producers present the wines of Northeastern Hungary in August; Agria International Folk Dance Festival, a convention of folk dance troupes in August; the Benediction of Wine on the day of St. John, the traditional celebration of new wine and wine exhibitions in late December.

ESSENTIALS

GETTING THERE   Eger is a 2 hour 20 minute **train** ride from Budapest if you take one of the seven direct trains daily departing from Budapest's Keleti Station. Tickets cost 2,870 Ft for first class or 2,290 Ft for second class, for a one-way trip. There are other trains that leave every half hour, but you will have to change trains, which can get confusing if you are an intrepid traveler or in a hurry. For this inconvenience, you will pay more: 3,320 Ft for first class, 2,810 Ft second class.

The train station is not located in the center of the city; it is about 1 mile out. The walk is pleasant, but if you have luggage, take a taxi. It should not cost more than 1,000 Ft to reach your hotel if you are at any of those listed here.

If you're **driving** from Budapest, take the M3 motorway east to Kerecsend, where you pick up Route 25 north to Eger. There is a toll and toll tickets will be going up in price in the near future, so check at all MOL gas stations.

VISITOR INFORMATION   For information, contact **Tourinform,** at Bajcsy-Zsilinszky u. 9 (✆ **36/517-715**). The office is open in summer Monday through Friday from 9am to 6pm and on weekends from 9am to 1pm; during off season, the office closes an hour earlier on weekdays and is closed on Sunday. For private-room booking, try **Eger Hotels** at www.egerhotels.com or **Egertourist** at the Tourinform office above (✆ **36/510-270**). The office is open Monday through Saturday from 10am. Note that the telephone city code for Eger is 36, the same as the country code for Hungary. To call from abroad, you would use 36/36 and then the local six-digit number.

EXPLORING OLD EGER

Eger's main sites are fairly concentrated once you have made it to the city center, within easy walking distance of each other and of **Dobó István tér** ★★★. Like many European cities and villages, life revolves around the town square, but before you get there, you may want to check out the **Town Under the Town** ★★ (✆ **06/20-961-4019** mobile phone only; www.varosavarosalatt.hu). Enter from Széchenyi u. through the Érsek-udvar. It is a cave-like structure built by Archbishop Fenessy for protection from the Turks and as a wine cellar. The incredible part is the lake. Tours in English are 50 minutes long and offered daily on the hour from 10am to 7pm. Admission and tour is 800 Ft for adults and 400 Ft for pensioners.

The town center is particularly attractive and large for a city this size. The **Minorite Church** sits on Dobó István tér with many believing it to be one of the most beautiful baroque churches in Europe. It is in razor-sharp contrast to the nearby solemn edifice of the friary. One of the greatest masters of European baroque, Kilian Ignaz Dientzenhofer, designed the church.

The Tourinform office offers a guided walking tour on Saturdays June to September that lasts 2 hours and costs 300 Ft. In the center of the square, there is an impressive statue of the town defender, Dobó, flanked by a knight and a woman. Erected in the 1960s, it was created by Alajos Strobl, one of the country's leading turn-of-the-20th-century sculptors. Strobl's execution of the work did not hold back on his feelings about the battle against the Turks. Strobl's other works include the statue of King Stephen on Buda's Castle Hill and the statue of poet János Arany in front of the National Museum in Pest.

The reconstructed ruins of **Eger Castle** (✆ **36/312-744**; www.egriva.hu), visible from just about anywhere in the city, are easily reached by walking northeast out of the square; take the path out of Dózsa György tér. You can wander the grounds free of charge daily from 8am to 8pm in summer and daily 8am to 6pm in winter. Climbing the castle ramp and walking the ramparts is a lovely stroll in warm weather, taking in the rooftop views of the old town area. To walk along the top of the castle wall will cost 600 Ft for adults and 300 Ft for children. You can also explore the two museums on the premises. The **István Dobó Castle Museum** (✆ **36/312-744**), as the name implies, offers the castle's history along with displays of some Turkish artifacts. The **Eger Picture Gallery** displays pieces from the same 19th-century Hungarian artists who are featured in the **Nemzeti Galéria (Hungarian National Gallery)** (p. 138). The museums are open Tuesday through Sunday from 10am to 5pm, and until 4pm in winter. Admission to each is 1,200 Ft for adults and 600 Ft for children. A photo ticket is 1,000 Ft, while video is restricted.

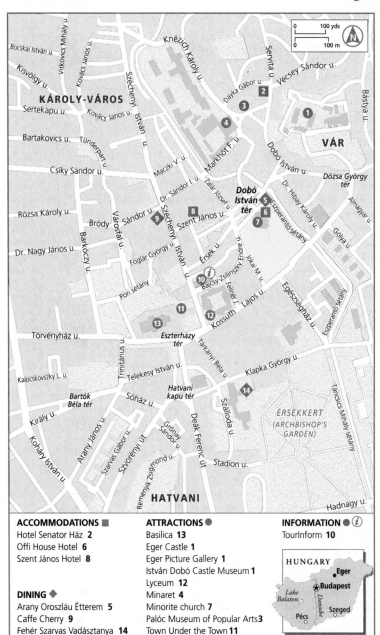

ACCOMMODATIONS ■
Hotel Senator Ház **2**
Offi House Hotel **6**
Szent János Hotel **8**

DINING ◆
Arany Oroszláu Étterem **5**
Caffe Cherry **9**
Fehér Szarvas Vadásztanya **14**

ATTRACTIONS ●
Basilica **13**
Eger Castle **1**
Eger Picture Gallery **1**
István Dobó Castle Museum **1**
Lyceum **12**
Minaret **4**
Minorite church **7**
Palóc Museum of Popular Arts **3**
Town Under the Town **11**

INFORMATION ● ⓘ
TourInform **10**

Just to the west of the castle, on Harangöntő utca, is Eger's most visible reminder of the Turkish period, its **minaret** at Knézich u. 1 (© **36/410-233**). The minaret survived, though the mosque under it was destroyed in 1841. The minaret is 14-sided, 33m (108 ft) tall, and in good enough condition that for an admission charge of 200 Ft, you can climb to the narrow top. It is open from April to the end of October, Tuesday to Sunday 10am to 6pm. If you suffer from claustrophobia, I warn against it. The scramble up is steep, on a cramped spiral staircase, but because the space is so narrow you can't turn back if anyone is behind you. Those who are successful, however, are justly rewarded with a spectacular view.

You can't miss the massive **basilica** (© **30/337-2398**), it is the second-largest church in Hungary, the largest being Esztergom's basilica and it competes in size with the basilica in Pest. You just need to walk a few blocks south on Eszterhazy tér. It is the only classicist building in Eger. Ordered by Archbishop Pyrker József, it was designed by architect József Hild, who was one of the architects of St. Stephen's Basilica in Pest. He completed this church in 1837 in the grandiose neoclassical style of the time. It's open daily from 6am to 7pm. If you are visiting in the high season, wander in at 11:30am Monday through Saturday or at 12:45pm on Sunday for a free organ presentation. Admission is free to the church at other times.

Next you will find the **Lyceum** at Eszterházy Square 1 (© **36/325-211**) built in late-baroque style. Count Eszterházy Károly ordered it to be built as a university at the end of the 18th century. It is now a college. (Colleges generally offer 4-year degrees, while universities require 4 to 6 years of more specialized study.) The Lyceum houses the nationally famous **diocesan library** *(kö nyvtár)* on the first floor with an impressive ceiling fresco of the Council of Trent by Johann Lukas Kracker and József Zach. The only original letter written by Mozart, in Hungary, is on display here. You can visit March 1 to September 30 Tuesday through Sunday 9am to 3pm, the rest of the year, on Saturday and Sunday only from 9am to 1pm. Admission is 350 Ft. Entrance to the balcony is free. Concerts are frequently performed in the yard of the Lyceum during July and August, so ask at Tourinform for the schedule and ticket information.

The **Palóc Museum of Popular Arts,** Dobó u. 12 (© **36/312-744**) presents exhibitions of the folk arts of the Palóc, inhabitants of Northeastern Hungary. Wood carvings made by shepherds, including crooksand drinking spoons, and hand-woven fabrics of mainly household textiles, tent sheets, shawls, haversacks, male and female clothing, and ceramics, are displayed. The museum is open January 1 through May 23 Tuesday through Saturday 10am to 4pm; May 24 to September 30 Tuesday to Sunday 10am to 4pm. Admission is 600 Ft for adults and 300 Ft for students.

If you missed visiting a spa or bathhouse in Budapest, check them out in Eger. Northeastern Hungary is rich in thermal waters; ask at Tourinform for a list of spas in the region. Eger is called the Spa of Northern Hungary.

WHERE TO STAY

Eger has some delightful hotels to stay right in the center of the town. On my most recent visit, I toured three such places, all of which I would highly recommend. Eger is small, so you don't want to be too far out unless venturing to a health spa hotel. **Hotel Senator Ház** ★★★ (© **36/320-466**; fax 36/411-711, www.senatorhaz.hu) sits right at Dobó tér 11. This small 11-room 18th-century townhouse hotel has tremendous charm decorated with numerous antiques throughout, including the lobby area on each floor outside the rooms. The rooms are spotlessly clean and although it is right on the square, it was quiet and relaxing. The **Szent János Hotel** ★★ is located at Szent János u. 3

An Excursion to Bükk National Park

Just to the northeast of Eger lies the Bükk mountain range, a lush, rugged terrain of cliffs and forest land. Established in 1976 this region encompasses the **Bükki Nemzeti Park** (Bükk National Park; © **36/411-581;** www.bnpi.hu/english). This mountainous national park presents a different persona with each season. If you visit in the spring, the palate of colors from countless wildflowers covering the backdrop will be your reward. The park is 43,200 hectares (106,750 acres) of which 97% is covered with forest. There are several unique and rare wildlife species in the mountains; more than 900 caves are known to exist. There are also numerous hiking trails. In the village of **Szilvásvárad**, you will discover where the world-famous Lippizaner horses are bred. The Lippizaners have more than 400 years of history in this area. You are able to discover the area by horseback. On the Szilvásváradi rail line, you can take a narrow gauge train along a 5km (3 mile) railway line through the mountains going through trout ponds and ending at **Veil Waterfall**, where the water falls 17m (56 ft) and resembles a gauzy veil. From here, you can hike to the prehistoric Istállóskö Cave or to the Bükk Plateau.

A public bus from Eger stops here.

(© **36/510-350**; fax 36/517-101, www.hotelszentjanos.hu) with 11 rooms in an attractive baroque building. Room charges vary according to which floor they are on. A double with two beds or one double costs from 15,000 Ft to 21,000 Ft, which includes breakfast, but not tourist tax. Another choice is the **Offi House Hotel** ★★ (© **36/518-211;** fax 36/518-211, www.offihaz.hu) placed at Dobó István tér 5 within minutes of the central square. This tiny hotel has only five rooms making it quaint and quiet. The rooms are large and tastefully decorated. They are associated with the adjoining restaurant, so guests receive a 10% discount on meals. Double rooms range from 19,500 Ft to 26,000 Ft depending on the season. The apartment is 26,000 Ft all year. Tourist tax of 360 Ft per person, per night is not included.

Travelers on a tight budget should consider renting a private room through Egertourist (p. 268). Rates in Eger are as low as 6,500 Ft for a bed with a shared bathroom and as high as 15,000 Ft for an apartment with bathroom and kitchen.

WHERE TO DINE

The **Fehér Szarvas Vadásztanya (White Stag Hunting Inn)** ★, located next door to the Park Hotel at Klapka u. 8 (© **36/411-129**), a few blocks south of Dobó István tér, is one of Eger's best-known and best-loved restaurants. The menu offers a full range of Hungarian wild-game specialties. Award-winning regional wines are featured. A piano and bass duet plays nightly amid the kitschy hunting lodge decor. The restaurant is open daily from noon to midnight and reservations are recommended. Credit cards are accepted. The **Arany Oroszláu Étterem** (© **36/518–211**) is at the same address as the charming Offi House Hotel above. For something informal and more budget, try **Caffe Cherry** at Széchenyi u. 11. If your hotel does not include breakfast, you can get it here as they are open from 9am to 10pm daily.

The best place to sample local wines is in the vineyard country just west of Eger, in the wine cellars of the **Szépasszony-völgy (Valley of the Beautiful Women).** More than 200 wine cellars are located here, each offering its own vintage. Some cellars have live music. Although the wine cellars don't serve food, you can grab a meal at one of the local restaurants. Generally, the cellars open at 10am and close by 9 or 10pm.

The easiest way to get to the Szépasszony-völgy is by taxi, though you can also walk there from the center of town in 30 or 40 minutes. You could also take bus no. 13 to the Hatvani Temető (Hatvan Cemetery) and walk from there; it's a 10- to 15-minute walk. Remember if you are driving, Hungary has a zero-tolerance law.

---

3 TOKAJI: WINE OF KINGS, KING OF WINES ★

200km (125 miles) NE of Budapest

TOKAJ-HEGYALJA

Also in the northern regions of Hungary, you find the world-famous wine called Tokaji. Its fame and reputation transcends centuries of the history of the area, identifying it as a famous wine region of Hungary. Grapes were found growing in a 43km (27 mile) area when the first Hungarian conquerors appeared on the scene. The uniqueness of the wine is attributed to the growing conditions of the grapes. Starting with a volcanic soil, the area is protected by the Carpathian Mountains. They have a southern exposure with the autumn weather promoting the grapes turning to *aszu* (raisin). Other important grape varieties of the area are the Furmint, Hárslevelű or Linden Leaf, Yellow Muscatel, and Oremus.

Legend has it that a wine grower abandoned his harvest when there was a threat of a Turkish invasion. When it was safe to return to his fields, he feared his harvest had been ruined since the grapes had stayed on the vine too long, but he used them anyway to make wine. The product was Tokaji. The wine has a long history with royalty as well as with poets and writers. As poet Miklós Szemere from the 19th century exemplifies with his short verse:

Blessed Tokaji wine, how good you are,
your mere fragrance is enough to send death running;
for many ill people have been cured by drinking you,
though they were about to be taken away.
Drink of the gods, immortal nectar,
the land is blest where you grow!

The Tokaji wine was well established and popular as early as the 12th century. Admirers of the wine were King Louis XIV, Cromwell, Tsar Alexander the Great, and Tsarina Catherine. The Russians even stationed a small garrison in the surroundings of Tokaj to ensure continuous supply. Believing the wine had curative power, the doctors of Pope Pius I ordered him to drink Tokaj wines regularly to protect his health. The French king Louis XIV called it "the king of wines and the wine of kings."

ESSENTIALS

GETTING THERE Tokaj is only accessible by car or by taking a tour to the region. If you're driving, take the M3 motorway from Budapest to Miskolc. From Miskolc take

Route 37 to Route 38. Unfortunately, all tourist information is in Hungarian only. I suggest you take a guided tour to the region (see Chapter 7 "Exploring Budapest" for tour information). If you decide to venture there on your own with a car, then the **Tourinform** office can be of some assistance. You can contact them at Tokaj 3910, Serház u. 1 (© **47/352-259;** fax 47/552-070).

WHERE TO STAY

The Tokaj Hotel and Restaurant at Rákóczi u. 5 (© **47/352-344;** fax 47/352-759; www. hoteltokaj.hu) is found at the foot of Tokaj Mountain, at the fork of rivers Tisza and Bodrog. The hotel has 30 double rooms with a full bathroom and 12 double rooms with a shower that are modern and comfortable, but as high as the fourth floor in the attic. Rates are 10,900 Ft per person, not per room. Breakfast and taxes are extra.

The Sos Tavern and Pension looks like a large converted barn on Tokaj-Hegyalja Route 37 situated between Szerencs and Tokaj and with no specific address. Surrounded by vineyards, the pension has 11 rooms with showers and a restaurant, a sauna, and a traditional wine cellar for guests. The nearby Mádi Lake and the forests of Hegyalja are rich in game and offer excellent fishing facilities. For more specific driving directions, contact István Novák (© **47/369-139;** www.sosborhaz.hu).

WHERE TO DINE

The restaurant at the Tokaj Hotel has many regional specialties and offers special food programs as well. In summertime, the balcony overlooking the river is open and it offers a delightful view. The pension above also has a restaurant for guests.

---

4 AGGTELEK: AN ENTRANCE TO THE CAVES ★

224km (139 miles) NE of Budapest

Swaddled in the northernmost part of Hungary to the Slovak border, about 80km (50 miles) north of Eger is the **Aggtelek National Park (Aggteleki Nemzeti Park)** established in 1985 primarily to protect inorganic natural treasures, surface formations, and caves. A deciduous forest covers 75% of the park inhabited by over 220 species of birds, rare plants, and a rich collection of varied insects. Most fascinating to many is that it also has over 200 caves of various sizes, creating Central Europe's largest cave system. The **Baradla Cave** is the longest with a total length of 25km (16 miles), including side branches. One 5.6km (3.5 mile) section runs into Slovakia and is called by its Slovak name, Domica. The cave is a youthful 2 million years old according to geologists. Water from streams entered through cracks, dissolving and eroding the limestone, eventually widening the water's entry and formed the current passages. The lime content of the dripping water forms stalactites and stalagmites in a range of sizes, colors, and shapes embellishing the passages, inspiring those who discovered them to give them names such as Dragon's Head, Tiger, Mother in Law's Tongue, the Hall of Columns, and the Hall of Giants. Prehistoric people inhabited the caves according to archaeological excavations.

Guided daily tours are available lasting 1 to 2 hours *(roved)* covering roughly 1km (½ mile). The more rigorous 5-hour *(közép)*, or 7-hour *(hosszú)* tours cover a range of 7km (about 4½ miles) and include scaling, climbing ladders, and crossing water-filled gullies. They are available from the villages of Aggtelek or Jósvafő from April 1 to September 30

(**Tips** **Cool Caves**

Remember, no matter how hot it is outside, the Baradla caves are always damp and chilly (a constant 50°–52°F/10°–11°C), so take a couple of layers of clothes to add as the temperature decreases.

between 8am and 5pm and from October 1 to March 31 between 8am and 3pm. First-time cave visitors will be flabbergasted by the miraculous subterranean world of stalactites, stalagmites, and other bizarre formations that Mother Nature has created.

Classical and other music concerts are held in the beautiful Concert Hall of the Baradla Cave because of its superb acoustics; it provides a very special experience for visitors. For more information, call the Aggtelek National Park Jósvafő, Tengerszem oldal 1 (© 48/506-000; www.anp.hu, no English) for tour information.

The **Hotel Cseppkő** (© 48/343-075), in the village of Aggtelek, is a popular place to crash after a day in the caves. Double rooms start at 15,000 Ft and a triple is 21,000 Ft, breakfast included. Though it's very plain, it is clean and conveniently located. Camping is also popular in the area.

Travelers without cars can get to Aggtelek by bus from Eger. The trip takes 3 hours. From Miskolc, the trip takes 2 hours. Ask about transportation at the local tourist office (such as Eger's Tourinform or Egertourist), where you can also ask for help booking a room at the Hotel Cseppkő. Off season there is no need to book in advance.

Southern Hungary: The Mecsek Hills & the Great Plain

In southwestern Hungary, you will find the fertile Mecsek Hills; Pécs is the major city of this hilly region. Pécs has been named a European Capital of Culture for 2010, when the spotlight will be on highlighting its history and cultural life. On the other side of the Danube to the south and east, lies the mainly agricultural region of the Alföld (Great Plain), which begins not far outside of Budapest. This is the farmland of wheat and orchards—a broad, bleak, yet dramatic land mass that covers almost half the country. It is similar to the great prairies of the U.S. The last remains of the *Puszta* are in this region, where Hungarian folk legends have sprung from, and the land of the Hungarian cowboys or *csikós*. This is also the home of the famous Nonius horse, a powerful equine breed developed in Hungary in the 19th century, which won the title "Ideal Horse" at the Paris world exhibition in 1900. The main cities here are Kecskemét and Szeged. The Great Plain comprises approximately 51,800 sq. km (20,000 sq. miles).

1 PÉCS: A CITY WITH A 2,000-YEAR PAST ★★★

197km (122 miles) SW of Budapest

Pécs (pronounced *Paych*) is the largest and most beautiful city in the Mecsek Hills region. Although far from the Mediterranean sea, it has a Mediterranean feel with a generally warm and arid climate. Due to this, the hills produce some of the country's premium fruit.

Pécs is located just 32km (20 miles) from the Croatian border. Sopiane, as the Romans named it, has over 2,000 years of history still visible to speak of its past. In evidence are remnants of the Roman era which date back to around A.D. 350–400. The early Christian burial chamber dating back to the 4th century is the most noteworthy remains.

The later period of the Turkish rule and their structures are even more evident. The Turks occupied the city for over 140 years from 1543. The Inner City Parish Church is an incredibly beautiful place of worship, with an interesting history. It is located at the top of Szechenyi Square in the city center and you may not recognize it as a church, because it looks like a mosque. The Turks used the stones from St. Bartholomew's Church at the other end of the square, to build the mosque of Pasha Gazi Kassim. When the Turks were eradicated from the city in 1686, the mosque was occupied by Jesuits who restored it to a Catholic church.

It was in Pécs that the first university in the country was founded in 1367 while under the rule of King Louis the Great. While that university no longer exists, Pécs remains a university city. The current University of Pécs was founded on January 1, 2000, the merger of three institutions of higher learning: Janus Pannonius University, the Medical University of Pécs, and the Illyés Gyula Teacher Training College of Szekszárd.

Pécs continued to be a vibrant city through the 143-year Turkish occupation, in part because the greatest ruler of the Ottoman Empire, Suleiman II, made this his home. The Turks introduced a new culture with baths, and decorative and drinking fountains. Some of the most important Turkish remains in Hungary are landmark reminders of this historic time in the city life, such as the Mosque of Pasha Gazi Kassim.

The first public library in the country was created here by Bishop György Klimó in 1774. Maria Theresa, empress of the Austro-Hungarian Empire, gave the city the rank of Free Royal City in 1780. During the 19th century, four major companies opened factories: Littke (champagne), Hamerli (gloves), Angster (organs), and later in the century, Zsolnay (porcelain).

Those who live in Pécs declare it is the best city in the country. Pécs is a growing city. The people do not exhibit the inertia you might notice on a hot summer afternoon in Great Plain towns like Kecskemét or Szeged.

Walking up Janus Pannonius utca toward Széchenyi tér, about a block up the street, you cannot help but notice a small wrought-iron fence covered with padlocks. There are even padlocks hanging from padlocks in chains. The story goes that one young couple in love placed a padlock there as a token of their love. Others followed and now the fence is at risk from toppling under the weight. Someone started the same tradition on yet another fence just a minute's walk away from the original. If you look closely at the locks, you'll see names and dates engraved on them.

In 2010, Pécs will have the moniker "European Capital of Culture," sharing the title with Essen, Germany, and Istanbul, Turkey. Other than failed plans and the firing of the executives hired to spearhead the projects, it is uncertain at this writing what actually will be accomplished to celebrate this title. It has been fraught with problems that continued through the autumn of 2009.

Drinkers be aware that the consumption of alcoholic beverages in public areas was banned in Pécs from January 1, 2009. Violators are liable for a fine of up to 30,000 Ft. Smokers don't get any breaks either. No smoking is allowed within 50m of cultural, educational, health institutions, or churches, nor at bus stops or in playgrounds.

ESSENTIALS

GETTING THERE   Eight IC (InterCity) **trains** depart daily from Budapest's Keleti Station; others leave from Deli Station, but take considerably longer to get there. The fare is 3,780 Ft for a one-way, second-class ticket. You will need a reservation for these IC trains for an additional 520 Ft. An intercity train will get you there in just under 3 hours. The trains leaving from Deli Station take 4¼ hours, but you don't need a reservation, and the trains are not as good. If you are **driving** from Budapest, take the M6 south for approximately 3 hours (the distance is 210km/130 miles).

VISITOR INFORMATION   Once you leave Budapest, English speakers are harder to find except in hotels and some restaurants. The best source of information in Pécs is **Tourinform,** at Széchenyi tér 9 (*©* **72/213-315;** www.tedeempecs.hu). Tourinform is open April and May, Monday through Friday from 9am to 6pm; June through September, Monday to Friday from 9am to 6pm and on Saturday 9am to 2pm; October through March, Monday through Friday, 9am to 4pm. Tourinform can provide a list of local

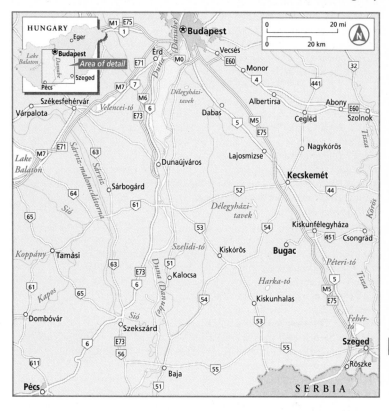

private-room accommodations, though you'll have to reserve the room yourself. You can also get city information online at **www.pecs.hu**. Look for the English link at the top.

EXPLORING OLD PÉCS

The old section of Pécs is really awe-inspiring with the differences in architecture side by side; there is plenty of eye candy to satisfy anyone. One of Hungary's most incredible central squares is **Széchenyi tér** ★★★. Starting with the mosque at the top of minor hill, it descends to St. Sebastian's Catholic Church, where there is an unusual fountain made of Zsolnay porcelain sitting in front. Walking down the square, make sure you stroll slowly and look up. The variety of architectural styles and colors within such a short area is just amazing. Grand pastel-colored buildings line the cobblestone streets that border the square.

Old Pécs has a reputation for its many museums and galleries; after Budapest, Pécs comes in second as a cultural center in Hungary. Most of the museums are relatively small, unlike the many grand ones in Budapest, so you can conceivably visit three or four in a day without feeling overstimulated.

14

Most of the museums are under the directorship of the Baranya County Museum's Directorate and therefore, the phone number is a central one while opening hours and admission are uniform throughout. As in Budapest, these museums charge extra if you're taking photos or video; see p. 123 for more information.

Amerigo Tot Exhibition ★   This museum closed in 2009 for renovations, but is expected to re-open in mid-2010. Check with Tourinform for further information regarding hours and admission cost. It displays the work of Hungarian sculptor Amerigo Tot who moved to Italy in 1937. He presented Pécs with his works *Baptism* (1938), *Madonna of Csurgó* (1968/1980), *Cross as Protest* (1969), and *Still Life in Transylvania* (1980), all of which are beautiful pieces.

Kaptalan u. 2. ✆ **72/324-822.**

Jakawali Hassan Museum   This museum is housed inside a 16th-century mosque, the most complete Turkish temple in Hungary. The mosque stands with its minaret still intact (though, unfortunately, you can't ascend it). At one time there was a religious house of the Dervishes and a religious college next door. Like the much larger mosque up in Széchenyi tér, this mosque was converted to a church after the Turks were driven from Pécs; however, in the 1950s the mosque was restored to its original form. The museum's main attraction is the building itself, although various Muslim religious artifacts are on display as well.

Rákóczi út 2. ✆ **70/626-7414** (mobile phone only). Admission 500 Ft. May–Oct Wed–Sun 9:30am–5:30pm. Closed Nov–Apr.

Tivadar Csontváry Museum ★   This small museum has a fine collection of the work of Tivadar Csontváry Kosztka (1853–1919), who claimed he had a mystic revelation wherein God told him to paint. He worked for 20 years preparing himself financially by opening a pharmacy, then did not start painting until he was 41 years old. His revelation was attributed to the fact he suffered from schizophrenia, which most likely also influenced his art. He is considered the first post-Impressionist artist of Hungary, thus shunned from the artistic community. He remained unknown during his lifetime and when he died, his family wanted to sell his paintings for the value of their canvases, not the work itself. Someone who realized their potential value bought the selection that is now on exhibit (which initially angered wagon makers who wanted the large canvas for their wagon making). Supposedly, Picasso once saw an exhibition of Csontváry's work and said, "I did not know there was another artistic genius in this century, besides me."

Janus Pannonius u. 11. ✆ **72/310-544.** Admission 700 Ft. Photo 300 Ft; video 600 Ft. Apr 1–Oct 31 Tues–Sun 10am–6pm; Nov 1–Mar 31 Tues–Sun 10am–4pm.

Victor Vasarely Museum ★   The late Victor Vasarely, internationally known father of op art, was born in the house that this museum now occupies, although he left early on for France. This is one of two museums in the country devoted solely to Vasarely's work (the other is in Óbuda, p. 143). While Vasarely's fame was achieved abroad, Pécs proudly considers him a native son. In addition to Vasarely's pieces the museum also displays the work of a few significant Hungarian artists whose work of geometric and kinetic styles are from the second part of the 20th century. Some international artists are also on display at different times. The museum will reopen after May 2010 once renovations are completed.

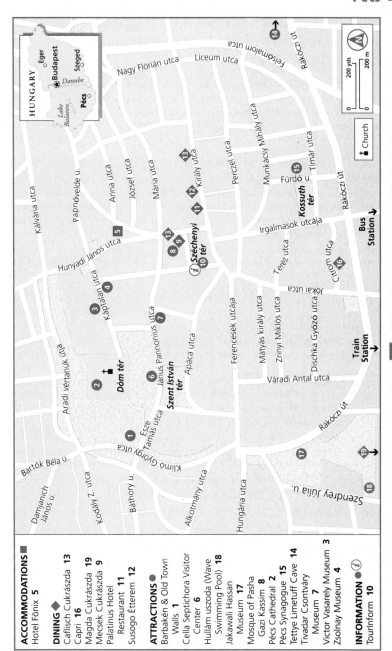

ACCOMMODATIONS ■
Hotel Főnix **5**

DINING ◆
Caflisch Cukrászda **13**
Capri **16**
Magda Cukrászda **19**
Mecsek Cukrászda **9**
Palatinus Hotel
 Restaurant **11**
Susogo Étterem **12**

ATTRACTIONS ●
Barbaken & Old Town
 Walls **1**
Cella Septichora Visitor
 Center **6**
Hullám uszoda (Wave
 Swimming Pool) **18**
Jakawali Hassan
 Museum **17**
Mosque of Pasha
 Gazi Kassim **8**
Pécs Cathedral **2**
Pécs Synagogue **15**
Tettye Limetuff Cave **14**
Tivadar Csontváry
 Museum **7**
Victor Vasarely Museum **3**
Zsolnay Museum **4**

INFORMATION ● *ⓘ*
TourInform **10**

Kaptalan u. 3. ✆ **72/514-040.** Admission 700 Ft. Photo 300 Ft; video 600 Ft. Apr 1–Oct 31 Tues–Sun 10am–6pm; Nov 1–Mar 31 Tues–Sun 10am–4pm.

Zsolnay Museum ★★★ This is one of a number of the small museums on Kaptalan utca, Pécs's "street of museums," and you shouldn't miss it. The Zsolnay Museum displays some of the best examples of Zsolnay porcelain, produced locally since 1852. There are vases, plates, cups, figurines, and even ceramic paintings. Once you've seen the museum, check out the Zsolnay fountain at the lower end of Széchenyi tér in front of St. Sebastian's Church.

Kaptalan u. 2. ✆ **72/514-040.** Admission 700 Ft. Photo 300 Ft; video 600 Ft. May 1–Oct 31 Tues–Sun 10am–6pm; Nov 1–Apr 30 Tues–Sun 10am–4pm.

OTHER SITES

Cella Septichora Visitor Center ★★ Dating back to the 4th century, this ancient Roman burial ground is now on display. From the street level, you can walk over 300 sq. m (3,229 sq. ft) of the glass cover over the burial chambers. Below several hundred tombs were discovered, of which there was a seven-celled tomb (Cella Septichora), and a three-celled pentagon-shaped tomb (Cella Trichora) excavated on two levels. This has been named a UNESCO World Heritage Site.

Dóm tér. ✆ **72/224–755**. Admission 1,200 Ft. Apr–Oct 31 Tues–Sun 10am–6pm; Nov–Mar 31 Tues–Sun 10am–4pm.

Tettye Limetuff Cave Cave in to your desire to visit an unusual cave. Partially formed by a waterfall, the water of which is used in Pécs, you can visit this limestone hole in the hill. I don't do caves, can you tell? This is recommended by the local Tourinform office.

Tettye tér. ✆ **72/517–200.** Admission 750 Ft. Mar 15–Apr 30 Mon–Fri 10am–5pm, Sat–Sun 10am–6pm; May–Oct 31 daily 10am–7pm; Nov–Mar 14 Mon–Fri 11am–4pm, Sat–Sun 10am–4pm.

HOUSES OF WORSHIP

Mosque of Pasha Gazi Kassim ★★ The largest Turkish structure still standing in Hungary was once a mosque and it now houses a Catholic church. It was built in the late 16th century, during the Turkish occupation, on the site of an earlier church. The mix of religious traditions is evident everywhere you look, and the effect is rather pleasing. An English-language description of the building's history is posted on a bulletin board on the left-hand wall. No photos or videos are allowed inside.

At the top of Széchenyi tér. ✆ **72/321–976.** Free admission. Apr 15–Oct 15 Mon–Sat 10am–4pm, Sun 11:30am–4pm; Oct 15–Apr 15 Mon–Sat 10am–noon, Sun 11:30am–2pm.

Pécs Cathedral ★ Originally built in the 11th century by Bishop St. Maurice, this four-towered cathedral has been destroyed and rebuilt more than once like many buildings during wars. The Turkish used it as a mosque and embellished it with a minaret (spire). At the end of the 19th century, the present neo-Romanesque exterior was added. The interior remains primarily Gothic, with some baroque additions and furnishings. The frescoes by leading 19th-century artists, Károly Lotz and Bertalan Székely, are inside. Organ concerts are performed in the cathedral throughout the year; inquire at the cathedral (no English spoken) or at Tourinform for the schedule.

The square in front of the cathedral and the beautifully landscaped park with a magnificent fountain beneath it is a popular gathering place, and occasionally the site of folk concerts, dances, and fairs. No photos or videos are allowed.

On Dóm tér. ☎ **72/513-030.** Cathedral admission (includes treasury and crypt) 1,100 Ft. Apr 1–Oct 15 **281**
Mon–Sat 9am–5pm, Sun 1–5pm; Oct 16–Mar 31 Mon–Sat 10am–4pm, Sun 1–4pm. The church is not
open to the public during weddings, which are often on Sat afternoon.

Pécs Synagogue ★   Pécs's grand old synagogue is incongruously situated in what is
now one of the city's busiest shopping squares, Kossuth tér. The gentleman at the door
speaks excellent English and is warm and inviting. Once inside, you will forget the outside world. Built in 1865 and consecrated in 1869, the synagogue has the original rich
oak interior to this day. It was the third synagogue built in the city in Hungarian romantic style for a Neolog Jewish community. Sadly, it is the only surviving synagogue in the
city after World War II. Prior to World War II, the synagogue had more than 4,000
members, of whom only 464 survived the Holocaust. Every year, Pécs's small and aging
Jewish community commemorates the 1944 deportations to Auschwitz on the first Sunday after July 4. Regular services are held in the smaller temple next door at Fürdő 1
(there isn't a sign; go through the building into the courtyard and cross diagonally to the
right) on Friday at 6:30pm.

Kossuth tér. 1–3. ☎ **72/315-881.** Admission 800 Ft. May–Sep 30 Sun–Fri 10am–noon and 1–5pm. Closed
Oct–Apr.

SHOPPING

As you stroll through the city, you will be surprised at the number of pedestrian-only
streets, making shopping in Pécs a pleasurable activity. Many of the stores are standard
shops found in Budapest or any other large city, for that matter. For a more exotic shopping experience, visit the **Pécsi Vásár (Pécs Flea Market)** ★. At this crowded, bustling,
open-air market you can find everything from antique china and silver to Turkish T-shirts
and Chinese baby booties. The market is open Friday, Saturday and Sunday where the
Sunday is the first Sunday of the month. Take a special bus, marked VÁSÁRTÉR, which
departs from the Konsum downtown shopping center. You need two standard city bus
tickets for this bus; these are available at newsstands and kiosks or ask the bus driver, but
the prices are higher. You can also take the no. 3 bus from the Konsum (only one ticket
required), but you'll have to walk some distance from the stop to the entrance of the flea
market.

OUTDOOR ACTIVITIES

If you visit Pécs in the summer, plan for the heat. Air-conditioning is not common, so
cool off in the waves at **Hullám uszoda (Wave Swimming Pool)** on Szendrey Júlia utca 7
(☎ **72/512-935**). Admission is 900 Ft. The pool is open daily from 6am to 10pm
throughout the year. Another swimming pool complex, which belongs to the university
is at Ifjúság útja 6 (☎ **72/501-519** ext. 4195). There is a wading pool for kids as well as
a 25m (82 ft) lap pool. Admission is 700 Ft. It is only open to the public 6am to 8am
and 4pm to 6pm Monday to Friday, 8am to midnight on Saturday.

WHERE TO STAY

For the best little hotel right in the center of town, try the popular **Hotel Fönix** ★★, at
Hunyadi út 2 (☎ **72/311-682**). This unique hotel's structure is reminiscent of a building
from a children's fairy tale. It sits just off the top of Széchenyi tér across from the mosque.
With only 14 rooms and three apartments, this adds to its charm as does the fact that
each room has oddly angled walls and partial dormer-type ceilings. Some of the rooms
are a bit cramped, but all are clean with refrigerators and TVs and the common facilities

are well maintained. The three apartments have full facilities and their own entrance off the street. The staff is incredibly helpful and friendly. The hotel has Wi-Fi. Double rooms cost between 10,600 Ft to 14,000 Ft, triples are 15,000 Ft to 16,000 Ft, and apartments range from 20,000 Ft to 30,000 Ft. Rates include breakfast, but not tourism tax of 350 Ft per night per person. Call several days ahead to reserve a room. Credit cards are accepted.

If the Hotel Fönix is full, the management can book a room for you at a pension that they operate called **Kertész Panzió,** at Sáfrány u. 42 (© **72/327-551**).

WHERE TO DINE

Palatinus Hotel Restaurant ★★ HUNGARIAN   The interior of this restaurant is incredibly decorated with a combination of Art Nouveau and other styles with Zsolnay porcelain tossed in here and there. The peacock Zsolnay fountain will have you wondering whether to eat or stare at the colors and design of the building. Eat though, the food is excellent, and so is the staff. A friend of ours who was living in Pécs for 9 months had a poor experience with service on one visit, but ours was excellent. I would still say give it a try.

Király u. 5. © **72/889-400.** Reservations recommended. Main courses 1,900 Ft–3,600 Ft. AE, DC, MC, V. Daily 11am–11pm. Off main square.

Susogo Étterem ★★ HUNGARIAN MODERN   Given the Mediterranean feel of Pécs, it is not surprising that this restaurant incorporates a bit of French cuisine into its Hungarian menu. Two dining options are available by the same owners. On the first floor you will find the fine dining restaurant Enoteca, upscale, elegant, and great service. For a more casual cozy restaurant, you may want to try the Bistro Corso, on the ground floor with a youthful ambience.

Király u. 14. © **72/525-198.** Reservations recommended. Main courses Enoteca 1,500 Ft–3,900 Ft. Main courses Bistro Corso 1,150 Ft–2,390 Ft. MC, V. Enoteca Mon–Fri noon–2:30pm, 6:30–10:30pm, Sat 6:30–10:30pm. Bistro Corso daily 8am–midnight.

COFFEEHOUSES & ICE-CREAM PARLORS

If you have a sweet tooth, there are opportunities to satisfy it all over town. Pécs offers numerous places to enjoy coffee and sweets. Try **Mecsek Cukrászda,** on Széchenyi tér 16 (© **72/315-444**) for a quick jolt of espresso and any number of luscious-looking and inexpensive pastries. For people-watching on the pedestrian street, try **Caflisch Cukrászda** at Király 32 u. They also have a large selection of ice-cream flavors. **Capri,** a very popular shop at Citrom u. 7 (© **72/333-658**), three blocks south of Széchenyi tér, serves up various sundaes as well as cones, but their choice of pastries is limited. Another place for sweets and ice cream is **Magda Cukrászda** ★★ at Kandó Kálmán u. 4 (© **72/511-055**). It's out of the way but worth the walk. It is open daily 10am to 8pm and to 7pm in winter.

2 KECSKEMÉT ★

85km (53 miles) SE of Budapest

Kecskemét (pronounced *Ketch*-keh-mate), a city of just over 100,000 people in the western portion of the Great Hungarian Plain, definitely has a village feel. The name is derived from "*kecske*" meaning goat and "*mét*" being district. You will notice a goat in the coat of arms. A quiet, sun-baked city with wide, open squares and broad avenues,

Kecskemét is blessed with some of the most interesting architecture in the Great Plain region. The town's dizzyingly colorful Art Nouveau buildings may be the equal of any in the country outside Budapest.

Kecskemét was the birthplace of Zoltán Kodály, the early-20th-century musicologist, teacher, and composer who, along with his friend and colleague Béla Bartók, achieved worldwide renown for his studies of Hungarian folk songs and his compositions. Kodály also developed a method of teaching music that is used worldwide. Today, a music school in town bears Kodály's name.

Kecskemét is also famous for its many varieties of apricot brandy *(barack pálinka)*.

If you have interest in the famous feats of the Hungarian horsemen, this is the jumping-off place to see the *puszta*. You can arrange a day with a horse-carriage tour, a horse show, and wind it up with a goulash party at the end. Tourinform (see below) can assist with all of the arrangements.

ESSENTIALS

GETTING THERE An IC **train** departs Budapest's Nyugati Station every hour. The fare is 1,880 Ft–2,440 Ft one-way, depending on the train. You are required to pay an additional seat reservation fee of about 770 Ft. Travel time is 1¼ hours. If you're **driving** from Budapest, take the M5 motorway south—you'll have to pay a highway toll each way.

VISITOR INFORMATION The best source of information is **Tourinform,** at Kossuth tér 1 (©/fax **76/481-065;** www.kecskemet.hu). Their website in English is one of the most comprehensive available. In summer the office is open May 1 through June 15, Monday through Friday 8am to 5pm and from June 16 to August 31, it is open Monday through Friday 9am to 6pm, Saturday and Sunday 9am to 2pm. From October 1 to April 30, hours are Monday through Friday 8am to 4pm.

Piroska Tours at Szabadság tér 2 (© **76/483-493**) will be useful if you're planning a side trip to Bugac or any equine-based activities. Summer hours May to September 30, Monday to Friday 9am to 5:30pm, Saturday 9am to noon and from October to April Monday to Friday 9am to 5:30pm.

EXPLORING KECSKEMÉT

The museums mentioned here are in the immediate vicinity of Kossuth tér, Kecskemét's main square, a beautiful area with gorgeous buildings.

Photography lovers will not want to miss the excellent **Hungarian Photography Museum,** Katona József tér 12 (© **76/483-221;** www.fotomuzeum.hu), featuring the works of contemporary Hungarian photographers, including foreign photographers of Hungarian ethnicity. The English pages of the museum's website are complete and written with a touch of humor. Operation hours are March through November Wednesday to Sunday 10am to 5pm, and December through February Wednesday to Sunday 10am to 4pm. Admission is 400 Ft.

Visit the **Bozsó Collection,** Klapka u. 34. (© **76/324-625**). Open March 15 to September 16 Friday through Sunday 10am to 6pm. The Impressionist paintings of this native son are hauntingly beautiful. Admission is 400 Ft adult. You can make an appointment to visit for an extra 500 Ft.

Explore the work of the country people and its history at the **Museum of Hungarian Folk Art and Handicrafts** at Serfőző utca 19. (© **76/327-203**). It's open 10am to 5pm Tuesday through Saturday, January 15 through December 15. Admission is 300 Ft.

Hungary's largest toy collection can be found at the **Toy Museum (Játék-műhely és Múzeum)** ★, at Gáspár András u. and Hosszú u. (© **76/481-469**). This quaint museum has exhibits on toy design and manufacturing, as well as exhibits featuring actual toys. Families with children should try to come on the weekend, when youngsters are allowed to play with some exhibits. Admission is 450 Ft for adults, free for children 5 and under; free for everyone on Sunday. Open Tuesday through Sunday 10am to 12:30pm and 1 to 5pm. Closes 1 hour earlier in winter.

City Hall ★, Kossuth tér 1 (© **76/513-513**), built in 1893 by Ödön Lechner and Gyula Pártos, is a delightful Art Nouveau structure and a must-see for aficionados of Lechner's later Budapest buildings: the former Post Office Savings Bank (p. 178) and the Applied Arts Museum (p. 128). Like the buildings in the capital, Lechner's Kecskemét masterpiece is generously decorated with colorful Zsolnay majolica tiles. The council chamber *(dísz terem)* contains ceiling frescoes by the artist Bertalan Székely, whose work is on exhibit in Buda's National Gallery. If the building is closed when you arrive, admire it from the outside while you listen to the bells playing music by Kodály and others throughout the day (usually on the hour). Admission is 400 Ft, by appointment only. Open Monday through Friday 8am to 4pm.

WHERE TO STAY

Fábián Panzió ★, Kápolna u. 14 (© **76/477-677**), a small family-run guesthouse, is situated in the center of Kecskemét. Six rooms are located in the garden building and 4 smaller rooms are in the main building, all with private bathrooms. Doubles range from 9,000 Ft to 10,800 Ft without breakfast or 11,000 Ft to 12,080 Ft with breakfast. Taxes are included.

Hotel Háry is located at Kodály Zoltán tér 9. (© **76/480-400**). It features 21 rooms in a small conference-hotel setting. Doubles are 13,500 Ft and triples 16,500 Ft. Rates include buffet breakfast, use of the sauna, and VAT. Tourist tax of 250 Ft per person per night is extra.

WHERE TO DINE

Háry Restaurant can be found in the Hotel Háry above. Serving traditional Hungarian meals, it also offers occasional live concerts and performances on its small stage. The wine list has more than 100 choices from all over Hungary. Enjoy the outdoor terrace for summer dining. Entrees cost 1,100 Ft to 2,900 Ft. It is open daily 7am to 11pm.

Another good dining option is **Liberté,** Szabadság tér 2 (© **76/509–175**). The restaurant serves Hungarian cuisine for 1,150 Ft to 2,900 Ft. There's outdoor terrace seating in summer. It is open daily 9am to 11pm.

3 SZEGED: HUNGARY'S SPICE CAPITAL ★★

168km (104 miles) SE of Budapest

Historically, Szeged (pronounced *Seh*-ged), was destroyed on March 12, 1879, when a distant dyke collapsed and flooded the city. Locals were given financial aid that was collected in other European countries and sent to Szeged to help the rebuilding; hence, there are streets named Rome, Brussels, Berlin, Paris, London, Moscow, and Vienna honoring their contributions. After the catastrophic flood, Szeged was redesigned with the engineer's precision of a compass and ruler to become the most modern town in Hungary. Its

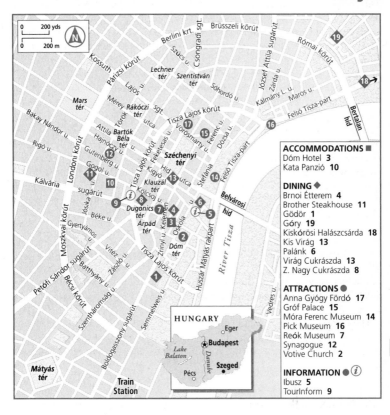

ACCOMMODATIONS ■
Dóm Hotel **3**
Kata Panzió **10**

DINING ◆
Brnoi Étterem **4**
Brother Steakhouse **11**
Gödör **1**
Góry **19**
Kiskőrösi Halászcsárda **18**
Kis Virág **13**
Palánk **6**
Virág Cukrászda **13**
Z. Nagy Cukrászda **8**

ATTRACTIONS ●
Anna Gyógy Fördő **17**
Gróf Palace **15**
Móra Ferenc Museum **14**
Pick Museum **16**
Reők Museum **7**
Synagogue **12**
Votive Church **2**

INFORMATION ● ⓘ
Ibusz **5**
TourInform **9**

broad avenues and boulevards along with its extravagant center won the Europa Nostra Award, granted annually to outstanding heritage achievements.

It is the proud capital of the Great Plain in Csongrád County; an interesting hospitable city, large by Hungarian standards with a population of 177,000 making it the fourth largest in the country. World famous for its paprika and salami (Pick *Szalami*), Szeged is also home to one of Hungary's major universities, the University of Szeged as it was renamed in 2003. From 1962 until its renaming in 2003, the university was József Attila University, named for a poet who did not gain fame until after his death. His statue stands in front of the university's main building on Dugonics tér. There is another statue of him next to the Parliament building in Budapest on Kossuth tér, sitting on the steps of the embankment.

The people of Szeged, many of whom are students, love to stroll along the riverside, sit in cafes, and window-shop on the just reconstructed elegant **Karász utca** ★★, the town's main pedestrian-only street. Dóm tér, a beautiful, wide square, is home to the **Szeged Open Air Drama Festival** ★, which has continued annually since 1931. It is a popular summer-long series of cultural events, with the majority in Hungarian, but they have opened competition to the festival, so other languages may be represented in the future. **THEALTER,** an association of artists was founded in 1991 with the mission to introduce and support the work of experimenting, innovative artistic communities. They bring the best artists from minority-marginal positions to Szeged to perform during their festival. There is an emphasis on introducing well-known groups from Western Europe as well as local artists to create progressive schemes and ways of viewing artistic performances. During the last 16 years, the Old Synagogue has become synonymous with THEALTER, forming a close alliance. THEALTER has presented more than 130 groups from 27 countries to Szeged; some of them making their Hungarian premier performance here in the town of Szeged. For more information about these festivals, contact Tourinform. This smaller city is a delightful travel destination for a day or two of visiting.

ESSENTIALS

GETTING THERE On a daily basis, there is one InterCity **train** every hour, departing from Budapest's Nyugati Station. The fare for an IC train is 3,820 Ft plus an additional fee for a seat reservation. The travel time is 2½ hours. Once in Szeged, the building to the left of the station is where you can buy a one-day transportation pass for 750 Ft. Directly in the front of the station is tram no. 1, which will take you to Széchenyi tér, a perfect starting point for exploring the city. If you're **driving** from Budapest, take the M5 motorway south through Kecskemét and Kiskunfélegyháza.

VISITOR INFORMATION The best source of information is **Tourinform,** at Dugonics tér 2 (© **62/488-699;** www.szeged.eu), located in the renovated 19th-century courtyard of the fine pastry shop Z. Nagy Cukrászda (p. 289). The office is open Monday through Friday from 9am to 5pm. In summer, there is a Tourinform kiosk on Széchenyi tér, open on weekends 9am to 5pm. For private accommodations for the daring, stop in at Ibusz at Oroszlán u. 4 or call © **62/471-177.**

MAHART, the Hungarian ferry-line company, organizes boat tours up and down the Tisza River from April 1 through mid-October. For information, contact the MAHART boat station in Szeged at Felső-Tisza part or call © **62/425-834.** The Tourinform office can also assist in arranging excursions.

EXPLORING THE TOWN

In addition to the listings below, you should wander past the **Gróf Palace** ★★★ (© **47/580-400**; www.hotelgrofdegenfeld.hu), a piece of architecture worthy of a few photos. Located at the corner of Lajos Tisza körut and Takarektar utca, the building was designed by Ferenc J. Raichl and was built in 1912 for citizens who could afford "higher rent"; it's not a hotel. Shamefully, there are a couple of broken windows, but the elegance still shines brightly. Nearby, see or visit the **Reök Regional Art Center** ★★★ (© **62/541–205**); www.reok.hu) in Gaudian style at Lajos Tisza körut and Kölcsey utca. This is considered one of the most beautiful Art Nouveau buildings in Europe. Open Tuesday to Saturday 10am to 6pm.

Anna Gyógy Fürdő This newly remodeled and reopened bath is just the cure for what ails you. Great if you have a medical need or just want to explore the healing powers of the Hungarian mineral waters, which contain alkali-hydrogen-carbonic, and it is recommended for anyone with joint ailments. Originally opened in 1896, it has a freshness and intriguing architecture.

Tisza Lajos krt. 24. © **62/553–330.** Admission 1,200 Ft. Daily 8am–8pm; and Mon–Fri 9pm–midnight for bathing under the stars.

Móra Ferenc Museum As the name suggests, paintings of Ferenc Lucs are the main attraction here, but also on display are the History of Chemists (a natural sciences exhibition),

Avars (an archaeological exhibition), and folk art of Csongrad county (an ethnical exhibition). Temporary exhibits are also displayed throughout the year.

Roosevelt tér 1–3. ℂ **62/549-040.** www.mfm.u-szeged.hu. Admission 600 Ft. Tues–Sun 10am–5pm.

New Synagogue ★★★   A tribute to the once-thriving Jewish community in Szeged, this synagogue was built in 1907. Created in a number of architectural styles, it is a monumental 49m (161 ft) tall Moorish Art Nouveau building. The space between the right and left exterior curve of the arch is an ornamentally decorated space. In the enclosing right angle is a rib-like wall in Gothic style, directly above an organ."Roman columns support the galleries. The most beautiful part is the dome, but everywhere you look is awe-inspiring. This is considered the masterpiece of architect Lipot Baumhorn, who was a disciple of Ödön Lechner and the most prolific and renowned synagogue architect in modern Europe. It occupies a full block, making it the second-largest synagogue in Hungary. The synagogue is fully functioning and holds services at 6pm every Friday.

If you find the synagogue closed when it should be open, go to the address that's posted near the entrance and the caretaker will open the synagogue for you.

Jósika utca. ℂ **62/423-849.** www.zsinagoga.szeged.hu. Admission 300 Ft. Apr 1–Sep 30 Sun–Fri 10am–noon and 1–5pm; Oct 1–Mar 31 Sun–Fri 9am–2pm. Services Fri 6pm. Closed for Jewish holidays. From Dugonics tér, walk right on Tisza Lajos krt., and turn left on Gutenberg u.

Pick Museum ★★   This is a must for anyone interested in food or cooking. The museum contains the history of Pick brand salami and Szeged paprika, both world famous as Hungarian products that developed from this city. Follow the history and evolution of salami production from 1869 to the present day. On the first floor, follow the history of paprika production, all with puppets in period dress.

Felső Tisza-part 10. ℂ **06/20-980-8000** (mobile phone only). www.pickmuzeum.hu. Admission 800 Ft. Tues–Sat 3–6pm.

Votive Church ★★   Built by the residents after the flood that destroyed the city, this church sits in a square that is exactly the same size as St. Mark's Square in Venice. In the church, you'll see an unusual representation of the Madonna created in mosaic by Ferenc Márton over the baldachin of the high altar. It's nicknamed the "Madonna in a fur coat," because she is depicted wearing a richly decorated fur coat, typical of this region, with red slippers typical of Szeged. There are many magnificent pieces of artwork throughout the church. It houses Europe's third-largest church organ with 9,040 pipes. Mass is held here at 6:30am, 7:30am, and 6pm every day.

Also on the square is the oldest historic monument of the city: the St. Demetrius Tower with a foundation dating back to the 11th century. The lower, squared Roman-styled section and early Gothic upper sections are dated to the 13th century. If you're lucky enough to be on Dóm tér at 12:15pm or 5:45pm, you will be treated by the unique-to-Hungary musical clock that performs at these times with music and wooden figures that come out announcing the time.

Dóm tér. Free admission. Mon–Sat 9am–6pm; Sun 9:30–10am, 11–11:30am, and 12:30–6pm. Mass daily 6:30am, 7:30am, and 6pm.

WHERE TO STAY

Dóm Hotel ★★   Located on the square near the cathedral, the Dóm opened in 2004 offering clean modern rooms with easy access to all sights. Two apartments with a separate living room and bedroom are available for two to four people.

Bajza u. 3–6. ℭ **62/423-750.** Fax 62/423-750. www.domhotel.hu. 16 units. 25,000 Ft–26,600 Ft double; 34,800 Ft–43,400 Ft apt. Rates include breakfast but not VAT or tourist tax. AE, MC, V. Parking 1,000 Ft / day. **Amenities:** Sauna. *In room:* A/C, TV, minibar.

Kata Panzió ★★ This charming pension moved across the street to expand, but is still in a quiet residential neighborhood, just a short walk from central Klauzál tér. It features plenty of common space and sunny balconies on each floor. There is a small spa in the basement at an added cost: Jacuzzi (1,400 Ft), sauna (1,200 Ft), and solarium (500 Ft). Guests receive a 10% discount at Brother Steakhouse below.

Bolyai János u. 20 (between Gogol u. and Kálvária sgt.). ℭ **62/311-258.** www.katapanzio.hu. 17 units. 18,900 Ft double; 26,500 Ft deluxe double; 26,500 Ft apt. Tourist tax of 2€ per person per night. Rates include breakfast. AE, MC, V. Free parking. *In room:* A/C, TV.

WHERE TO DINE

Brother Steakhouse ★ INTERNATIONAL Around the corner from Kata Panzió is this rustic restaurant with thick slab wood tables and benches to match. If you aren't hungry for steak or other meat offerings, they serve pizzas as well.

Gogol u. 20. ℭ **62/424-044.** Main courses 790 Ft–5,500 Ft; pizza 690 Ft–1,350 Ft. MC, V. Mon–Sat 10am–10pm.

Brnoi Étterem ★ INTERNATIONAL Close to the center of the city, this pleasant peachy colored restaurant has indoor and outdoor seating for casual dining without feeling overwhelmed by prices.

Kelemen u. 3. ℭ **62/310-040.** www.brnoisorozo.hu. Main courses 1,350 Ft–2,950 Ft. No credit cards. Daily 9am–midnight.

Gödör ★★ HUNGARIAN Located next to the Hero's Arch right in the center of the city is where you will find this eatery. It is frequented by university students, teachers, and tourists alike, most likely because of their reasonable prices. Two of us had a filling meal for the same cost as one meal in Budapest. From spring to late summer you can enjoy your meal on the terrace.

Tisza Lajos krt. 103. ℭ **62/420-130.** Main courses 1,300 Ft–1,800 Ft. No credit cards. Mon–Sat 11am–10pm; Sun 11am–5pm.

Gőry ★ HUNGARIAN A varied menu offers something for everyone at this old-fashioned Hungarian restaurant. They claim to be the most floral restaurant in the area with garden dining all year round (with the aid of heaters).

Liszt u. 9. ℭ **62/422-157.** Main dishes 1,650 Ft–3,600 Ft. No credit cards. Daily 11am–11pm.

Kiskőrösi Halászcsárda ★ HUNGARIAN If you are brave enough to sample the local fish and the famous Szeged fish soup, then this authentic riverside restaurant is the place to try it. The fish soup is rather unglamorous-looking at best, but those that love fish, say the taste is excellent. Not me, thank you very much. Paprika and onions are the spices of choice for hearty fish stews and bisques alike.

Felső Tisza-part 336. ℭ **62/495-698.** Reservations recommended. Main courses 1,000 Ft–2,200 Ft. MC, V. Sun–Thurs 11am–midnight; Fri–Sat 11am–2am.

COFFEEHOUSES & ICE-CREAM PARLORS

Sándor Árvay and his son Kálmán created a patisserie, which became famous by the end of the 19th century because of the quality of their goods. It was nicknamed the Gerbeaud of Szeged. The Virágh brothers bought it in 1922 continuing the quality reputation and renaming it **Virág Cukrászda,** located on Klauzál tér. The menu has expanded to include meals with main courses ranging from 1,190 Ft to 2,440 Ft. Pastries cost from 310 Ft to 510 Ft. It is open daily from 8am to 10pm. This square has more than its share of pastry shops with the **Kis Virág (Little Flower)** ★★ directly across the square, where pastry prices are slightly cheaper ranging from 250 Ft to 510 Ft. Their specialty is *rakott rétes* (layered strudel), which is the divine local version of the traditional Jewish pastry *flodni.* Kis Virág is open daily from 8am to 8pm. There are other shops on or near the square vying for attention with *cukrászdas* almost outnumbering full restaurants.

Z. Nagy Cukrászda ★ on Dugonics tér, just off Karász utca (the pedestrian-only street) is yet another rivaling pastry shop. When the summer heat is beating down, head for the line of people waiting to be served at the most popular ice-cream shop, **Palánk** at Oskola utca 1 on the corner of Viktor Hugo. They are open daily from 10am to 9pm.

SZEGED AFTER DARK

Átrium Music Café at Kárász u. 9 (✆ **06/30-289-4466** mobile phone only) is a lively place with a variety of different music styles each night including jazz, funk, and soul with specific ladies' nights. **Szote Klub** at Dóm tér 13 (✆ **62/545-773**) is a definite disco with DJs knocking out the tunes, but the action doesn't start until 9:30pm and goes into the wee hours, whenever the action slows down. The famous **Jate Klub** of the university opened its doors in 1973. Originally it was an air-raid shelter located in the basement of the main building of the university. During the day, it operates as a cafe and in the evening it hosts parties, concerts, and cultural, theatrical, and literary events. It is open Monday to Friday 10am to the end of the program, Saturday 10pm to the end of the program, and closed on Sunday. The latest edition for the youth set is a club called **Sing-Sing** on Mars tér, pavilion C (✆ **62/311–314**), but their only regular hours are Wednesday 11pm to 5am with occasional Friday and Saturday events.

Fast Facts

AREA CODES The country code for Hungary is **36.** All telephone numbers in this guide are listed with the city code/telephone number. The area code for Budapest is **1.**

AUTOMOBILE ORGANIZATIONS The **Hungarian Auto Club (Magyar Autóklub)** operates a 24-hour free emergency breakdown service: Call ℭ **188** (note, however, that not all operators speak English).

The Autóklub also has an **International Aid Service Center,** at II. Rómer Flóris u. 4/a (ℭ **1/345-1744**), which was established specifically for international motorists; however, our attempts to get assistance with information were a bit frustrating. Stay on the line, you will be connected. Services provided include emergency aid, towing, and technical advice, but the center may refer you to the rental company first, which in turn may have to make the contact with the auto club.

BUSINESS HOURS Most **stores** are open Monday through Friday from 10am to 6pm and Saturday from 10am to 2pm with a few closing earlier at 1pm. The majority of stores are closed Sunday, except those in central tourist areas or malls. Very few shop owners and restaurateurs close for 2 weeks in August. On weekdays, food stores open early, at around 6 or 7am, and close around 6 or 7pm. Convenience stores, called "nonstops," are open 24 hours and just about every neighborhood has one.

Banks in general are open Monday through Friday from 8am to 4pm. Some banks open a half-hour later on some days, but stay open an hour later that day too.

There is no shortage of banking services or automatic teller machines (ATMs) in the city.

DRINKING LAWS The legal drinking age in Hungary is 18. Beer, wine, and hard alcohol are sold everywhere including grocery stores, nonstop convenience stores, and even some discount stores. A few neighborhoods within different districts have started to stop the sales of alcohol at 11pm for nonstop stores, which are the only outlets open at that hour, aside from bars and clubs. This is a district-regulated law and is not city-wide; sometimes it is only within a particular neighborhood within a district. Bars do not have legally mandated closing times, but they may have to close outside seating in warm weather and move patrons inside to keep the noise down. Don't be surprised if a bar is still open at 5am.

Although it is not uncommon to see people drinking alcohol on public transportation in the late evenings, it is illegal if caught. Drinking on the street is also, but that is totally ignored, unless someone is causing a disturbance. Don't carry open containers of alcohol in your vehicle. Don't even think about driving after having had a drink—Hungary has a zero-tolerance law for drunk drivers and this is strictly enforced if you're stopped.

DRIVING RULES See "Getting There and Getting Around," p. 33.

ELECTRICITY With the exception of the U.K., Hungary as the rest of Europe has the same double round prongs on their plugs. Electric is 220 to 240 volts AC (50 cycles) as in most of Europe, Australia, and New Zealand. For most things electrical, all you will need is an adapter to fit into the wall outlet. Adapters are easily found in any electric or most computer stores. For the most part, converters that change 110–120 volts to 220–240 volts are impossible to find, so bring one with you.

EMBASSIES & CONSULATES The **Australian Embassy** is at XII. Királyhágó tér 8–9 (② **1/457-9777**). The **Canadian Embassy** is at II. Ganz u. 12–14 (② **1/392-3360**). The **Republic of Ireland Embassy** is at V. Szabadság tér 7 (② **1/301-4960**); the **United Kingdom Embassy** is at V. Harmincad u. 6 (② **1/266-2888**); and the **United States Embassy** is at V. Szabadság tér 12 (② **1/475-4400**). New Zealand does not have an embassy in Budapest, but the U.K. Embassy can handle matters for New Zealand citizens.

EMERGENCIES The general emergency number in Europe is ② **112**. Dial ② **104** for an ambulance, ② **105** for the fire department, ② **107** for the police, and ② **188** for car breakdown service. ② **1/438-8080** is a 24-hour hotline in English for reporting crime.

GASOLINE (PETROL) Taxes are already included in printed prices at the pump. Prices may be shocking, but remember 3.8 liters equals one U.S. gallon.

HOLIDAYS Banks, government offices, post offices, most stores, some restaurants, and some museums are closed on the following legal national holidays: January 1 (New Year's Day), March 15 (Anniversary of 1848 uprising against the Austrian rule), Easter and Easter Monday (dates change annually), May 1 (Labor Day), Whit Monday (date changes annually), August 20 (Feast of St. Stephen), October 26 (Anniversary of the 1956 Revolution), November 1 (All Saints' Day, December 24 (stores close half day), December 25 (Christmas) and December 26 (Boxing Day). For more information on holidays, see "When to Go," in Chapter 3.

HOSPITALS See section 5, "Health," in chapter 3, "Planning Your Trip to Budapest."

INSURANCE It's always a good idea to have travel cancellation insurance, but especially so with the volatile state of some airlines. Travelers should contact their medical insurance carrier to see what their policy is for out-of-country medical expenses. U.S. travelers should note that Medicare does not provide any coverage outside of the U.S.

Travelers from the U.K. and the Republic of Ireland should carry their European Health Insurance Card (EHIC), which replaced the E111 form as proof of entitlement to free/reduced-cost medical treatment abroad. (www.ehic.org.uk/www.ehic.ie). Note, that the EHIC only covers "necessary medical treatment" and for repatriation costs, lost money, baggage, or cancellation, travel insurance should always be sought.

For information on travelers' insurance, trip cancellation insurance, and medical insurance while traveling please visit www.frommers.com/planning.

INTERNET ACCESS Most hotels now provide free Wi-Fi access. Outside of the hotel, you will find dozens of places where one drink will allow you to stay as long as you want to crawl the web. Look for Wi-Fi signs on windows, doors, and standing signs outside doors of cafes, restaurants, and bookstores.

LANGUAGE You will find more people who speak English in Budapest than you will in the outer regions. My rule of thumb on the streets is to ask a young person. Most young people will speak some English, although they may not be fluent. For basic survival Hungarian, see *Useful Terms & Phrases* in the back of the book.

LAUNDROMATS Finding a Laundromat is close to impossible, since every home has their own machines. There is a service in Budapest, but it is not self-serve. You leave your clothes and return for them later. It is simply named **Landromat-Mosómata** in district VI at 24–26 Ó utca, (✆ **06–20–392–5702**). The hours are Monday to Friday 9am to 7pm and weekends 10am to 4pm. Washing, drying, and folding will run 1,800 Ft for up to 9kg (20 lbs). Ironing is available for an extra charge. For dry cleaning services, look for **Tiszta Kék** at VII. Rákóczi út 2, (✆ **1/266–2379**). Their hours are Monday to Friday 7am to 7pm and Saturday 8am to 2pm.

LEGAL AID International visitors should contact their embassy or consulate as soon as possible. If an officer insists on a fine being paid immediately while on a highway, ask for a receipt to show the fine was paid to avoid problems later, especially if you have rented a car. If you have a minor traffic accident, generally the police will not get involved unless it is insisted upon. People generally just exchange insurance information.

MAIL The postal system is not the most efficient or honest, so take great care with sending or receiving packages. Even letters mailed "Registered with a Return Receipt Requested" card have not made it to their destination without issues. Most post offices are open Monday through Friday from 8am to 6pm; however, with the current state of the economy, many have or will be shortening their hours on an office-by-office situation. Sending postcards to the U.K. or Ireland is 210 Ft, while Australia, Canada, New Zealand, or the U.S. is 230 Ft. Mailing a letter under 20 gm to the UK is 270 Ft, but Australia, Canada, New Zealand, or the U.S. are all 300 Ft. For packages, note there is a high percentage rate that never arrive at their destination, so I would avoid it at any cost. FedEx or UPS are prohibitively expensive for even sending a document. For example, sending a letter to the U.S. can cost over 5,000 Ft.

NEWSPAPERS & MAGAZINES For local news or magazines in English, you can find *The Budapest Times* at most large newsstands or your hotel. *Funzine*, *Where*, and *Time Out* magazines are available at hotels, restaurants, or the Tourinform offices. For other newspapers or magazines, see the Shopping chapter p. 189.

PASSPORTS See "Embassies & Consulates," above, for whom to contact if you lose your passport while traveling in Hungary. For other information, please contact the following agencies:

For Residents of Australia Contact the **Australian Passport Information Service** at ✆ **131-232,** or visit the government website at www.passports.gov.au.

For Residents of Canada Contact the central **Passport Office,** Department of Foreign Affairs and International Trade, Ottawa, ON K1A 0G3 (✆ **800/567-6868;** www.ppt.gc.ca).

For Residents of Ireland Contact the **Passport Office,** Setanta Centre, Molesworth Street, Dublin 2 (✆ **01/671-1633;** www.irlgov.ie/iveagh).

For Residents of New Zealand Contact the **Passport Office** at ✆ **0800/225-050** or ✆ **04/474-8100,** or log on to www.passports.govt.nz.

For Residents of the United Kingdom Visit your nearest passport office, major post office, or travel agency or contact the **United Kingdom Passport Service** at ✆ **0870/521-0410** or search its website at www.ukpa.gov.uk.

For Residents of the United States To find your regional passport office, either check the U.S. State Department website or call the **National Passport Information Center** toll-free number (✆ **877/487-2778**) for automated information.

POLICE Dial (✆) **107** or general emergency dial ✆ **112.**

SMOKING You will find most hotels and restaurants accommodate both smoking and nonsmoking guests. It is not legal to smoke on public transportation or in shops. Cigarettes are a fairtrade item meaning a pack of a particular brand, size, and blend will be the same price everywhere in the country.

TAXES Hungary has a value-added tax (VAT) on everything, but the rate depends on the service or product. Hotel VAT is now 18% and VAT on goods in shops is 20%. When you are shopping the VAT is included in the posted price. However, some stores will break it down showing a "*netto*" and "*brutto*" price. You want to pay attention to the *brutto*, as this is what you will pay at the register.

TELEPHONES Many convenience stores, kiosks, and Internet cafes sell **prepaid calling cards** in denominations up to 5,000 Ft; for international visitors these can be the least expensive way to call home. Many public pay phones are not properly serviced, but most require the use of a specific pay phone calling card also available as above.

TIME Hungary is in the Central European Time zone. This is the same time zone for all of Western Europe, with the exception of the U.K. It is 1 hour ahead of Greenwich Mean Time, except during daylight saving time. Hungary is 6 hours ahead of New York City and 9 hours ahead of San Francisco.

Daylight saving time is in effect from 2am on the last Sunday in March to 2am on the last Sunday in October. Daylight saving time moves the clock 1 hour ahead of standard time.

TIPPING In hotels, tip **bellhops** at least 500 Ft per bag (750–1,000 Ft if you have a lot of luggage) and tip the **chamber staff** 500 Ft per day (more if you've left a disaster area for him or her to clean up). Tip the **concierge** only if he or she has provided you with some specific service (for example, calling a cab for you or obtaining difficult-to-get theater tickets). Tip the **valet-parking attendant** 500 Ft every time you get your car.

In restaurants, bars, and nightclubs, tip **service staff** and **bartenders** 10–15% of the check (see p. 88 for more information), and tip **valet-parking attendants** 500 Ft per vehicle.

As for other service personnel, tip **cab drivers** 10% of the fare and tip **hairdressers** and **barbers** 10–15%.

TOILETS In some areas, you will find public toilets on the streets. You will be required to pay the attendant to use the facility. Keep small change handy as it can cost from 50 Ft to 100 Ft. Because they are attended, safety is not a concern, but have extra paper with you—what they provide is minimal. If you think you can run into a fast-food restaurant, be prepared as they will charge unless you have ordered food. Your receipt is your admission ticket, but only good for one person. Split your order for more receipts. Other facilities are found in hotel lobbies if you hunt for them, bars, restaurants, museums, railway and bus stations. Some full-menu restaurants, cafes, and bars reserve their restrooms for patrons.

VISAS British and Irish nationals can visit Hungary as a tourist without a visa. Visitors from Australia, the U.S., Canada, and New Zealand may visit for 90 days as a tourist without a visa (see p. 31).

Note that in 2009, the Hungarian government announced it would be closing four embassies and a large number of missions, though the final list was not available at the time of this writing. Check this government website for current information: **www.mfa.gov.hu/kum/en/bal/missions/missions_abroad/**.

Australian and **New Zealand** citizens can obtain up-to-date visa information from the Hungary Embassy, Canberra, 17 Beale Crescent Deakin, ACT 2600 (© **6282/2555**). The embassy website is www.mfa.gov.hu/emb/canberra.

In Sydney, the Consulate General's office is at Edgecliff Centre 203–233, Suite 405,

New South Head Road (© **9328–7859**) or check the consulate's website at www. mfa.gov.hu/cons/sydney.

British subjects can obtain up-to-date information from the Hungarian Embassy at 35 Eaton Place, London SW1X 8BY (© **020/7201-34-40;** www.mfa.gov.hu/ kulkepviselet/UK/en/mainpage.htm).

Irish citizens can obtain up-to-date information through the Hungarian Embassy, 2 Fitzwilliam Place, Dublin 2, Ireland (© **01/661-2902, 661-2903;** www. mfa.gov.hu/emb/dublin).

VISITOR INFORMATION **Tourinform** office locations in Budapest and other cities are provided elsewhere, but the main websites are **http://tourinform.hu** and www.hungary.com. Other helpful sources are www.funzine.com, the online portion of the printed Funzine magazine that comes out every other week, listing current events and fun things to do. For relevant regional news, you can go to the Budapest Times online at www.budapest times.hu. For news that is sometimes irreverent, check out Caboodle's site, www.caboodle.hu. For information for gays and lesbians, join the Budapest Yahoo group by sending an email to gaybudapest info-subscribe@yahoogroups.com.

WATER You will see plenty of people drinking bottled water, but water from the faucet is completely safe to drink. It is just a matter of personal preference.

Help with a Tough Tongue

Many travelers are leery to enter a land where the language is so incomprehensible, and they cannot make any connection to their mother tongue. This is certainly true of Hungary and the complex and unusual language of the Hungarians, Magyar. There are only an estimated 15 million people worldwide who use Hungarian as their mother tongue, so if you don't, you are still in the majority. For years, it has been lumped in the Finno-Ugric language family with only two other distant cousins: Finnish and Estonian. However, Finns and Estonians have as much trouble with Hungarian as anyone else, having less than a handful of words in common. Their grammar is also very different. Recent scholarship is now questioning the theory of where Hungarian really has its leaf on the tree of world languages. Magyar originated on the eastern side of the Ural Mountains, but exactly where is still uncertain.

The Hungarian language has long been one of the country's greatest obstacles and continues to be as many business and tour websites, especially for smaller cities and villages, are in Hungarian only. Nevertheless, the Hungarian people are intensely proud of their language to the point of creating laws to keep foreign language business names at bay whenever possible. Our transcription of Hungarian pronunciations is of necessity approximate. Stress is always on the first syllable of any word, and all letters are pronounced, but there are no *Q, X,* or *Y* in Hungarian unless the word has been borrowed from another language. With that said, you will find *Y,* but it is a consonant combination letter like *gy, ly,* or *ny,* making the two letters one letter unto themselves. Hungarian has 44 letters and 14 of them are vowels.

Fortunately, for the modern-day traveler and Hungary's ascension into the European Union, many Hungarian young people have taken their foreign language studies much more seriously than ever before. Numerous young people speak English and most people in tourism venues do to some extent. Do not be daunted if you attempt some polite words and find a confused Hungarian staring at you. The difference between an *o* and *ó* can not only change the meaning of the word, but since the Magyar people are so unaccustomed to hearing strangers attempt their language, they are also a bit befuddled to the point of not understanding. At the least, try to learn the polite words and stick with them.

One more thing: Both "hello" and "goodbye" in Hungarian is *hallo* (sounds the same in English) or *szia* (sounds like see-ya). You will often see people saying goodbye to each other and saying "*hallo, szia*" as they depart. They often do the same on the phone before ending a call.

A printable phrase book is available at www.single-serving.com/Hungarian/print.php.

Vowels

a t*au*t	ó same as above but held longer
á b*ahh*	ö s*u*b
e *e*ver	ő same as above but held longer
é d*ay*	u l*oo*k
i m*i*tt	ú b*oo*t
í t*ee*n	ü d*o*ve
o b*o*ne	ű same as above but held longer

Consonants

Most Hungarian consonants are pronounced approximately as they are in English, including the following: *b, d, f, h, k, l, m, n, p, t, v,* and *y.* There are some differences, however, particularly in the consonant combinations, as follows:

c g*ets*	r slightly rolled
cs *ch*ill	s *sh*eet
g *g*ill	sz *s*ix
gy he*dge*	z *z*ero
j *y*outh	zs *az*ure, plea*s*ure
ny as in Russian *ny*et	

---

1   MENU TERMS

GENERAL TERMS

Bors black pepper	**Paprika** red pepper/paprika
Fóételek main courses	**Sajt** cheese
Fózelék vegetable purée	**Saláták** salads
Gyümölcs fruits	**Só** salt
Halak fish	**Tészták** pasta/dessert
Húsételek meat dishes	**Tojás** eggs
Italok beverages	**Vaj** butter
Kenyér bread	**Zöldság** vegetables
Leves(ek) soup(s)	

COOKING TERMS

Csípős hot (peppery)	**Pirított** toasted
Forró hot (in temperature)	**Pörkölt** stew
Főtt boiled	**Rántott** fried
Friss fresh	**Roston sült** broiled
Fuszerezve spiced	**Sült** roasted/baked
Hideg cold	**Sútve** baked/fried
Párolt steamed	**Töltött** stuffed

SOUPS (LEVESEK)

Gombaleves   mushroom soup
Gulyásleves   goulash soup
Húsleves   bouillon
Karfioleves   cauliflower soup
Krémleves   cream of ... whatever is
before it

Lencseleves   lentil soup
Paradicsomkrémleves   cream of
tomato soup
Zöldborsóleves   pea soup
Zöldségleves   vegetable soup

EGGS (TOJÁS)

Kolbásszal   with sausage
Rántotta   scrambled eggs
Sonkával   with ham

Szalonnával   with bacon
Tükörtojás   fried eggs

MEAT & POULTRY (HÚS ÉS BAROMFI)

Agyonsütve   well done
Bárány   lamb
Bécsi szelet   Wiener schnitzel
Borjú   veal
Csirke   chicken
Félig nyersen   rare
Gulyás   goulash
Kacsa   duck

Kotlett   cutlet
Közepesen kisütve   medium
Liba   goose
Marha   beef
Pulyka   turkey
Sertés   pork
Tokány   ragout

FISH (HALAK)

Csuka   pike
Fogas Balaton   pike-perch
Halászlé   fish stew

Pisztráng   trout
Ponty   carp
Tonhal   tuna

VEGETABLES (ZÖLDSÁG)

Bab   beans
Burgonya   potato
Fokhagyma   garlic
Gomba   mushrooms
Hagyma   onion
Káposzta   cabbage

Paradicsom   tomato
Sóska   sorrel
Spenót   spinach
Tök   squash
Zöldbab   green beans

SALADS (SALÁTÁK)

Fejes saláta   green salad
Lecsó   stewed pepper, tomatoes, and
onion
Paprikasaláta   pickled-pepper salad

Uborkasaláta   cucumber salad
Vegyes saláta   mixed salad

Alma apple
Barack apricot
Cseresznye cherry
Dinnye watermelon
Körte pear
Málna raspberry
Meggy sour cherry

Narancs orange
Őszibarack peach
Sargadinnye cantaloupe
Szeder blackberry
Szilva plum
Szóló grapes

DESSERTS

Almás rétes apple strudel
Dobos torta layer cake with caramel candied frosting
Fagylalt ice cream
Ischler chocolate-dipped shortbread cookie sandwich

Lekváros palacsinta crepe filled with preserves
Meggyes rétes sour-cherry strudel
Túrós rétes cheese strudel

BEVERAGES

Barna sör dark beer
Fehér bor white wine
Kávé coffee
Koktél cocktail
Narancslé orange juice

Sör beer
Tej milk
Víz water
Vörös bor red wine

---

2 BASIC PHRASES & VOCABULARY

QUESTION WORDS (IN THE NOMINATIVE)

English	Hungarian	Pronunciation
Where	**Hol**	hole
When	**Mikor**	*mee*-kor
What	**Mi**	mee
Why	**Miert**	*mee*-ayrt
Who	**Ki**	kee
How	**Hogy**	hohdge

USEFUL PHRASES

English	Hungarian	Pronunciation
Good day/Hello	**Jó napot**	*yoh* napoht
Good morning	**Jó reggelt**	*yoh* reg-gelt
Good evening	**Jó estét**	*yoh* esh-tayt
Goodbye	**Viszontlátásra**	*vee*-sont-lah-tahsh-ra

English	Hungarian	Pronunciation
My name is . . .	**Vagyok . . .**	*vodge*-yohk
Thank you	**Köszönöm**	*kuh*-suh-nuhm
You're welcome	**Kérem**	*kay*-rem
Please	**Legyen szíves**	*ledge*-yen *see*-vesh
Yes	**Igen**	*ee*-gen
No	**Nem**	*nem*
Good/Okay	**Jó**	*yo*
Excuse me	**Bocsánat**	*boh*-chahnat
How much does it cost?	**Mennyi bekerül?**	*men*-yee *beh*-keh-roohl?
I don't understand	**Nem értem**	*nem* ayr-tem
I don't know	**Nem tudom**	*nem too*-dum
Where is the . . . ?	**Hol van a . . . ?**	*hohl* von a . . . ?
bus station	**busz állomás**	*boos ahh*-loh-mahsh
train station	**vonatállomás**	*vah*-not-*ahh*-loh-mahsh
bank	**bank**	*bahnk*
museum	**múzeum**	*moo*-zeh-oom
pharmacy	**patiká**	*paw*-tee-kah
theater	**színház**	*seen*-hahz
tourist office	**turista iroda**	*too*-reesh-ta *eer*-ohda
embassy	**nagykövetség**	*nahdge koo*-vet-shayg
restaurant	**étterem**	*ayt*-teh-rehm
restroom	**wc**	*vayt*-say
Right	**Job/Jobbra**	*yob*/*yob*-ra
Left	**Bal/Balra**	*ball*/*bal*-ra

RESTAURANT SERVICE

English	Hungarian	Pronunciation
Breakfast	**Reggeli**	*rehg*-geh-lee
Lunch	**Ebéd**	*eh*-bayd
Dinner	**Vacsora**	*vah*-choh-rah
I would like . . .	**Kérnék . . .**	*kayr*-nayk . . .
a table	**egy asztalot**	edge *ah*-stah-lot
a menu	**egy étlapot**	edge *ayt*-lah-poht
a glass (of water)	**egy pohár (vizet)**	edge poh-har (*vee*-zet)
to pay	**fizetni**	*ee*-zeht-nee
I have a reservation	**Foglaltam már**	*fohg*-lawl-tahm mahr

TRAIN TRAVEL

English	Hungarian	Pronunciation
A ticket, please	**Egy jegyet kérek**	*Edge ye*-dget *kay*-rek
Seat reservation	**Helyjegy**	*heyh*-yedge
One-way only	**Csak oda**	*chalk oh*-da
Round-trip	**Oda-vissza**	*oh*-dah-*vees*-sah

English	Hungarian	Pronunciation
First class	Elsó osztály	*ell*-shooh *oh*-stahy
Arrive	Érkezik	*ayr*-kez-eek
Depart	Indul	*inn*-doohl
Track	Vagány	*vah*-ghine

POST OFFICE

English	Hungarian	Pronunciation
Airmail	Légiposta	*lay*-ghee-posh-ta
A stamp, please	Egy bélyeget kérek	Edge *bay*-yeh-get *kay*-rek
A postcard . . .	Egy képeslapot . . .	Edge *kay*-pesh-law-poht
An envelope . . .	Egy borítéket . . .	Edge *bohr*-ree-tay-ket

USEFUL WORDS

English	Hungarian	Pronunciation
Map	Térkép	*tayr*-kayp
Police	Rendórség	*ren*-du(r)r-shayg
Hospital	Korhéz	*kohr*-hahhz
Emergency	Szükséghelyzet	*soohk*-shayg-hey-zet
Theft	Lopás	*loh*-pahsh
Passport	Útlevél	*oot*-leh-vayhl
Pillow	Parna	*par*-na
Window	Ablak	*ab*-lock
Man/Men	Férfi	fear-fe
Woman/Women	NőI	*noy*

SIGNS

Bejárat	Entrance	**Tilos a dohányzás**	No Smoking
Érkezések	Arrivals	**Toalettek**	Toilets
Indulások	Departures	**Veszélyes**	Danger
Informácio	Information	**Vigyázat**	Beware
Kijárat	Exit		

NUMBERS

1	**egy**	edge	12	**tizenkettó**	*teez*-en-ket-tu[r]
2	**kettó**	*ket*-tu[r]	13	**tizenhárom**	*teez*-en-hahh-rohm
3	***három***	*hahh*-rohm	14	**tizennégy**	*teez*-en-naydge
4	**négy**	*naydge*	15	**tizenöt**	*teez*-en-u[r]t
5	**öt**	*u*[r]*t*	16	**tizenhat**	*teez*-en-hawt
6	**hat**	*hawt*	17	**tizenhét**	*teez*-en-hayt
7	**hét**	*hayt*	18	**tizennyolc**	*teez*-en-nyohlts
8	**nyolc**	*nyohlts*	19	**tizenkilenc**	*teez*-en-kee-lents
9	**kilenc**	*kee*-lents	20	**húsz**	*hoos*
10	**tíz**	*teez*	30	**harminc**	*hahr*-mints
11	**tizenegy**	*teez*-en-edge	40	**negyven**	*nedge*-vehn

Side margin: HELP WITH A TOUGH TONGUE · **16** · BASIC PHRASES & VOCABULARY

50	**ötven**	*u[r]t*-vehn	90	**kilencven**	*kee*-lents-vehn
60	**hatvan**	*hawt*-vahn	100	**száz**	*sahhz*
70	**hetven**	*het*-vehn	500	**ötszáz**	*u[r]t*-sahhz
80	**nyolcvan**	*nyohlts*-vahn	1,000	**ezer**	*eh*-zayr

DAYS OF THE WEEK

English	Hungarian	Pronunciation
Monday	**hétfő**	hait-fo
Tuesday	**kedd**	kedd
Wednesday	**szerda**	ser-dah
Thursday	**csütörtök**	chew-tor-tuk
Friday	**péntek**	pain-tek
Saturday	**szombat**	sahm-bat
Sunday	**vasárnap**	vasha-ar-nap

Days of the week are not capitalized.

INDEX

See also Accommodations and Restaurant indexes, below.